BETWEEN THE LAYERS

Spiderwoman Theater, Storyweaving, and Survivance

The Spiderwoman Theater, the longest-running Indigenous theatre company in North America has heralded the revolutionary methodology of Storyweaving for generations of Indigenous artists. Storyweaving is a distinct methodology that governs the dramaturgical structure and performed transmission of the company's plays on the contemporary stage. The practice of Storyweaving predates written history. It has been (and remains) specific to tribal storytellers across the continent.

The reclamation, then, of this aesthetic legacy by contemporary Indigenous storytellers is a crucial act of recovery. Jill Carter, an Anishinaabe-Ashkenazi theatre-worker and scholar, examines the process and development of Storyweaving. She studies how Storyweaving imagines and develops a functional framework that is being adopted and adapted by artists from myriad nations to create works (on the page and stage) that facilitate the healing, transformation, and survivance of their communities. *Between the Layers* pays respects to the teachers and visionaries that moulded this practice and encourages future generations to continue its legacy, while making a much-needed contribution to the study of Indigenous theatre and performance.

In its painstaking documentation of the Storyweaving artform, *Between the Layers* refuses the devaluation, erasure, and suppression of Indigenous culture, while contributing to the dissemination and celebration of Indigenous Knowledge Systems.

JILL CARTER is an Anishinaabe-Ashkenazi theatre-worker and Associate Professor in the University of Toronto's Centre for Drama, Theatre, and Performance Studies; Transitional Year Programme; and Centre for Indigenous Studies.

Between the Layers

Spiderwoman Theater, Storyweaving, and Survivance

JILL CARTER
WITH SPIDERWOMAN THEATER

UNIVERSITY OF TORONTO PRESS
Toronto Buffalo London

Toronto Buffalo London
utppublishing.com
Printed in Canada

ISBN 978-1-4875-0791-6 (cloth)
ISBN 978-1-4875-5906-9 (paper)
ISBN 978-1-4875-3721-0 (EPUB)
ISBN 978-1-4875-3720-3 (PDF)

Library and Archives Canada Cataloguing in Publication

Title: Between the layers : Spiderwoman Theater, storyweaving, and survivance / Jill Carter with Spiderwoman Theater.
Names: Carter, Jill (Jill L.), author | Spiderwoman Theater, author.
Description: Includes bibliographical references and index.
Identifiers: Canadiana (print) 20250154587 | Canadiana (ebook) 20250154625 | ISBN 9781487507916 (cloth) | ISBN 9781487559069 (paper) | ISBN 9781487537203 (PDF) | ISBN 9781487537210 (EPUB)
Subjects: LCSH: Spiderwoman Theater. | LCSH: Storytelling. | LCSH: Indian theater – United States. | LCSH: American drama – Indian authors – History and criticism.
Classification: LCC PN2270.I53 C37 2025 | DDC 792.089/97073 – dc23

Cover design: Will Brown
Cover images: (Front) Photo by Théo Coté. Courtesy of Spiderwoman Theater. (Back cover, from left to right) Gloria Miguel, Muriel Miguel, and Lisa Mayo (Spiderwoman Theater). Promotional photo for the "New Tribe" exhibit (2005–6). Courtesy of the National Museum of the American Indian, Smithsonian Institution.

We wish to acknowledge the land on which the University of Toronto Press operates. This land is the traditional territory of the Wendat, the Anishinaabeg, the Haudenosaunee, the Métis, and the Mississaugas of the Credit First Nation.

This book has been published with the help of a grant from the Federation for the Humanities and Social Sciences, through the Awards to Scholarly Publications Program, using funds provided by the Social Sciences and Humanities Research Council of Canada.

University of Toronto Press acknowledges the financial support of the Government of Canada, the Canada Council for the Arts, and the Ontario Arts Council, an agency of the Government of Ontario, for its publishing activities.

Canada Council for the Arts | Conseil des Arts du Canada

Funded by the Government of Canada | Financé par le gouvernement du Canada | Canada

"We all know that what makes us so funny is an underlying set of hurts and scars and pain. You don't hide it. You turn it into something new."

– Lisa Mayo, *LA Times* (1990)

"We're afraid to get hurt. We're afraid to die. We're afraid to get sick. We're afraid of a lot of things. And that I think is part of the solution is how do we make it so we're not afraid – not afraid when we jump the hurdle and we don't know what's on the other side."

– Muriel Miguel, *Segal Talks* (June 2020)

Contents

List of Illustrations ix

Acknowledgments xi

Spiderwoman Theater: A Performance History xiii

Introduction: Between the Layers 3

1 Persistence of Violent Delights: "It's All the Same Bullshit Again" 20

2 "An Indian Is an Idea a Man Has of Himself" 65

3 An Indian Is *More* than Just an "Idea": By Their Acts, Ye Shall Know Them 110

4 Towards a Poetics of Re-Worlding: Becoming (and Then Staging) the New Human Being 151

5 The Published Texts 202

6 The Three Sisters from *There* to Here: Spiderwoman's Issue and the Project of Re-Worlding 265

Appendix 1: The Fittin' Room *(Spiderwoman Theater), "Pam's Ed. (March)"* 309

Appendix 2: From the Walter Havighurst Special Collections and University Archives (Miami University Libraries, Oxford, Ohio) 313

Appendix 3: From the Walter Havighurst Special Collections and University Archives (Miami University Libraries, Oxford, Ohio) 315

Works Cited 317

Index 333

Illustrations

0.1 Lisa Mayo in *I'll Be Right Back* (1984) at La MaMa Experimental Theatre Club 2
0.2 *Misdemeanor Dream* performance at Knutson Theatre at the University of South Dakota, 27 February 2024 8
1.1 *Material Witness* fabric installation at La MaMa ETC, 2016 46
1.2 Gloria Miguel as Du Tu Kapsus in *Material Witness* 53
2.1 Antonio and Elmira Miguel in costume for their upcoming *MOHICANS* spectacle in New York City, circa 1930s 78
2.2 Lisa Mayo and her puppet dance partner in *The Three Sisters from Here to There* 98
3.1 Muriel Miguel in front of the signature backdrop during a production of *Women in Violence* 122
4.1 A rendering of Jan Derrick's teaching model of a traditional Haudenosaunee community 172
5.1 Gloria Miguel in *Sun, Moon, and Feather* 222

Acknowledgments

This project began (although I mayn't have realized it just then) in 1990 when I first saw Monique Mojica's *Princess Pocahontas and the Blue Spots*. It lifted me up, set me on my feet, and suggested to me a purpose – to re-member my broken shell in and through the stories that reminded me to remember who I was born to be. Since this time, I have been privileged to work with and to witness the works of not only Mojica and Spiderwoman Theater, but also hundreds of burgeoning and established Indigenous artists from all disciplines and from all four directions across Turtle Island. Again and again, my life has been saved; my soul, restored; my hope, renewed. And through this project I attempt to dis-cover just how it is that these Indigenous artists can unfailingly effect repair, restoration, and renewal in the communities they labour to serve.

Between the Layers: Spiderwoman Theater, Storyweaving, and Survivance is a communitist project built upon the outrageous love, explosive creativity, intellectual courage, and immoderate generosity of a whole host of artists, scholars, and mentors. I owe an incalculable debt to my teachers and research partners Elizabeth, Gloria, and Muriel Miguel. **This book is not *about* these grandmothers. It is *theirs*, standing as it does upon the knowledge that they have preserved, developed, created, and passed on.**

My debt extends to all the artists who have been a part of Spiderwoman Theater since its inception, who have created work with the Miguel sisters, and/or who continue to pass their teachings on. These lights include Deborah Ratelle, Monique Mojica, Murielle Borst-Tarrant, Floyd Favel, Oswaldo DeLeón Kantule, Michelle St. John, Jani Lauzon, Erika Iserhoff, Candace Brunette, Ange Loft, and Penny Couchie.

Between the Layers began over a decade ago as a doctoral project (completed in 2010). And I acknowledge here what is owed to my supervisor

Paula Sperdakos and committee members Daniel Heath Justice and the late John Astington, who guided this work with gentle patience, infinite grace, and uncompromising rigour to make it what was and to show me what it could be. Paula, Daniel, and John, Chi Miigwetch for your profound investment in this project and for all the teachings that you have left with me. In this book, your teachings are cradled, as they are cradled in my heart.

In the intervening years, between the completion of my dissertation and the publication of this book, I have been a grateful beneficiary of the unconditional support of so many mentors, colleagues, and friends. Good-hearted, uncompromising, and wise, you are Keith Barker, Christine Bold, Antje Budde, Susan Hill, LeAnne Howe, Stephen Johnson, Ange Loft, Ric Knowles, Lee Maracle, and Tamara Trojanowska.

I would be remiss here if I did not also acknowledge the invaluable support and considerable assistance of William A. Wortman, former Head, The Department of Steward and Sustain: *The Walter Havighurst Special Collections, Preservation & University Archives*, housed at Miami University, Oxford, Ohio, and the assistance of this collection's current Head, William M. Modrow.

To my family – those who survived that I might live – I offer these pages with my love. I remember – now and forever.

And finally, with utmost gratitude and humility, I declare my thanks to God who created me and who has unfailingly sustained my hope, resolve, and breath throughout the beautiful moments (of which there have been many) and throughout those times when my heart broke and courage failed me.

Spiderwoman Theater: A Performance History

1976	*Women in Violence*	Washington Square Methodist Church, New York, NY
1977	*Women in Violence*	First European Tour
1977	*Lysistrata Numbah!*	La MaMa ETC, New York, NY
1978	*Trilogy: Friday Night, Jealousy, and My Sister Ate Dirt*[1]	Theater for the New City, New York, NY
1979	*Cabaret: An Evening of Disgusting Songs and Pukey Images*	Theater for the New City, New York, NY
1980	*Oh, What a Life*	WOW Festival, Theater for the New City, New York, NY
1980	*The Fittin' Room*	The Theater Project, New York, NY
1981[2]	*Sun, Moon, and Feather*	Newfoundland Theater, New York, NY
1982	*I'll Be Right Back*	Theater for the New City, New York, NY
1982	*The Three Sisters from Here to There*	Theater for the New City, New York, NY
1984	*The Banana Bunch*	Theater for the New City, New York, NY
1985	*Neurotic Erotic Exotics*[3]	At the Foot of the Mountain Theater, Minneapolis, MN
1985	*Women in Violence*	Tenth Anniversary Celebration

1 One-woman show, written and performed by Lisa Mayo.

2 This is when the split occurred in Spiderwoman Theater. Two contending factions within the group shared a grant. The Miguel sisters created *Sun, Moon, and Feather* based upon their family history. Lois Weaver, Peggy Shaw, and Pam Verge created *Split Britches* – a show based upon the family history of Weaver. Both shows enjoyed significant success. In the wake of this success, the "trial separation" became a permanent arrangement.

3 A collaborative project with AFOM.

1986	*3 Up, 3 Down*	American Indian Community House, New York, NY
1988	*Winnetou's Snake Oil Showfrom Wigwam City*	Theater for the New City, New York, NY
1990	*Reverb-ber-ber-rations*	Theater for the New City, New York, NY
1992	*Power Pipes*	Randolph Street Gallery, Chicago, IL
1992	*The Pause that Refreshes*[4]	American Indian Community House, New York, NY
1995	*Daughters from the Stars: Nis Bundor*[5]	Dance Theater Workshop, New York, NY
1996	*Trail of the Otter*[6]	Aboriginal Arts Programme, Banff Centre for Arts and Creativity, Banff, AB
1999	*Fear into Sacred*	Mending the Sacred Hoop: STOP Violence against Indian Women Conference, Flagstaff, AZ
2002	*Persistence of Memory*	Banff Centre for Arts and Creativity, Banff, AB
2007	*Persistence of Memory*	Miami University, Oxford, OH
2010	*Red Mother*[7]	La MaMa ETC, New York, NY
2012	*The Elders' Project: Among the Living*[8]	La MaMa ETC, New York, NY
2014	*The Elders' Project: Something Old, Something New, Something Borrowed, Something Blue*[9]	Produced by Native Women in the Arts at Native Earth Performing Arts, Toronto, ON
2016	*Material Witness*[10]	La MaMa ETC, New York, NY
2017	*MisdemeanorDream*	Currently in development

4 A one-woman show written and performed by Lisa Mayo, *The Pause that Refreshes* won an Obie Award for Outstanding Production.

5 This piece emerged from Lisa Mayo's solo-show *Voices from the Criss Cross Bridge.*

6 This is a solo performance created and performed by Muriel Miguel.

7 This one-woman show was written and performed by Muriel Miguel.

8 Lisa Mayo began to create this show in 2011 after her dementia had been diagnosed. Her youngest sister Muriel Miguel supported her as co-author, and the show was performed by Lisa Mayo and Danielle Soames under the direction of Muriel Miguel in March 2012.

9 This one-woman show was created by Gloria Miguel and Steve Elm and premiered in Toronto in November 2014.

10 *Material Witness* has emerged from a creative partnership between Spiderwoman Theater, Loose Change Productions, and Aanmitaagzi.

BETWEEN THE LAYERS

Figure 0.1. Lisa Mayo in *I'll Be Right Back* (1984) at La MaMa Experimental Theatre Club.

Photographer: Jerry Vezzuso. Courtesy of La MaMa Experimental Theatre Club Archive.

Introduction: Between the Layers

Some of us you will not see because we are spirits. But you will hear us. The door has been left ajar.

– Gloria Miguel, *Daughters from the Stars: Nis Bundor*

On 24 November 2013, Red Feather Olo Nadile-Naga Gilyai passed out of mortal existence to disappear between the layers.[1] In her 89 years on this earth, Elizabeth Miguel (more popularly known as Lisa Mayo) trained to become an accomplished mezzo-soprano and actor; co-founded North America's longest-running Indigenous (and feminist) theatre company Spiderwoman Theater; co-wrote and performed more than 25 shows worldwide; wrote and performed three solo shows; helped to raise her youngest sister Muriel; mothered a stepson; taught and mentored countless Indigenous youth and women; served her community as an AIDS activist and as a board member of the American Indian Community House in New York City; won countless awards; and was awarded an Honorary Doctorate from Miami University in Oxford, Ohio.

Born 15 November 1924, the eldest daughter of a Guna sailor (Antonio Miguel) and his Rappahannock wife (Elmira Miguel), Lisa Mayo grew up in Red Hook, Brooklyn, as a poor, brown girl who dreamed of being a folk singer (Mayo, Interview). In 1992, during an interview with Kathy A. Perkins, Mayo spoke movingly of her artistic journey. As she recounted this journey, it became clear that her story is not one of a singular dream pursued and finally attained. Rather, as I consider

1 When Lisa Mayo has introduced herself by her Guna name, she has translated it as "First Daughter to Come from the Stars – Interpreter of Dreams."

the lessons I have taken from Mayo's eventful life and prolific career, I understand that her journey teaches us to follow our passions, trust the process, and embrace the work that is put before us to do (Mayo in Perkins). Lisa Mayo followed her passion for folk music and eventually encountered a teacher who steered her towards operatic training. Her easy embrace of Italian arias and German *Lieder* led her to develop her histrionic instrument at the HB Studio with the legendary Herbert Berghof and his wife Uta Hagen (Mayo, Interview).[2] As she developed her actor's craft, Mayo regarded herself as a "tragedienne." However, her outward manifestation of the tragic roles to which she was attracted left little doubt that she was (as she remained throughout her life) an incredibly gifted comedienne with a cheeky flair for the burlesque (see fig. 0.1). Indeed, this tension between "inside" and "outside" and Elizabeth Miguel's desire to align her inner life with her outer life are motifs that arise within each of her works – from her earliest collaboration with Spiderwoman Theater as the Perfect Woman in *Women in Violence* to her final solo show *Among the Living*. Her life's work echoes with the refrain, "I'm alone, using my dreams to make inside more like outside" (Miguel and Mayo). Perhaps, at the end of her life, trapped as she was within a failing mind (dementia) and a failing body (cancer), she knew that she had accomplished her life's goal. In *Among the Living* (part of Spiderwoman Theater's *Elders' Project*), she tells us that she is, at last, "seeing [herself] from the inside out" (Mayo, "Among").

On 27 July 2017, Spiderwoman Theater presented the Toronto remount of *Material Witness* at the Living Ritual Festival in Toronto, Ontario.[3] As I watched, I was reminded of Lisa Mayo's view of herself as a human conduit in an eternal chain, connecting ancestor to descendant through her practice. *Material Witness*, directed by Muriel Miguel, performatively revisits Spiderwoman Theater's *Women in Violence* (1976) – the historic production that launched the troupe onto the world stage and that altered the course of Lisa Mayo's artistic life. Resisting the positioning of women as victims/survivors of violence, Spiderwoman's original production presented a raw interrogation – at once personal confession and social indictment – of women *in* violence. Four decades later, a new generation of storytellers complicated the weave of a dark tapestry, layering

2 In 2007, Mayo told me that she had intended to take a class (at the HB Studio) with Ozzie Davis, but Davis was playing Hamlet in Denmark. She ended up (contrary to plan) studying under Berghof and Hagen for over a decade. Lisa Mayo's training will be discussed at length in chapter 2.

3 The 2016 premiere of *Material Witness* will be discussed at length in chapter 1, while its progenitor *Women in Violence* will be discussed in chapter 3.

personal stories that speak not only to the myriad brutalities that mar the lives and scar the souls of countless Indigenous women and children but also to the brutal acts perpetrated upon the earth that threaten all life. The historic intervention set into motion by Lisa Mayo and Spiderwoman Theater has continued, as a new generation of aesthetic heirs rigorously unpacks the violent mechanisms of a racist system that facilitates the spiriting away of children from their families, that continues to turn its blind, complacent eyes away from the ever-growing numbers of our missing and murdered Indigenous sisters, and that sows poisonous seeds of dissension within our communities.

It is here perhaps that the lessons we can take from Lisa Mayo's life in art truly reverberate. As an artist, she was absolutely committed to the discovery and revelation of *truth*. Yet, as she testified in 1992 (Mayo in Perkins), her early life, in many ways, was directed by an instinct to flee from the truth, just as she resisted the "interesting" but "scroungy" Storyweaving process that was being developed by her youngest sister Muriel Miguel (Mayo in Perkins). It was within this process, however, that Mayo discovered "[she] could write," and that she could free herself from the institutional boxes that constrained her within her professional career (Mayo in Perkins). As she collaborated in the process of making the performative mola that was *Women in Violence* – "Cut. Bring up stories. Stitch" (Miguel and Mayo) – Lisa Mayo "came out" on stage as an Indigenous woman; here, with characteristic charm and humour, she was at last able to acknowledge and work through the violence she had experienced in the private and public spheres she inhabited throughout her life.

Furthermore, with this self-revelation, Lisa Mayo joined her younger sisters, Gloria and Muriel, on an arduous journey back to source – first, to the dining room floor on which she was born in Brooklyn, New York (Spiderwoman, *Sun*) and later, following an ancestral bloodline, to her father's birthplace in Gunayala to "break the conflicting enchantment" that so upset the balance between inner truth and outer life (Miguel and Mayo). Here, and throughout her career with Spiderwoman Theater, Mayo's artistic process radically informed her *life*, bringing into convergence the outer expression of self with ontological truth. It is almost a decade since she passed on from this world; still this First Daughter to Come from the Stars continues to realize herself as an intermediary agent, holding space in which ancestral past and unrealized future converse in the living present. Every show that she has authored, co-authored, and performed with Spiderwoman Theater has carried her ever deeper into the layers of existence within the seen and unseen worlds, connecting her with ancestor, with immediate family, with all her Indigenous relations, and with the personal responsibilities conferred upon her when she was named Olo Nadile-Naga Gilyai in her father's birthplace in Gunayala.

Nearly 50 years after its inception and a decade after Lisa Mayo's death, Spiderwoman Theater continues under the direction of Muriel Miguel, the "baby" sister whom Mayo had helped to raise. Penny Couchie (Anishinaabe), Cherish Violet Blood (Blackfoot), and Ange Loft (Kanien'kehá:ka) join original cast members Gloria Miguel and Donna Couteau (Sac Fox) to continue a healing journey initiated by three brown girls from Brooklyn, NY. Throughout *Material Witness*, echoes of Mayo's irreverent voice with her insouciant optimism momentarily surface from beneath the show's ever-thickening layers, infusing the horrors with which it wrestles with the promise of healing and a celebration of survivance. "The footprints of the stars that walked around all night are still fresh in the sand" (Miguel and Mayo).

Indeed.

Lisa Mayo still speaks to us from somewhere between the layers. In *Daughters from the Stars: Nis Bundor*, this daughter from the stars declared, "I am connected to my ancestors through the stories they passed down to me. And I am connected to and living through the next generation" (Miguel and Mayo). Today, her stories live on, and those connections continue to manifest themselves through the works of Spiderwoman Theater, her sisters, and the generations that have worked with and learned from them.

I write this in a time of global crisis, just over a century after a terrible flu pandemic, carried to myriad nations by soldiers returning from their tours of duty in World War I, ravaged the world. Once again, a flu virus has emerged to consume the hearts and minds and lives of people from every nation. I write in recovery, having spent two weeks "between the layers," hovering between this world and the next, as my body battled COVID-19.

I write with a head fuzzy with amorphous, half-remembered dreams and visions of my own final resting place. I write in the light, but part of my consciousness still wanders in a place of darkness and silence, sifting through the fragments of broken, fevered dreams. I tell you this because, to my mind, my own brief journey to a dark waiting room between worlds feels like yet another invisible thread that provides a point of connection – that ties me to the story of these Elders, artists, mentors, friends. This story, now, is one of loss, grief, fear, unknowing, and of a determination to continue.

Weeks before lockdown across North America, I was able to travel to New York City to witness a riotous workshop of Spiderwoman Theater's performative response to William Shakespeare's *A Midsummer*

Night's Dream. This was the third developmental phase of the project, which began at the Stratford Festival in 2017 under the direction of Muriel Miguel with an exploration of dreams. The following year, the company began to explore Indigenous relationships with the non-human creatures with whom we share our biotas. And in the 2020 workshop performance that I witnessed, the company members began to find themselves in stories of little people and in the myriad Indigenous origin stories that recount a descent of our human forebears from the stars. For 2021, the company planned to explore yet another realm and then to integrate all the realms they had navigated throughout this process for the premiere also scheduled for that year. The North American lockdowns that began only weeks after this workshop production halted those plans. Now, on the eve of this book's publication, *Misdemeanor Dream* has undergone several phases of development, had several showings in New York City, and has toured successfully in the United States.

Where Shakespeare's comedy navigates the tensions between humans and the natural world, between the generations, between lovers, between conquest and victor amidst a *collision* between the seen and unseen worlds, Spiderwoman Theater's *Misdemeanor Dream* curates the convergence of seen and unseen worlds, utilizing Indigenous "logic" or "what some might consider magic" to tackle the question of human origins, human being, and "human experience" (H.J. Tarrant qtd. in "The Magic"). Perhaps, then, we had entered one of the myriad portals (at least in our consciousness) between the familiar, quotidian world and a new realm. Perhaps, too, as rumours of a global pandemic began to increase in volume and urgency, we were already hovering on the precipice of a re-creation story.

This workshop production explored origins. It carried us through portals between worlds, recounting in mythic proportions an intergenerational birth story that takes us through the delivery of Penny Couchie (choreographer and performer) to her mother and, later, the delivery of her own daughter and fellow performer Animikiikwe Couchie-Waukey, who plays one of the fairy guides, ushering us in and through realms within the story. In this birth story, a Lynx Woman who falls in love with a weeping human enters the rift between darkness and light and takes up a new existence as a growing foetus in her womb. While the human woman loves her baby girl, she weeps when she is born. The new mother's tears (fear for the baby's future?) fall into the newborn's eyes and blind her. The blind child grows up fearful but strong and determined despite the fears she has inherited. And when she has a baby the tears that fall from her eyes wash her blindness away,

Figure 0.2. *Misdemeanor Dream* performance at Knutson Theatre at the University of South Dakota, 27 February 2024. Performers (left to right): Donna Couteau, Henu Josephine Tarrant (projected image), Chingwe Padraig Sullivan, Darylina Powderface.

Photo: Raimondo Genia, 2024. Courtesy of Spiderwoman Theater.

so that she can fully apprehend the beauty of her daughter (Spiderwoman, *Misdemeanor Dream*).

In a heart-piercing moment, the performer Penny Couchie approached that beauty and danced with Animikiikwe, the beautiful girl who grew up to follow her mother and to unite with her as a beautiful creation in a co-creative act of beauty and Indigenous logic. Herein are made apparent the layers of creation and re-creation. Through its navigation of fleshly and immaterial realms, this third developmental workshop offered a vision of what it means to be born into an unending Creation Story and a peripheral glimpse of how small, yet infinitely important, each life is in its moment of living.

During a compelling pre-performance address, Muriel Miguel (the show's director) related an experience she had had while sitting on a far shore and watching the tide come in. She spoke about how small she felt within this grand creation. She spoke about death and her conviction that mortal death is only a movement from one realm to another. "We all matter," she told us. We are small but infinitely precious. We are stardust, and "our beauty blends with the beauty around us" – enhances it, compliments it, adds to its wondrous store (M. Miguel in Spiderwoman, *Misdemeanor Dream* Talkback). Witnessing this workshop production, I felt keenly that I was witnessing a ceremony of recovery – a performative intervention that navigates Indigenous stories of beginning, that recoups language after the suppressions and losses, and that looks towards the future for all.

Elder Baba Nana (embodied by Gloria Miguel) became the thread binding the generations more tightly together and extending a web of care outwards to the "babies in cages" separated from their migrant mothers at the US border. What could she, a woman who has occupied this realm for more than nine decades, do to take care of those babies, she asked. What actions could she take to affect a healing intervention on the angry youth whose rage drives them to attack and kill each other (Spiderwoman, *Misdemeanor Dream*)? How can we all take care of that beauty and ensure its continuance?

With *Misdemeanor Dream*, Spiderwoman Theater has extended its circle of care. As it approaches its fiftieth year with an intergenerational project (that includes performers who range in age from their early twenties all the way up to a nonagenarian Elder), *male* performers and their stories have been intentionally included in the performative mix.[4] This

4 Joe Cross (Caddo) and Sheldon Raymore (Cheyenne River Sioux) appeared in *Fear of Oatmeal* (Amerinda in association with Spiderwoman Theater). This premiere was

male presence on Spiderwoman's stage is a new phenomenon for the company, which has been celebrated as the longest-running "feminist" troupe in North America. It bespeaks an explicit address of the company's *womanist* leanings – of its commitment to uplift an *entire* community and to performatively dissolve the colonially imposed oppositional binaries that divide and destroy families and nations.[5] After all, as our origin cycles remind us, our existence within the creation is sustained by dualism – by the balance of oppositional forces: light with darkness, hunger with satiation, flesh with spirit, male with female.[6]

> Ensemble: When she awoke, she looked out into the universe, and there he was. His light burned so brightly. She called him over. When they came together, it was magic! Stars shot across the sky, collisions happened, and in the space between them a portal opened. Animals and humans and spirits and fairies and other than human beings travelled between earth and sky, sky and earth. In the shadow of the sun and the moon, the earth

---

launched at the Theater for the New City in New York, NY, 8–24 June 2018. However, these performers played the roles and performed a text that had been written for them. Although *Fear of Oatmeal* is also an exercise in Storyweaving, it is a memory play and an exploration in the crafting of dialogue authored by a singular individual – Muriel Miguel – who is also the show's director (M. Miguel in Interview with Jill Carter 2018). The piece features Gloria Miguel in her childhood home in post-depression Brooklyn. Clothed in her mother's dress, Gloria presents a future vision of her baby sister Muriel now largely immobilized and isolated in the family home. As she sits at a kitchen table, she opens the show in song and sifts through the material remains of the generations who created and lived in this family home. Meanwhile spirits (played by Joe Cross, Soni Moreno, and Sheldon Raymore) dance in and out of her peripheral vision, singing to her and offering glimpses of the storied past and prophecy for the future.

5 Womanism and feminism as they pertain to the spirit, intent, and work of Spiderwoman Theater will be discussed later in chapter 4 of this work.

6 To my mind, acknowledgment and acceptance of dualities in our universe does not constitute a turn towards a worldview that structures itself around oppositional binaries. Because we love the light, we do not seek to obliterate the peace and beauty night brings. To eradicate one or the other would throw the world into imbalance. Indeed, destructive actors in many Anishinaabe teaching stories are not utterly destroyed; instead, they undergo radical transformation within these stories and grow into creative agents whose acts then become life-giving acts undertaken for the good of the creation and not simply self-serving acts that sate the appetites of one while destroying others. Light and darkness, good and evil, selfishness and self-sacrifice are contained within us all and may be balanced and called into service to sustain the lives of all. For further discussion around the distinction between dualism and thinking that is governed by oppositional binaries, readers are encouraged to refer to *As We Have Always Done* (2019) by Leanne Betasamosake Simpson (201).

began to die. The sun and the moon went to opposite sides of the sky to love each other from afar, but every once in a while, they come together and … (Spiderwoman, *Misdemeanor Dream*).

Witnesses to the 2020 workshop of *Misdemeanor Dream* were welcomed into Spiderwoman's space by Muriel Miguel's late son-in-law Kevin Tarrant (Ho-Chunk and Hopi). Kevin Tarrant was the youngest son of the late Josephine Mofsie-Tarrant for whom Spiderwoman Theater is named. As the leader of the Silver Cloud Singers, Tarrant welcomed us into the space with an address that remembered all the nations who had and who continue to steward Manahatta (Manhattan) and in song. This was a task he continued to fulfil throughout the run of the show. For me, this was yet another first. This was the first time I had seen a land acknowledgment delivered within an American theatre space. Sid Bobb (Stó:lō), who is the partner of co-performer Penny Couchie, joined the cast and wove in stories from his ancestral territories. He told us of sea slugs and of a napping "fat-ass" bear. At the height of summer, this bear had feasted on berries, stuffing himself into a stupor. Satiated and napping, he was spotted by a "crooked crow" with desires much bigger than his/her diminished raptor stomach could accommodate. And as the hapless sleeper was about to be eaten by this greedy, "crooked" creature, he suddenly reared up to declare, "I'm not done yet" (Spiderwoman, *Misdemeanor Dream*).

As a new era begins, Spiderwoman calls in the coming generations. This troupe is not "done yet." A new era is beginning, and *we* are "not done yet." Despite the rapacious acts and genocidal schemes of colonial agency; despite the relocations, re-education, child theft and murder; despite a centuries-old campaign to eradicate Indigenous presence from this continent, Indigenous Peoples "are not done yet." Where the agents, profiteers, and beneficiaries of the colonizing project have shrugged in the face of these crimes against Indigenous humanity, characterizing them as "misdemeanours," which we too must learn to shrug off – to "get over" – Indigenous bodies today still bear the scars. These are not the stuff of aggravating dreams of petty slights that melt in the light of morning. These are the stuff of living nightmares.

As I write today, Canada is cautiously celebrating its imminent emergence from the nightmare of the global pandemic; at the same time, Indigenous Peoples within this nation state have been catapulted back into a perennial nightmare by the material manifestation of state-sanctioned infanticide with the unearthing of over one thousand children (at the date of this writing) in unmarked graves on the grounds of several residential schools in Western Canada. As survivors of these schools across these lands, and around the world, navigate the grief and conduct ceremonies for these erstwhile "disappeared," it is understood by all that the nightmare will continue. Thousands more within the grounds of Canadian re-education camps lie sleeping in darkness awaiting discovery. This nightmare does not emerge from the shock of a grisly revelation. Residential school survivors have been speaking about this publicly for decades. The unmarked graves of stolen, abused, and murdered babies are not simply markers of misdemeanor to cloud the national imaginary for a moment only to be buried and forgotten. These mark crimes that require redress. These mark crimes for which their perpetrators need to be named and "held accountable" (Christian qtd. in Quan).

Such reflections are not part of some thought experiment. They are neither whimsical nor capricious. These reflections emerge from the knowledge that the governing bodies and citizens of both Canada and the United States of America hold (and have held for some time) a very different story (and interpretation of their history and origins) than the Indigenous nations whose lands they continue to occupy. Beneath the earth and between the layers, countless unsettling truths – truths that can do no less than crack the very foundations of the current North American imaginary – are now being spoken into the world. And yet, a story may be told or received in countless ways. Truths may be obfuscated. Genocidal crimes may, as Muriel Miguel's pre-show address reminded us, be cast by the perpetrators and their beneficiaries as minor wrongdoings – as "misdemeanours" (Spiderwoman, *Misdemeanor Dream*).

MisdemeanorDream's treatment of the Origin Story of Sky Woman forcefully brings this point home, even as it tickles its rapt witnesses with its whimsy and irreverence. Throughout this workshop production, we are carried by an inter-First-National cast through myriad accounts of creation. These stories – Anishinaabe, Apache, Chickasaw, Guna, Ho-Chunk, Hopi, Innu, Maya, Mi'kmaq, Rappahannock, Stó:lō, and Yaqui – trace the threads of connection between people and nations and between earthbound existence and celestial origins. Each story from each nation identifies the stuff of life as stardust and locates the beginning and ending of life in the stars. And the troupe's whimsical iteration of the saga of Sky Woman is but one of these "visual narratives of empowerment, self-awareness and connection" (Programme Note). For all its uproarious humour, Spiderwoman's telling of Earth's creation provides a sly, cautionary note – a reminder that no telling is fixed: one man's dream may be another's nightmare. Where one characterizes wrong action as "misdemeanor," the story of another may reveal that action as a gravely criminal act.

The story of a celestial female entity who fell from her world to collaborate in a project of re-worlding speaks to the formation of the earth upon which we now live and to the origins of humankind within this biota (see fig. 0.2). It is shared in various forms and iterations by myriad nations across Turtle Island (North America). For those readers who are not yet familiar with this creation/re-creation story as it has been told for millennia by the Haudenosaunee and Anishinaabeg, I offer a skeletal distillation of this long and complex saga:[7] Long before the emergence of human beings, this world was a water world, inhabited only by creatures who could thrive and survive within such a biota. And these creatures did thrive; they loved this world of water; they were content with their way of living. Meanwhile, up in Skyworld, in a biota much like the terrestrial biota we inhabit today – a tree had been uprooted, and a powerful and very pregnant woman fell through the foundations of her world, hurtling straight towards the water world below. When the water creatures began to perceive her imminent and dramatic arrival, a flock of white winged birds flew upwards, caught her mid-flight and gently escorted her towards the water. When it was perceived that she could not long survive in the water, Turtle offered his back, as a place upon which she could rest. But she and her unborn baby could not be provided with the necessaries of life on the hard shell of Turtle's back. So, at her request, the water creatures began to dive in turns to acquire a clod of earth from the floor of their watery home. Eventually, the least likely seeming creature (some say Muskrat; others say Otter) succeeded. Sky Woman spread that earth on Turtle's back and began a dance. As she danced, this stuff of life expanded and deepened. The rock-hard shell of Turtle's back became a rich, loamy bed in which Sky Woman could plant the medicines she had brought with her from her own world. So it was that the inhospitable shell of a most hospitable amphibian could become a green and fertile place – a place of plenty to support a new creation.

With *Misdemeanor Dream*, Spiderwoman Theater strips this mythic fall of its romance, weaving two interpretations of the same event:

---

7 I have drawn here upon several published and/or publicly performed accounts. These accounts appear in *Braiding Sweetgrass: Indigenous Wisdom, Scientific Knowledge, and the Teachings of Plants* by Robin Wall Kimmerer (Milkweed Editions, 2020); *Chocolate Woman Dreams the Milky Way* (written and performed by Monique Mojica, 2011), and *Material Witness* (Spiderwoman Theater, 2016).

DONNA [COUTEAU]: And at the council meeting, they decide to send up seven of the biggest geese in V formation. And they flew up and spread out their wings and caught the falling woman on their backs.

HENU [TARRANT]: They weren't seven strong geese. They were seven little assholes. And they come over saying they're gonna help me because I'm a poor woman with child for Christ sakes. I have a child inside me and I'm falling out of the Goddamn sky.

DONNA: So they begin to circle around and circle around but after a while, "Honk! Honk! Oh, please help us! We didn't know she was big AND pregnant!"

HENU: I'm not big.

DONNA: Well anyway, they started to complain. They said, "We got to find a place to put her down right now. She's so heavy."

HENU: Those assholes! I made them! And you leave me![8]

DONNA: I hope you have a parachute.

HENU: This is my story! (Spiderwoman, *Misdemeanor Dream*)

This *is* Sky Woman's story. It is a spiritual tracing that belongs to generations upon generations of those who have come after her – those whose lives have been directed by the teachings they have absorbed in each new telling. For better or for worse, the purposes to which this elemental female force devoted her existence manifest themselves now as an ongoing legacy, lighting a way forward for the generations that follow. Such stories, regardless of who is telling them, offer us only the tracing of a life – a glimpse of spiritual essence. It is into this essence that the living witness to historic doings is invited to breathe new life, investing it with the flesh and colour that belongs, for a moment, to the mortal sojourner in this material realm. These thoughts guide my reflections around the backdrop of human silhouettes, which the actors created for this workshop production. Here, Spiderwoman's signature mola backdrop (which has travelled with the troupe since its inception) had been replaced by structural drawings of the performers' spiritual essence. Here, we witnessed flesh and spirit commune, as a new generation of Spider-people followed their Creation Stories back to an originary self.[9]

---

8 I quote here from the workshop script provided to me by Muriel Miguel and Deborah Ratelle. In the performance I saw, Sky Woman shrieked, "Those sons of bitches dropped me," casting doubt upon the intentions of her would-be helpers and further emphasizing the differences between the spirit and intent that exert their influence upon our recounting and reception of memory.

9 Visual artist and arts educator Sherry Guppy was born in Temagami. Since 2009, Guppy has been a core artist with Aanmitaagzi where *Misdemeanor Dream* was

I write in a time of uncertainty and in a time of deep mourning. In February 2020, I felt my soul expanding as I witnessed the workshop production of *Misdemeanor Dream* and gleefully anticipated its completion and 2021 premiere.[10] One month later, the rumours of a global plague had manifested themselves as a new, global reality. On 09 April 2020, cast member Tyree Giroux (Chickasaw) passed away from complications due to COVID-19. On 04 May 2020, Kevin Tarrant was snatched from his wife Muriel Borst-Tarrant, his daughter Henu Josephine Tarrant, and his mother-in-law Muriel Miguel. He too had died from complications due to COVID-19. Confined to their homes, Gloria and Muriel Miguel could not attend his funeral. Confined to their homes, Gloria and Muriel Miguel could not hold, hug, or comfort his widow who was herself battling the virus. They could not hold, hug, or comfort his daughter. They could not meet in ceremony. They could not meet to work. They could not share "touch" or "breath" – key practices in the business of living, key practices in the business of making theatre. As the world wondered how (and if) we were going to survive this historical moment, Muriel Miguel asked, "How are we going to do the future?" (M. Miguel in *Segal Talks*).

Since that time, millions the world over have been vaccinated. Nations, towns, and cities have opened up. Humans are once again congregating to teach, learn, work, rehearse, and witness. Yet the future remains uncertain, and it remains, now, to be seen – in the wake of all our losses, amid escalating social unrest, amid calls for justice in an unjust world – just how that future will be done. Like Sky Woman before us, it seems, we are falling away from an old world – a world in

---

developed in its Big Medicine Studio (Nipissing, ON). Here, Guppy led a body-mapping intensive during which the devisor-performers of *Misdemeanor Dream* each created a full-scale body map through which to explore personal "narratives of empowerment, self-awareness, and connection." Together, then, they created a collective map and the initial design for the set. In the following year (2020), the devisor-performers' body maps were incorporated (via life-size panels) into the backdrop under the guidance of Sherry Guppy, Megan Lozicki Paulin, Tasheena Saraxin, Chris Couchie, and Gayle Weston (see Couchie). In performance, these body maps co-perform with their three-dimensional creators, marking corporeal sites of wounding and energy centres (sites of healing). Within each tracing, we see a soul in conflict. Tranquil confidence and fluid forward momentum pull away from the wounded soul paralyzed by fear and rage. In February 2020, *Misdemeanor Dream* was publicly workshopped at the Abrons Arts Centre in New York. And it is of this production I write here.

10 In March 2020, the COVID-19 pandemic forced the world into lockdown. *Misdemeanor Dream* ultimately premiered at the Ellen Stewart Theater in New York and was presented by La MaMa ETC in collaboration with Aanmitaagzi and Loose Change Productions.

which, perhaps, "we got too comfortable" (M. Miguel in *Segal Talks*) – clutching memories and medicines to sustain us in whichever world we land. Perhaps, this calamitous time is just another phase in an eternally cycling origin story. Perhaps, we are living a re-creation story.

The work I attempt to accomplish here is my own *re-creation of a Creation Story*. Within this work, I attempt to document several journeys towards becoming. First, there is the two-pronged journey of each Miguel sister: The quest to discover one's humanity through art, and the human being's discovery and development of a potent art form that emerges out of her deepening knowledge of her Indigeneity. Between these layers nests my own story of becoming – the journey of a mixed-blood, urban Anishinaabe-Ashkenazi learner towards a greater sense of her own humanity and a more profound understanding of her artistry through her apprenticeship with Spiderwoman and its issue and in her retracing of her teachers' steps to map their lives in art. Finally, with this work, I attempt to document the creation of a community (Spiderwoman Theater and those they have influenced) and to map the making of a process – a process through which the vehicles that carry the stories of our origins might be invested with the power to heal, transform, and contribute to the formation of Indigenous human identity. Like Sky Woman before it, Spiderwoman Theater has prepared a bundle for the Indigenous theatre workers and audiences who will follow, and it is my profound hope that this work will inspire others to take up this bundle and create potent medicine for their communities.

I began this project with a simple objective: I had encountered two teacher-artists (Muriel Miguel and Monique Mojica) who had profoundly influenced my life and art; they had given me the tools with which I was beginning to write a new story for myself. I wanted to document their process. I intended to create a historical record that would clearly attribute authorship of the Storyweaving Practice[11] to Muriel Miguel (founder of Spiderwoman Theater) and that would mark the stages of its evolution in the works of Spiderwoman's inheritors. *Spiderwoman Theater's practice of Storyweaving is significant, unique, and specifically Indigenous.* Admittedly, it has been informed to varying degrees by the work of Joseph Chaikin, Uta Hagen, and Lee Strasberg in the application and adaptation of some of their exercises. But these exercises have been adapted in the Spiderwoman studio in accordance with the world view/lifeway of Spiderwoman Theater's Guna-Rappahannock founders. Theirs is a process that directs the creation of

11 Muriel Miguel now refers to Storyweaving as a "practice," not a methodology.

story, the dramaturgical framework that contains it, and the mode of its performance.

Just as the artistic investigations and resultant exercises of many Western teacher-artists in the theatre have been documented, so like *respect* is owed the teacher-artists who are Spiderwoman Theater for what they have created and for what they continue to create. This concept of respect is a highly complex and multi-layered "animal." First, there is the respect of the student for her teachers and for the knowledge they have given me – the tools with which they have gifted me to enhance my capacity to live well. This aspect of respect speaks to my esteem for my teachers/research partners and to the reciprocal relationship that exists between us. It is very personal; as such, it renders this project a highly personal act. There is also, here, the respect that renders this project a political act – an act (which like the process I have laboured to disseminate) speaks, for me, to the anti-colonial project of re-worlding. If the process of colonization necessitated the devaluation, denigration, and ultimate suppression of Indigenous Knowledge Systems, its reversal requires the evaluation, celebration, and dissemination of those knowledge systems – those that we have recovered and those that Indigenous Peoples are creating now.

This project began as a processual "primer" and grew into a Creation Story. As a "primer," it was never intended to replace the teacher. Rather, it was intended to remind the student of lessons learned, exercises tried, and principles activated. It will, I hope, inform coming generations of the existence, history, mechanics, and development of the Storyweaving Practice, of its applicability to their own projects, and of the teachers whom they might seek if they wish to pursue it. I hope it will inspire young Indigenous artists to seriously interrogate the stories they wish to tell, to consider the containers that house them, to experiment with modes of transmission, and to develop their own frameworks and methodologies informed by Indigenous Knowledge Systems and the aesthetic principles emerging from their nations. Ultimately, I hope that this work will add to a growing body of processual theory upon which coming generations of Indigenous artists and culture workers can draw.

In chapter 1 ("Persistence of Violent Delights"), we encounter Spiderwoman Theater as it approaches its fiftieth year of existence to discuss the troupe's most recent completed work *Material Witness* (introduced here) and the new generation of performers who have joined forces with original troupe members to untangle a web of violence that continues to be a defining experience for Indigenous women today. *Material Witness* continues the work that was begun in 1976 with *Women in Violence* – the show that catapulted the troupe to the world stage. Extractivism, voyeurism, and the continuing murder and disappearance of Indigenous women will be considered in light of the question, "What good is theatre, anyway?" as we explore despair and hope in the time (and times again) of violent crisis and the emergence of Spiderwoman Theater as creative response in an "irredeemable" moment.

Chapter 2 ("An Indian is an Idea") carries us back to the beginning before Spiderwoman's beginnings. Here, we encounter the early personal and professional histories of Spiderwoman Theater's founding mothers. Through an exploration of their socio-economic positioning, their difficult home life, the racialized narratives by which they were defined outside the home, and their artistic development within these impossible conditions, this chapter unpacks instances of personal and familial resistance to colonial agency and reveals the seamless weave that so inextricably binds art and life.

Moving beyond the "idea" of Indigeneity into "acts" of Indigeneity, chapter 3 documents the early history of Spiderwoman Theater and offers a processual analysis of its transformation from a multi-racial, feminist collective to the longest-running *Indigenous* theatre troupe in North America. In this exploration of early (unpublished) Spiderwoman productions, I attempt to map the intersection of a personal project of Indigenous self-recovery with the politically (re)vital(izing) creation of a decolonizing/re-worlding aesthetic. The next chapter ("Towards a Poetics") affords us the opportunity to engage more deeply and intimately with Spiderwoman's Storyweaving Practice. Discovering its connections to the aesthetic principles of the Miguel sisters' Guna forebears, chapter 4 moves us into the contemporary rehearsal studio to methodically unpack how this aesthetic works within and through the living bodies who utilize it in the creation of works for the contemporary stage.

Chapter 5 ("The Published Texts") carries us through a chronological examination of Spiderwoman's published works – *Sun, Moon, and Feather; Winnetou's Snake Oil Show from Wigwam City; Reverb-ber-berations;* and *Power Pipes*. This chapter attends to the realization of these works on both page and stage, as it attempts to illuminate the ways in which Spiderwoman's Storyweaving Practice has shaped the effect of these seminal works on the artists and their audiences.

Finally, this project concludes in this historical moment where I have chosen to begin. "The Three Sisters from There to Here" names and evaluates the benefits of Spiderwoman Theater's legacy by charting the adoption and adaptation of its Storyweaving Practice by its genealogical and aesthetic heirs. Works created and performed by Turtle Gals

Performance Ensemble, the Chocolate Woman Collective, and The Collective Encounter are among those explored in this concluding chapter. The threads of connection, binding these works one to the other and to their methodological progenitors emerge, as we contemplate *Persistence of Memory*, the Miguel sisters' final collective creation. Reflecting upon memory and survivance, the ethics of witnessing, and the potential for redemption in irredeemable moments, this chapter invites us to weigh the bundle that Spiderwoman Theater has prepared for a coming generation of Indigenous artists and witnesses and to consider its application in myriad projects of re-worlding, re-treating, and relational repair.

As we move forward towards an uncertain future, "the door has [indeed] been left ajar." This work contains the bundle that I clutch as I move unseeing through the portal that Spiderwoman Theater has opened for us. It contains the teachings that I have received and that I believe I comprehend. I remain aware, however, that the bundle I have received and attempt to pass on here does not contain *all* the teachings Spiderwoman Theater has offered. But for better or worse, I have tried and tested the teachings that I have received, and so this is a bundle that *owns me* and a bundle to which I am responsible: I am responsible as an artist to use it in a good way, as a scholar to represent it faithfully, and as an educator to pass it on in a way that respects and honours my teachers and those who taught them.

1 Persistence of Violent Delights: "It's All the Same Bullshit Again"

What's Theatre Good For, Anyway?

Some years ago, I saw Professor J. Edward Chamberlain (now emeritus, English/comparative studies, University of Toronto) read from *If This Is Your Land, Where Are Your Stories?* During the discussion that followed, Professor Chamberlain passionately asserted that the purpose and function of story is to help us stand and withstand in the face of death (Chamberlain), and this assertion resonated deeply with me, as a mixed-blood, Anishinaabe-Ashkenazi woman fattened upon story when food was scarce. And through the myriad accounts of Creation upon which I have been feasted, I have come to learn that for the Anishinaabeg, the whole of the ongoing creation is a web of story. Each of our lives is a fragile filament in the web. We live forever within story because we have been woven into it. Our tellings of that story on the page, on birchbark, through earthworks, or through our corporeal instruments reflect and affirm this knowledge. With each new telling, we invoke (literally re-*present*) those who continue to live in the story although their sojourn on this earth has been concluded. We recall/re-call them to the present moment because our need to see them is so great. We need to remind ourselves that human life does matter, that human actions do resonate – that we do indeed continue on and that our struggles are not in vain. Indigenous methodologies reflect this understanding. Indigenous reception of the story reminds us of this teaching. The "actors" become subjects of their telling: mimesis is not an art they need to master, a goal they need to pursue; it nests within their bones, awakened by story to activate breath, muscle, tendon. It courses through their blood. And if they weave the story respectfully, the nerve centres of their witnesses respond – tugging at our limbs, prompting us to retrace ancestral steps. As ancient pathways are recharted and ancient portals opened, a profound transformation – of teller and witness – ensues in the moment of the retelling.

This is the work of re-worlding that so many Indigenous artists (i.e., Floyd Favel, Monique Mojica, Yves Sioui Durand, Jani Lauzon, and Debajehmujig Storytellers, to name a very few) have undertaken. This is the work that concerned the Miguel sisters in 1976 and that has continued for almost half a century with their Spiderwoman Theater. This is work that summons, for a moment, our dead into the circle and that bids them dance. It is work that asserts life in the face of death, that enlists hope to smother despair, that re-members the dismembered and connects the fragments of a dislocated sense of self and personal history. It is work, which knits into our bones the certainty that our Indigenous ancestors dreamed our coming and that they rejoice because we are still here. This is work that reaches back into a timeless Indigenous imaginary to recover traditional epistemologies and practices and to distil from these the aesthetic principles through which to craft communal healing.

Yet, despite all the good work that has been accomplished, doubt slithers to the surface to whisper its unsettling questions – questions that demand address: What precisely do we change as we tell our stories and perform our histories? What shifts do we effect in our own lived reality or the lived reality of our descendants through this dedication of breath and corporeal effort? If the sum of our existence and the ways in which we express existence amount to no more than the stories we have chosen to believe, tell, and retell (King 2), what are we? What do we become? What changes? What remains unchanged? What are the stories we need to be telling – to and of ourselves, to and of our children, to and of each other?

As I write this, it has been some years since the Truth and Reconciliation Commission of Canada released its 2015 Final Report on the Indian Residential School System with its 94 Calls to Action. Across the nation, educational institutions, government offices, and public theatres have fallen over themselves to publicly declare their commitment to redress past misdeeds and contribute to the establishment of right relations between the settler populations they represent and the Indigenous Peoples whose lands they occupy. And yet, 2016 saw the publication of an Angus Reid poll that indicated that while most Canadians were happy to support the launch of a national inquiry into Missing and Murdered Indigenous Women and Girls (MMIWG), the same respondents also voiced their belief that such an inquiry would change absolutely nothing (Global News, "Most Canadians"). This is baffling. The respondents to this poll were advocating for a cosmetically correct action: They expressed no qualms about investing hundreds of thousands of tax dollars (dollars that could have gone directly to an Indigenous community or to an urban organization that serves Indigenous people) in an investigation that *they believed would bring no justice* and that *they believed would do nothing* to help stop the slaughter of Indigenous women and girls. For these Canadians, the *gesture* was enough. Its effects held little interest. Two years later, in February 2018, a Canadian jury delivered a "not guilty" verdict in the case of a Saskatchewan farmer who shot and killed a Cree youth – Colten Boushie.[1] And not two weeks after that, a second jury vindicated the man accused of the brutal murder of a 15-year-old Anishinaabe girl.[2]

In 2019, Canada's prime minister *mocked* a young Indigenous woman who had raised and paid $1,500 to attend a fundraising dinner at which

---

1 In 2016, five Indigenous youths (three young men and two young women) drove onto a Saskatchewan farm when a tire on their vehicle went flat. Were they seeking help, or were they, as the farm's owner Gerald Stanley maintained, about to commit robbery? Gerald Stanley and his son met these youth with loaded guns, attacking their compromised vehicle with a hammer. The encounter ended with the death of Colten Boushie, a 22-year-old Cree man whom Gerald Stanley shot in the back of the head (Austen). Upon Boushie's death, seven RCMP officers were dispatched to the home of his mother Debbie Baptiste to inform the family of this tragedy. Accounts of this visit to Baptiste's home (by the family and noted in the Final Report of the Civilian Review and Complaints Commission) do not indicate that the announcement of Boushie's death was delivered with any note of compassion or accompanied by any expressions of condolence. Instead, the distraught mother's home was surrounded by armed officers. She was repeatedly asked if she had been drinking and told to "get it together." Although no warrant had been obtained, officers conducted a thorough search of the Baptiste home. Less thorough, it seems, was their investigation into the shooting of Colten Boushie: The failure to maintain the integrity of the crime scene; laxity on the part of forensic investigators; and failure to instruct the accused and his son to not discuss the case before being independently examined are some of the concerns noted in a 2018 report published by the Civilian Review and Complaints Commission for the RCMP (see, for example, Civilian Review and Complaints Commission Findings 25, 26, 37, 9, and 13). Throughout his trial, Stanley maintained that he was in fear for his property and that his close-range shooting of Colten Boushie had been the result of an accidental discharge. Given the lack of diligence in the investigation of the shooting of an Indigenous person, the failure to hold his killer to any account whatsoever, and the callous treatment of an Indigenous woman overcome by shock and grief upon hearing the news of her son's death, is it any wonder that Indigenous people harbour such distrust of law enforcement officials and the system these officials have been tasked with upholding?

2 Despite being wrapped in plastic and fabric and being weighted down with rocks, the lifeless body of Tina Fontaine (of Sagkeeng First Nation) was found floating in the Red River on 17 August 2014. Four years later, the man accused of her murder, Raymond Cormier (53), was acquitted on the grounds of a lack of evidence. The

he was speaking. "Mr. Trudeau, people at Grassy Narrows are suffering from mercury poisoning," she told him. "You committed [yourself and the nation you represent] to addressing this crisis" (Global News, "Trudeau"). Amid laughter and applause from his supporters, Canada's leading man answered this witness to a nation's suffering with a lighthearted quip completely devoid of empathy – a jest, more suited to the court of the last royal family of France than a "progressive," elected leader of a twenty-first century "democratic" nation. "*Thank you for your donation,*" he responded. Thank you for your donation, indeed!

Later that year, the Final Report of the National Inquiry into Missing and Murdered Indigenous Women and Girls was released. In his initial statement of response to the report, Prime Minister Justin Trudeau promised that Canada would break its historic inertia and begin to act to protect the rights and well-being of Indigenous girls and women and of 2SLGBTQQIA people. At a subsequent gathering of women – likely, responding to criticism for his refusal to use the word "genocide"[3] in

---

Crown has not appealed his acquittal; nor have any other suspects been investigated or apprehended. Fontaine and Boushie are only two of thousands of Missing and Murdered Indigenous Children for whom justice (from within Canada's legal system) is not and will not be forthcoming.

3 Throughout this book, I use the terms "genocide" and "genocidal" to characterize the actions and intentions of the European settlers and their governing bodies who eventually claimed "ownership" of Turtle Island (North America). An early reviewer of this book has challenged my use of these terms and has suggested that I define these terms as I intend them to be understood and to offer historical and/or statistical proofs. To build this case with the rigour and gravitas that should be accorded it would require a series of books and/or reports – many of which have already been published and may easily be accessed. That said, I offer my own understanding and some very scant examples for those readers who may be discomfited by my characterization of historic and ongoing relations between Indigenous and non-Indigenous Peoples within these lands now known as "Canada."

My understanding and use of the terms genocide and genocidal accord with Article II of the *Convention on the Prevention and Punishment of the Crime of Genocide* (PPCG) adopted by the United Nations on 9 December 1948. Article II states that acts perpetrated with the intent to significantly reduce the numbers of or to entirely eradicate an ethnic group are genocidal acts. Such acts include the deliberate murder of individuals from the targeted group; any act that causes "serious bodily or mental harm" to members of the targeted group; imposing untenable living conditions on the group, which have deleterious effect(s) on its members (bodily and otherwise); enacting measures to prevent or significantly reduce births within the group; and removing children from the group by force to place them with another group (see National Inquiry into Missing and Murdered 51).

An intentional series of violent actions and covertly violent legislative policies enacted upon Indigenous Peoples across this continent through the eighteenth and nineteenth centuries for the purposes of "extirpation," "elimination," and "assimilation," may be traced by reviewing the Indian Act (1876) and its various amendments throughout the late nineteenth and early twentieth centuries. Myriad published historical accounts (too numerous to cite here) may be easily accessed. These speak to massacre, to the deliberation fomentation of distrust and division among Indigenous nations, to treaty negotiations undertaken with an intent to placate and deceive, and to a deliberate and long-sustained campaign to legislatively effect the removal of Indigenous Peoples (as distinct political bodies) from these shores.

The systematic and ongoing destruction of land and waters that once sustained Indigenous nations across these territories; the relegation of Indigenous Peoples to reserves where they would be dependent upon insufficient (and often withheld) treaty payments of basic foodstuffs, tolerable living conditions, and monies; the Residential School System (1884–1996) in Canada by means of which Indigenous children were removed from their homes (by force or coercion) and set apart from their communities during their formative years have been well documented. And this knowledge is readily available to all who wish to better understand this fraught history. One has only to review the Final Report of the Truth and Reconciliation Commission of Canada (freely available online) to comprehend the significant damage (physical, emotional, and spiritual) that was visited upon Indigenous children and to further comprehend the trauma suffered by the generations of children and grandchildren who were either snatched up by these institutions themselves or who were raised by survivors.

As Canada's Residential School System began to crumble, Indigenous children were removed from their homes by state care workers and adopted into non-Indigenous homes in the 1960s and the decades that followed. The Sixties Scoop (as this period is called) has evolved into the "Millennium scoop." Now, Indigenous children who have been removed from their homes and communities are being placed into state-run institutions and long-term foster care at an increasing rate (Sinclair 68). Such institutions are subject to little oversight, and too many of these young people, placed into the "care" of predators, experience unendurable abuse, exploitation, and sexual trafficking (see, for instance, Russell, Jarvis, and Wroebel). In 2021, Statistics Canada reported that only 8 per cent of children across Canada age 14 and under were Indigenous. Yet, in the same year, 53.8 per cent of all children in care within that age group were Indigenous (Needham).

Further, a concerted effort to prevent the birth of Indigenous children has continued from the 1930s into today. For more information about the ongoing forced sterilization of Indigenous women in Canada, please refer to "Indigenous Women – Forced Sterilization Saskatchewan, Canada," a fact sheet published by the Saskatoon office of Maurice Law; Yvonne Boyer and Dr. Judith Bartlett's "External Review: Tubal Ligation in the Saskatoon Health Region: The Lived Experience of Aboriginal Women"; *Sacred Bundles Unborn* by Mercredi and Fire Keepers Collective; Maria Cheng's "Indigenous Women in Canada Forcibly Sterilized Decades after Other Rich Countries Stopped"; and the 2022 Report of the Standing Senate Committee on Human Rights.

Across the globe there are many Truth/Truth and Reconciliation/Transitional Justice Commissions, and more are being established each year. For each nation within which she rages, genocide wears a different face. She may move carefully and surreptitiously over decades or centuries; she may descend in a lightning strike to devastate a people unashamedly and with brutal rapidity. Her bundle of tactics is immense and varied. My intent here and throughout this book is neither to conflate genocidal events that have historically occurred and that currently occur around the world or connection with the MMIWG crisis – he observed that the *authors* of the report had "found that the tragic violence that Indigenous women and girls have experienced *amounts to genocide*" (Global News with Connolly, emphasis mine). Questions around how *he* (as this nation's leader and representative) might characterize the violence *his* nation has visited upon Indigenous bodies, minds, and spirits for the past 150 years remain unanswered.

Despite the Juno Award–winning Indigenous musicians; despite a mountain of Indigenous scholarship, poetry, fiction, film, visual art, theatre, drama, and performance art; despite blockades and occupations; despite declarations by activists; despite all of the stories that have been communicated via myriad media, the living Indigenous body with its immediate concerns has been too often rendered and remains even now, largely, invisible: Entire communities living for generations without potable water in one of the most water-rich land bases on this earth. We are telling these stories, but what changes? Our young men spirited away in the night in police vehicles, stripped of their boots and winter jackets, and left to die on the frozen outskirts of some city or town. We are telling these stories, but what changes? Our girls and women taken, consumed, and discarded without ceremony, without leave-taking, in ditches, over highways, under farmers' fields, in water. We are telling these stories, but what changes? Our children spirited from their families to be murdered (in body or spirit) by the agents of the state who have been entrusted with their care. We are telling these stories, but who is listening? What changes?

As Monique Mojica asks, "What is it we have to do to be seen?" (Personal Communication 2017). How does the Indigenous body, disrobing to reveal the violence perpetrated upon it, reconfigure colonial sites of viewing – our contemporary *theatrons*? How do we reflect back to our viewers their own *visibility*; their own *complicity* within a system of oppression that, by turns, punishes, spectacularizes, and disappears Indigenous bodies; their *accountability* to the living Indigenous body; and their *responsibility* to respond to that body as witness, not consumer? *What do we have to do to be seen and not eaten?*

---

to weigh one genocide against another. Nor is it my place here to comprehensively document and enumerate the crimes committed against Indigenous Peoples on this continent and worldwide. My intent is simply this: to discuss the aesthetic strategies of several Indigenous theatre workers who have survived the colonial onslaught on these shores and who have dedicated their lives and art to teaching the rest of us how we might do the same.

Story-ing the Human Being

Acoma Pueblo poet Simon Ortiz has stated, "We are not born as human beings; we have to be made into human beings through tradition and ceremony" ("Land"). Teachings from Indigenous nations across the globe identify the pursuit of a way of living that ensures that all created life – with which we interact and upon which we are dependent for the continuance of our own lives – lives well as the primary goal of all human action, interaction, and thought. And a primary function of every ceremonial act – be that the act of storytelling, hunting, planting, gathering, dancing, singing, speaking ancestral languages, praying, or creating – has always been to gradually *transform the individual from a "random," animated carbon formation into a fully developed human being*, an integral "actor" invested with meaning and purpose, who would walk softly on the earth and work collaboratively to ensure the sustenance of a healthy, productive life for every member of his/her immediate community and the greater community to which we all belong. The process of becoming, then, is inextricably bound up in and beholden to story. After all, as Kiowa novelist and scholar N. Scott Momaday so poignantly reminds us, "*Our very existence* consists in our imagination of ourselves" (103, emphasis added). Hence, the right to imagine or to recover traditional imaginings of self, the right to control the story, and the right to shape the vessel that contains Indigenous life are central to the ongoing struggle for Indigenous sovereignty. Indeed, the struggle for control over story is as crucial and immediate, in this century, as the struggle for lands and self-government (Weaver 33). Within myriad Indigenous societies globally, story has long been a primary mechanism within the larger matrix of teaching and learning (Cajete, *Igniting* 54). Other mechanisms around which this matrix is composed include experiential learning, ceremony (initiation), dreaming, apprenticeship, and creative synthesis (artistic expression) (Cajete, *Igniting* 55). But it is upon story that these are carried and through story that they are articulated. Story, then, is a container for knowledge, a vehicle of its transmission, and indeed a site of its production. And the goal of education – the goal of the acquisition, preservation, and transmission of knowledge – for Indigenous Peoples has historically been bound up in the search for life (or a way of living appropriately) through an ontological interrogation of individual *selfhood*. The *self* is understood as an integral component of a complex social mechanism, which is itself an integral component of the larger matrix of Creation (Cajete, *Igniting* 54). It follows, then, that if story contains and communicates knowledge, and if the highest form of knowledge is *self*-knowledge and if story is also a site of knowledge production, then it is within and by means of story that identity may be re-constituted and/or refashioned: Within story, individuals, communities, and nations could conceivably imagine (or re-imagine) themselves into being. And story, at the end of the day, is the archive of a life well lived, or of a misspent existence. The life we "write" for ourselves will become the story that will be written about us and told by the generations that follow us. The process of creating story, then, is not simply the process of "telling" life; it is the process of *doing* it.

Doing, not being, is the cornerstone of human essence. And that essence can only be discovered and fully realized within the context of active relationship to our communities. Such relationships, however, risk undergoing subtle but dangerous transformations if we unwittingly integrate the Western concept of mimesis (in its oral or written manifestations) into our own consciousness as we react to non-Indigenous analyses and disseminations of Traditional Stories. For the Western reader/viewer (informed by Aristotle's reading of the ceremonial performatives of his Attic ancestors), mimesis constitutes an imitation of an action either fictive or finished. But here on Turtle Island, long before contact, oral transmission was a key component in the greater ceremonial matrix (Allen, *Sacred Hoop*, 100); so, it remains.

Engagement in performative or mimetic acts for ceremonial purposes *recreates* action, brings it into the here and now, and effectively transforms the "players" and the world they inhabit in that moment of their re-creation: *Time after time, within each new telling, Nanabozho breathes on a clot of damp earth, and in each new exhalation, the lands and waters that sustain us are made anew.*

Many of the foundational stories that belong to tribal Oral Traditions have been written or are narrated in the third person. And, as Anishinaabe scholar David Treuer observes, this is certainly true of the cycle of stories, which chronicle the life and doings of the Anishinaabe transformer Elder Brother/Nanabozho/Wenabozho/Nanabush (54). So, it is very likely that this is how we will experience these stories if our only point of contact with them is on the page or in the lecture hall. But the Oral Tradition in which these stories were meant to unfold does not simply affect the transmission of words and ideas, which hover in the space between speaker and listener existing independently of either. Rather, the story takes possession of the storyteller who gives it *body*, moving fluidly through the encounter, assuming a new shape with each new moment to become the vessel through which the original actors again live to recreate historical events. In the moment of its telling, this third person narrative simultaneously communicates and comments upon historical actors and their doings even as the storyteller enters the story to become protagonist, antagonist, and supernumerary acting in the here and now (see Manossa 126–7).

The stories that chronicle the process of becoming fully human in an Anishinaabe sense – that is, the process that transforms an isolate mass of carbon molecules, nerve endings, and warring impulses into a community member working creatively with the collective for the general good – are key pedagogical tools in which personal investment and active engagement, on the part of the learners, are required if they are to remain efficacious catalysts of transformation, healing, and development for tribal individuals. Always, we should remind ourselves that when we encounter characters on the page, they must not be read as "the thing itself." To do so robs these stories of their efficacy by stripping our culture heroes of their colour and corporeality, thereby reducing them to bloodless spectres forever dancing in a one-dimensional universe. To ensure that the timeless beings on whom the self-actualization of the tribal individual and body politic rests are not diminished to what Anishinaabe novelist and scholar Gerald Vizenor has termed "simulation[s] of survivance" (78), we might foster and cultivate an organic understanding of the textual archive as a notation of kinetic and oral movement – a series of *blocking notes,* as it were – that exist not merely to be read or said but to be done that *we* might become the thing itself and not the stuff of alien imagination.

Gerald Vizenor explains that survivance denotes "an active sense of presence, the continuance of native stories, not a mere reaction, or a survivable name" (vii). Survivance stories, then, contain the lives and recount the doings of living human beings who are profoundly aware of and connected to their histories without being somehow "frozen in a time before." Histories, languages, and lifeways evolve and develop with each successive generation of living cultures, and so it is with the Indigenous Peoples who continue to survive despite a centuries-old onslaught of colonization and conquest.

I liken Vizenor's "simulation of survivance" to Poundmaker Cree playwright/director Floyd Favel's concept of the "artificial tree" on stage (Favel Starr 71). With every simulation of survivance, we see a carefully arranged picture of nobility, stoicism, courage, spiritual power, "savagery," or resistance. Such representations have been so curated because "America embraces romantically not the absence of real people, but the simulated spiritual presence of the Indian in a kind of New Age movement" (Vizenor qtd. in Isernhagen 83). Such simulations on the page, on the stage, or echoing for posterity in a digital universe constitute the erasure of actual life and organic growth and infuse the national imagination with a romantic longing for what no longer exists (if it ever did) coupled with an aversion to the contemporary survivors of the colonial project who do not reflect the romantic "purity" of their shadowy representatives.

Where Vizenor's "simulation of survivance" denotes the *literary* reduction and erasure of living humans, Favel's "artificial tree" denotes the reduction and erasure of the spiritual essence of the humans themselves. A contemporary theatre practitioner, Favel regards contemporary theatre as "the younger brother of tradition" (Favel, "Theatre" 30). Since 1991, he has laboured to draw upon Indigenous Knowledge Systems, cosmologies, and ceremonial praxis to develop a methodology, which is dramaturgically and performatively workable. He does not represent "realistic" fragments of actual ceremonial performatives (oratory, kinetic performance, or opsis) on the public stage. This, he warns us, is an empty exercise. The work emerging from such endeavours will ultimately lack an essential centre – a spiritual core. This empty, spiritless work is, for Favel, an "artificial tree." And artificial trees can be deadly.

Favel rejects material mimesis, favouring instead metaphysical mimesis. He seeks to draw upon that "animating spirit," to infuse his theatrical works with that spirit, to place that invisible spirit centre stage, to communicate that spirit to his audiences, and to thereby nourish them from "the source of the river of our cultures, country and ourselves" (Favel Starr 72). Throughout this book, we will encounter Floyd Favel and his investigations into Native Performance Culture within which he has developed long-standing partnerships with such artists as Muriel Miguel and her niece Monique Mojica. However, for the moment, it may prove instructive to illustrate just *exactly* what an "artificial tree" or a "simulation of survivance" might look like and the dangers this presents for storyteller (fabricator) and witness alike.

Some years ago, I was teaching an undergraduate course on Indigenous Theatre in North America. Generally, non-Indigenous students outnumber Indigenous students in the course (which is largely a reflection of the Academy's demographic as a whole). Hence, students were invited to present something to the class that fulfilled the mandate (for the presenter) of "Indigenous drama" – defined within this diverse context as an expression of each student's personal landscape. Having studied various instances of contemporary Indigenous theatre as vehicles of healing, facilitators of pedagogy, community-unifiers, transmitters of oral history and language, or avenues of re-writing and re-righting distorted histories and re-appropriating sites of misappropriation, presenters were invited to explore like possibilities in pieces of their own making, arising out of their own personal histories, languages, and cultures, for specific audiences of their own imagining (mixed audiences, children, senior citizens, or individuals from particular communities), which their "vehicles" would be designed to affect in specific ways.

One non-Indigenous student chose to create a "restorative justice circle," in which she revealed herself to be a victim of domestic, childhood sexual abuse. In the past, many deeply personal revelations have emerged from within such presentations within the context of profound trust, a strong super-objective, and the application of artistic process to transform personal struggle into hope, healing, inspiration, valuable life lessons, or community-unifiers. However, this student's presentation was different from those aforementioned, in that it *explicitly imitated* a "justice circle" in which the audience (comprised of myself and of fellow students in the course) was *compelled* to participate. This student explained that she had heard about such justice circles from a therapist with whom she was working through her abuse. Her therapist had explained that victim, perpetrator, those immediately affected, and those less immediately affected by a particular breach would form a circle "so healing could occur within the entire community."

Although I was very sensible of the profound trust and courage this student was demonstrating by reaching out and "showing her throat," as it were, to her classmates, and although I felt deep sympathy for her and profound outrage on her behalf, I was discomfited by the exercise. "Why?" I wondered. "Am I so horrified by the notion of theatre as a vehicle for the artists' healing as well as for audience healing? Am I the one to judge when and where she should make her disclosures, and to whom? Why do I (a woman who has been abused herself) feel so repelled, so violated? Is her disclosure somehow violating me? Is she endangering her classmates?"

When the exercise was over, many of her classmates hugged her and thanked her for her trust. Others, however, did not. Interestingly, the "huggers" were largely male, and all were non-Indigenous. Those who sought to politely avoid her were female. I was mystified. Upon reading the final journals for this class and reading the students' responses to the presentations of their colleagues, I was interested to come upon entries (written by females who also revealed themselves to be victims of domestic childhood sexual abuse) that expressed the exact ambivalences I had felt and that expressed the same guilt I had felt for those ambivalences. "What kind of person am I?" they asked. I began to wonder anew. What kind of people were they? What kind of person am I? What was wrong or broken or lacking within us that we could not reach out and unreservedly embrace this young woman, her exercise, and the trust she had demonstrated?

Gradually, I began to apprehend that the "wrongness" lay neither with them nor with me; it lay within the "justice circle" that had been fabricated. The shape and function of a particular communal rite of restoration had been staged. And we were, by this final class, a community of sorts. But this could never be a justice circle: The perpetrator was absent; the family, common to both victim and perpetrator, was absent; others who were linked to this family or who had been affected by this terrible violation were absent; the Elders who would have conducted such a circle (at the time, within a location, and in the manner *they* deemed most appropriate) were absent. *And the community of supportive individuals who formed this circle had been co-opted into a collective, complicit fabrication of an "artificial tree" from which not healing, nor justice, nor restoration were to be had.* This student's choice to disclose her terrible secret was not the violation. The violation lay in her choice of "container" – in her attempt to literally recreate a frame of which she had no personal knowledge, to which she had no personal connection, and in which she had no personal experience. More troubling, this frame has been carefully constructed by peoples who are not her own and finds its foundation upon a world view of which she has only rudimentary knowledge, to which she had no personal connection and in which she had no personal experience. In attempting to produce a materially mimetic experience (based upon an *oral simulation* of the "Native" model of restorative justice), this student produced a stunted shadow of a shadow and effectively eradicated the affective essence around which the original event has been constructed.

For colonized peoples around the world, the process of healthy self-actualization has been interrupted. Forced relocations, confinement to reservations, re-education in the residential schools and in the churches, and restrictive legislative policies have prohibited the peoples' speaking and subverted our patent and metaphysical doings. Ironically, this series of colonial interventions designed to re-order the world by re-forming its myriad peoples into second-rate shadows of the colonizing superman has affected little more than New World disorder. We speak his language, adopt his diet, and live in accordance with his laws, but the transformation is incomplete: As Homi Bhabha has observed, we are little more than "the effect[s] of a flawed mimesis, in which to be Anglicized is emphatically not to be English" (125). Generations of Indigenous children were forcibly taught the English language not that they might communicate as equals with the settlers but that they might forget their own languages and that they might understand the orders and the dictates of those whom they were being trained to serve. Indigenous girls were rigorously trained in English domestic arts (cooking, serving, polishing, cleaning, etc.) not to set up their own households in homes of their own but to serve in the households of settler women. Generations of Indigenous people graduated from residential schools as liminal people speaking, dressing, and trained to "do life" in accordance with settler tastes and customs;[4] like the South Asian colonial subjects, they were being shaped into a "class of interpreters between [the English] and the millions whom [the English] govern[ed] – a class of persons [Indigenous] in blood and colour, but English in tastes, in opinions, in morals and in intellect" (Macaulay qtd. in Bhabha 124). And just as it was for the South Asian colonial subject, it must have oft-times felt to those ancestors that "[they] pretended to be real, to be learning, to be preparing [themselves] for life" (Naipaul 416). Mortal shades cut off from their languages, communities, histories, knowledge systems and lifeways – from the very foundations of their humanness and from the processes of ontological investigation and self-actualization – and struggling against the hegemonic denial of their humanity, they nonetheless struggled to retain and transmit their organic understanding of that humanity and fragments of those foundations from which successive generations might begin to build themselves anew.

In the struggle to recover the Indigenous self, all strategies – be they the reclamation and transmission of ancestral languages; the assertion of intellectual property rights; the assertion of land and Treaty Rights; the generation and control of artistic representations of our peoples; the reimplementation of ceremonial praxis; or the recovery and reinstitution of traditional, social, jurisprudential, and political infrastructures – ultimately require us to negotiate our way through that interrupted process of *becoming*. At every level, the project of re-Indigenization is a creative project through which to transform the chaos that defines a colonized existence; it is a project, which requires us to remember, re-member, recover, and devise effective methods with which to dramaturg the ordered existence we imagine for our children and grandchildren. This is a key challenge that has become an integral part of the creative process for Indigenous writers and artists seeking to serve their communities in a meaningful way through their works.

---

4 I borrow the expression "do life" from Althea Prince (260) whose commitment to participatory action and interaction as a reader, witness, writer, and speaker infuses her work and provides a vital (and commonsensical) model for all scholars who labour to contribute to the project of decolonization (see Prince 259–68).

Spiderwoman Theater: Identity, Survivance and Communitism in Action

Spiderwoman Theater began in 1976 and has gone on to become the longest-running Indigenous theatre company and the longest-running feminist troupe in North America. The story of Lisa Mayo, Gloria Miguel, and Muriel Miguel (the three Guna-Rappahannock sisters who, with Lois Weaver, founded the company) is, in itself, an epic saga of becoming. And the formation of Spiderwoman Theater constitutes a historic act of survivance. Indeed, it may be read as an organic and necessary phase in the trio's process of becoming – first, separately as women, as artists, as wives and mothers, as political entities and feminists; finally, communally as sisters, urban matriarchs, community builders, and Guna-Rappahannock artists in America.[5] The company not only stands as testament to survivance but also has served as the vehicle of survivance for its founders, guest artists, and audiences. Its service to myriad Indigenous (and non-Indigenous feminist) communities is a manifestation emerging from the performances, which have remembered, united, affected, and empowered witnesses the world over. And this service has been vigorously realized within the Miguel sisters' projects of activism, outreach, community building, and artistic training – projects, which have affected and galvanized Indigenous creative efficacy, presence and, indeed, survivance for nearly five decades.

Jace Weaver has identified "a quest for identity" as a common preoccupation that manifests itself in contemporary Indigenous writing (26–7). As a key factor of survivance, then, the location of identity requires action that remembers and affirms who we are and "that we are" and that simultaneously frees us from the lie of who we are *not* – a lie, which divides, destabilizes, and debilitates us. The "quest for identity" as an act of survivance may be located in the foundational questions that have engendered Spiderwoman's dramatic works, in the aesthetic models that characterize these works, and in the dramaturgical and performative process that underpins them. Meanwhile, an examination of the founding of *the company* provides a map to the generations of young

5 Although the Miguel sisters are also Rappahannock on their mother's side, they ultimately recovered and asserted their Guna heritage throughout their works. Their mother's strong Christianity (and the conflicts this created), her emotional withdrawal from her daughters, their frequent exposure to their father's culture and his uninhibited expression thereof will be discussed at length in the following chapter. Taken together, all these factors may help to explain why it is that Spiderwoman's works ultimately anchor themselves and their creatrices to their Guna inheritance.

Indigenous artists yet unborn: In itself, this history constitutes a specifically Indigenous "morality play" around the true nature of identity in an Indigenous context; it speaks to Indigenous survivance even as it distinguishes the Indigenous quest for self-knowledge from "heroic" individualism, romantic isolation, and/or wrong-headed struggles for dominance that divide and destroy.

The identity that contemporary Indigenous Peoples seek to recuperate is an identity that traditionally has had to be located within the context of community: Individuals found meaning and identified their role within Creation by discovering the "self in society" as opposed to the "self and society" (Weaver 39). Hence, in the struggle to create and maintain a literature of survivance, which properly locates and represents Indigeneity, the artist does not undertake a solitary quest. This quest is undertaken as a "communitist" project – that is to say, it is an activist intervention undertaken with the survival of community as its sole aim (see Weaver 43). Indeed, Weaver's theoretical lens "communitist" has been engendered through the fusion of the terms "activist" and "community" to indicate that action is required and that the impulse of this action, its affect and effects must grow out of and express a proactive commitment to the continuance of an Indigenous community (see Weaver 43) if it is to effect survivance for the individual artists and for those to, of, and for whom they speak.

Once upon a time, three little brown girls dreamed of escape from the racism that surrounded them in their Brooklyn neighbourhood, from poverty that confined and defined them, and from domestic violence that threatened their peace:

> GLORIA: When I grow up, I'm going to marry a man from far away across the sea AND he's going to take me away from all this and I'll never come back again.
>
> LISA: I'm going to marry a rich man and he's going to give me things like a fur coat and a refrigerator full of food.
>
> MURIEL: I'm going to get me an apartment. (Spiderwoman, "Sun" 308)

Each of these sisters had sought escape in the exercise of her creative talents. As each matured, she separated herself from her sisters and her family home and sought her place in an artistic community wherein she might develop and utilize her voice – wherein she might come to self-knowledge and reveal and assert her presence. Ultimately, while each sister began by seeking her identity as an artist apart from the others, it was only within their work together within a collaborative venture spanning almost five decades that each was able finally to come into her *self*: "Storytelling is the way you feel and know where you are within your family, your clan, your tribal affiliations, and from there into the history of how you fit into the world. Storytelling starts at the kitchen table, on your parent's lap, on your aunt's and uncle's laps" (M. Miguel qtd. in Haugo, "Weaving" 225).

In the development of a dramaturgical process through which they were able to pose questions, to issue challenges, to answer each other with stories (often opposing versions/visions of a single event) and to weave those stories into a unified design, they were at last able to locate themselves in relationship – as sisters; daughters; granddaughters; Guna-Rappahannock women; wives; mothers; lovers; aunties; grandmothers; healers; teachers; activists; diasporic survivors; and preservers and transmitters of oral histories extending beyond self, family, community, and nation. In reuniting to revisit, re-member, and reconfigure the story that contained their lives, the Miguel sisters found themselves by finding their rightful place within an orbiculate superstructure through which we are all connected within the larger community of all that has been created: "There's [sic] always circles upon circles upon circles," Muriel Miguel asserts. "And that's how Spiderwoman approaches theater, through circles upon circles upon circles" (Haugo, "Weaving" 225).

The story of Spiderwoman Theater offers a window into a contemporary, urban context of an ancient process of becoming. It is a story that is powered by the generations that precede its principal actors and that provides a power source for the generations that follow them. This book, which attempts to disseminate their story, also attempts to disseminate their *process* – a process, which imagines into being, a pathway to becoming. The story I hope to transcribe here is not simply the story of "a life in art"; *it is the story of an art well lived.* This is a story of three women who severally sought to transcend personal circumstance, family history, and the external limitations imposed upon them, as American Indians and as women.[6] This is a story of three women

6 Throughout this work, I will refer to the three founding members of Spiderwoman Theater and to their family members as they have chosen to refer to themselves. When speaking of themselves or of other Indigenous people in terms of general ethnicity, they often use the term "Indian" or "American Indian." They also use the term "Native" – particularly when they are speaking with interviewers who are speaking with them from the territories commonly referred to as "Canada." Although it is crucial that this work addresses and refers to their specific Guna and Rappahannock nations, it is also crucial to note that their art and activism speak to and work for a pan-Indigenous community. Since its inception, Spiderwoman Theater has been called to perform for, empower, and partner with Indigenous peoples from Alaska to New Zealand and everywhere in between.

who severally sought to transcend the denial of Indigenous humanity and suppression of Indigenous and female voices by the colonial and patriarchal forces that have governed this continent for more than two centuries by gaining entrance into its paradoxically exclusive margins – the artists' training grounds – and forcefully asserting their individual lives in art. As each sought to discover, affirm, and assert her own humanity, she found her way back to her sisters, her family, her clan, her community, her nation. She came to know and to occupy her rightful place within the larger story. This is a story of three women who sought to find their unique and separate lives in art, and who instead found their art in community. This is the story of three American Indian women who imagined themselves as artists and of three artists who, in the exercise of their life's work, found a way to imagine themselves as Guna-Rappahannock women and to show other First Peoples who have been disaffected by separation, loss, self-hatred, and forgetfulness, how we may do the same.

Communitism and "Critical Generosity" as Pedagogical Models and Research Methodology

As a young urban woman of mixed ancestry (Anishinaabe-Ashkenazi), I began to find myself in the stories that the Miguel sisters publicly shared, in their powerful performances, and in the Storyweaving Workshops facilitated by Muriel Miguel and her niece Monique Mojica. Their works gathered me into a community of active witnesses: Their stories intersected with ours; ours, with each other's, and the threads that bound individual to community manifested themselves within the theatrical event. As I began to perceive the intersections, those commonalities of experience that connected each Indigenous individual in the theatre on a given night to others – present or absent, vocal or silent, living, dead, or yet to be – I began to discover and to accept my responsibility to the stories and to those who live within them. With such a sense of connection and responsibility came the realization of my own "self in community."

As a theatre practitioner, I sought to learn from them that I might share with others what they have given me. As a scholar, within this work, I seek not only to discuss the works and life's work of Spiderwoman Theater as communitist projects, but also to create a communitist project of my own. I hope that this endeavour will work to tighten the weave in the fabric of a growing and vibrant community of Indigenous culture workers insofar as it encourages our artists to document aesthetic process and to come together to discuss, exchange, and develop methodologies based on specific objectives pertaining to specific communities for and with which artists wish to create. As well, it is crucial that my own process (research) and performance (archived/published document) are undertaken and realized within a communitist model. I regard the Miguel sisters and their daughters, Monique Mojica and Murielle Borst-Tarrant, as *research partners* as opposed to research "subjects," and I undertake this quest to comprehend, analyse, and record a body of Indigenous Knowledge as an Indigenous woman in partnership with other Indigenous women who have held, developed, and shared this knowledge over several generations.

Kanien'kehá:ka scholar Marlene Brant Castellano reminds us, "The ultimate test of the validity of knowledge is whether it enhances the capacity of the people to live well" (33). The knowledge these artists hold has already been tested on the stage, on the page, in workshops, studios, and sharing circles. They have used their knowledge to enhance the lives of Indigenous people globally, and this will be discussed and demonstrated at length throughout this work. The questions remain: How can I ensure that my own work "passes the validity test?" What must I do to not only honour but also to reciprocate the myriad gifts these Elders, teachers, and artists have given so freely? Partnership, after all, necessitates reciprocity.

The late Anishinaabe Elder Art Solomon often utilized the image of fire as a metaphor for Minobimaatisiiwin (the way of living well within the Creation), which is the body and purpose of Anishinaabe Knowledge. As we seek to discover identity – our own meaning and purpose – we must sift through the embers of a fire that has been all but smothered by the forces of colonization (see Castellano 25). But sifting through embers is perforce slow, painstaking work. Stir too vigorously and a conflagration may spring to life. Sift with too heavy a hand, and the fire might be forever extinguished. Mix it up too rapidly and crucial sparks may be overlooked or even lost.

In November 2006, I was driving Muriel Miguel back to her residence from one of a series of workshops she was facilitating at the University of Toronto's Graduate Centre for Study of Drama.[7] During the drive, I asked her to comment upon something I had read about her former colleagues in Split Britches. The conversation began to turn towards academic scholarship in theatre in general. Laughing heartily, she offered a rueful observation around her encounters with articles,

7 Since 2011, the Graduate Centre for Study of Drama at the University of Toronto has been known as the Centre for Drama, Theatre, and Performance Studies.

which purported to analyse and clarify productions of artists whom she admired: So often, she noted, the scholars' theories bore little relation to the artists' work as it was realized on stage. She could not recognize the production(s) she had witnessed in the theoretical work that she was reading. Rather than outrage, what Muriel Miguel expressed that evening was sympathy, sympathy for the artists whose work, she felt, the "experts" had so grossly misrepresented. It is important to note here that the artists and theorists Miguel spoke of that evening were white women with feminist leanings. These artists and scholars shared (at least, some) commonalities of gender, life experience, cultural cosmology, political philosophy, and commitment to political activism. The ubiquitous misrepresentation of Indigenous experience by non-Indigenous "experts" is a phenomenon, which Indigenous artists have come to expect. And it is a phenomenon against which contemporary Indigenous culture workers are now actively fighting, as scholarly misrepresentation has historically provided grounds for legislative strategies designed to contain, assimilate, and oppress Indigenous Peoples and to suppress our languages; spiritual praxis; and traditional societal, pedagogical, and governmental structures.

As an Indigenous culture worker and researcher, I remain very aware that I must guard against any hubristic assumption that the danger of misrepresentation would "naturally" be eradicated with the replacement of the non-Indigenous scholarly "expert" with the Indigenous "expert." Inspired by Hawaiian scholar Leilani Holmes's reconfiguration of the research paradigm, I position myself within this project as the *research subject*. As I assume this position, the requisite analysis, and interrogation, so integral to this field of endeavour, will turn their lenses not only upon the knowledge communicated to me by my research partners but also upon myself as I am forced into a transparent reckoning with my own understandings of and responses to the works I have encountered and the experiences I have been granted. This research/learning paradigm, then, will contribute much to my own location of "identity" as it will force my discovery and public revelation of the "non-neutral and limited nature of my own language and perspectives" (Holmes 39). Furthermore, repositioning the researcher as subject in the research project will, I believe, go far to realize a manifestation of the "critical generosity" called for by David Romàn. It will, I hope, transform the isolate scholarly quest to acquire, document, analyse, and quantify knowledge systems into a "cooperative endeavor and collaborative engagement with a larger social mission" (Romàn xxvii). And such, I believe, is what traditional models of Indigenous pedagogy have always been structured to be.

As African Canadian scholar Njoki Nathani Wane reminds us through the revelation of her own experiences as a researcher in Kenya, active engagement within the community from which one seeks to learn is a crucial requisite of any research undertaken in an Indigenous community (56). Indeed, apprenticeship, as a processual pedagogical element in traditional Indigenous societies, may afford, for the contemporary researcher, a way into critical generosity. To be sure, the apprentice often begins her "tour of duty" with her own assumptions, her own questions, and her own agenda. But she very quickly learns humility: Her research partners direct her investigations and unfailingly lead her down paths she may never have discovered for herself. They answer the questions they deem important, often revealing the emptiness of her own pre-prepared questions, and they answer those questions when *they* deem it appropriate – when they are satisfied that the learner is ready for the lesson. They follow a "lesson plan" of their own making, regardless of the learner's preconceived agenda or timeline. As Leilani Holmes has observed, "Knowledge is given through the context of relationships and for the purpose of furthering relationships" (41). And all relationships are ultimately orchestrated within and negotiated through action. So, while the more formal interview certainly plays a part in this research process, its importance to the overall project has been eclipsed (even as it has been informed) by the more "prosaic" activities and lessons related to apprenticeship. Action and relationship are certainly required to generate critical generosity; however, the catalyst that will ensure its realization is intellectual humility without which true creative growth cannot occur.

Syilx writer Jeannette Armstrong is a contemporary artist who teaches other artists and who rigorously sifts through her own language and traditions to create a specifically Indigenous pedagogical model within which to train and nurture her students. She has named the creative writing school she founded for this catalyst *Enow'kin*. This is a verb that privileges a dualistic principle by inviting opposition. The gift of opposing perspectives allows us to "understand how [we] need to challenge [our] thinking to accommodate [another's] concerns and problems" (Armstrong 283). Rather than simply recording research and a singular analysis of my "findings," I strive to employ Armstrong's "Enow'kin Principle" by approaching this project as a dialogue between artist-mentors and apprentice. Where my interpretations do not coincide with the artists' original intent, both sides of the discussion will be included, so as not to privilege the student's interpretation over that of her Elders and teachers. A story about storytelling, about the stories that make and unmake us, and about the traditional, contemporary, and specifically

Indigenous methodologies around making those stories must perforce be as dialogic, collaborative, and communitist as the Oral Traditions from which the contemporary Indigenous human draws inspiration, identity, and survivance.

This project is not my story; nor is this solely the story of the Miguel sisters and their family. This story begins at a kitchen table in a "house of mirrors" in Red Hook, Brooklyn. But like a stone tossed into quiet waters, it reverberates across and within the stories of so many others, catching them up in endlessly extending ripples, and weaving them together in a living biota … So, while the story of Spiderwoman Theater begins at the kitchen table in a modest house in Brooklyn; while it begins in the stories told around that table, I am choosing to begin its telling in an uncertain time – a time during which I am still mourning the death of the eldest Miguel sister (2013) and witnessing the physical decline of the two sisters who survive her; a time during which I am witnessing not the creation of Spiderwoman Theater but its re-creation, as a new generation of Indigenous artists enters the performative web to rework old stories; a time during which I have watched as Indigenous people have achieved some significant success in the struggle to claim a platform from which to voice our own stories; a time during which I have (with many friends and colleagues) wondered, "Who is listening?" (see Nolan, *Medicine Shows* 16); and a time during which I am caught between a pull towards silence (to refuse any attempts to be understood by the settler demographic) and a pull towards keeping the channels of communication open.

What is theatre good for? I ask in this time. Of what possible benefit are our stories if nobody is listening and nothing changes? Perhaps, I am asking the wrong question. Perhaps, I should be asking this: For whom is our theatre good? Whom does our theatre serve? And so it is from here that I shall begin this story almost five decades after its beginning – with a re-creation story that carries us into a performative space of refusal, an "irreconcilable space" from which to bear witness in a time of "reconciliation."

Mean Men and Material Witnesses: A Re-Creation Story

Imagine a woman
A wife with two daughters
A sibling with two elder sisters
A daughter with two parents …
Her mother silenced by a husband whose
voice booms with intoxicated rage, as his fists fly …
Sometimes.

Sometimes.
Imagine that.
Imagine her
Tall and strong
Fierce and dark
Rich of voice
This activist
This activist's wife
A brown woman capsizing in the first white wave
A brown woman with a brown husband with brown, angry fists
Imagine this activist
This activist's wife – he of the brown, angry fists
Imagine her eyes
Dark and deep,
Looking into you – right into you
Unafraid
Imagine this activist,
Who would carry the world
With her ready hands,
Who would comfort the world
In deep, honied tones
And easy laugh
If only we were listening …
Imagine this woman
Who has travelled from far
To be part of a moment in history
A moment to change everything
Imagine this brown woman who has travelled from far
To make coffee for the activists who want to change everything
To make coffee for those brown men with their brown, angry fists.
They are handsome and strong
Like her husband
Like her father
They are intoxicated by rage
With booming voice
And booming fists
Like her husband
Like her father
Imagine one evening
This activist
With other women
Brown women

Who have travelled from far
To be part of a moment
A moment to change everything.
Brown women like her
With honied voices, ready hands, easy laughter, and soft, dark eyes.
In this moment
Within a moment to change everything
Imagine this evening filled with soft laughter and soothing voices
Broken by a cry
Followed by another cry
Crying in the dark,
They stop their chatter
They cease their laughter
Listening hard.
They hear weeping
Begging
"Please, don't hurt me"
That crying woman who is not with them in this moment is just like them.
A sister, a daughter, a lover, and soon-to-be wife
She is speaking with a brown man
A leader of men who will be remembered as one who changed everything.
She begs him to stop
She begs him to calm his angry fists
To save that anger for those who oppress those he has come into this
moment to
Defend …
Defenseless against her defender she weeps
And the brown women
Listen silently
Hands covering mouths
Breaths short and shallow
Breasts heaving
Rage mounting
"In a revolution, women are equal"
Enough!
It is enough.
They have had enough
Of bad men
Of angry fists
Of defenders who
Rend and
Wreck and

Wreak their havoc
"We heard her pleading."
"We heard her crying."
Muriel tells us.
They heard the bad man drag his lover, his partner, his beautiful brown soon-to-be-wife
Outside
To the River
His angry fists, sated with blood and bone, with spit, and salt tears
Itched to drown the witch
"In a revolution, women are equal"
The women flew to her
They tore her from his grasp, as he threatened
And spit curses at them all
At these brown sisters
Who had travelled from far
To land in a moment that changed everything.
Imagine a woman
A brown woman
From Red Hook, Brooklyn
Who travelled to dance beneath a burning sun
To stand against violence
To say, "Enough!"
To dedicate her body in dancing and prayer
To a ceremony of re-creation
In a site of old violations
Remembered woundings
To be part of a moment that would change everything.
Imagine Muriel Miguel – a young mother
A woman in violence
Once again
A woman in violence
Once again …
A woman …
Violence …
Once again …
Imagine a beater of women
A mean man
A man of violent means
Progenitor
Destroyer
Imagine a moment within the moment that changed everything …

Out of the emergency
Emergence ...
Out of an ending
New beginnings
Muriel tells us, "That was the beginning of Spiderwoman Theater because something had to be done."

Reiteration, Redemption, Regeneration: A Re-Creation Story

During a public talk in January 2020, Muriel Miguel declared that "The beginning of Spiderwoman started because of [a celebrated Indigenous rights activist who laid hands on his romantic partner]" (M. Miguel, *RedTalk*). She then went on to tell the late Mi'kmaq host and interlocutor Candy Palmater this story of redemption and regeneration – of the birth of Spiderwoman Theater in an irredeemable moment. She was attending her first Sun Dance – an historic first Sun Dance hosted at Wounded Knee, the site of violent colonial invasion, the site of murder and massacre. It was 1973, and American Indians from tribal nations across Turtle Island had gathered to participate in this re-creation story. A leading activist had brought his fiancée to the camp and "disappeared" one evening. During his absence, his fiancée had been visited by a male acquaintance in her tent with whom she talked for some time. When the activist finally returned to the tent, he attacked her physically, accusing her of infidelity – of sleeping with her visitor. "We heard her pleading. We heard her crying," Muriel told us. Finally, he dragged her outside of their tent and dragged her towards the nearby river, threatening to throw her in. Miguel and a group of women who had heard everything ran outside and intervened, tearing the wounded woman away from her attacker, packing her things, and driving her to Rapid City where she presumably caught a bus for home. Muriel Miguel never saw her again. But out of this catastrophic male-on-female violence, something was born: Enough was enough; Muriel Miguel was determined to assemble a troupe, build a theatre company, and take a place at the table.

But where are you when you have fought bitterly for that seat at the table only to discover (after more than 40 years of concerted effort) that "Now all you have is a black eye" (Spiderwoman Theater and Aanmitaagzi)? I began this chapter with this question, writing in a fraught time, where the trending project within Canada (up until COVID-19) has been "truth and reconciliation" and where an ever-growing chorus of Indigenous voices calls for resistance and refusal. Why should Indigenous people participate in the life of the settler state, which has been built upon the theft of Indigenous lands and unconscionable acts of violence perpetrated on Indigenous bodies and minds (Simpson, "Savage")? Why should we sit at a table that is not of our own making? What will it profit us to stay? With *Material Witness*, Spiderwoman Theater joins a growing cohort of Indigenous artists, scholars, and activists in a retreat (both material and spiritual) from this proverbial "table."

Indigenous protocols, globally, have required us to pause in a liminal space never touching that place where water kisses land, never venturing into the clearing beyond the dense forest, never stepping off the tarmac until we have sent out the call announcing our presence and intentions and until we have received a response – an invitation to step into the territory of another. In this historical moment, across disciplines and within myriad media, a mounting impulse to curate spaces of retreat – spaces in which the Indigenous Peoples will be able to identify and get on with the work we need to do to strengthen ourselves and our communities and in which non-Indigenous Peoples might discover the work they need to accomplish before the project of relationship building can be realized – is being activated. Before restor(y)ation, re-treating, or re-imagining can occur, we need to retreat from each other into what Métis Curator David Garneau conceives of as "irreconcilable spaces of Aboriginality" (26–7). Such spaces are spaces, Stó:lō scholar Dylan Robinson explains, "outside of Indigenous knowledge extractivism, where our knowledge is not simply a resource used to Indigenize" (20). Perhaps, too, these are spaces in which to re-integrate, what Stó:lō-Cree/Métis scholar, writer, and Knowledge Keeper Lee Maracle terms, the "split mind" and affect relational repair.[8]

On a sunny afternoon in late May 2016, I enter an "irreconcilable space" curated by Spiderwoman Theater. Here at La MaMa ETC, a

8 I first encountered the term "split mind" while curating a performance intervention *Medicine Walk: Breath Tracks* on the University of Toronto (St. George) campus for *ScotiaBank Nuit Blanche 2011*. Lee Maracle contributed the "Breath Track" in the form of a recorded story, which provided the heart of the project's soundscape. The story introduced listeners to a fragment of the Stó:lō origin cycle, recounting the history of a Double Headed Serpent, which for me (a listener) came to embody the warring impulses of creation and destruction, rage and forgiveness, selfishness and selflessness that exist in all humans. Later, in 2019 when I directed the collective creation *Encounters at the "Edge of the Woods,"* Maracle offered a much longer and more detailed telling of this story during early workshops that she co-facilitated with her daughter Columpa Bobb. This telling became a *call* to which each member of the company was invited to respond by telling "the story back different but the same." The "split mind" work accomplished with Maracle during *Encounters at the "Edge of the Woods"* will be discussed in the final chapter of this book.

Figure 1.1. *Material Witness* fabric installation at La MaMa ETC, 2016. Photo: Théo Coté. Courtesy of Spiderwoman Theater.

historic hub of performative exploration and creation, I will witness a historic re-creation. As my eyes adjust to the sudden gloom of the performance space, I find myself surrounded by a fabric installation, collectively created by community members in Aanmitaagzi Big Medicine Studio from personal items representing each fabricator's story and from items donated by individual women from other communities (see fig. 1.1). This is more than installation; it is set overspilling itself, breaking down the liminal threshold between stage and house – between performer and witness. No family, after all, remains untouched, no nation remains healthy when its women are being attacked, when its mothers are weakened, wounded, dying. I am swathed, on all sides, in a "story-quilt" (Ozawabineshi) – a fabric world formed of items that have been solicited from and contributed by Indigenous women from across Turtle Island. This material world has been formed of the stuff of myriad stories, myriad hopes, myriad acts of care. It carries and communicates a collective testament offered by living women in this historical moment – an offering of mutual support through which the stories of both witness and performer are upheld (Ozawabineshi).

Grandmothers smile out at us from a snug nest of soft layers, lush fabrics, and bright colour. Hands reach up to catch or cradle a beloved mother, aunty, or sister. Hands reach up and out to touch a girl-child lost somewhere in a grand and terrifying darkness. "Have you seen her?" the material witness cries out to us. "She's 12 years old."

Here, I find myself borne up by a multitude of sister-artists who join the actors to speak back from the stage through the backdrop to which so many have contributed for the over four decades of Spiderwoman Theater's life; to speak back through the story-quilt, which has been created by participants in the various Pulling Threads Fabric Workshops that travelled to various First Nations communities 2012–16 (as the production was being developed) and to tell their stories from a place of witnessing during the several panel discussions and talkbacks that follow various performances during this run. I am borne up too by the company's invitation to contribute a scrap of my own story to this quilt – to leave a material trace of myself, my family, my spirit in this world built by female agency. Sewn into the larger backdrop, perhaps, these fragments may aid me as I attempt to re-member "what has been torn apart" (Couchie and Miguel 227), layering pieces of my own story into a larger story, which envelops me and which invites me to anchor these fragments of self – invested now with worth and meaning – in the long ago, in the current moment, and in the time to come.

Onstage, the quilted backdrop, like the theatre company with which it travels, has been almost five decades in the making. Like the performers to whom it has been entrusted and like the work that it supports and upholds, these lovingly assembled fabric fragments testify to the beauty that may be conceived within and birthed in the aftermath of violence and ugliness – to new worlds that might emerge from the emergency. So welcomed, I enter a dimly lit theatre space and claim my seat. Something is beginning …

> Onstage, a fabric mound – rich and brown as the soil it represents – begins to heave – folding and rolling, as if moved by the shifting of its ancient, tectonic bone structure. Slowly, cautiously, a woman – herself ancient and mound-like – emerges. She pulls against gravity, rising to her feet and leaning on her cane. Walking the land of the stage, this Elder composed of earth and stardust and received knowledge and earned knowledge walks the stage, blessing it and inscribing a circle of protection. She addresses the children, the Warriors, the biota that protects us, and ancestral spirits whom she calls upon to enter, witness, and protect the storytellers on stage: "Don't be afraid / Here in this circle you are free to tell your story" (Spiderwoman Theater and Aanmitaagzi).

So begins the world premiere of *Material Witness*. Here, a new generation of performers has been invited to revisit and enter into conversation with Spiderwoman Theater's historic bombshell *Women in Violence* – the 1976 production that thrust Spiderwoman Theater onto the world stage.[9] Joined on stage by original cast members Gloria Miguel and Donna Couteau under the direction of troupe-progenitor and guiding artist Muriel Miguel, *an all-Indigenous* feminine collective[10] wrestles with the bundles of stories belonging to preceding generations, converses with their former tellers, and engages with contemporary witnesses (many of whom are, ourselves, Indigenous women in violence) to weave all of our experiences into a greater whole. Together, we revisit an urgent project, as we (all of us – in house or on stage – *witnesses*) work to untangle a web of violence that continues to be a defining experience for Indigenous women today. The thousands of Missing and Murdered Indigenous Women and

9 *Women in Violence* will be discussed at length in chapter 3.

10 The core creators of this work (esp. in its forthcoming published iteration) are Cherish Violet Blood, Penny Couchie, Donna Couteau, Ange Loft, and Gloria Miguel under the directorial and dramaturgical leadership of Muriel Miguel. In the May 2016 performance, which I address in this chapter, Tanis Parenteau was a cast member and co-creator.

Girls bear silent witness to only one arm of a genocidal campaign, which has been characterized on every front (academic, institutional, jurisprudential, educational, environmental, societal, and personal) by a targeted onslaught of extractivism, voyeurism, and opportunism that has persisted throughout the centuries since first contact.

Nine decades into this onslaught, Gloria Miguel observes, "I don't protect myself as much anymore. What have I got to lose? [...] You've got to lick your wounds and go on" (*Segal Talks*). Onstage, this Elder has shed the protective layers she had assembled for *Women in Violence*. Emerging from a fabric cocoon to prepare the space for her collaborators and their witnesses, she takes up her Guna name Du Tu Kapsus ("Flower of the Night"). And in her acceptance of this identity, Gloria Miguel takes up all the responsibilities that name carries. Here, on a twenty-first century stage, she "initiates the crack in the fabric/sky/earth," inviting her younger colleagues "towards voice and those initial steps towards health and wellness" (Couchie and Miguel 224). As the fleshly interface that draws past, present, and future into ceremonial conflation, Miguel/Du Tu Kapsus presences hope – the hope that birthed Spiderwoman Theater almost half a century ago and the hope with which this generation of storytellers will be able to stand in the face of the relentless violence and enduring danger that assail them. She has, after all, lived to tell and tell and tell again ...

As in the original *Women in Violence*, a ragtag group of clown figures who "wear [their] trauma and survival within [their] costumes stitched and glued together" (Couchie and Miguel 27) conduct a performative search for self, revisiting the violence that has fragmented their lives and struggle to story order, reason, and hope out of chaos, unreason, and despair. Like its 1976 progenitor, *Material Witness* indicts women (and those who identify as women) for the violence we inflict upon each other (in thought and word and deed) with the selfsame vigour it exercises in its indictment of those who identify as male for the violence they visit upon the female body.

From the instant the accusing "clowns" (Cherish Violet Blood, Penny Couchie, Donna Couteau, and Angela Loft) tumble onto stage and begin introducing themselves to each other, witnesses are swept into the siege, as one clown sabotages another's attempt to create order by undoing the neat piles of fabric she has frantically been sorting and folding. Moments later, disruption and sabotage escalate into violence, as Loft's "Entrance" (the one who struggles to maintain order within the chaos) is punched by Couteau's "Warrior Woman" because "she deserve[s] it" (Spiderwoman Theater and Aanmitaagzi). And suddenly, whimsy turns to dark reality ...

A little girl is constantly groped by a little boy at school because she "want[s] it." Teenage girls bully their schoolmates, pulling off the clothing of some to humiliate their victims by exposing their underclothing for public display and administering brutal beatings to others. Drunken fathers humiliate their wives; then, smash their faces. Women slice up other women because "you don't fuck with anyone else's boyfriend" (Spiderwoman Theater and Aanmitaagzi). Little girls are fondled by their mothers' boyfriends; young women are brutally raped because their attackers "love" them; and missing daughters are "plucked" lifeless and violated from dank waters, as the numbers of Missing and Murdered Indigenous Girls and Women spiral ever upwards (Spiderwoman Theater and Aanmitaagzi). It gets very real, indeed.

Woven into the palimpsest of this testimonial weave are the shameful jokes – delivered as were the jokes of *Women in Violence* – to indict those who tell and retell such jokes, those who receive such jokes with permissive silence, and those who receive them with laughter, signifying the hearers' sympathy and approbation. Now, more than ever, as real and virtual spaces have become the sites of actual, irreconcilable struggle (#BlackLivesMatter, #SayHerName, #MeToo, #ThisIsZeroHour, Idle No More, #MMIGW, or #IWearRed), perpetrators and their targets alike understand all too well how rapidly and with what ease violent, ugly words are driven home with violent, ugly deeds.

In 1976, the members of Spiderwoman Theater introduced a specific methodology (informing story creation, dramaturgy, design, and performance) by which to navigate a series of questions around the roots of violence that had been visited upon their own bodies, their own collusion in violence against other women, and their positioning as women within both the American Indian Movement and the feminist movement. The resultant performative intervention (*Women in Violence*) emerged as an answer – sounded as a public alarum – to the very personal questions they had posed to themselves. And while it delivered an uncompromising indictment of the very liberatory movements, which promised to uplift them, it concluded with a declaration of certain hope: *"In a revolution, a woman is equal"* (Spiderwoman, *Women in Violence*, italics added) and a plea for positive change in the famous words of Oglala Sioux Spiritual Leader Wallace Black Elk:

> The first peace, which is the most important, is that which comes within the soul of people when they realize their relationship, their oneness with the universe and all its powers [...] The second peace is that which is made between two individuals, and the third is that which is made between

two nations. But above all you should understand that there can never be peace between nations until there is known that true peace, which, as I have often said, is within the souls of men. (qtd. in *Ya-Native*)

Encountering *Material Witness* almost 50 years later, I found myself overwhelmed with questions: What peace have we achieved between then and now? What has changed for Indigenous women? What has changed for our children and grandchildren? While *Women in Violence* extended its artists' reach beyond the stage into the real world, affecting significant change in specific instances (see chapter 3), has the centuries-old assault on the bodies and minds of Indigenous women ceased? Have incidents of violence against Indigenous women lessened in the intervening years? Have the interventions curated and activated by earlier generations of Indigenous women been enough to facilitate the peace and safety of the women born after them? Are these what *Material Witness* shows us?

On the surface, it may seem that very little has changed for Indigenous women and their children. The young "clowns" who pull us into the same violent worlds their creatrices have been navigating for much of their lives attest to this fact. They bear material and corporeal witness to the epigenetic transgenerational legacy of trauma, which has been visited upon racialized bodies by colonial agency since first contact. Temporally and spatially unbounded, this web of trauma has altered the shape and course of ancestral life as it continues to alter the shape and course of the lives of the descendants who live today and the lives of those yet unborn. The weight (material and immaterial) of this legacy seems only to have increased and accumulated density in the years between Spiderwoman Theater's 1976 performative intervention and its twenty-first century reiteration. As was true in the very beginning of Spiderwoman, "something [still remains] to be done." And there are questions that still require answers: When it is done, what will have changed? And if nothing changes, why do it at all? How are we to receive and interpret this insistent revisitation of a performative intervention, this re-creation story – as an inspiring exemplar of perseverance or as a fruitless and fatal exercise in perseveration? And if the second, then to what end does the troupe continue its labours? What good has been produced?

Redeemable Moments in Irreconcilable Space

Du Tu Kapsis [sic] holds the space for us to tell our stories [...] We accept that in this space, the "holding cell," we are safe to tell our stories. We

> witness one another's stories so that we can begin the process of putting down what makes it difficult for us to move forward. (Couchie and Miguel 228)

Since that moment in 1976 when *Women in Violence* burst onto the world stage, violence against women (and particularly against BIPOC women and girls) has seen no decrease. Certainly, the autobiographical accounts of violence upon which Spiderwoman Theater's twenty-first century ensemble has built *Material Witness* attest to its escalation in frequency and ferocity. And yet, for me, it is heartening to reflect on a profound shift that I believe is occurring. For some, the stories told in *Material Witness* may present themselves as iterations of a very old story, but the intent of the storytellers in this historical moment has changed, as has the affect they have engineered.

In 1976, the troupe's founder Muriel Miguel gathered a *multi-ethnic* cast to shake the complacency of their "socially aware," "progressive" audiences by reflecting their bigotry, hypocrisy, and violence back to them through a performative mirror glazed in memory and mimesis. At that time, a newly divorced Gloria Miguel was struggling to assert herself as artist and as human being. Gloria's struggles, fears, and fantasies played themselves out in Spiderwoman's inaugural production through the clown that she created and embodied for *Women in Violence*. To explore the violent forces that shaped and defined so much of her offstage life, Gloria's clown donned a hard hat to protect her head, sported a plethora of mirrors to deflect cruel assumptions and distorted views of her person, and carried a flashlight to aid her as she searched for herself – a whole and healthy self in the detritus of the onstage chaos that was merely an extension of her offstage life.

More than four decades have passed; still, the violence has not abated. While the searing consequences of a genocidal colonial project continue to story themselves upon this erstwhile clown and upon the bodies of the Indigenous women born throughout these decades, Gloria Miguel no longer requires a clown persona to protect herself. Surrounded by the younger women, confronting and navigating their own stories of violence, she gracefully shrugs on the mantle of Elder who tethers her younger colleagues to the "holding cell" she has prepared and holds safe with blessings, prayers, and guardians. This space is a space of display upon which the material witness to the continued assault on Indigenous bodies is laid bare – a body to be scrutinized and known for the price of a theatre ticket. At the same time, it is a protected space, an Indigenous space – rendered impenetrable to all except those who meet the actors as fully engaged witnesses, as compatriots, as helpers who

Figure 1.2. Gloria Miguel as Du Tu Kapsus in *Material Witness*. Courtesy of Spiderwoman Theater.

have come not to observe a spectacle but to engage in a collaborative process of healing. Here, in this space, Du Tu Kapsus reminds us, the voice reverberates; through our words, we extend ourselves outwards to others, mingling with other essences contained in other words. But there is always a return to self: "Don't be afraid / Here in this circle you are free to tell your story" (Spiderwoman Theater and Aanmitaagzi). In this space, the teller is safe; she will not lose herself; she will not be left vulnerable. Here, Du Tu Kapsus embodies and enacts a dramaturgical process, which Dione Joseph terms "cradling space" (8). Within this process (and on Spiderwoman's stage), her ministrations, her words, and her very presence "gift life into [Spiderwoman's] practice, enabling it to extend outwards to serve, heal, shift and empower, and move space" (Joseph 8).

As both material witness to and fleshly container for nine decades of injustice and abuse, Miguel announces herself with her Guna name. She wears the Guna regalia (see fig. 1.2), which has been made for *her* – for Gloria Miguel, for Du Tu Kapsus.[11]

11 Gloria Miguel wears a mola in this production. Molas will be discussed at length in chapter 3.

The events of her life – the violent incidents with which she has had to contend – have not altered. And the conditions under which, the tenor and the frequency of the violence she has endured remain unchanged (where they have not worsened). As she carries her traditional name onto a twenty-first century stage, Du Tu Kapsus re-*presents* Gloria Miguel. No longer searching for a missing part of self, she is now fully plugged in to the agency she wields within the communities she serves (Couchie and Miguel 224). In this historical moment, as the numbers of Missing and Murdered Indigenous Women and Girls continue to mount; as Indigenous children continue to be removed from their parental homes and communities on the thinnest of pretexts; as lateral violence continues to destroy more women and their children; and as legislative policies continue to sever the connections between those women, their children, and their communities, Gloria Miguel's recovery of her traditional Guna and Rappahannock names signals hope. This woman has walked through fire, sifted through the embers, stitched the fragments that could be salvaged and emerged as Du Tu Kapsus to continue a difficult conversation that Spiderwoman Theater began as a revolutionary intervention upon revolution.

But to where does the conversation turn if nobody is listening? In 1976, Spiderwoman Theater held up a mirror to its audiences, inviting them to reflect upon their complicity in a centuries-old campaign of colonial violence, to shift hateful attitudes, and to cease hate-fuelled behaviours. As company member Penny Couchie has observed, "When you come from a culture that has those values, and that worldview, and you try to engage with another society and culture with an opposing worldview, that's where the problems start" (Couchie and Miguel 233). More than 40 years since, the violence persists. And it seems that the conversation has redirected itself and turned inward. With *Material Witness*, a new generation walks away from the violence and refuses to be penetrated by an ossifying, colonial gaze. Instead, it weaves a circle of protection in sovereign territory, inviting the Indigenous witness into this irreconcilable space of condolence to begin to map the first steps of a journey towards healing.

At once heartbreaking and strangely empowering, this graceful refusal – manifested in the development/re-development of its inaugural production – is a most significant development in the life of Spiderwoman Theater. And it is a phenomenon that is being enacted across Turtle Island by multiple generations of Indigenous artists, thinkers, activists, and leaders who have come to accept a bitter truth: Amid the political posturing and empty gesturing towards redress and "reconciliation," political, institutional, and personal violence upon

Indigenous lands, Indigenous minds, and Indigenous bodies has not abated. Certainly, in the realms of theatre, drama, and performance, publishers, pedagogues, funding agencies, and institutions continue in their failure to "provide safe working environments for BIPOC and marginalized members of [the] artistic community" (Harvey, "To: Arts Leaders"). It is unsurprising, then, that a significant shift in intention and praxis among a growing number of Indigenous culture workers is occurring. A "time of reckoning" has indeed arrived (Harvey, "To: Arts Leaders").

The exercise of reckoning the *immense* investment of time, labour, and goodwill that has been required of Indigenous culture workers to show institutional leaders exactly how they might make these spaces of knowledge creation, if not "safe," at least saf*er* provides a distressing proof. Indeed, Spiderwoman Theater has invested over four decades of labour to the task of performative bridge-building – crafting those liminal spaces in which Indigenous and non-Indigenous Peoples might meet to begin a collaboration built upon the foundations of active listening, generous reception, reciprocal compassion, and mutual understanding. And Spiderwoman Theater has not been alone in this. Across the decades of this troupe's existence, numerous Indigenous culture workers have laboured to build like bridges of understanding between the peoples who co-habit these lands. All to no avail, it seems. Our audiences never quite cross that bridge. And this wilful refusal to do so – this disingenuous insistence on endless reiterations of lessons that could quite easily be grasped by open minds and willing hearts – has edged Indigenous culture workers onto a hamster wheel on which we rush to create and recreate in an endless cycle that numbs minds, strains hearts, tears muscle, and breaks bone. As Toni Morrison has observed, this wheel upon which Indigenous, Black, or other racialized culture workers have been relegated to iterate and reiterate their humanity to others who refuse to see and hear has been deliberately engineered to "distract" us from the more vital, life-affirming, and life-preserving work we need to do within, with, and for our own communities (Morrison 7). And in this observation is a dire warning: We collude (unwillingly) in our own imprisonment, as with each new project, in each successive generation we dedicate our efforts to the crafting (and then replication) of bridges of understanding, which the colonial mind refuses to cross.

When it becomes apparent that healthy perseverance has morphed into toxic perseveration, the only course remaining is self-preservation: "One foot in front of the other, in front of the other, in front of the other. Walk, keep walking, walk away" (Spiderwoman Theater and Aanmitaagzi). In this moment, historic colonial refusal is increasingly being met with *Indigenous refusal*. Scholars such as Kanien'kehá:ka activist Audra Simpson asks why Indigenous Peoples should continue to entertain the promises of occupying states – promises of "redress," "restitution," and "reconciliation" (A. Simpson, "Savage"). Such promises (popularly expressed as "diversity," "inclusion," "equity") might best be represented by the acronym "DIE." And to DIE is not to decolonize. Apologists for the diversity, inclusion, and equity agenda require from the Indigenous body – as payment for its admission into colonial institutions – a series of cognitive, corporeal, and ontological contortions – or outright amputations – by means of which we may, however awkwardly, squeeze ourselves through their doors. So, the question remains: Once the Indigenous body arrives, what of that body will remain? We can be reconciled, and right relations can be established, they seem to say, if *we* are willing to change to fit ourselves into their machinery. But true "[d]ecolonization is about how [these institutions shake their foundations and shift their shapes] *to fit into us*" (Blight qtd. in Maracle, emphasis added). As Indigenous artists experience this subtler series of assimilative tactics, they have begun to devise means – *material and immaterial* – by which to refuse the very institutions that once prevented Indigenous entry and that now constrain Indigenous agency.

Such refusals take myriad forms. Increasingly, we are seeing Indigenous, Black, and Artists of Culture remove themselves (and the work they have produced) from settler-run theatre companies, training grounds, and production houses. Others refuse to conform to time-honoured conventions and praxis within these organizations. Still others enact subtle subversions that reconfigure the spaces of viewing into spaces of dual reception where the affect and messaging absorbed by the Indigenous witnesses differs markedly from that received by their non-Indigenous neighbours (see Carter, "My!"; Carter, "Indigenous Rage"). Each fraught experience brings in its wake a new mode of refusal, and each refusal carries a significant cost.

After a lifetime of working in theatre, the octogenarian founder of Spiderwoman Theater, Muriel Miguel (Guna-Rappahannock), has issued a public refusal of colonial control over her work. In recent years, she has called for a curation of space "that is not colonized – [a space] for Native people, taken care of by Native people" (*Segal Talks*). And until the COVID-19 pandemic initiated a global lockdown, Miguel's dream of an Indigenous theatre space in New York City seemed to loom large and clear on the horizon. A gathering of Indigenous theatre-makers and Elders (who would discuss the space, its design and upkeep) had been scheduled for May 2020. A meeting via Zoom occurred a year later, but this is the beginning of a project that will take much time to be realized.

And yet, even in this moment – a moment of suspension in which she feels herself "frozen," Muriel Miguel imagines herself as an Indigenous artist leaping "over the hurdle" to a time and space where she is not continually being reshaped, constrained, and instructed "how to" by the very people who invite her into settler-controlled spaces to speak, to teach, to create, or to perform (*Segal Talks*). The only way through is over. The vehicle of transport is the story, and the fuel is *listening*.

Spiderwoman Theater began almost half a century ago as an act of faith engendered by the realization of "how many women were being beaten" (*Segal Talks*) and a desire to do something about it. It continues today despite an added layer of institutional violence, but in this historical moment, something has changed: The violence continues – escalates, even – *but the story has shifted*. Where hope may have once been sought in telling the story, affecting the sensibilities of witnesses, and calling upon them to re-right that story, hope now manifests itself within the lens of clear-eyed self-reliance. This story will not be re-righted by outside agency. *Indigenous hope resides, not in the appeal, but in the refusal*. "Hope is getting out of a bad situation," Du Tu Kapsus tells us (Spiderwoman Theater and Aanmitaagzi). When all else has failed, our best hope may lie in simply walking away.

Leanne Simpson and Elder Edna Manitowabi remind us that the cycles of Indigenous origin stories provide the "lens" through which we can see beyond what has been devastated in the wake of colonial invasion and through which we can imagine a process through which to repair, rebuild and re-world (280–1). These are not only stories of human-to-land relationships; *they are the stories that teach us to survive ecological disaster*—the utter collapse of a once- thriving world. Indeed, as Muriel Miguel reminds us, those origin stories that sprout, flower, seed, and re-root themselves in the communal hearts and minds of diverse peoples the world over are stories of exile – of a fall from the familiar into an alien landscape in which the exiled must learn to sustain herself, build a home, and nurture functioning relationships with her host community. Wheresoever they are told, in whatever language and with whatever narrative flourish or discrete detail, their essence remains the same: "[S]ky woman falling, and all the stories of daughters from the stars, your Anishinaabe stories about coming from the stars, and our [Guna] version of the star family; I think they are the same thing" (Couchie and Miguel 226). These Creation Stories – lessons in recovery from an epic fall – are iterated and reiterated in each new generation. The human body is a vessel holding, in its deepest recesses, the muscle memory of an originary fall – the fall of human beings from Eden; Sky Woman's plummet to Earth; the eviction of the human child from her mother's womb and her sudden slide into the world in a rush of water; our first steps – falling, falling, and then, thankfully, fall recovery. In each new life stage until that final slide from this existence into an unknown plane, these stories teach us we must continue to "land" – to recover from the fall and set ourselves to rights. But in each new generation, as we reiterate that originary fall, something changes, and we "land" differently.

And, as Karyn Recollet (Nêhiyaw) and Jon Johnson caution us, "'land-ing' […] entails radical relations of care with the land, the stories, and one another" (178). In 1976, Spiderwoman Theater landed – first in North America and then in Europe – armed with a performative mirror with which to incite change. Four decades later, a new generation, scrambling to recover from the fall refuses the ongoing and escalating violence against Indigenous women on this continent and curates, within the spaces of public witness, an irreconcilably Indigenous space of healing for Indigenous storyteller and witness alike. Subtle as this shift may be, it is powerful: In this generation, after decades of effort, Spiderwoman's storytellers walk away from the fruitless task of confronting settler audiences with their "failure to uphold relational obligations" (Recollet and Johnson 186), evidenced by the ongoing and intensifying assault on Indigenous Peoples and the biotas they have stewarded over millennia. In focusing their intervention on the healing of Indigenous dis-ease, rather than on trying to redirect ingrained patterns of colonial thinking, the artists of Spiderwoman Theater refuse perseveration and model, instead, a dogged perseverance that is so necessary to hold on to hope, to hold on to life.

Outside of Spiderwoman Theater, these young artists and their cohort persevere in their escalation of refusal. No longer interested in educating settler audiences or tailoring its works and modes of working to garner the approbation of those audiences, this generation of Indigenous culture workers is enacting its own re-creation story. Stepping/falling away to "land" outside the colonial "theatre estate" (Kershaw 32), its artists focus on communal health and healing. Playwright/director Kim Senklip Harvey, for instance, has emerged as a potent and revolutionary voice with *Kamloopa: An Indigenous Matriarch Story*. She has publicly declared that she would rather forgo professional advancement (e.g., a national tour of her work) than risk the safety of the Indigenous artists (cast, crew, and designers) who make up her team. If she has been characterized by arts leaders in particular spaces as a "contrarian," it is because she will not back down in the struggle to ensure that the Indigenous individuals with whom she works are not subjected to "spiritual wrongdoing" (*Kamloopa*). Meanwhile, playwright/performer

Yolanda Bonnell (Anishinaabe-South Asian), who has worked with Muriel Miguel, is also part of *Kamloopa*'s creative team. Bonnell shares Harvey's contention that the "industry of theatre" in Canada has been and continues to be unsafe for all racialized artists.

In early 2020, Bonnell excited controversy by enacting a courageous refusal and requesting that *only* non-Caucasian writers review her recent production *bug* at Theatre Passe Muraille.[12] It was a risky move. Mainstream critics – by and large, white males (see Nolan, "Why it Matters") – have historically held and continue to wield no small degree of power over the reception and lifespan of a production. But Bonnell enacted this "contrarian" move because she is driven by the need to carve out spaces of "safety for artists of colour" rather than the desire to appease the "gatekeepers of success" (Bonnell, "Why"). With this refusal, Bonnell has flipped the script, restoring respect to the communities for whom she creates this work and investing them with rightful authority as the final arbiter of a production's merit: As a performative mechanism of healing for and by Indigenous people, *bug* requires and invites community consultation and feedback, rather than a colonial stamp of approval or disapprobation. And, as Bonnell has testified, the personal cost for this refusal has been inordinately high.[13]

Nonetheless, with director/playwright/performer Carmen (formerly, Cole) Alvis (Métis) and their manidoons collective, Bonnell continues to push back against institutional constraints that may endanger the health and safety of her colleagues (Sur). Characterizing her work as "artistic ceremony" (Bonnell qtd. in Nestruck), Bonnell advocates for the engagement of Elders and Traditional Healers at every performance to support all of those who come to witness her work (Bonnell, *bug* 29). She and Alvis curate the spaces of devising and rehearsal as ceremonial sites. Here, action is governed by Respect, Love, Humility, Honesty, Bravery, Truth and Wisdom – the Seven Grandfather Teachings of the Anishinaabeg.

---

12 Bonnell credits Harvey for her inspiration here. With the 2018 production of *Kamloopa* (in which Bonnell performed), Harvey did not invite reviewers. Instead, she sought community feedback by soliciting "love letters" from Indigenous women who had seen the show (Nestruck).

13 Threats, shaming, and violently racist vitriol have constituted key weapons in online assaults aimed at Yolanda Bonnell and at Kim Harvey Senklip in the wake of Bonnell's request that white critics refrain from reviewing *bug* (Sur). And such incidents are not rare. Racialized artists and students of the art have been and continue to be subjected to microaggressions and macro-assaults within the "theatre estate," as are Indigenous individuals and communities in the larger Canadian context.

As it has always been with Spiderwoman Theater, the artists of the manidoons collective are encouraged to bring their lives and entire human experience into the space of co-creation and to share their whole selves with their colleagues in the talking circles with which the rehearsal day begins. The places in which manidoons' artistic ceremonies unfold are entered with protocol and appropriately acknowledged, as their caretakers are honoured (Sur). So too are all witnesses cared for. Each time I have attended a performance of *bug*, those Elders and Knowledge Keepers engaged to care for the audience stood with Bonnell and Alvis to welcome all of us into the space and ensure our comfort. We were invited to leave cell phones on (in case of emergency) and to leave and re-enter the space as needed. Just as this generation of storytellers who are carrying forward the legacy of Spiderwoman Theater have done with *Material Witness*, so Bonnell and the manidoons collective have carved out a "holding cell" – an "irreconcilable space" – in which to presence and address the epigenetic transgenerational legacies of embodied trauma (Indigenous) and sustained perpetration (non-Indigenous). In performance, Bonnell's scripting of an irreconcilably Indigenous, *protected* space flips the colonial centre, as, heretofore, *marginalized* bodies are invited to join Bonnell and to occupy an inner circle from which to fulfil the role of witness and so travel with her through those dark spaces where trauma is born into the luminescence of hope.

Non-Indigenous witnesses are invited to seat themselves in the margins *outside* the ceremonial circle. From here, they are invited to witness this healing work and to use this teaching to heal the very specific epigenetic transgenerational dis-ease that took root in the bone and swam in the blood of European refugees fleeing plague, starvation, oppression, and a thousand years of violence visited by one European body upon another. This is a dis-ease those refugees brought to these shores, a disease that moved their bodies and directed centuries of crimes against those adjudged by the White Body to be other-than-human (Menakem). There is a healing that needs to occur in this space also. And the responsibility to intervene upon and eradicate this destructive condition rests solely on the shoulders of its carrier – the European settler.

Aanmitaagzi: "S/He Speaks" in Mounds

> Throughout *Material Witness*, there are heaps, piles, and mounds. They are sacred and irreverent, beautiful and ugly, profound and mundane. It's all piled one on top of the other, our storied lives, and very long histories. It's all woven together. (Couchie and Miguel 228)

Spiderwoman Theater's "holding cell" is an irreconcilable space in which to speak in safety. As welcoming and comforting as it has been curated to be, it is, nonetheless, a space of preparation, not a permanent home. It is a space in which the most secret and sacred truths emerge, are painstakingly layered one atop another, and shaped into a performative earthwork. And through this collective labour, it becomes a crucible in which to uplift the voices of Indigenous storytellers and Indigenous witnesses who are a part of (or apart from) the communities they have invited to collaborate with them on this healing work. Co-producers Penny Couchie (Anishinaabe) and Sid Bobb (Stó:lō) of Aanmitaagzi ("S/He speaks") have successfully collaborated with Muriel to transport their Big Medicine Studio to any site upon which *Material Witness* is performed, and thereby to transform the storytelling event into a rite of healing. The protected space here has been extended beyond the stage to include and envelope the *theatron* (the place of witnessing) itself. Onstage, Du Tu Kapsus walks the space, blesses the space, and sings in spirit guardians from all four directions. Offstage, Indigenous women from across Turtle Island have stitched their stories and memories of the women whom they miss – women missing from their lives – into a "material witness" that greets us upon entry, envelops us, and invites us into the conversation. Like the fabled backdrop[14] that has travelled with Spiderwoman Theater since its inception and that has extended itself and thickened with each new scrap of fabric that has been offered by a collaborator, a grateful community, or an affected audience member, this installation also fulfils the function of binding fragments into story, of repairing what has been torn, and of mapping the greater constellation(s) of which we are all a part (Couchie and Miguel 227). This installation is a material call that demands response. It reminds those who have come to see a show that the one who sees is charged with responsibility: We are *material witnesses* to former, current, and ongoing crimes of violence against women. Perhaps, some of us have played the part of perpetrator; others, perhaps, have only colluded with the perpetrator – bearing witness and burying our knowledge within the folds and layers of the myriad skeins of fabric with which we all adorn our bodies, our homes, our playthings, pets, and children.

Imbedded in these adornments, too, is the trauma of the violated body. Entrance simultaneously prepares and protects her fists, as she

14 This too is "mola," and I will be speaking at length about this signature backdrop in chapter 3.

wraps them in fabric, readying them for violence. Penny Couchie carries us into the memory of a little girl, desperately trying to protect herself from the sexual advances of an adult visitor to her home on the night of her kindergarten concert: Her dress, the dress her mother made with such love, cloaks her vulnerable little girl body, even as it invites predatory eyes – "Little red and white flowers, pearly white buttons, a scoop neck" (Spiderwoman Theater and Aanmitaagzi). In yet another memory, Cherish Violet Blood's character Cholula remembers tearing off a schoolmate's shirt, shaming her in front of her teenage peers by revealing the torn bra beneath (Spiderwoman Theater and Aanmitaagzi). The fabric itself bears witness to these violent acts and to their resultant scars. Masking the scarred body or proclaiming (in its colour and cut) profound psycho-spiritual truths, this fabric may also bear the tokens of violence – tears, stains, loose threads. In such tokens, a dark history may be read. And in loose threads, such tangled histories may be unravelled, rendered visible, and/or woven into a larger history of survivance (Couchie and Miguel 227).

In a particularly potent moment Penny Couchie recounts an exciting period in her life when, finally, after many years of training as an actor and a dancer and too many years of playing "too many trees and too many whores," she receives the opportunity to dance as an *Indigenous woman in an Indigenous story*. Here, Couchie quips, she "danced genocide, danced smallpox, and danced Indigenous reclamation." During the rehearsal period, the choreographer tells her that she must lose weight to fit into the costume. But throughout her telling (in the present moment of performance), Couchie keeps dancing, demonstrating the power, beauty, and grace with which she was originally able to illuminate the story she had been hired to tell. As the pressure to lose weight mounts, her movements become more panicked and inchoate. The scene peaks as Couchie dances herself to the ground, madly shimmying to get into an unseen costume, while a chorus keeps time by madly chanting "Go fatty! Go fatty! Go fatty!" Once the beautiful dancer's body has been squeezed into the unsuitable costume, Couchie struggles to her feet, constricted and hobbled, her natural grace and dignity stifled. "Fuck, why didn't you just get me a bigger costume? Like, seriously, how hard was it?" she asks (Spiderwoman Theater and Aanmitaagzi).

How difficult is it for the settlers who occupy Indigenous lands to acknowledge and desist from an historic campaign of violence perpetrated on these lands and the Indigenous Peoples who have stewarded them? How difficult is it to listen to Indigenous humans, to acknowledge Indigenous humanity, and to agree that "this" – land theft, femicide, eugenics, re-education, child theft, starlight tours, language suppression, spiritual prohibition, racist policies, etc. – "isn't normal"? (M. Miguel qtd. in Commanda).

Fifty years after *Women in Violence*, this new generation of storytellers continues to sift material mounds and memory in search of "humanity in these stories and how to heal" (M. Miguel qtd. in Commanda). What has changed, however, is that these carriers of Indigenous story have taken up this work solely for themselves, for their communities, and for their children. This work is not presented for the entertainment or edification of its non-Indigenous audiences. The "material witness," which dresses Spiderwoman's set and envelopes the house, both proclaims and protects the story of its makers. Collaboratively created by Indigenous women across Turtle Island during the Pulling Threads workshop series hosted by Spiderwoman Theater and Aanmitaagzi, each embroidered inlay and each loose thread cradle answers to these questions: "[W]hat piece of material reminds you of yourself? What is your darkest secret? What is your legacy? What do you want to leave behind?" (M. Miguel qtd. in Commanda).

Work-worn hands. Hands that have cradled babies, tanned hides, stroked fevered brows, braided hair, warded off blows, cleaned fish, stirred broth, stitched hides, mended clothing, dug roots, picked berries, and/or clasped each other in prayer have pulled at loose threads, worried them, and ultimately reconfigured the personal stuff of darkness, of heart break, of incalculable loss into a living document that orders the chaos of desperate thoughts and fevered imaginings. And in so doing, these hands teach us how to "make hope actionable" (Morriseau qtd. in Annie Smith 85). The secret lives of these hands are written into the layered fabrics that constitute this living document and they may be read in the fleshly witnesses on stage who endlessly fold and mound clothing to create order in the chaos, who craft love medicine, who hold a finger to the lips or clamp a hand on their own mouths to hold back dangerous utterances and who raise wrapped fists to ward off violence or to deliver it, all the while reminding themselves that "In a revolution, a woman is equal. In a revolution, a woman is equal" (Spiderwoman Theater and Aanmitaagzi).

As these women make the decision to refuse the violence of their domestic partners, declaring that they will run "to the mountains," "to my mum's," to "a bunker," "to Canada," it is well worth reminding ourselves of the refusal out of which Spiderwoman Theater was engendered: *"I found rape; I found abuse. And I could not be with [countenance, or tolerate such violence any longer]"* (M. Miguel, *RedTalk*). It is significant also that Spiderwoman Theater began with a *working of the hands*. Indeed, as is discussed in the next chapter, Spiderwoman Theater accomplished its North American emergence with a performative weave of Creation Stories, underscored by one Hopi artist's practical "gest" of finger weaving. Weaving, interweaving. Creation, re-creation. More than 40 years since the company's inception, its outreach, growth, and influence are apparent in the many, many hands that craft emergence from within the emergency – that weave re-creation for Indigenous Peoples five centuries after incalculable catastrophe battered this continent. These hands still remember to hold on. As Du Tu Kapsus reminds us, "That's instinct. Long ago, that's the way a baby stayed on its mother's body" (Spiderwoman Theater and Aanmitaagzi). Skin to skin. Hand to hand. Within and, perhaps, despite the wrappings that swaddle and contain us. "You look into a palm. You see the future" (Spiderwoman Theater and Aanmitaagzi). Perhaps, you make that future for yourself.

2 "An Indian Is an Idea a Man Has of Himself"

We are what we imagine. Our very existence consists in our imagination of ourselves. Our best destiny is to imagine, at least completely, who and what and <u>that</u> we are. The greatest tragedy that can befall us is to go unimagined.

– N. Scott Momaday 103

A Short, Ugly Episode Around Naming and Claiming

Muriel Miguel likes to tell this story when she is speaking about the creation of Spiderwoman's *Winnetou's Snake Oil Show from Wigwam City* (1989). And while chapter 5 will explore this important production at length, it may prove instructive to discuss one of the stories behind its creation immediately. It is a familiar story in Indian Country, and in its various incarnations (constructed upon myriad incidents) it never fails to elicit eruptions of outraged laughter at the sheer audacity of its protagonists who seem to be insensible to the unconscionable absurdity of their violations, which they continue "with the best intentions" to perpetrate on Native individuals and Native communities across North America.

The late Rosemary Richmond and Muriel Miguel had enjoyed a lifelong friendship that endured over seven decades, since they were both 12-years-old (M. Miguel, Interview 2007). And it was from Richmond, director of the American Indian Community House (AICH) in New York City (1987–2010), that Miguel received this story. Like many Indigenous urban leaders, Richmond took care to support American Indian artists and artisans within her city and its environs by purchasing some of their works for the Community House. One day, a European man who had attended many community events at AICH paid her a personal visit during which he presented her with some exemplary pieces of beadwork, which were characterized by a distinctly Indigenous aesthetic.[1] She complimented the pieces and asked him who had crafted them, thinking, perhaps, that he had purchased them from an Indigenous artist. "I did," he answered. Again, she complimented the work and remarked upon his skill. But he had not come to her for compliments; he wanted her to purchase his work and display it at AICH. When she declined, he became agitated and shouted at her, telling her that his work was far superior to any of the works by American Indian artists then on display at AICH. And for this reason alone, he argued, she should purchase and display his work (M. Miguel, Personal Communication 2006). Cue eruptions of outraged laughter …

The point of this story is not to condemn this artist for his imitation of a form that has been developed within a culture to which he is not indigenous, or for his attempt to sell the product of his considerable study and labour.[2] What is disturbing, however, is the unconscionable

---

1 An early reviewer of this book suggested that I clarify some key points in this story. This reviewer wondered if the craftsman discussed here might have been displaying work emerging from his own European traditions. Perhaps, this reviewer argued, Richmond was being presented with an opportunity to curate an aesthetic "conversation" between bead workers emerging from differing communities and to showcase their distinct traditions. This is not the case. Quite simply, a Euro-American bead worker (whether through independent study or through attendance at Indigenous beading workshops) had developed considerable proficiency in imitating Indigenous beadwork, and now he was seeking profit and validation.

Indigenous beading carries a distinct aesthetic. Forms that are represented, pattern-flourishes, and colour schemes are specific to each nation, and the culturally literate "reader" is able to read, encoded within these details, the nation to which the wearers belong, the clan to which they belong, and the nation to which the maker belongs. It is also important, I think, to note here that Indigenous service organizations generally operate on a very tight budget and do not operate as for-profit entrepreneurial enterprises. In other words, AICH was not purchasing and displaying Indigenous work as a gallery might – to eventually sell for profit. Rather, in purchasing works from local Indigenous artists, Rosemary Richmond was doing what she could to offer financial support to talented individuals whose financial situations are generally precarious because they are artists and who live doubly precarious lives simply because they are Indigenous.

2 Spiderwoman Theater does not condemn non-Indigenous theatre workers for utilizing their Storyweaving Practice to create original works that speak to their own unique questions, histories, and cultural practices (assuming, of course, that those who utilize the process, credit its authors). The deployment of an artistic process belonging to another's culture does not have to lead to the manufacture of an "artificial tree." When it does (and it often does), the work produced reflects profound disrespect for the process, for the community from whom the process was "borrowed," and for the intended audience. Ultimately, such work reveals the spiritual torpor of its makers who have not followed a processual path to arrive at their own truth but who have co-opted aesthetic principles (alien to themselves) with which to cloak the spiritual enervation that will otherwise pervade their works.

arrogance of an individual who has the audacity to co-opt the voice of another, to imitate that voice, and then to declare his imitation to be superior to the original. After centuries of concentrated – albeit, unsuccessful – effort to assimilate and/or to eradicate the Indigenous voice on this continent, contemporary beneficiaries of the colonizing project now claim ownership of that voice and presume to "teach" Indigenous Peoples how to manifest it in the manner that *they* deem most appropriate and most authentic. In so doing, they continue their appropriation of Indigenous voice as they dispossess the Indigenous human of her sovereignty – of her inherent right to "imagine [and proclaim] who and what and *that*" she is (see Momaday 103). It is heartening to remember, however, that such incidents, even as they assault and work to degrade the tribal voice and erode Native identity, can work as crucibles in which the objects of their violation put their identity "to the test" by confronting and questioning not only those who co-opt Indigenous voices and try to exercise control over Indigenous agency but also themselves, their understanding of, and their relationship to these. Paradoxically, such "trials by fire," contrary to the spirit and intent upon which they were engendered, can work (or force us to work) to embrace and strengthen that identity.

In 1980 Spiderwoman Theater produced *Oh, What a Life* at Theater for the New City and *The Fittin' Room* for the Theater Project in New York City. Set in a six-cubicle representation of an in-store dressing room with racks of garish, outlandish clothing, which served as a metaphor for the containment and pigeonholing of women, *The Fittin' Room*[3] presented a series of songs and sketches through which its performers resisted and subverted the stereotypes and labels with which they had been defined, upending the popular "truism" that "one size fits all." Choosing to forgo the presentation of fictional characters, each performer presented herself as herself, highlighting myriad contradictions, each containing a portion of her truth as opposed to defining moments purporting to represent absolute truths about her life and essence. The flaws they sought to reveal were flaws of perception; and these, they built into a dialectical dramaturgical structure, which provided a deceptively loose framework that easily accommodated blatant contradictions in tone, style, and content, and which alternatively turned its focus from the

3 No complete textual artifact of this script exists. The Walter Havighurst Special Collections & University Archives (Miami University Libraries, Oxford, OH) houses hand-written fragments (donated by various performers) of *The Fittin' Room*. Please see Appendix 1 for a running outline of the show (from Pam Verge's notes).

doings on stage to the audience itself. Indeed, as the show began, the "spotlight" was turned upon the audience as its members were rigorously coached and rehearsed to perform their own identities:

> Hello everybody. How is everybody tonight [?] You look wonderful. It's wonderful to be here in _____. Before we begin there are a few things I want to go over with you. Now when I go like this (gesture) I want everybody to clap. When I go like this (gesture) it means stop. When I go like this (gesture) I want you to cheer. When I go like this (gesture) laugh. (**Practice.**) Now, what's green on the inside, white on the outside and hops? A frog Sandwich (laugh) (clap) (cheer) (stop)
>
> - Anybody here from _____?
> - Anybody here from out of town?
> - Where you from?
> - Anybody else?
> - Are there any feminists in the audience?
> - Any gays? (cheers)
> - Any straights? (cheers)
> - Anybody out their [sic] own a cat? (cheers)
>   - Now, without further ado – Here's Spiderwoman. ("Spiderwoman Papers," emphasis added)[4]

As the troupe members entered, Pamela Verge called out characteristics belonging to each performer as she whipped the audience into a physical and emotional frenzy: "I said straight. I said gay. I said young. I said old. I said fat. I said feminist" ("Spiderwoman Papers"). And audience members continued to perform their own declarations of identity by alternately raising and lowering their hands and standing and sitting (Giuliano 9D). Within this slyly subversive pedagogical "workout," audience members were induced to perceive and examine their own intersectionality and to perceive and acknowledge the complex intersections that challenge our understandings of self and other, often drawing us into alliance with those whose lives and context may, at first glance seem to differ radically from our own. If an audience member stood to align herself with the "fat" category, she might find herself still standing with those who self-identified as "thin" in the "gay" category

---

4 This text is titled "Pam's Intro." It was written and performed for *The Fittin' Room* by Pamela Verge who joined Spiderwoman Theater upon her graduation from Bard College. She remained with the troupe until the 1981 split.

and these might find themselves still standing with those who self-identified as "straight" in the "old" or the "young" categories. Alternatively, an audience member might find herself jumping up and down in her seat and raising and lowering her hand repeatedly. Through her own exertions, such an audience member would begin to organically understand that her identity, like those of the performers she had come to see, could not be comfortably contained in one "box."

Some popular ballads and show tunes were satirized in performance to expose the ridiculous premises upon which they had been built. Indeed, one reviewer declared, "'Feelings,' '42nd Street' and 'The Way We Were' [had never been] sung in quite this campy way before" (Giuliano 9D). Others, by contrast, were approached seriously and celebrated for the beauty they revealed: "Gloria [Miguel] actually uncovers poetry in, or imparts it to, the lyrics of '(You're not a dream) You're a Man'" (Blumenthal). And sketches were alternately presented as rollicking caricatures or in absolute earnest, while the troupe interrogated its audiences with the same questions about feminism and the female condition around which its predecessor *Cabaret: An Evening of Disgusting Songs and Pukey Images* (1979) had been constructed, obliging its audiences to turn their gaze upon themselves and each other as keenly as it had been turned upon the spectacle on stage.

> Self-revelation, on the part of the performers, was never simple or one-dimensional. And through it, each performer issued a challenge to all those who had sought to neatly categorize her on the basis of partial evidence or who had challenged her identity because she did not neatly fit into the societal box that had been specially constructed for her as a "feminist," a "lesbian," a "woman," "wife," "mother" or an "American Indian." For instance, Muriel Miguel revealed herself as a lesbian lover and then gave a lesson on how to be sexually attractive to men: "... if you purse your lips and say prunes – that's sexy." ("Spiderwoman Papers")

And Peggy Shaw presented herself as both a butch lover of women and as a sentimental, nurturing grandmother, while Gloria Miguel's personal testimony overturned a hilarious examination of the American "Metonyndian":[5]

GLORIA: This is my class photo. Can you pick me out? I'm always the same. Always Gloria.

5 I have coined this term by combining Homi Bhabha's "metonym" with the European misappellation of the original peoples on this continent as "Indians."

MURIEL: Did you know your Cancer sun is in conflict with your Scorpio sun?

GLORIA. NO.

ALL: Ohh

PAM: Do you do beadwork?

GLORIA: No.

ALL: Ohh

EVA: Are you an actress that's a feminist or a feminist that's an actress?

GLORIA: I'm a woman. I'm a mother, a mother of a man and a woman. I'm a grandmother. I love women – I have great friendships with women. I love men. I have sexual relations with men. I don't have to apologize for my life. ("Spiderwoman Papers")

Despite the fierce insistence of its performers to forge and assert their own identities; despite its cries for liberation, this project offered no easy answers. Rather, it left its audiences to ponder a rather plaintive question: "Now that I'm free, what do I do about being alone?" (Giuliano 9D).

Ironically, in this year as the women of Spiderwoman were performatively declaring their right to carve out and lay claim to identities of their own choosing, corporate America mustered its forces and began its own assault on the troupe and the name with which it had chosen to identify itself. In 1980, lawyers for Marvel Comics sent a letter to Spiderwoman Theater, collectively addressing the troupe's members as "Gentlemen" and accusing them of copyright infringement, ordering them to "cease and desist" identifying themselves by the name "Spiderwoman." Marvel had copyrighted and trademarked the female counterpart to its "Spiderman;" and in its eyes, the theatre troupe's appellation, "Spiderwoman Theater," constituted a "dilution of the distinctiveness of the Spiderwoman Mark" (see Appendix 2). Outrageously, Marvel's arguments could not even rest on the corporation's claim that its creation and naming of its mutant female with her keen "spidey senses" pre-dated the 1975 formation and naming of the feminist theatre company, which it was attacking. After all, "Marvel's Spiderwoman" had only been in existence since 1979 (Baker and Davidson). Marvel simply *owned* the name (or so it claimed) by virtue of the copyright, which it had purchased. Spiderwoman Theater responded by engaging the services of William Kunstler and took their case to the people, writing an open letter to the New York City press, laying claim to their name and accusing the Marvel Group of yet another act of cultural appropriation perpetrated against the original peoples of this continent.

The case did not last more than two years and ended well for Spiderwoman Theater, which still retains its name. Various commentators tend to cite this battle with the Marvel Group as little more than a worrisome, inconvenient incident with no lasting consequences. Indeed, it has been largely regarded as a mere footnote in a sea of struggles, which included the day-to-day battles to find performance venues, to perform for people who could pay, to negotiate travel expenses, suitable accommodations, and per diems – in short, to be treated with the respect and consideration that Spiderwoman's craft and professionalism warranted, particularly amongst those producers and festival organizers who deemed themselves sister-soldiers in the feminist struggle. By 1997, the Marvel incident was being cited as little more than a pithy title for the exhibition that featured Spiderwoman's private papers at the Walter Havighurst Special Collections Library at Miami University in Oxford, OH: This exhibition was titled *Spiderwoman Theater: The Real Marvel*. It explored the troupe's origins, travels (throughout the 1970s and the 1980s), "travails" (of which the Marvel incident was deemed by its organizers to be the least significant), works (including partial scripts), audience reception, and critical commentary.

But this short, ugly episode around naming and claiming is not insignificant. It resonates at multiple levels, connecting Spiderwoman Theater to the history of its inception; to the people for and by whom it had been originally designed to speak; and to the history of misappropriation, dispossession, and misrepresentation that has characterized the relationship between the founding fathers of America and the pre-existing Indigenous nations whose existence complicated their project of Manifest Destiny. For Muriel Miguel, the issue was quite simple: Demonstrating the selfsame *hubris* upon which America had been built, the Marvel Group had created its mutant female, whose existence was entirely reliant upon questionable science and endowed her with the name of a Hopi deity whose existence pre-dated both creator (Marvel) and creation (its comic book heroine). "Spiderwoman," for Marvel (and for its public, it hoped) would now and forever identify its creation – and *only* its creation – because Marvel had "discovered" the name. Citing a "centuries"-old history of misappropriation, Muriel and the troupe attacked Marvel and other US corporations, which identified their goods by appropriated names – Winnebago, Pontiac, Thunderbird, Mohawk, etc. – and challenged their right to "appropriate and claim the exclusive use of names from a people's cultural heritage" (see Appendix 2).

Spiderwoman Theater had been named for the Hopi creatrix as a tribute to Josephine Mofsie-Tarrant (Hopi-Winnebago) whose initial work with Muriel had inspired and engineered its engenderment and process. Although the troupe was largely identified as a "heterogeneous," "feminist," and lately "lesbian" group, the existence of three Native American members was consistently emphasized in publicity materials around this identity skirmish as it had been for all Spiderwoman productions since *Women in Violence* (1976). Further, the name with which the troupe identified itself, did not simply constitute a tribute to its founding "grandmother" Josephine Mofsie-Tarrant or to the American Indian heritage of its director and her sisters, it also reflected essence and action: Muriel Miguel had named her troupe for the process and presentational style it would (and did) follow. This process is rooted in the philosophic and aesthetic traditions of Miguel's own nations as well as of Mofsie-Tarrant's. This is a process within which Mofsie-Tarrant and Miguel (and later, Miguel's older sisters) rooted themselves as they began to construct a communitist project designed to facilitate their own survivance and the survivance of tribal peoples around the world.

With its open letter to the New York media, Spiderwoman Theater had appealed to its audiences and to the larger community for support. The community responded. Through 1980 and 1981, New York City papers followed the case and expressed full support for the troupe. It is interesting to note, however, that while all commentators sympathized with Spiderwoman Theater's position and uniformly descried Marvel's misappropriation of the Hopi deity's name as cultural theft, this assault on Indigenous cultural identity was, for some, less politically charged than the Marvel Group's historically troubled relationship with another marginalized and oppressed cultural group.

Citing the overt lesbian content within Spiderwoman's repertoire and Marvel's long-standing conflict with the gay community, some pundits expressed the belief that Marvel's suit had been conducted in the spirit of targeting the troupe's lesbian orientation (see Tyler 5; Goldstein 42). Just what it was the troupe had become – its right to identify and name itself in accordance with its *becoming* – was being written externally, in corporate boardrooms and in the court of public opinion through a chorus of contending stories serving conflicting agendas. Internally, each performer was *becoming* as she wrote and re-wrote herself into herstory. But even as each of Spiderwoman's artists imagined the community in which herstory would play itself out and in which she could discover, assert, and play out her own identity, the connective filaments of the web that bound the troupe's women together were tearing away from each other.

Spiderwoman Theater, then in its fifth year, was just barely out of its infancy. The work had just begun, and suddenly it seemed as if it was about to end. A split was imminent. As it turned out, however, the split that finally occurred did not affect the end of the troupe; rather, this split was the catalyst, which would initiate a new beginning …

Herstory: The "Beginning of the Beginning of the Beginning"

Lisa Mayo,[6] Gloria Miguel, and Muriel Miguel were born in the traditional way on the floor of their maternal grandmother's house in Brooklyn, NY – the house that Muriel Miguel occupies today.[7] All were delivered by their mother's mother who was as gifted as a midwife as her daughter was a seer. And the umbilical cords and afterbirth of all three have long since integrated with the soil of that Brooklyn yard behind the house in which they were delivered and raised. That all three sisters were born into a life of struggle is now, by virtue of the candid interviews they have offered over the years and the confessional nature of their stage works, a matter of public record. That these sisters longed to escape the grinding poverty and racism, which had defined their young lives and the domestic unrest (set into motion by their father's alcoholism and their mother's withdrawal) and which had threatened their peace and disrupted their sororal relationships, resonates throughout their works demanding redress and reconciliation.

Their father Antonio Miguel, born in Gunayala (in the San Blas Islands off the coast of Panama), was a middle child in a family of 12 children.[8] When he was six years old, a British family adopted him, taking him to Jamaica, presumably to educate him and to offer him a "better" life.[9] While their intentions may have been good, and while he had always maintained that they treated him well, Antonio was

6 Lisa Mayo is the stage name Elizabeth Miguel concocted early in her career in a bid to recreate herself as an ethnically indeterminate performer. Close friends and family generally call her Elizabeth or Liz.

7 In actuality, Gloria was born two houses away – in the home of her aunt. But like her sisters, she was born on the floor and delivered by her grandmother. For all intents and purposes, she grew up with her elder sister Lisa, although Lisa lived for a time with their grandmother and aunt.

8 No birth certificate exists for Antonio Miguel. He never knew his exact birth year or month; however, he used to say that he was born sometime around 1900 (Mojica, Personal Communication. 15 July 2023).

9 This would have occurred in the early twentieth century – approximately 1906. During this time, he was renamed Jim Foster and retained that name until he settled in New York City (Mojica, Personal Communication 2023).

unhappy. He missed his birth family; he felt constricted by the schoolroom atmosphere; and he felt constricted in the suits, stiff collars, and shoes he was forced to wear. Realizing that he was not attending school and that he would not willingly or easily acclimatize himself to the life for which they were trying to groom him, Miguel's adoptive family finally sent him back to his home in Gunayala (Mayo qtd. in Burns and Hurlbutt 170–71).[10]

At the age of 15, Antonio Miguel, along with several of his brothers and his friends, became a merchant seaman, travelling the world on schooners and steamships. During a leave in New York City, one of Antonio's friends who had been dating a young Rappahannock woman invited him to come along and meet his date's younger sister, Elmira. These sisters had been born and raised in Red Hook, Brooklyn. Their Rappahannock ancestors hailed from Virginia, and their nation is part of the Powhatan alliance into which Pocahontas had been born and Captain John Smith had been adopted in 1606. The Rappahannock people have been influenced by over four centuries of contact with European invaders, settlers, and missionaries; consequently, Elmira's people had been practising Christians for generations. Sitting at a window in her mother's Brooklyn house to catch a glimpse of her older sister's "gentleman caller," Elmira saw his tall, handsome companion, Antonio, and at that moment she knew she was looking at her future husband. Such is the stuff of family legends.

Of course, there were complications. These, too, comprise the stuff of family legends – the stuff that may remain unspoken, "forgotten," buried beneath the layers. But while a stone cast upon the waters may only create momentary surface ripples, which cease and are forgotten when it sinks, this stone imbeds itself deep within the layers of the sediment that form the riverbed, forever altering its topography and its elemental nature and redirecting the path of the waters cradled therein.

Antonio Miguel was a traditional Guna man. He was not Christian. He was not an American Indian. And so, Elmira's mother was opposed to a marital union between the affianced couple. So, Antonio Miguel went home and stayed away for three years. In those three years, he married a Guna woman (in an arranged marriage) with whom he had a son (Mayo

10 Reflecting on this, Muriel Miguel has noted that her father had been "scooped," like so many Indigenous children around the world. His hair was cut; his name had been changed; and he began to fear that he would lose his language. This, Miguel notes, created indelible scars, which were never addressed. "He never talked about it," she has told me, and this deep wounding would have, certainly, contributed to his alcoholism in later life (Miguel, Personal Communication, 2023).

qtd. in Burns and Hurlbutt 171). According to family legend, the petite, beautiful Elmira had been born with a caul, and she was gifted with psychic abilities, which she passed on to her daughters and to their children.[11] Although she was a practising Christian, along with her psychic abilities, she had also inherited medicinal knowledge from her mother, and she utilized this medicine to bring her fiancé back to her (Mayo qtd. in Burns and Hurlbutt 172). They were married, and in 1924 Elizabeth Miguel (Lisa Mayo) made her grand entrance on to the family "stage." In 1926, Gloria was born, and in 1937, "baby" Muriel joined the family.

But the initial "stones" – resentments, secrets, and betrayals real or perceived – that had rippled the waters of Antonio and Elmira's budding romance were silently ensconced in the riverbed; they were joined by other "stones" – racism, difficulties with acculturation, and economic impoverishment. And these "silent partners" began to direct individual choices, familial relationships, and quotidian events that would later discover themselves to the Miguel sisters as concomitant sources of wounding and vehicles of healing through which they would fully realize themselves as human beings and through which they would teach others to do likewise.

"We Were Talking about that Layer of Worthlessness, Selflessness"

Lisa Mayo has revealed that upon the birth of Gloria, her grandmother convinced Elmira to give Elizabeth over to herself and to Elmira's older sister Ida, who was unmarried and childless. So, Elizabeth went to live next door where she was "like a little princess" and given everything she wanted "except [her] mother" (Mayo qtd. in Burns and Hurlbutt 172). But while Elizabeth's "layer of worthlessness" is woven into the birth of her sister, Gloria has had her own issues around rejection and abandonment with which to contend:

> Elizabeth, do you remember when Aunt Ida and Uncle George and Uncle Frank used to take you out and leave me home? I used to sit at the window for hours wondering, why I couldn't go [...] I used to think there was something terribly wrong with me. (Spiderwoman, *Sun* 294)

11 Indeed, her considerable psychic gifts became the subject of Spiderwoman's *Reverb-ber-ber-rations* (1990). After exploring and sending up the ersatz glamour of "plastic shamanism" in *Winnetou's Snake Oil Show from Wigwam City*, the Miguel sisters were ready to revisit the less "glamorous," less profitable, genuine spirituality (which had sometimes discomfited and embarrassed them in their childhood). *Reverb-ber-ber-rations* (1990) was the result.

It may very well be that the extended family was trying to ease Elizabeth's trauma by showering her with extra attention to assuage her feelings of being rejected by her mother. But these are things that children cannot be expected to fully comprehend and reasonably accept. Eleven years after Gloria's birth and Elizabeth's "exile" from the parental home, Muriel was born, and by that time, their mother had become completely withdrawn. Muriel Miguel has stated on numerous occasions that she is the "only child" of her two sisters and that her mother never spoke to her. Living in a home infested with bedbugs and cockroaches with a deeply depressed mother, who had given up and withdrawn, and with a father who frequently came home inebriated and who was often out of work or who "drank away" his pay cheque when he was working, the Miguel daughters could not help but attribute their circumstances to either some "lack" in themselves as individuals or some congenital deficiency passed onto them by their cultural heritage and ethnic genealogy: All they could know at that time was all they saw; what they saw was that "being Indian meant a drunken father, a depressed mother, and no food, and being dispossessed from your house. It was [indeed!] ugly" (Mayo qtd. in France and Corso 181).

What they couldn't see (what they were not allowed to see) at that time was their father's "secret life": the extra-marital affairs in which he engaged; the abandoned son in Gunayala; another son in New York City for whom his brothers cared; Antonio's guilt for the children he had engendered but not *fathered*; a seaman's frustration at being landlocked; a man's frustration at not always being able to provide for the household in which he was an active father; his indignation at the relentless racism (a daily experience, which would have humiliated him personally; enraged him when he witnessed or heard how it affected his daughters, extended family, and friends; and effectively impeded his access to employment opportunities); and his resentment in the knowledge that his wife's mother did not consider him worthy of her daughter, did not consider his people as being on an equal footing with her own, and did not allow him to communicate his Traditional Knowledge and world view to her granddaughters. He drank to forget. He drank to bury the guilt and perhaps the resentments. And although he continued to practice Guna ways, his excessive drinking must certainly have interfered with his practice and compromised his instruction of Guna tradition and lifeway for his children[12] (Mayo qtd. in Burns and

12 Alcohol consumption is not compatible with the practice of traditional spiritual ways. Indeed, alcohol consumption is strongly discouraged by traditionalists of

Hurlbutt 175). Religious confusion – particularly, for the older sisters – added another opaque layer, which further separated them from the knowledge of themselves as human beings belonging to and valued by a specific community (or pair of communities). Elizabeth, Gloria and, eventually, Muriel attended their local church. They sang in the choir. And Elizabeth went through the rite of Communion. Meanwhile, their father would remind Elizabeth that she was "not *really* a Christian" and that their attendance of Church was simply a concession to her mother. It did not reflect who she was. "'I'm not [a Christian]?' I would say [...] *What am I?*" (Mayo qtd. in Burns and Hurlbutt 175, emphasis mine).

It is no great marvel, then, that the elder Miguel sisters began their quest for identity by rejecting their Native heritage. Elizabeth took a more radical approach than her sisters, declaring, "Fuck this Indian Shit. I'm going to see what I can do" (Mayo qtd. in Burns and Hurlbutt 175). She resolved never to marry an Indigenous man; she underwent a full conversion to Judaism, which she practised for a time. And she eventually adopted the stage name "Lisa Mayo" by which she is publicly known. Gloria Miguel dealt with her own ethnic "shame" by identifying herself as a *human being*, and although she maintained a greater connection with her Indigeneity than did her elder sister, she resisted being defined or confined by it.

Of the three, the youngest sibling Muriel maintained the greatest connection to her Indigenous roots, although, in her early professional career, she too resisted being packaged and labelled as an "Indian." Perhaps because her mother had so totally withdrawn by the time she was born, she spent more time with her father than her sisters had. By the age of eight, Muriel had quit the Methodist Church in which her sisters had been choristers, and by the time she was beginning to study and to pursue extra-curricular activities with her peers, the American Indian community in New York was creating social groups for the youth (Mayo qtd. in Burns and Hurlbutt 175). At the age of 12, Muriel Miguel

most (if not all) Indigenous nations across Turtle Island (North, Central and South America). Until quite recently, if individuals did occasionally imbibe in their daily lives, they were expected to abstain from alcohol from periods of between one day and several weeks (depending upon the nation and the ceremony) before handling medicines or participating in ceremonial activities. This has changed to some degree (in some communities) with the recognition that those who may be addicted to harmful substances may benefit greatly if they are included in the ceremonial life of their communities. Nevertheless, then (as now), it would have been inappropriate – dangerous, even – for a man who was frequently and regularly inebriated to attempt to instruct his daughters in ceremonial praxis.

Figure 2.1. Antonio and Elmira Miguel in costume for their upcoming *MOHICANS* spectacle in New York City, circa 1930s. Miguel Family Photo. Courtesy Muriel Miguel.

co-founded, with Louis Mofsie (Hopi–Ho-Chunk), the Little Eagles learning and performing dances from various nations across America, and as a teenager, she continued to work with the Thunderbird American Indian Dance Company (the Thunderbirds) – the company into which the Little Eagles evolved (Spiderwoman, "About").

Although many obstacles confronted Antonio Miguel as he struggled to make ends meet (particularly, during the depression years), Miguel proved himself a creative and resourceful man. Capitalizing on his personal magnetism, his artistic abilities and on America's romantic (albeit twisted) fascination with the "vanishing Indian," he began to perform America's fantasy, turning it into a "family business," which endured for more than two decades and included three generations of performers. He concocted snake oil in the family bathtub to sell on street corners after movie theatres had disgorged their patrons. His daughters stood atop floats, ballyhooing to draw customers to the local cinemas when John Wayne westerns were playing.

"They posed for tourists in their buckskins and feathers and danced for the boy Scouts" (Mojica, "Stories" 17–18).

These performances (as demeaning as the Miguel sisters may have ultimately felt them to be) became the first training ground for the young artists. And while they eventually rebelled, refusing to "play Indian" in their father's projects, they could not, nor did they attempt to, suppress the talents they had already begun to discover and develop in his *Mohican*[13] spectacles (see fig. 2.1). They were, indeed, "show biz Indians." It is no surprise, then, that each began a pursuit of her own individual identity by exploring the avenues that would best facilitate the development of her unique artistic voice in opera (Lisa), acting (Gloria), and modern dance (Muriel). Ultimately, they would not perform on the same stage again until 1976, when they came together to form Spiderwoman Theater as women who were now entering their middle years.

Notably, it would be Muriel (the "baby" of the family and raised by her older sisters) who would envision the creation of Spiderwoman Theater, who would develop its working methodology, and who would pull her sisters into a working relationship that has spanned nearly five decades. Lisa and Gloria have both credited their younger sister with "outing" them as feminists. And Lisa has further testified that her involvement with Spiderwoman has forced her to "come out ... to the world as an Indian" (Mayo qtd. in Burns and Hurlbutt 168).

Muriel Miguel had trained as a modern dancer and worked intensively with Joseph Chaikin's Open Theater. However, she had also maintained her commitment to traditional dance. Influenced, perhaps, by her parents' activities in the organization of inter-tribal, urban powwows,[14] which drew otherwise isolated, urban Indians into a pan-Indian

13 *Mohicans* was the name Antonio Miguel gave to his Medicine Shows – perhaps, in honour of his family back in Gunayala.

14 A powwow is a gathering, hosted by one community and attended by many individuals from various tribal communities. Here, individuals and families have the chance to gather, to exchange news and information, to share dances and songs and to trade goods. The inter-tribal, urban powwow, then, might best be described as a gathering specifically formed for the benefit of Indigenous individuals (regardless of their nation) living away from their home communities. Its objective is to counter the acute isolation experienced by such individuals by providing them with an opportunity to meet and network with other American Indians, to share their languages, lifeways, ceremonial praxis and strategies for surviving in the city, and to celebrate the survival of all our peoples through the free exercise of ceremonial acts and cultural expression.

community, and which facilitated ties between individuals and their home communities and encouraged profound and enduring inter-tribal relationships, Muriel was a founding member and co-director (with Louis Mofsie)[15] of the Thunderbird American Indian Dancers. Today, her daughter playwright/performer Murielle Borst-Tarrant, and her granddaughter Henu Josephine who is the daughter of Borst-Tarrant and Kevin Tarrant, have maintained this connection with the Thunderbirds. In 1990, Kevin Tarrant started the SilverCloud Singers, which he continued to lead until his death in 2020.

Since the formation of Spiderwoman Theater, all three Miguel sisters have embraced an inspiring, unflagging agenda of community-building work with the American Indian Community House in New York City, the American Indian AIDS Task Force, Off the Beaten Path Theater (which served as a training ground and production company for Indigenous performers) and countless tribal communities throughout North America and around the world in addition to their individual artistic projects and company productions. Spiderwoman does not simply show the way to healing; *it passes on its process*, so that others may affect healing for themselves. It is this process that constitutes the centre of this study, the centre of the lives of its practitioners, the cornerstone of their becoming. And so, if we are to begin to grasp it in its entirety, we must begin by exploring the constituent elements of this process – the "threads" that make up its grand design.

Muriel Miguel and The Open Theater

By his own account, Joseph Chaikin's earliest training began with encounters with various disciples of Stanislavski's method (including Uta Hagen and Herbert Berghof) as he pursued a means to access and to manifest his own "inner truth" (43). As his political consciousness

15 I will take this opportunity here to, once again, remind readers of the intergenerational web of aesthetic relationality out of which Spiderwoman Theater emerged and into which it remains inextricably bound. Josephine Mofsie-Tarrant was Muriel Miguel's best friend from childhood; she performed in the 1974 workshop production, out of which Spiderwoman Theater eventually emerged in the year following her death. It is in her honour that Spiderwoman Theater was named. Louis Mofsie is the late Josephine Mofsie-Tarrant's brother, and Kevin Tarrant (husband to Muriel Miguel's daughter Murielle Borst-Tarrant) was her youngest son. Although Josephine Mofsie-Tarrant died before she had reached the age of 40, her best friend still maintains profound connections to her through her work with Louis Mofsie and through their granddaughter Henu Josephine Tarrant.

began to develop during his work on Bertolt Brecht's *Man is Man* with the Living Theater, Chaikin became increasingly dissatisfied with the limitations of realistic drama and Method acting as vehicles of the representation of human experience: "Reality is not a fixed state," Chaikin declared (8). Instead, he encouraged his students to consider the Latinate root of this word: *res*, he pointed out, translates as, "that which we can fathom," as opposed to that which we can see, touch, or hear (Chaikin 8).[16] For Chaikin, any pretensions of representing "reality" would ultimately result in the perpetuation of stereotypes because he felt very keenly that theatre, as a commercial enterprise, had largely become a business and that the *business* of acting teaches actors to think in and as stereotypes – that is, as recognizable and palatable and eminently digestible products for public consumption.

Dissatisfied with what he perceived as an undue emphasis on the internal mechanisms of the actor's instrument and with the depth of inquiry into "universal" human truth that he had encountered within his training, Chaikin united with a group of colleagues – all theatre practitioners who had been studying under Nola Chilton before she relocated to Israel in the early 1960s.[17] Together, as The Open Theater,

16 This definition of "reality" connotes Chaikin's sensitivity to (and perhaps a search for) metaphysical realities as opposed to material "reality." Cosmological belief, ceremonial praxis, and artistic expression of the Indigenous nations across Turtle Island all reflect the understanding that the physical world is only a shadowy reflection of metaphysical reality. Certainly, this is a key concept in Guna cosmology, which imagines the world of spirit (neg burbaled) enveloping the material world (neg sanaled) and residing inside each material element, animating it with its life force (Chapin 219–20). Hence, to transfigure substance (e.g., to heal a sick body), the healer works in the metaphysical realm, descending through eight layers of the spirit realm to locate the corrupted or stolen soul (burbagana) and so restore it. In restoring the soul (which is the spiritual copy of the physical body), the Guna healer restores the body and effects a material transformation from illness to health (Chapin 219–20).

While Chaikin would certainly have no knowledge of Guna healing practices or cosmology, his perception of "reality" and his implicit willingness to investigate that which can be fathomed beyond (or beneath) the material would certainly have attracted Muriel Miguel's interest in his work and her desire to join him in his investigations.

17 Chilton, a daughter of Russian émigrés, was born and raised in New York City. During the 1940s she trained as an actor with Lee Strasberg. Eventually, she rejected her Method training because she felt that actors who mined their own emotions and impulses could only produce "fossilized" performances – that is, *representations* of their *conditioning* (qtd. in Ben-Zvi 46). Searching for a process that would facilitate the integration of theatre with social activism, she began to develop her own improvisations

they began to work through a series of "open questions," which ultimately would allow them to challenge "the big set up" – the socio-political matrix that strips humans of their humanity by fixing the ways by which we can identify and differentiate one human being from another (Chaikin 12). They began by deepening the traditional questions that an actor asks of a character: For instance, "What do I want?" would inevitably lead Chaikin's actor to ask, "What makes me want what I want?" (75). And they chipped away at the tyranny of psychology (as an indicator of "human truth") by exploring physical impulse, foregrounding the actor's body, and developing "a spare language of tasks which speak of life and nature" (Chaikin 65). To this end, Chaikin began to seek out dancers to join his troupe and encourage his colleagues to *move*.

By 1963, Muriel Miguel was already a highly trained and promising modern dancer (having trained at the Henry Street Playhouse with Eric Hawkins, Alwin Nikolais, and Jean Erdman).[18] But she was becoming dissatisfied with dance as a sole medium for the stories she was trying to tell.[19] As her training intensified, her choreography was becoming

---

and exercises designed to help actors deepen their self-awareness and move beyond the constraints of patent reality. This has been one of Chaikin's primary objectives in the development of his own work (Chaikin 2–3). In 1963, Chilton relocated to Israel to live out her commitment to social activism in her art (Ben-Zvi 47). The students she left behind in New York City, led by Joseph Chaikin, formed The Open Theater.

18 Jean Erdman was trained by Martha Graham and began her own highly influential modern dance company (the Jean Erdman Dance Group) in 1944. In addition to her own celebrated performances, her company, and her teaching, Erdman also won an Obie Award (1962–63) for her off-Broadway play *The Coach with Six Insides*, and she won a Tony Award (1972) for Best Choreography in *The Two Gentlemen of Verona*.

19 Muriel Miguel had not consciously decided, at this time, just what stories she did want to tell; she was simply compelled to explore. Perhaps, however, "explore" is not an accurate term for what she sought. Perhaps, she sought to integrate two seemingly disparate fragments of her being.

> The reason I left dance was because I felt like I was going upstream. I wasn't going where anybody else was going. I did modern dance to pop music. I did modern dance; I had a trombone that I played. I can't play a trombone! I just blasted it! I did a modern dance with a yellow chair with sitar music. I did that for an audition with Julliard. I didn't get in [laughs]! It was out there! You know what I mean? I did a lot of "out there" stuff. (M. Miguel, Interview 2007)

For Miguel, it was all about process. She had traditional dance (with the Thunderbirds) and she had "process" (which she pursued through modern dance). Sometimes, she tried to infuse her traditional work with the "process" by inserting experimental bits into her performances with the Thunderbirds. But she followed her instinct to protect her Traditional Knowledge and kept both forms separate. "People didn't understand that [she] was an Indian" (M. Miguel, Interview, 2007). And Miguel's later experiences with The Open Theater eventually convinced her that there was no room in the one world (of contemporary art and process) for her cultural and familial sensibilities:

> They really didn't understand it. So, [they didn't understand] a lot of the ways I looked at things: For instance, at Open Theater, I remember I said, "It's Father's Day, I can't come." And they all looked at me: "You can't come? It's Father's Day?" And then I'd say, "Well, yeah." And then, I'd say, "I have to buy five presents." And they'd say, "You have five fathers?" And I'd say, "My father and all my uncles." You know? *"Duh.* What's wrong with you?" was my [reaction]. And they looked at me like I had two heads: you know… that kind of thing. (M. Miguel, Interview 2007)

She was expected to leave her cultural sensibilities "outside the door." If we regard Miguel's dance life as a metaphor for her socio-political life as an American Indian woman, it is readily apparent that forces outside herself were forcing her into conflict – forcing her to choose her community and hence her identity. She was constantly negotiating between living artfully as a proud American Indian woman or making art as a contemporary, urban artist in New York City. And the sum of her artistic life might well be regarded as a series of contemporary, urban liminoid "acts," which tore through the "veil" separating two worlds and facilitated a *liminal* transformation and the (self)creation of a "new" human being.

To gain some insight into just what stories, Miguel wanted to tell through her dance, what these might have looked like and how they may have differed from the works of her contemporaries in modern dance, it may prove instructive to consider a somewhat more recent manifestation of her work. On 6 September 2008, I attended the fifth annual Choreographers' Workshop produced and presented by Earth in Motion: World Indigenous Dance. This particular year, Muriel Miguel was one of the four featured choreographers, and she had utilized this opportunity to choreograph a section of her one woman show *Red Mother*, which is her own adaptation of Bertolt Brecht's *Mother Courage and Her Children*. The program notes for this workshop state:

> *Red Mother* is the story of Belle, who roams across the continent with her horse and companion, Blue Fred. In this section, Red Mother mourns her dead horse. She passes through times of wars and conflicts that have changed the very core of life on this land. She has witnessed massacres and has survived through lying, cunning and capitulation. (Earth in Motion, 6 September 2008)

I had deliberately put away my program without consulting it before the evening began because I wanted to try to identify each choreographer's work for myself. Interestingly, although I believed that I could boast greater familiarity with the choreographic styles of the other artists on the program that evening (Penny Couchie, Julia Jamieson, Alejandro Ronceria), Muriel Miguel's piece was the only piece I correctly identified and attributed to its artist.

During the talkback, which followed the performances, Miguel told us that during the earlier phases of *Red Mother* (in which she is the solo performer), she had taken "the easy way out" after the death of Belle's sole companion Blue Fred. For this event, she mapped Belle's inner landscape onto the body of dancer Nadine Jackson to explore the terrible turmoil experienced by a bereaved woman who looks at the corpse of her last friend on earth and sees only "fresh meat."

If this piece, in any way, can speak to the artistic objectives and aesthetic sensibilities that distinguish(ed) Miguel's dance projects from those of her colleagues, it may be by comparing Miguel's unflinchingly naked presentation of raw, ugly honesty increasingly dramatic and multi-disciplinary (cited in Abbott 168–69). And she was starting to integrate her talent for improvisation with her dance. As a child, she had been rather silent and withdrawn. Her concerned sisters had encouraged her to pursue dance as a means of self-expression and creative nurturance. Now, in her 26th year, Muriel Miguel was ready to develop her vocal instrument and add another "colour" to her artistic palette. She was attracted to Chaikin's way of working and his aesthetic sensibility; and initially, at least, she was attracted to his vision – his willingness to challenge Eurocentric aesthetic, economic, political, and social systems; his commitment to creating pieces that were founded on "open" questions for which answers might never be found; and his aspirations to find new ways to discover and somehow represent human truth.

Tellingly, Lisa Mayo who had meanwhile spent a decade of intense study with Uta Hagen and who was absolutely committed to one

---

and her refusal to beautify, sentimentalize, or soften one moment of the experience she and the audience share. Unlike the other presentations, which seemed at times to "milk" the painful moments or, alternatively, to make meaning in them by investing them with beauty, Miguel, in no way, stretched our willingness to suspend disbelief. Somehow, her presentation was "realer" than anything I have ever seen although it was deliberately presented in a most anti-realistic manner (lacking even a representation of "meat" to tantalize the dancer until she succumbs and gorges herself on it). The material signifiers or lack thereof did nothing to detract from the raw, irrepressible spirit of hunger, which refused to be denied.

Dressed in a raggedy skirt, backless leotard (which revealed every muscular twitch) and awash in red streamers, which swirled about her like frantic blood vessels exploding out of a body wracked by harrowing grief, Miguel's dancer alternately careened and floated between maniacal grief, ravenous hunger, and preternaturally serene nostalgia. Nostalgic moments were sent up and presented as excessive indulgence, as if Miguel were inviting us to laugh at the human tendency to sugar-coat pain and mask the raw ugliness of mortal resistance to mortality. Jackson was magnificent here: Her hands spoke; her very back "spoke," and every emotional nuance etched itself upon her own youthful visage, which took on the years of her choreographer as the piece progressed. The piece reverberated with fury; it screamed with need. And through it all, I was reminded of the furious grief Miguel had surely been experiencing daily, since May 2008 when her eldest sister Lisa Mayo was diagnosed with Non-Hodgkin's Lymphoma. It was not until I read the program later that evening that I realized that the piece had been dedicated to Mayo and just how real this spirit that impotently rages against the implacable forces governing mortal existence and its conclusion is.

If, as a septuagenarian, Miguel's work marked her so unmistakably from artists who are her peers, her former students, and her colleagues (and with whom she had and continues now to frequently work – artists who are trained in the same techniques as she), there can be little doubt as to how far her earliest work set her apart when Miguel was working alongside those who did not share her cultural sensibilities, her spiritual beliefs, or her aesthetic understandings.

version of the Method against which The Open Theater was rebelling spoke of Chaikin's methods (later *adapted* by Muriel Miguel) as she looked back upon the 20-year history of Spiderwoman Theater in 1996. In an interview with Larry Abbot, Mayo observed that while she had "admired" the work of The Open Theater, the process they employed to devise scripts "wasn't [her] way of working." And when she began to work on *Women in Violence,* she initially resisted the process. Within a week, however, she had begun "to see the possibilities": *"It wasn't that different from the way I worked. It was a different approach, but it was getting to the truth, which is what acting is about: getting to the truth of the character and what is real"* (qtd. in Abbott 169, italics mine).

It cannot be denied that elements of Chaikin's process appear to have been adopted by Spiderwoman Theater and *adapted* to serve Spiderwoman's specific aesthetic and to serve the specific concerns of the Miguel sisters as American Indian women in the twentieth and twenty-first centuries.[20] The foundational exercises utilized in The Open

---

20 To illustrate, in the creation of Spiderwoman Theater's *Women in Violence* (1976), the troupe combined CR (consciousness raising) sessions at the table and regular drills in "Transformations." The "Transformations" exercise originated in The Open Theater and has since become a foundational exercise in the Storyweaving Workshops of Muriel Miguel and Monique Mojica. The "Transformations" exercise will be discussed at some length in chapter 4. But for the purposes of this discussion, it may be helpful to examine the influence of Chaikin's other exercises (i.e., "Odets Kitchen" and "Perfect People") in the development of *Women in Violence.*

Lisa Mayo has stated that guided by her younger sister, she accessed her Trickster persona through the "Inside/Outside [Odets Kitchen] exercise" (Mayo, Interview 2007). Odets Kitchen "was named for [Clifford] Odets, but [owing to its purpose and essence] Chayevsky, Miller or Inge would have done as well" (Pasolli 12). This exercise calls upon actors to first improvise a scene and then to play out the scene again, giving voice to the inner motivations behind each action and articulation of the original. For instance, a man may come home late from work bearing romantic gifts – a bouquet of red roses, a box of candy, etc. His loving wife, in total disarray, may be struggling to salvage a burning dinner as he enters. He drops his briefcase, throws down his jacket, declares that he is "beat" and presents her with the gifts. She accepts gratefully and demurely comments on how she "must look a sight." He tells her that she is always beautiful to him. They embrace. Meanwhile, dinner burns. In the second scene, the actions of the first are recreated exactly. However, this time an "inner monologue" is articulated along with the original text. In Chaikin's studio, either the original actors articulated the inner monologue or other members of the company articulated that inner life as they replayed the external score. He comes home, declares that he is "beat." The inner monologue might be fraught, however, with guilt (for an affair) or aggression towards his wife. His spouse gratefully accepts his gifts, uttering her thanks, while her inner voice reveals her suspicions and/or pent-up aggression towards him. She self-consciously refers to her rumpled

Theater manifest themselves in Storyweaving Workshops facilitated by the Miguel sisters and by Gloria Miguel's daughter, playwright/performer/dramaturg Monique Mojica. As well, Chaikin's approach to questioning is reflected in Spiderwoman's work. Chaikin asked questions. Through these questions (for which the company may or may not have found "answers"), character could be explored; stories, created. Such explorations held out the possibility, at least, of discovering some of the answers to the greater questions around who we are as human beings. After all, the primary question asked by the actor of his character, "Who am I?" ultimately, speaks to the larger human question, "Who are *we*" in relation to God, to each other, to the rest of the Creation? For Spiderwoman, *I*-dentity (Who am *I*? Who am *I* in relation to the "I" I play?) is discovered through specific questions out of and around which each of its productions has been crafted. Like Chaikin before her, Muriel Miguel looks for questions to explore rather than statements to assert, and what is played out before us on Spiderwoman's stage is an exploration of these questions – the embodied quest for self-knowledge. Doubtless, Chaikin's active resistance to stereotypes (which purport to carry absolute answers, thereby simplifying human truth and degrading human existence) would have held a great attraction for Muriel Miguel. Indeed, every layer – private, political, and professional – of her existence had been contained and defined by the "Metonyndian" of settler imagination. From the Medicine Shows, in which her family had had to perform to make ends meet, to the neighbourhood children

---

state, while her inner voice (much less demurely) expresses her rage at being enslaved in the kitchen or the fact that she has given up entirely, because he has not noticed her in years. And so it goes …

Of the exercises that Muriel Miguel brought to the rehearsal studio for this production, Mayo has only been able to specifically recall and identify the "Inside/Outside" exercise as a significant vehicle of her character's creation. But it would not be illogical to speculate that coupled with this, Chaikin's "Perfect People" exercise may have also contributed to the development of her clown persona. The "Perfect People" exercise differs from Odets Kitchen in that it deals solely with surface behaviour and calls upon actors to choose icons of perfection (from media representations) and to improvise the events of their ongoing perfect lives after the movie, commercial, or magazine spread has ended. Ultimately, all the exercises as utilized by Mayo for the creation of her "Perfect Woman" affected a **balancing** of inner life and outer life in the performer, rather than merely highlighting a dichotomy between "text" and "subtext" or constructing a biting social commentary. As Muriel Miguel has observed, the revelation of the American Indian actress beneath the mask of Mayo's "Perfect [Caucasian] Woman" was the "most healing moment in [*Women in Violence*]" (M. Miguel, Interview 2007). For further information, Robert Pasolli's *A Book on the Open Theatre* provides a detailed account of each of these exercises and of Chaikin's exercises in transformation through sound and movement.

who verbally assaulted the sisters with war whoops and called them "Injun Joe," to the professional roadblocks she encountered as a performer "[b]ecause [she is] an Indian" (Billotte), Muriel was hyper-aware of and actively resistant to a system that forms and disseminates the stereotype to justify oppression: "Sometimes what happened to me in the beginning was that agents would call up: 'I have the best part for you!' 'Get down here, you have to read for this part!' [...] I had to go, and it would be some 'Indian Princess.' [...] In those days, it was really degrading stuff, really degrading stuff" (M. Miguel qtd. in Beaucage 5).

While the aforementioned factors would certainly have drawn Muriel Miguel to The Open Theater, Chaikin's embrace of storytelling as a key working element in studio work was likely a factor in her decision to work with the company for as long as she did. For Chaikin, storytelling was a *new* way of working (116). But Muriel had lived with and been intensively trained in this art from birth. Her understanding of and abilities in storytelling were rooted in her being "from the toenails up" (Miguel qtd. in Abbot 169). When she finally left The Open Theater, she wanted to deepen her exploration of storytelling and what it might affect: "That's what we did; we used stories to make different stories" (qtd. in Abbott 169).[21]

As detailed examination of key Spiderwoman productions (and their processual foundations) will demonstrate, Chaikin's studio explorations of "emblems" and "jamming" and "transformations" to reconfigure narrative and tease out performance texts from raw story have found their way into Spiderwoman's practice of Storyweaving. Indeed, the processual links between Open Theater and Spiderwoman Theater are apparent. Less apparent, however, are the *contextual differences of spirit and intent* that direct the application of the exercises, affect the performer in profound ways, and determine the "fruits" engendered by her labours. Nor, at this point can we be entirely sure of authorship/ownership when it comes to these exercises. To what extent might Muriel Miguel, steeped as she was in powerful and enduring aesthetic Indigenous traditions, *have influenced* studio rehearsals and experiments at

21 Lee Maracle, renowned worker in story, joined the cast of *Encounters at the "Edge of the Woods,"* a devised show I directed for Hart House Theatre, University of Toronto (6–8 September 2019). In early devising workshops with the cast and crew (storytellers, all), Maracle told a Traditional Story, instructing us to "allow the story to wash over you." The story became a "call" to which we were instructed to respond by allowing the story to work itself through us and then "tell[ing] the story back different but the same." Hence, a show about the history of a specific university campus and about the experiences of those whose lives have taken them onto that campus formed itself around multiple retellings of a timeless origin story emerging from a territory thousands of kilometres removed.

The Open Theater? To what extent might Chaikin's exercises have been borrowed from the misappropriative and ethno dramaturgical traditions of the Living Theater? These are questions for which we may never reach definitive answers; nor, are these questions for which this study can purport to offer answers. But if such questions do nothing more than highlight the complexity of a processual matrix wherein threads double back upon themselves even as they twine themselves around other threads spun from other stuff, on other looms, by other hands, they will have done enough. We can certainly discern the threads spun by The Open Theater in Spiderwoman's processual web; let us continue to unravel the design to isolate and identify the other stuff of which this web is constructed.

Lisa Mayo Encounters *Respect*

> I see myself and my sisters acting as mentors for Native people. My teacher Uta Hagen is 76, and she strove for the best, for the highest goals, and what I do I learned from her. I think of her every day of my life. She's part of my life, that woman is. Her ideals are so high, I want to keep that within myself, so I can work with the young Native people of this country and the Indigenous people of Central and South America and Mexico who want to study and do their own theater. (Mayo qtd. in Abbott 180)[22]

While Gloria Miguel and Muriel Miguel have expressed some reservations around the rigid pedagogical practices through which performance methodologies have historically been imparted to students within North American studios,[23] Miss Hagen's methodology warrants

22 Miss Hagen passed away in January 2004, eight years after this interview. She was 84 years old.

23 During the Honoring Spiderwoman Theatre Conference presented 19–21 February 2007 by the Walter Havighurst Special Collections & University Archives, Miami University Libraries (Oxford, OH), Dr. Ann Haugo facilitated a talking circle during which the Miguel sisters discussed their process and their influences (21 February 2007). Gloria and Muriel Miguel spoke of the historical rigidity of actor training within various acting studios (including the HB Studio). Like Miss Hagen and her contemporaries, Muriel Miguel works to inspire self-discipline in her student-actors and an organic understanding of all the tools at their disposal with the ability to use these tools. At the same time, however, Muriel Miguel is very conscious of the experience of racialized and historically oppressed communities and prioritizes the safety of her students within the training process – a practice that is now only beginning to be adopted by instructors and within the institutions that train performers across this continent. Of primary importance for Muriel Miguel is identifying and "asking

serious examination for its influences – however indirect – on the process authored by Muriel Miguel and utilized by Spiderwoman Theater. With her husband Herbert Berghof, Miss Hagen was one of Joseph Chaikin's earliest influences; it was, after all, at the HB Studio where Chaikin sought and acquired his first serious, professional training in the craft (Chaikin 43), and it was in opposition to this training that his own experiments at The Open Theater were attempted. While the purpose of this project is to transcribe and disseminate Spiderwoman Theater's methodology of Storyweaving as an Indigenous-authored process, reliant upon and specific to Indigenous models of aesthetics and pedagogy, it will be necessary to address, also, its concatenations with seemingly disparate models, and thereby to chart the ways in which the stories, written on the road to self-knowledge, intersect and reverberate around and within each other.

Lisa Mayo was determined to be neither poor nor Indian. But she was deeply sensible of just how strong her cultural roots are, and she was not satisfied with the idea of simply "blending" into the anonymous sea of White America. So, she searched for an alternate community in which she could forge an alternate identity of comparable potency with that she was trying to escape and deny. Attending Brooklyn College, she met a young Jewish man named Julius (Jules).[24] She fell in love with him, with his community, and with the strength of his Judaism, which she instinctively felt and with which she immediately connected; indeed, each of the sisters has for a time been married to a Jewish man, "because there was a strong religion, a strong whatever that we were attracted to" (France and Corso 184). As well, Lisa has reflected that she

---

the right questions," so that students don't feel called out – don't feel challenged to fit into an accepted norm. The questions she crafts are questions through which to acknowledge the full humanity and lived experience of all of her students – and particularly the lived experience of Indigenous students, many of whom have been historically denied access to training and professional opportunities. Muriel Miguel works carefully with her students, asking, at each stage of the work, "How does it make you feel? Where are you coming from? Do you want to do this?" In cases, for instance, where her students may be most comfortable working within a language other than English, Miguel works with these individuals to allow them to create and perform work in the language(s) in which they are most comfortable. When students have been allowed to work in this way, Miguel testifies, "It was like a flower blooming." Further, she observes, "If we don't ask them the [right] questions," our students may simply disengage and "remain silent" (Personal Communication, 28 August 2023). In Miguel's studio, healing is balanced with discipline.

24 During our interview (2007), Lisa Mayo explained that they had met in an amateur folk dancing group of which they were both members.

was drawn to Judaism because of the ceremonies she witnessed (and in which she later participated); such festivities were seasonal, she has noted, marking the profound connection between the Jewish people and the earth (Mayo qtd. in Burns and Hurlbutt 174).

Although Elmira Miguel was initially against the match, she gradually came to appreciate the young man who loved her daughter. Hence, despite Antonio Miguel's objections, the couple was married; Mayo underwent a conversion, kept a kosher house, and promised to raise any children they might produce in the Jewish faith. For his part, Jules contributed significantly to the development of Lisa Mayo's artistry. He paid for all her schooling and for her singing lessons.[25] However, when she started to receive professional offers to travel abroad and sing in European opera houses, he was less supportive. After receiving an invitation to perform in several small opera houses in Germany for three months, the limits of Jules's support became apparent. Elizabeth Miguel was his "wife." Her duty was to stay with him and take care of their home: "This was in the 1950s, you know. And I said, 'Why can't I go? Why can't you come?' But he said no, so that was impossible" (Mayo qtd. in Burns and Hurlbutt 174).

Already an accomplished (albeit, professionally frustrated) mezzo-soprano, Lisa Mayo had begun to expand her operatic abilities through intense work in the performance of German *Lieder*. To this end, she began studying the craft of acting with Uta Hagen in the early 1960s to perfect her storytelling abilities and to allow these to manifest themselves through her entire instrument. As she has testified, what was to have comprised a summer of intense study at the HB Studio became a decade of "hard labour" as a key student of Uta Hagen, Herbert Berghof, and Charles Nelson Reilly (Haugo, "Native Playwrights" 327).

Like Chaikin, Uta Hagen believed that those who pursue theatre do so because they are dissatisfied with the status quo and that the very choice to become an actor constitutes a conscious, political choice to enact resistance. For her, it was only through rigorous investigation into self and community that actors could identify just what they were resistant to and from there choose what aesthetic strategies to employ and what stories to tell that would best serve the objective of facilitating

---

25 Lisa Mayo testifies that she didn't know that her husband was wealthy until they had been married for one year; one day he showed her some bankbooks and told her that this was her money. He suggested that she use this money to take a real estate course to learn a profession so that she could support herself. She decided instead to invest in her training as an actor and a singer (Interview 2007).

change (Hagen 15). Of course, to understand themselves as political agents is to presume that individuals feel themselves to be firmly entrenched in a community. The personal only becomes political when it resonates beyond the individual and produces repercussions within a larger group. So, before the "person" can act in a meaningful and politically efficacious manner, she must find her place within a larger social group, which values her and her actions: S/he must acquire self-knowledge – *I*-dentity.

Acting for Hagen was never about "losing oneself" in the story, as so many of her detractors have claimed, but about *finding oneself* in the language, history, philosophical beliefs, spiritual praxis, fears, fantasies, conflicts, artefacts, edifices, and artistic works of the communities one wishes to transform and be transformed within. Indeed, she asserted that the first task of the burgeoning actor is to "find your own sense of identity and then *enlarge this sense of self*" (Hagen 22, emphasis added). The burgeoning artist, Hagen explained, would find that sense of self *in community* through extensive travel (immersion in landscapes), visits to museums, immersion in history and biography, immersion in visual arts, keen observation of one's contemporaries (intimates and passing acquaintances), and by becoming conversant with classical music and linguistic studies. Indeed, in her first acting "primer," which she later repudiated,[26] the parallels – albeit, unconscious and unintentional – between Hagen's observations on America (e.g., America's "lack of respect for the past" and the disconnection of its people from the natural world) and observations posed by Native scholars like Vine Deloria Jr. or N. Scott Momaday are compelling (see Hagen 30).

Compelling, also, is Miss Hagen's emphasis on *place* as the authorizer of Story as opposed to time. In *Respect for Acting*, she writes about those connections she has intuited – profound connections between herself and humans (of various European nations to which she was foreign and who had lived and died long before she was born) "on the very cobblestones" and "in every cell, corner and courtyard" (30). It is through connection to place that her belief was ignited – that a story long past

26 While Miss Hagen's philosophical and aesthetic sensibilities had not drastically altered between 1972 when she co-wrote *Respect for Acting* with Haskell Frankel and 1991 when she published *A Challenge for the Actor*, she revealed to her students in a Master Class (conducted July–August 2000 at the Robert Gill Theatre in Toronto, ON) that the older text was "full of mistakes." As well, she reveals in her Introduction to the 1991 text that many of the exercises notated in the earlier text had been subject to misinterpretation by readers and that the 1991 primer presents the exercises with greater clarity, precision, and detail (see Carter, "Poisoned" 299–340).

became real and momentous. So too, for Indigenous Peoples across this continent, those connections to the generations that precede us, to each other, to the greater community of Creation and to the generations that will follow us are ultimately bound up in our connections to land. The late Vine Deloria Jr. (Standing Rock Sioux) has explained, "The Navajo, for example, have sacred mountains where they believe they rose from the underworld [...] No one can say when the creation story of the Navajo happened, but everyone is fairly certain *where* the emergence took place" (Deloria 138, emphasis mine).

Miss Hagen was of Teutonic stock. The stories she loved – and to which she chose to dedicate her voice – had been penned by Chekhov, Shaw, Brecht, Ibsen, Strindberg, Shakespeare, and the Euro-American writers who were her contemporaries. These were the stories of *her* world, history, world view, and ancestry. These were the stories she chose to tell; these were the stories in which she searched for self and meaning – for the relationships and responsibilities that bound her to communities (physical and metaphysical) beyond herself. These were the stories in which she searched for human truth. These were not the stories she insisted that others tell. However, as she has taught so many generations of actors, *we find ourselves in the stories of our nations*. And if we are lucky, we earn the privilege of becoming storytellers by immersing ourselves so deeply therein that they become part of us and we become a part of them (see Carter, "Poisoned" 309–10).

These briefly and aforementioned parallels warrant attention because they demonstrate how some of Miss Hagen's key teachings intersect with Indigenous-authored pedagogical and aesthetic models: These models constitute a centre around which my investigations into the work of Spiderwoman Theater revolve because *the rediscovery, formation, and/or implementation of such models constitute crucial steps in an anti-colonial project of re-worlding*. Hence, the story of Spiderwoman Theater writes itself, for me, like a communitist "morality play" – an *Every-Indigenous-Man* or a *People's Progress* – through which a path towards personal and communal decolonization may be painstakingly charted.

It is important to state, however, that while Miss Hagen's methods may intersect with Indigenous pedagogies of decolonization, there are crucial differences between her objectives as an artist and the objectives, which her "key student" Lisa Mayo and her sisters came to adopt as they came to discover self, meaning, and their truths as Guna-Rappahannock women. Hagen, ultimately, did not advocate for a "process of decolonization" through the work. Indeed, such a concept could not be said to have been part of her personal or artistic lexicon. As Mayo has testified, Miss Hagen knew little to nothing about the Indigenous Peoples of this continent. Certainly, she did not know what to make of her own American Indian scholarship student; she "didn't understand Native people," and she consistently demonstrated this early on in their relationship by casting Mayo in African American roles, believing these to be the only roles in which Mayo had a chance to find employment (Mayo, Interview 2007).

Furthermore, although Miss Hagen dreamed of building a theatre *cum* training ground that would nurture the spiritual life of America – her adopted nation – she was very careful to separate her work from any therapeutic function (Hagen 49–50). Art might facilitate some healing in its witnesses, but her process was engendered in the pursuit of artistic excellence and she deplored the notion that artists might utilize her methods to any therapeutic effect for either themselves or their audiences. For Hagen, art and medicine were distinct and separate enterprises. America's dis-ease, in her estimation, consisted of a deadly combination of spiritual malaise and intellectual laziness. And while she hoped, through revelation of human truth, to stimulate an enervated public, she was not explicitly and expressly engaged in the task of healing communities through her artistry or intervention.

While the story of the Miguel sisters, their works, audiences, and the artists they developed is entwined with Miss Hagen's story and the process she developed in her pursuit of artistic excellence – and while the Miguel sisters hold themselves to the highest standards of artistic excellence and professionalism – it seems to me that one of the most striking differences between the artists of Spiderwoman Theater and this significant "inspirator"[27] speaks to the dichotomy between Western knowledge systems and Indigenous Knowledge: For Spiderwoman Theater (as it is for myriad Indigenous artists working in all genres), art *is* medicine. And it is a medicine of which the communities of contemporary Indigenous Peoples in North America have a dire need. Many Indigenous artists, however consummate, are not simply in pursuit of aesthetic excellence or of the revelation of "human truth." Although these are certainly key elements in their works, our communities require much more: Across Turtle Island, Indigenous Peoples continue a centuries-old battle to survive.

---

27 I borrow this term from Miss Hagen. It is a term she coined to describe her late husband, Herbert Berghof, in the dedicatory page of *A Challenge for the Actor*, published in 1991.

Miss Hagen's artist was responsible to "an art form" (Hagen 20), and the art form to which she was responsible was a "*communal* adventure" (19, emphasis mine). Although the Miguel sisters own their responsibility to an "art form," in their creation of Spiderwoman Theater, they have engineered *a communitist* project, thereby extending their responsibility to communities beyond their own communal adventure. In 1996, reflecting upon two decades of collaboration with her sisters, Lisa Mayo asserted that "healing" was the troupe's primary objective, while "survival" had been a central theme in "almost" all of their productions: "We're concerned for future generations and as we get older now we're passing on our information to younger Native people and young people in our own families who have decided to enter theater as a profession. So we're passing it on. That's part of survival, too" (qtd. in Abbott 179).

As we have already considered in chapter 1, Spiderwoman Theater continues to exercise its responsibility beyond the purview of the stage. Beginning with their first production *Women in Violence* (1976), which toured Europe through 1977, the Miguel sisters infused their art with activism. This piece began as an exploration of violence in women's lives; and during the process, the sisters began to examine the violence in their own lives, "as far back as [they] could remember" (Abbott 170). Ultimately, *Women in Violence* was autobiography transformed through process into a story that spoke to women across the globe. During the One World Festival of Theatre in Nancy, France, an audience member was inspired to tell the Miguel sisters her own story. She had been brutally beaten in the streets by an inebriated man. And although her attacker had been apprehended by the police and identified by her, he had been released with no penalty (Canning 96). The Miguel sisters told her story night after night during performances, solicited their audiences for ideas, and organized a mass demonstration at which they performed and at which, because of their intervention, feminist groups across the French provinces were able to network and mobilize (Canning 96).

Since this time, the Miguel sisters have continued their communitist projects, facilitating talking circles and workshops, developing the political and artistic voices of children with the American Indian AIDS Task Force, and offering up the Storyweaving Practice (through workshops) as a tool for Indigenous people to generate art, honest dialogue, and healing.

> This is what I mean by a legacy. We went to Salt River [...] Afterwards we went into the audience talking to people. Women were coming up

to me and saying, "That happened to me." "That happened to me, and I got pregnant." "This happened." Women were just surrounding me, and then one of the women said, "We should really have a talking circle" [...] Women came in from Phoenix for this talking circle. They wanted to know how. *How do you do this? How do you take these stories? What do you do with these stories? How do you get to these stories?* But more than that, everyone talked in that circle. (M. Miguel qtd. in Haugo, "Weaving" 223, emphasis mine)

The Miguel sisters, in stark contrast to Hagen, take seriously their duty to protect when facilitating workshops and talking circles or when leading a rehearsal. While Uta Hagen forcefully decried acting instructors and directors who push performers into accessing experiences and memories which they have not yet processed without any concern for their actors' emotional/psychological well-being and without the skills to close what they have opened or fix what they have broken, she often took no special pains to protect the fragile emotional core of even the students she considered most gifted – her "key" students. Lisa Mayo who has always expressed the utmost admiration and respect for Hagen has testified that even she (whom Hagen characterized as "wonderful") was sometimes uneasy in Hagen's presence (Interview 2007).

Similarly, Muriel Miguel has decried those who forcefully "open up" *Indigenous* performers during the course of studio work or rehearsals. Such instructors and directors neither know nor care about the psycho-spiritual state of their student-actors; nor do they possess the ability to suture the wounds they have opened: "There was no taking care of these Native people. So, if you opened them up and you showed everything, then you expected them to show up at ten o'clock the next day and you're shocked that they went on a drinking spree? You had no idea who these people were" (M. Miguel qtd. in Haugo, "Weaving" 231). Self-determination then – control over process and product – is necessary for Indigenous artists if we are to transcend exploitation and/or profound psychic wounding at the hands of irresponsible and culturally insensitive "professionals" who feel no sense of responsibility to their students, colleagues, or audiences (Haugo, "Weaving" 231). And while Muriel Miguel has declared the need, as an American Indian artist, to protect herself, her process, and her product, and has so done through the formation of Spiderwoman Theater, she and her sisters have shouldered the responsibility to *respect and protect others* (where Hagen did not) and gift them the tools to protect themselves: If theatre is to heal our peoples, then healing mechanisms must be built into the process. Those who facilitate the process must be prepared to tread carefully and to remain conscious of and faithful to the concept of art as medicine.[28]

Particularly intriguing is a story that Lisa Mayo has shared about her work with Miss Hagen several times. Although Mayo told this story to illustrate both her abilities as a comedienne and the importance of arriving at "appropriate choices" as actors, it highlights a compelling (and perhaps irreconcilable) difference between the Western and Indigenous world views. Further, it speaks to an important phase in the process of self-discovery and to an important lesson in the process of becoming:

> We are comediennes, and that's something we didn't work hard for. It's with us, with me, that's our way. It just makes me laugh because I remember when I was in acting school, I was given a scene from one of the Chekhov plays. It wasn't a funny scene but people were laughing and I realized that the choices that I had made were very natural choices but they were not right for that particular scene. The teacher, Uta Hagen, laughed. She said, "I wish I could get laughs like that. You are a natural comedienne, but you have to learn to make other choices." (qtd. in Abbott 174)

Although Lisa Mayo herself never questioned Miss Hagen's judgment, it is worth considering whether Chekhov himself mightn't have approved of Mayo's reading of his scene. Certainly, he was vociferous in his insistence that his plays are comedies, and as his surviving correspondence and the written testimony of Stanislavski demonstrate, Chekhov did not hesitate to vocalize his irritation, frustration, and even despair at the inability of acting companies (including the Moscow Art Theatre), audiences, and even his own family to "get" his humour (see Benedetti 72, 114, 190). Is it possible that Chekhov's sense of the absurd may have more closely aligned itself with an Indigenous sense

---

28 In February of 1994, Lisa Mayo and Gloria Miguel visited Gunayala to research Creation stories for their production of *Voices from the Criss-Cross Bridge*, later renamed *The Guna Project* and finally named *Daughters from the Stars:Nis Bundor*. As well, they facilitated workshops for a local theatre troupe Ibeler Uagan (Grandchildren of the Sun) for whom they rented studio space (which the troupe could not otherwise afford).

Ultimately for Lisa and Gloria, *Daughters from the Stars* was "about healing, and making [themselves] whole" (Mayo qtd. in Haugo, "Native Playwrights' Newsletter" 322). And during this time, all the sisters and their children (in person or in absentia) received their Guna names. Through these names, the Miguel sisters and their female children have been "reclaimed" (as it were) – woven back into the fabric of Antonio Miguel's community of origin.

of comedy than it did with that of his own compatriots who shared his history, language, and presumably his world view? The point here is not to argue with Miss Hagen's classroom direction; but it is worth observing that this instance speaks to a separation of world view, which ultimately speaks to artistic choices, methodologies, and audience reception. Shared laughter, after all, indicates shared experience and shared perceptions. It is often through our laughter or through our silence amidst the laughter that we declare ourselves as insiders or as Others.[29] And often, as Lisa Mayo has reminded us, it is when we find the courage to reveal our scars and find the strength to laugh in the face of our brokenness that we can sift through the wreckage of our lives and re-make the shards we find "into something new" (Mayo, qtd. in Koehler).

More importantly, perhaps, the first show in which Spiderwoman's artists expressly began to tackle questions around their *I*-dentity as bi-national, diasporic Indigenous women is directly linked to their interest, appreciation, exploration, and reception of Chekhov's works, through which they discovered similarities between his preoccupations (or those of his characters) and their own:

> That play [*The Three Sisters from Here to There*] came from *The Three Sisters* by Chekhov. We found a way that we could do it by making all the males big, life-size puppets. We had to do a lot of research into Chekhov. It was

29 In 1978, Spiderwoman performatively demonstrated this idea during their European tour of *Women in Violence*. As one critic noted, "They retell old jokes at times, children's sick jokes or sex jokes that seem all in good fun ... Much of the material is funny and handled with a joyous expansiveness but some of society's ideas of humour look strange when faced with the pointedly forced laughter of the company" (Chaillet 12). As Chaillet's comments demonstrate, audiences were lulled into the show's sense of "it's all in good fun." Popular jokes of the day – many of which were egregiously racist and/or sexist – were considered "harmless" in day-to-day life, often told in mixed company and generally elicited raucous laughter. (Indeed, three decades later they still *are* and *do* in many circles). The social gest of performing *falsely* in this instance was juxtaposed with the very real (and decidedly unforced) organic reactions of their audiences who were only reacting to familiar instances of what they regarded as normal, harmless, and amusing. Throughout the production, these audiences performed their complicity in and tacit acceptance of racist and classist attitudes, which they might elsewhere decry and deny. And this complicity was highlighted and tacitly condemned by the performing Others who patently manifested their own outsider status (and hence lack of complicity) by offering up a flawed signifier (forced laughter) as an indication of "solidarity" with the laughing "insiders." The mechanics behind such dis-coveries in this production will be discussed at greater length in chapter 3.

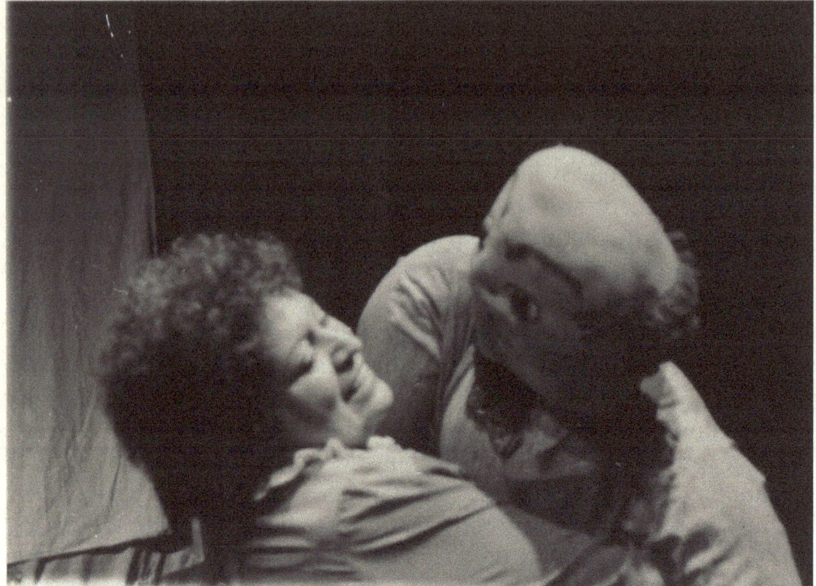

Figure 2.2. Lisa Mayo and her puppet dance partner in *The Three Sisters from Here to There*. Courtesy Walter Havighurst Special Collections and University Archives, Miami University Libraries (Oxford, OH).

> a challenge. During our research we discovered that we had a lot of personal information and that we could create another show, our show. The next year, after we did *The Three Sisters*, we decided to embark upon *Sun, Moon, and Feather*. In *Sun, Moon, and Feather*, parts of our Rappahannock names, we found our own "three sisters." We were three sisters, Indian sisters, living in Brooklyn trying to get to Greenwich Village. (Mayo qtd. in Abbot 175)

With Miss Hagen, at the very least, Lisa Mayo found herself as a comedienne and began to find her way into the stories she wanted to tell and the communities for whom she wanted to tell them. Perhaps, Miss Hagen ultimately inspired Mayo with questions relating to her own instinctive reception of Chekhov. Perhaps, it was she who convinced her sisters to embark upon such a profound exploration of his story and the stories he told to a troubled nation. And perhaps through this exploration, three Indigenous sisters from Red Hook, Brooklyn, were able to find their way back into their own story.

Gloria Miguel Comes "Home"

I am an actress
I realize the words
of others
These words are not enough
It leaves a hole in my belly
As a woman, a native
woman
I survive by telling my stories (G. Miguel qtd. in Perkins and Uno 298)

At the age of 13, Gloria Miguel's ambitions began to extend well beyond the family business of performing in sideshows, Medicine Shows, and carnivals. In high school, she began to take voice lessons to develop the considerable singing ability she had inherited from her father. Sadly, after high school, her financial circumstances did not permit her to continue her training (during which would have been the most crucial years in the development of her vocal instrument). Instead, she attended Brooklyn College and upon graduation began to pursue a career in early childhood education. After her marriage, Gloria Miguel created a home at Oberlin, Ohio, as a faculty wife and mother of two. At this time, she was able to take advantage of the Indian Education Act, and so she enrolled as an undergraduate student of drama at Oberlin, studying both classical and experimental performance methods with Bill Irwin and Herbert Blau. In 2007, she spoke to me at some length about this experience and the impact it had upon her:

> I studied with Herbert Blau. Basically, it was all Stanislavski movement. We did workshops and so forth. Bill Irwin was there; he worked with Herbert Blau [...] Herbert Blau had a series of exercises where you start out with your body, body movement, standing on your head – just freeing your body so that you would be able to walk on the stage [...] I did the regular class exercises, which involved somersaults, walking, standing on your head. I wasn't very successful in it; but I did it. And we sat down in a circle and talked about problems of the world, problems with ourselves – our life. And we would read certain classics that the college had on their roster – well, that Herbert Blau wanted. And it was an all-morning exercise class. And I got so much out of that: just the whole idea – even taking the one word "projection." And if somebody projected on you, we took hours working on our body reaction, our intellectual reaction to the projection and what we would do about it. You know, HOURS – just doing little movements like that. And all those – I'm jumping a little bit now, but

> I'll go back – all little exercises, all those BIG exercises ... And then we'd have people coming in as guest teachers; and they would give us their theory. And one year, we had a guy from Europe who did the *Kaspar* stories. I don't know too much about that. And we had someone who did Tai Chi and someone who did Kabuki. It was really, really, really cool.
>
> And that mixed with my past life, as being a child of a guy who did these Snake Oil Shows and Circuses and all the Cowboys and Indians in my house singing at night, and all those stories were still in my head. And the way that Guna men used to come and visit and talk and sing; and I watched that as a child. And so, in those exercises of going sense-memory and all that, I went back to that! Those are my connections as a child: listening and talking and *feeling* how I felt when those old men used to come into the house and sing [she sings in Guna by way of illustration] – and all different nations, as well as the Guna. It was really something. But that always came back. That always came back. (Interview 2007)

During this time, Gloria's younger sister, Muriel, who had left The Open Theater, was trying (unsuccessfully) to convince Gloria and their eldest sister Lisa to collaborate with her on a theatrical project. But Gloria was firmly entrenched in her obligations as a wife and mother and in her own development as an artist and as a "*human being*."

Gloria Miguel had gone out into the world "seeking intellect" (G. Miguel qtd. in Elm 3). And she found it in an intellectual Holocaust survivor from Paris named Mathis Szykowski with whom she built a life in Oberlin, Ohio, where he had obtained an academic post teaching French literature. Lisa Mayo has observed that each of the sisters had developed her own way of "dealing" with her Indigeneity (Mayo cited in Burns and Hurlbutt 174–75). Gloria's way was to assert herself as a "human being," as she developed her talents and expanded her intellect psycho-spiritual life. She maintained a home and tried to support her husband's career by conforming to his expectations and the expectations of the community into which he had drawn her. But however strenuously she tried to conform, her humanity – her very *I*-dentity – experienced repeated assault, and as her resentment grew, she began to rebel:

> So she tried to be a faculty wife at Oberlin. She went to the teas and all. But she resented her husband saying, "Don't you wear beads and buckskin." "Damn it, why not?" she thought. So she went to tea one day wearing a mola, the way the Cuna [sic] women dress. Everybody had a reaction. One of her husband's male colleagues said to her, "Is that decorative, or are

> you making a political statement?" She was stunned and didn't answer him. Then she thought about it and got angry. "Damn it, this is WHO I AM!" So Gloria tried to be a human being, which is sort of like being everybody, one big mishmash. It's not quite possible. (Mayo qtd. in Burns and Hurlbutt 174–75, italics added)

Perhaps this is exactly what her husband had been trying to do – to blend into the great, white "mishmash" of Middle America. As a self-avowed Trotskyite, he would certainly have denied any connection to the God of his ancestors; certainly, he would have eschewed any celebrations, any feasts, any rites or paraphernalia belonging to the worship of that Deity. And he had learned first-hand just how dangerous it is to be Other. Perhaps, Szykowski's misspoken and inappropriate directive to his wife was an attempt to protect her and their children – to censor *identifiable* cultural expression and in so doing to transform a family of Holocaust survivors (from three distinct nations) into a family of generic "human beings." But, as Gloria was beginning to discover, such a strategy (as attractive and logical as it might appear at first glance) was ultimately impossible. She was already starting to feel that in denying the family, community, and nations into which she had been born, she was ultimately suppressing her own human agency. Further, without these communities in which to exercise that agency, she could not fully realize herself as a human being.

By 1971, however, several shifts had occurred. First, the Miguel patriarch had died. And Gloria (along with his brother-in-law, her Uncle Joe) took the trip of which her father had been dreaming until his death: She enacted his (unrealized) return home to the San Blas Islands in Panama to meet the son (her half-brother) he had left behind and to discover herself as a Guna woman with kinship and communal ties that bound her to a world far beyond Red Hook, Brooklyn; Oberlin, Ohio; and the Broadway and Off-Broadway stages of Manhattan (G. Miguel, "Ibeler" 30). Second, Gloria's divorce finally freed her to leave Ohio and to reunite with her sisters in New York City. Lastly, a few years later, Josephine Mofsie-Tarrant (who had also been her friend) was gone – forever. Gloria's sister Muriel, who had been Mofsie-Tarrant's best friend, was grief-stricken and *grief-driven*. The force of her determination must have been overwhelming: "If I was going to do the work I was going to do, I was going to do it NOW and it didn't matter what the obstacles were" (M. Miguel qtd. in Beaucage 7). Gloria had returned from Panama with stories of their family, stories from their people, and a large mola[30] that had been given to her by their father's family. And Muriel had returned from a Sun Dance[31] at which she had received a collection of quilts and fabric during the community give-away that followed the ceremony. Gathering their voices, their stories, and their talents, the three sisters constructed Spiderwoman Theater's first show, *Women in Violence*. Gathering their fabrics, they constructed the company's signature backdrop into which has been layered Spider-woman's performance history, the personal stories of the Miguel sisters, and the material mementos of all of those who have passed through Spiderwoman. It is, as Muriel Miguel has asserted, "our history" (qtd. in Haugo, "Weaving" 225). And at the very centre of that histori-cal text(ile) lies Gloria Miguel's mola – the story of her homecoming, the story of being Guna, being female, making art. At the very centre sits Gloria Miguel's mola – the beginning of a story of three sisters *becoming …*

But I get ahead of myself here.

"I am Woman. Hear me Roar": Muriel Miguel Closes the Door on The Open Theater

Muriel Miguel had finally left The Open Theater. Ultimately, as she has revealed, its members, including Joseph Chaikin were all "middle class," "privileged" people, where she was not (M. Miguel, Interview 2007). As she began to recognize that her colleagues in The Open Theater were merely tourists to the "bare fork'd" existence (rife with fear, privation,

---

30 As molas and the craft of mola-making will be discussed at length in the next chapter, it is enough for now to state that these are intricately designed fabric panels belonging to the traditional dress of Guna women. Molas are created by layering panels of fabric – one over the other – and cutting away sections of the top layers to reveal precise sections of the lower layers to create the design. Molas vary in thick-ness, intricacy of design, and colour scheme; and the process of their construction is handed down from Guna mother to Guna daughter as a crucial and mandatory element of her epistemological development.

31 The Sun Dance is one of the most sacred ceremonial obligations practised by the people of the Plains, including the Arapaho, Blackfeet, Cheyenne, Comanche, Crow, Kiowa, Lakota, Plains Cree, etc. While purpose and praxis vary slightly among nations, it is generally conducted as an active rite of prayer to pray for renewal for the lands, waters, creatures of the earth, and peoples of the world. For participants, who have pledged themselves (often for several years) to dance in this ceremony, this is a grueling act of self-sacrifice. After going through a purification ceremony, participants dance for days at a time, fasting and praying in the hot sun. And while not all Sun Dance Ceremonies include piercing, this was practiced by some of the celebrants with whom Muriel carried out her ceremonial obligations.

violence, and struggle) that was her world, she began to weary of the empty, dime-store idealism that was constantly voiced but seldom lived by the troupe's members. She had been offended when fellow actors who were still receiving parental support tried to borrow money from her to support recreational drug use – money she required to pay rent and to feed and clothe her children (M. Miguel, Interview 2007).[32] "Equality" and "ensemble" lost their meaning during tours as some performers were billeted at "fancy hotels," away from their poorer fellows who had to make do with meaner accommodations. And these words began to ring with even more hollowness as Chaikin himself began to separate himself from his theatrical family, refusing to accompany the troupe to certain, less desirable destinations on their tours (M. Miguel, Interview 2007).

At the end of the day, Chaikin's commitment to challenging the "big setup" through his art became as hazy and surreal as his politics. Although by 1974, he had embraced the idea of the personal as political, he expressed his conception of community (that is, *the collective body through which the personal becomes political*) as "my *whatever* – you know, whatever group" (Chaikin qtd. in Canning 55, emphasis mine). "Whatever" communities can only breed confused, "whatever" individuals spouting "whatever" politics. For Muriel, as for other women who had worked with The Open Theater, "whatever" politics was no longer enough.[33] The explorations undertaken in Chaikin's "whatever"

32 Muriel Miguel identified one such colleague by name during our interview. Her story, here, is tinged with bittersweet irony, because, as it turned out, this fellow ensemble member went on to achieve considerable artistic and financial success in the theatre world. Upon achieving this success, this former colleague remembered those colleagues who had been so generous with him and repaid them very generously with interest! Sadly, as Miguel has laughingly pointed out, she "was not generous" (M. Miguel, Interview 2007).

This story points to the conflict between middle-class values and the values belonging to those possessing fewer resources. Although, she was not yet a single parent, Miguel and her family were engaged in a day-to-day struggle to survive. Had she encountered another in greater need than herself, it is likely that she would have been willing to sacrifice to help that person. And this would have been an incredibly "generous" act. But those who sought to "borrow" from her with no guarantee of repayment were not in dire straits. They regarded her as "mean," because she would not sacrifice her children's welfare to finance their fun (M. Miguel, Interview 2007).

33 Tellingly, although Muriel Miguel worked on the development of every one of The Open Theater's most influential productions, including *The Serpent*, *Terminal*, *Ubu Roi* and *America Hurrah*, she was never mentioned in Chaikin's book (which lists and pays tribute to many members of the collective) or in the credits to all (but one) of the published plays.

community could no longer approach the answers or generate the questions that drove Miguel, an American Indian mother, living in New York City in the late twentieth century.

The quiet little girl, who had struggled to create an autonomous self who would transcend the poverty, racism, fraternal friction, and parental dysfunction that had contained her childhood, had, by the early 1970s, come to know herself as an artist in relationship with a community of other artists and as a mother in relationship with her own children and the children of her sisters. The time had come to explore and assert her identity as an Indigenous woman and activist in the largest and wealthiest city in America in the last decades of the twentieth century.

In 1972, Muriel was invited to join a fledgling feminist theatre group:

> Feminist theatre, what was that? It was this "consciousness raising." I was busy with my kids and trying to make a living and I resisted. I really resisted. Every week I would go there and every week I would tell them I'm not coming back, and I really started to talk! I also realized I had a lot to say – I had accumulated a lot! *These two women were listening to me like I was a real person,* that I was important and that I really had something to say and that was amazing to me. (M. Miguel qtd. in Beaucage 6, emphasis mine)

And so, despite her initial resistance, Muriel moved from The Open Theater to form Womanspace with Laura Foner and Carol Grosberg. At that time, Foner, a former Weatherwoman,[34] and Grosberg who was just then coming out as a lesbian, were untrained theatre practitioners. They were, however, invested with a powerful commitment to work with other women on behalf of the burgeoning feminist movement and to the practice of Consciousness Raising (CR). These were the heady, early years of the second wave of the feminist movement. And CR sessions during which singular, personal experiences were articulated as stories, received by a group, and answered by other personal stories had been largely embraced by feminists as a praxis that would connect the individual with herself (self-exploration and identification) and with a community of her "fellows." For feminist theorists and historians, "The very act of focusing on women and asking them 'to speak for themselves' [presented] a challenge to traditional male-centered history"

34 The Weatherwomen were a fringe group of extreme feminist radicals. Many of its members resorted to violent acts to communicate their message.

(Armitage qtd. in Canning 18). For theatre practitioners, including many of the early feminist theatre companies and mixed-gendered alternative companies that sought to challenge the status quo, collaborative exploration through CR/storytelling challenged the authority of the playwright and freed the creative spirit of the performer from the aesthetic "superstructure" that constrained the impulse of the actor's instrument and contained its expression. Julian Beck, co-founder of the Living Theater and champion of the "Beautiful, Non-violent, Anarchist Revolution," has (without naming it) identified CR as an essential facet of collective creation:

> A group of people come [sic] together. There is no author to rest on who wrests the creative impulse from you. Destruction of the superstructure of the mind. Then reality comes. We sit around for months talking, absorbing, discarding, making an atmosphere in which we not only inspire each other but in which each one feels free to say whatever she or he wants to say. Big swamp jungle, landscape of concepts, souls, sounds, movements, theories, fronds of poetry, wildness, wilderness, wandering. Then you gather and arrange. In the process a form will present itself. The person who talks the least may be the one who inspires the one who talks the most. At the end no one knows who was really responsible for what, the individual ego drifts into darkness, everyone has satisfaction, everyone has greater personal satisfaction than the satisfaction of the lonely 'I.' Once you feel this – the process of artistic creation in collectivity – return to the old order seems like retrogression. (Beck 46)

Once again, Muriel Miguel was immersed in a process she had learned at the kitchen table in Red Hook, Brooklyn, and knew "from the toenails up" – sharing stories, discovering questions, seeking connections. Ultimately, despite her earlier resolution to abandon the group, she was compelled to return. While her Womanspace collaborators lacked the skills and training of her earlier collaborators at The Open Theater, they listened to her and acknowledged her. And as she has testified, the very fact that these women had (at least, initially) demonstrated respectful recognition of Miguel as a fellow human being was "amazing" to her. Their simple regard was simply not treatment to which she had become accustomed elsewhere in her professional life. So, Miguel kept coming back. For eight months, she continued to share experiences with Foner and Grosberg. And out of these gatherings, emerged Womanspace's first and only production.

Cycles, created over eight months in 1972, toured the Northeastern United States throughout 1973. It was a piece that turned its focus upon a facet of each member's identity (the class and race barriers separating one from the other) to discover "some common ground" and to "work out their problems in dramatic terms" (Chevigny qtd. in Canning 94). However, despite the supportive reception that greeted this project, the show did little to alleviate "their problems." If anything, it highlighted them. Ironically, these problems hinged upon questions around identity – *authentic* identity: "I expected them to know that if you say onstage that you love somebody and offstage you hate their guts, at that moment that moment is really true. They were calling me a bullshitter, a hypocrite. They couldn't maintain that kind of professionalism, that kind of craft" (M. Miguel qtd. in Canning 94). Miguel, here, is referring to an actual incident that occurred during an offstage argument. In heated terms, Foner and Grosberg expressed their distrust at her "hypocrisy," which for them manifested itself in her ability to say, with absolute conviction and believability, "I love you" onstage to the same scene partner with whom she was engaged in an offstage dispute. The subject of the dispute has long since been forgotten; it may have erupted around disagreements over labour division, authority, production content, financial matters, etc. No matter. The point here is that Muriel Miguel's partners chose to privilege the "reality" of petty, day-to-day, material concerns over the expression of something greater on the stage. Perhaps, they were, in the end, interested more in the documentation of daily socio-political concerns (in the manner of Piscator's agitprop, documentary-style theatre) than in peeling away the layers of material reality to reveal the connective tissues (sympathy, empathy, gratitude, admiration, humility, fragility, brokenness, mortality – *love*) that constitute the essence of being and the cornerstone of human identity. Perhaps, they were less interested in the art than in the politics. Either way, it seems that there was no room in their philosophy to *imagine* that the "love" being articulated on stage could be just as real as the bad feelings engendered within an offstage argument. Nor was there room in that philosophy to entertain the idea that perhaps the very articulation of the word "love" could carry the power to *imagine* healing and to facilitate the repair of broken trust and ruptured interpersonal relationships.

Charlotte Canning has suggested that Womanspace finally disbanded because "group and group process eventually became more important than creating new works" (94). But perhaps, the process had merely revealed, in this instance, that *there was no group*: Womanspace was not a "community" in which Miguel could realize herself as an individual *and* as an integral part of the whole. The questions of her collaborators ultimately were not and could not be her questions. They were activists, where she is both activist and artist. This separated them, as Foner and Grosberg vociferously articulated their distrust of her artistry – condemning it as a mask of untruth (designed perhaps to discourage action and activism) rather than celebrating it as a vehicle of transformation and a revealer of truth.

While all were impacted by and deeply concerned with the oppression of women, Foner and Grosberg, as "whitestream feminists," were not terribly concerned with racism or classicism – manifestations of oppression that did not directly impact them. Nor were they interested in exploring their own complicity in a system that may oppress all *but that does not oppress all equally*. I borrow the term, "whitestream feminism," from Quechua scholar Sandy Grande. She has noted that there exists a "historical divide" between feminists and those women who are racialized, who live with financial precarity, or who have been marginalized because of other challenging circumstances into which they have been born . The movement that has purported to represent "universal" female interests has been "not only dominated by white women but [is] also principally structured on the basis of white middle-class experience, serving their ethnopolitical interests and capital investments" (Grande 125). Indeed, during the meetings, workshops, and CR sessions of the 1970s, the feminists who gathered to network and share were fuelled by an objective to identify and overturn patriarchal oppression. For these women, questions of race and class were inessential. In their view, all women experienced the same oppression at the hands of the same oppressor. And within their project, as Audre Lorde has noted of others in the movement, these women acknowledged no "need at that time to examine the contradictions of self, woman as oppressor" (130).

In 1990, Miguel stated to Charlotte Canning that her decision to part company with Grosberg and Foner rested on the fact that "they weren't committed as theater people" (Canning 95). I am intrigued, however, by an unrealized possibility: While Muriel Miguel remains a committed, professional, and consummate artist, she may perhaps have found a way to reconcile herself to Grosberg's and Foner's lack of theatrical experience (and artistic sensibility) had she been able to envision herself in community with them. She is after all a highly skilled teacher and director with remarkable vision; and like many great teacher-directors before her, she might very well have transformed these women into fine theatre practitioners. These women may have lacked Miguel's degree of commitment to the theatre, but the eight months they devoted to the co-creation of *Cycles* bespeaks some commitment and some ability to produce pertinent and compelling work. Ultimately, it appears that Grosberg and Foner lacked commitment to (or indeed, any interest in) the questions that drove Muriel Miguel – questions that did not invite simple answers. A politically aware artist, Miguel had sought community among other artists who sought to challenge and transform the status quo. But that community had proven itself no respecter of women. A woman, she had sought community amongst active feminists, but this community had commanded her allegiance without reciprocity; within it, she would find no sympathy for or consideration of her very specific concerns as an Indigenous woman born into poverty in one of the wealthiest cities on the globe. Nor would this community undertake or even countenance any questions surrounding its own relative privilege and collective gains bolstered and made possible by race-based exploitation and oppression. The flyer for *Cycles* informs us that the show, which had grown out of the trio's CR sessions, was intended as a vehicle through which three contemporary females living in the United States of America would be able to "find common ground as political women of different class and racial origin, and to work out their problems in dramatic terms" (Production Flyer qtd. in Canning 94). Ultimately, *Cycles* failed in this noble objective. Instead of alleviating the "problems" of its creatrices and building bridges between them, the experience of touring and performing *Cycles* seemed to exacerbate differences and widen the chasm between the members of the fledgling troupe. Issues around race and class and the divisions they produce were not acknowledged or addressed. Instead, the craftswoman (Miguel) was singled out by and forced to separate herself from the activists who condemned her *artistry* as falsehood and who labelled her a "hypocrite." To fully integrate the artist self, the female self, and the Indigenous self, Muriel Miguel would have to find or form a new community.

Undaunted, Muriel Miguel threw herself into building the community of which she dreamed: She contacted her sisters and tirelessly worked to convince them to collaborate with her on a collective creation for the stage. As lack of funding at this time rendered their participation untenable (Gloria could not afford to come into New York City from Oberlin, and Lisa was seeking paying gigs), she joined forces with Josephine Mofsie-Tarrant and a non-Indigenous feminist performer, Lois Weaver. Out of this collaboration, in 1975 Spiderwoman Theater stepped onto the off-off-Broadway boards with a workshop. This workshop was formed around a series of experiments through which Miguel, Mofsie-Tarrant, and Weaver explored their spiritual experiences through improvisation; finding connections; layering sound, movement, images, narrative, and action; and finally presenting their work to a live audience, which the performers wove into the fabric of the theatrical event, teaching American Indian hand games and thereby transforming passive spectators into active "players." As a brief overview of Spiderwoman's history ("Origins") prepared by the Native American Women Playwrights Archive (Walter Havighurst Special Collections & University Archives, Miami University Libraries, Oxford, OH) states, for this event, the performers "rehearsed and structured the basics of their stories and dreams," and these were brought to life in improvisation during the live event ("Spiderwoman Papers").

The workshop was performed at the Washington Square Methodist Church. Its "anchor" was Josephine Mofsie-Tarrant who recounted an Origin Story about Grandmother Spider, the Hopi goddess of Creation who wove first man and first woman into the fabric of the universe. While she articulated the story, Mofsie-Tarrant *recreated the genesis of her people, as she played out the traditionally Hopi activity of finger weaving*. Muriel, who had just returned from a Sun Dance, wove her experience of ontological emergence into that of her best friend, while Weaver recounted her experiences of being brought up as a Baptist, weaving these with a dream she had had of a sexual encounter between her and Jesus of Nazareth (M. Miguel, Personal Communication 2006). At once connected and held apart by a "river" that wound its way across the stage, each storyteller occupied her own realm, as she recounted her origin story. As Mofsie-Tarrant worked on creating the belt that was suspended before her, she recreated the genesis of her own people in *action* and then extended that action to weave her colleagues and the Creation Stories that directed their lives into her own within the inscribed textile, thereby anchoring three lives (and the communities from which they emerged) together (M. Miguel, Personal Communication 2006). Hence, it is to her that Spiderwoman Theater owes not only its name but also elements of the distinctly Indigenous ontological, epistemological, and cosmological underpinnings of the process out of which it has, for nearly half a century, woven story on the world stage.

Muriel Miguel identifies this workshop as the beginning of Storyweaving ("Performance Lecture"). But this auspicious beginning was marred by tragedy: Several months after this workshop performance, Josephine Mofsie-Tarrant who was not yet 40 years old died suddenly leaving behind a husband, five children, and her best friend, Muriel Miguel. And just as suddenly, for Muriel, "it clicked." If she was going to survive to reach the age of 40, she had better take *action* and push harder to create a community to facilitate that survival; if she was going to form a theatre company with her sisters, she had better "do it NOW" (M. Miguel qtd. in Beaucage 7, emphasis in the original).

3 An Indian Is *More* than Just an "Idea": By Their Acts, Ye Shall Know Them

N. Scott Momaday's 1970 pronouncement that "an Indian is an idea, which a given man has of himself" (97) does not imply that Indigenous identity is simply a matter of choice; nor, on the other hand, is it merely an accident of birth. Traditionally, one born into a particular clan of a particular nation was mentored and rigorously trained to become a member of that nation. Choice (with regards to identity and membership) was a non-issue. After more than two centuries of colonization, relocation, removal, legislative assimilation, intermarriage and rape in North America, issues around identity have increased in complexity. Many Indigenous people today are bi- or tri-racial. Others may be wholly Indigenous, even as the blood of two or more disparate First Nations flows through their veins. For some mixed-blooded peoples, these issues can invite pain, shame, a sense of isolation/alienation; for others, they challenge the individual to "bust borders" and to melt down metonyms by de-essentializing identity: Mestizo performance artist Guillermo Gómez-Peña (with whom Monique Mojica and Turtle Gals Performance Ensemble have worked) has designed processes to teach artist and audience member that identity "can be altered or reshaped at will through conscious and strategic use of costumes, makeup, props" (Gómez-Peña 117). Perhaps, then, Plato was correct: Inner life arranges itself to mirror outer life (*Republic*, Book III 15). We become the masks we wear.

Of course, these masks must *live*. On stage, the efficacy of a performer is not assessed by outward appearance alone. The audience has not come to see an artful mannequin. So too in life, while outer accoutrements may aid in human transformation, their influence is indirect. In the most prosaic arenas of life, the clothing, wigs, makeup, footwear, hair extensions, dental veneers, and cosmetic surgery *influence* gesture, behaviour, action, and interaction. In life, the idea (the imagination of self) engenders the mask; and new masks require the human host to *act* in ways that will accommodate them. And as so many instances of American Indian and First Nations Oratory demonstrate, human action not only reveals human essence but also *transforms* it. This understanding should not present itself as a completely foreign concept to the Euro–North American reader. Method acting instructors (like Uta Hagen) remind us that we cannot convey – we cannot "play" – a state of being (i.e., being in love) and that an audience can only perceive and appreciate a character's essence/internal state as it is realized in action (e.g., What does one *do* when one is in love?). And European folklore runs amok with lumpish, low-born boobies who, *by virtue of their actions*, transform themselves into sages, heroes, and princes. Likewise, identity, in Anishinaabe teachings, is not solely formed in the regalia that one wears or in the ceremonial paraphernalia that one possesses but in the *actions* through which relationship between self and world and the interrelationships between human and "mask" are played out by the Indigenous human.

In the 1990s, Oogima Ikwe, an Anishinaabe woman from the eastern Upper Peninsula of Michigan, offered this teaching to demonstrate that who we are (cultural identity) is determined by what we do and that symbol without praxis is ultimately empty:

> I said, "what happens if all the pipes were gone?
> Creator just took all the pipes away?
> No more eagles,
> No more eagle feathers,
> No staffs,
> No pretty regalia …
> No pretty regalia,
> No fans,
> No breastplates,
> No nothing …
> Are we not Indian anymore …
> Where does my identity lie?" (Ikwe 188)

Preoccupied with these questions, the Anishinaabe speaker, finally goes to the water, lays her tobacco, and waits for a teaching. And the water gives her this:

> You *are* the pipe,
> You *are* the drum,
> You *are* the feather,

You *are* the buckskin,
You *are* the Earth,
You *are* all of these things.
All these things are is a reminder,
A tool. (Ikwe 189)

These "tools" remind us of who we are and, as the water goes on to teach Oogima, these alone do not bring us into our *selves*; ultimately, identity is formed through action.

If we were really *walking* in that way we're supposed to be walking,
Or should be walking,
We won't need those things,
'Cause we'll be those things. (Ikwe 191, emphasis mine)

It is necessary to return to this idea – the process of "becoming" (Indian) *here* because it is precisely at this point that Muriel Miguel took the first crucial steps of her transformational journey from an artist, who also happened to be an American Indian woman seeking to locate herself in the feminist struggle, into the Guna co-founder of and driving force behind a "feminist" American Indian Storyweaving collective with "womanist" leanings – a collective that would inspire, impact, and transform Indigenous and mainstream communities across the globe for more than three decades. It began with an idea, which generated an action, which generated another, which …

And once the "mask" took hold, there was no turning back.

Survivance: Act One

In 1975, in the wake of Josephine Mofsie-Tarrant's death, Muriel Miguel received a grant for which she had applied while she had been working with the now-defunct Womanspace. She channelled these funds into the mobilization of a new, multi-racial, feminist collective. And Spiderwoman Theater was born. Amid loss, mourning, love, disappointment, and irrepressible life, its creation was an *act of survivance* through which the Miguel sisters and three non-Indigenous colleagues wrote their resistance to the violence they had and by which they had been affected. Muriel had been thinking about "violence in Indian homes" ("Performance Lecture") and about the verbal and/or physical violence that every woman who lives in an urban centre can expect to encounter on the streets at least once in her life. Certainly, on the eve of a "family reunion" that would bind the Miguel sisters together within an intense professional and creative partnership, which would span three decades, Muriel Miguel was undoubtedly thinking about the violence she had both encountered and witnessed as a child and as a young woman and about the violence that had occurred in her marital home. After all, to effect healing within the greater community, these sisters would have to heal themselves as individuals and repair the sibling relationship, which had been compromised by the domestic explosions that had been brought into being by an alcoholic father and that continued to reverberate throughout the consciousness of each. Muriel Miguel was angry, and that anger was reaching its boiling point: "I really had to examine it [that anger] or get killed before it killed me" (M. Miguel qtd. in Beaucage 6).

But this performative investigation of violence and rage was not intended to present a diatribe that positioned women as victims/survivors of violence; this could not simply be a show about women *and* violence, although this too was a vital layer in the investigation. Certainly, some of the questions that preoccupied Muriel and her collaborators emerged from personal (or witnessed) experiences that ranged from the quotidian humiliations of verbal catcalls to which most women had (and have) been subjected on public thoroughfares to domestic violence, muggings, rape, and femicide. However, Muriel and her sisters brought other – perhaps, more pressing – questions to the table. These questions demanded unflinching encounter with the physical and mental violence we, as women, perpetrate upon ourselves and the violence we perpetrate upon each other.[1] Spiderwoman Theater's first collaborative creation was to offer a "constructive outlet" through which to articulate the "horror" of encountering oneself as a "part of the violence" – as a woman *in* violence (*Women in Violence* "Publicity Flyer" qtd. in Canning 167, emphasis mine). This performative investigation would yield an utterly honest examination of human brokenness that held up a mirror to the "oppressed" and reflected the face of an "oppressor."

Such biting honesty, albeit sweetened by a generous measure of humour, proved, for its audiences, a difficult pill to swallow.[2] Consequently, it set Spiderwoman in a liminal space between the three

1 No script of *Women in Violence* has survived. But for a complete "Scene Analysis" of the show, see Appendix 3.

2 Muriel Miguel continues to argue today for the necessity of producing work in which pedantry is seasoned with pleasure: "You get hit over the head. You get hit over the head. You get hit over the head. And you don't say anything except 'ow.' And you have to think about that. To have someone listen to you, you have to give them more than 'ow'" (*Muriel Miguel: A Retrospective*).

communities with which the Miguel sisters felt the strongest allegiance and in which they had hoped that their work would engender healing and transformation. Although the show received much well-deserved praise and recognition;[3] and although its communitist possibilities eventually manifested themselves across feminist communities throughout France, in America the reception of *Women in Violence* brought in its wake considerable controversy and effected polarization within the theatre, feminist, and American Indian communities.[4]

Women in Violence marks the historical moment in which Gloria Miguel and Lisa Mayo, mobilized by their "baby" sister, began to use their voices not simply to animate other people's stories but to create and perform their own stories to save lives – their own and others'. Within the context of a multi-racial, feminist troupe, dubbed by one critic as "a rainbow of American womanhood" (Chaillet 12), the Miguel sisters performatively asserted their identity as artists, as women – as *American Indian* women – and as feminists, working through problematic questions that spoke to their positioning as women in the American Indian struggle and as racialized women in a struggle that largely privileged the concerns of white, middle-class women. Ironically, this identity and their allegiances would be (often, vociferously) challenged by spectators for whom the troupe did not comfortably fit into imagined paradigms of authenticity (as bona fide members of either the feminist or American Indian communities) and by those discomfited by Spiderwoman's performative interventions, which had been

3 In 1977, Luis Valdez of Teatro Campesino saw *Women in Violence* at the Baltimore Theater. As a result of his passionate belief in the importance of their work, Spiderwoman Theater was invited to the One World Festival of Theater in Nancy, France, and became the first feminist company to perform at an international theatre festival (Canning 96).

4 American audiences were not the only audiences who reacted strongly to Spiderwoman's premiere production. It is instructive to mark the sites of polarization and denial in each locale. In Nancy, France, feminists received the show with much appreciation, where in America, feminist reception was far more ambivalent. As in America, French males expressed vocal disapprobation. They hissed at the troupe members and declared, "Oh, that's something American. We don't do that. We don't beat up our women" (M. Miguel, *Muriel Miguel: A Retrospective*). But in Nancy, France *Women in Violence* prompted a performance of the division between male and female, and the violence spilled out of the theatre. Fights erupted outside the performance venue, as "women were fighting the men that were hissing" (M. Miguel, *Muriel Miguel: A Retrospective*). In America, interestingly, when male audience members expressed disapprobation by walking out of the show or loudly (and sometimes, crudely) vocalizing their dissent, female audience members did not react by rising to the troupe's defense.

created to reveal, address, resist, and repair specific areas of communal dysfunction.

To illustrate, male audience members at New York City's American Indian Community House (where *Women in Violence* played on weekends in January 1976) demonstrated their displeasure with the troupe's work by stomping out of performances or loudly and succinctly vocalizing their critique for performers and audience alike: Indeed, Muriel Miguel recounts a story about a "famous Indian man" loudly exclaiming, "bullshit" during one of the shows (M. Miguel qtd. in Canning 122). And one non-Indigenous commentator lamented the fact that while she had appreciated *Women in Violence* and the fact that it spoke to "the family of women," her search for American Indian theatre in New York City had gone "unrewarded" (Cartwright 5). Apparently, this reviewer was disappointed by the absence of "traditional signifiers" (read: buckskin, blankets, feathers, and beads) without which she was unable to recognize or credit the ethnic "authenticity" of the Indigenous performers.

Although Spiderwoman Theater definitively allied itself with the feminist struggle, four of its members (the Miguel sisters and Naja Beye)[5] were women of colour. And the Miguel sisters were committed to deepening contemporary feminist analyses around violence by introducing the hitherto ignored layer of race: In North America, legislative policies designed to effect the eradication or assimilation of Indigenous Peoples have left our communities reeling from the horrendous legacy of forced relocations; forced removal of children from their families; violence; biological, ecological, and psychological warfare; land swindles; economic extortion; enslavement; indentured servitude; rape; cultural/spiritual rape (in the form of exploitation and misappropriation); and genocide. And while the Miguel sisters decried the frequent incidents of domestic violence and sexist behaviour still occurring in Indigenous homes and communities across Turtle Island, they refused simply to conform to the feminist party line that held the male, as upholder and

5 Little has been written about Naja Beye, and it seems she has become, for most commentators and archivists, little more than a footnote in the history of Spiderwoman Theater and Split Britches Theater. Beye performed with Spiderwoman from 1976 until 1980. In this year, Beye participated in the initial stages of the co-creation of *Split Britches* with Lois Weaver, Peggy Shaw, and Pam Verge. And in October of that year, the foursome performed *Split Britches* for the Women's One World Festival in New York City at the Allcraft Center (Case 7). Then, in 1981, Verge and Beye left the company, and Weaver and Shaw invited Deb Margolin to join the project (Case 5). Margolin stayed on with Split Britches to become a co-writer and performer. Currently, an instructor at Yale University and a playwright/performer in her own right, Margolin is credited with being one of Split Britches's co-founders.

beneficiary of the oppressive Western patriarchy, to be the sole oppressor of the female.

Certainly, the patriarchal attitudes imported by the settler nations and imposed upon Indigenous communities have been responsible for much of the societal chaos and individual brokenness that we experience today. But this patriarchy had often been actively supported by and had certainly afforded privileges to members of the very community that now challenged it. European, Euro-American, and Euro-Canadian women were among those who re-educated (and often physically abused) Indigenous children in residential/Indian boarding schools, whether these were nuns in the Catholic-run residential schools or the lay-teachers in Protestant or industrial schools. While much testimony around the frequent incidents of sexual abuse at these schools indicts male perpetrators, countless incidents of verbal abuse; daily humiliations; criminal neglect; physical abuse including confinement, severe beatings, starvation, and mutilations; and infanticide were perpetrated by school personnel of both genders.

Like violations of Indigenous Peoples continue today. The more subtle of these are acts of spiritual misappropriation, which, Andrea Smith reminds us, is "a form of sexual violence" (119). Cultural/spiritual misappropriation is a crime of "equal opportunity" perpetrated by both males and females (of European and, with less frequency, of Indigenous ancestry). And regardless of the ethnicity or gender of the perpetrator, it poses incalculable harm to Indigenous communities. Consider the sheer volume of financially successful "shamanesses" who have penned bestsellers that misrepresent Indigenous spiritual beliefs and praxis, who have facilitated workshops, and who have even "conducted" weekend Sweat Lodge ceremonies (for which they have charged thousands of dollars). These "shamanesses are, by and large, Euro-American women with no Indigenous ancestry whatsoever. Among the most successful and infamous of these are Lynn Andrews (see *Medicine Woman*), Evelyn Eaton (see *The Shaman and the Medicine Wheel*), O'Shinna "Fast Wolf," and Shequish Ohoho – to name just a few.

Indeed, Spiderwoman's *Winnetou's Snake Oil Show from Wigwam City* (1989) was created at the behest of the Circle of Elders as a performative intervention to address such acts of spiritual misappropriation. Unsurprisingly, its sly criticism of New Age icon Lynn Andrews and her acolytes was met with considerable resistance by some audiences: "We were talking about plastic shamans, and plastic shamans are somebody like Lynn Andrews [...] She has written [several] books, and she gives workshops all over the country. People come, mostly women, and they love her. She tells you how to use your shamanistic powers" (Mayo qtd. in Burns and Hurlbutt 176). Reactions to this show from individual audience members were intense and varied. Muriel and Gloria have both testified to receiving letters from outraged women who accused them of being spiritually "greedy" and who upbraided them for refusing "to share." Other reactions were less confrontational and more plaintive: "So when a woman said to me, 'It's not my fault if I wasn't born an Indian. What can I do?' I didn't know what to say to her. But Muriel said, 'Die and come back again. You'll be an Indian!'" (Mayo qtd. in Burns and Hurlbutt 178).

Muriel Miguel's instinct to challenge such performances of disingenuity is surely warranted. Previous gains made by the suffragette grandmothers of the movement have entitled Euro-American women to buy, sell, and own lands that had been stolen from Indigenous Peoples and to vote for national leaders who continue unjust policies against "their" Indigenous Peoples, refusing even to abide by the treaties signed by their ancestors and ours (see Grande 150–51). Nor could members of the feminist community distance themselves from their own complicit behaviours – whether these took the form of an "innocent," ethnic joke; a pointed verbal assault on another woman (be she mother, sister, acquaintance, or stranger); or a violent physical attack on a mother, daughter, sister, cousin, acquaintance, or stranger. Indeed, Spiderwoman Theater had already addressed this in no uncertain terms with the production that had catapulted the troupe onto the world stage.

In 1976, *Women in Violence*'s pre-show intervention bridged the lacuna between "actor" and "innocent bystander" by transforming the house (a space from which to see) into a space from which to be seen. Oblivious to the gaze, which had been turned upon them, spectators instinctively acted out and out of their personal animosities and prejudice and were ultimately forced into an uncomfortable reckoning with classist acts of subtle violence, which had become, for them, habitual patterns that informed and directed their social interactions.

Discomfiting Interventions: A Class (ist) Act

As the house begins to fill, there is a delightful buzz of anticipation in the air carried on the sounds of rustling clothing, bodies settling into seats, hushed murmurs bearing shared secrets, and punctuated with the occasional burst of laughter or joyous cry of recognition. In 1976, the members of this largely female audience possess the political and economic clout to decide how they will spend a Saturday night, to purchase their own tickets to the event of their choosing and to make their way to the venue alone, in pairs, or with a select group of 'sisters.' These women can afford the price of admission, and they are comfortable in their certainty that they possess the cultural capital to appreciate and assess the aesthetic and cultural values of the theatrical event they have come to witness. We could be in New York City or Baltimore or Nancy, France. We could be in Amsterdam. No matter. Tonight, this theatre is hosting a feminist audience, which has come to see Women in Violence created and performed by the newly mobilized feminist collective, Spiderwoman Theater. After the show, perhaps, these spectators will gather with their neighbours to enjoy a late supper or nightcap and discuss what they have seen. Others will retire to "rooms of their own" to write about the experience – not in private diaries but for local newspapers, academic journals or to prepare an upcoming lecture for the classes they teach or the women's groups they facilitate. It is "ladies' night," 1976. And it is perfect ...

It would be perfect, except amidst the comfortable and congenial groups of astute activists, there is one who doesn't belong.[6] Obviously, she doesn't belong; she is a 'bag lady.' Certainly, this human wreck could not afford the price of admission. Nor (judging from her tattered clothing and unkempt appearance), could she have amassed sufficient cultural capital to understand or appreciate the play they have come to see. But what is to be done? The front-of-house staff makes no move to eject her; so, she must be tolerated.

"Now, you will behave – won't you?"

It's a necessary question after all, tinged with the merest cautionary edge. That one obviously does not know how to dress herself appropriately; how can she be expected to behave appropriately? In answer to this question, the bedraggled interloper begins to misbehave.

Now, she's banging on some old tray she's brought with her! She's disturbing the peace! "Shhhh! Shoo! Stop it! Behave!"

The audience members are outraged. So intent are they in shutting her up and shutting her down that they are barely aware of the guttural growling on stage, which answers the Bag Lady's performance and builds in rhythm and intensity as she persists in her outrageous behaviour. This is not what they paid for – is it? Then again, maybe it is.

As it slowly dawns on them that this seedy infiltrator is part of the show, the spectators begin to relax and perhaps enjoy the fact that they have been fooled. (Carter, "Processual" 263–65)

6 Lois Weaver's clown character for *Women in Violence* emerged as a Bag Lady who was placed in the audience from the top of the show. While this description of a performance night in 1976 is largely constructed from my imaginings, the characterization of the audience and its reactions to Weaver's character remain true to the account shared with me by Muriel Miguel on 27 August 2007 in New York City during a personal interview.

As Muriel Miguel has observed of this intervention, "It showed exactly what these women [who made up their audience] were – upper middle class. They had no regard for homeless – homeless women. They had no regard for people of colour, certainly not women of colour" (Interview 2007). Women were supposed to present a morally righteous, united front against a common enemy, but in true Trickster fashion, Spiderwoman Theater had plunged headlong into the layers of an impossibly intricate socio-political web to reveal a vital flaw in its design. And the exposure of this flaw, embodied by the oppressor *within*, carried with it the potential to undermine political unity by upsetting the collective assurance in the moral rectitude of the feminist cause and its fighters.

As Muriel Miguel has explained, in that historical moment, feminist theater was a tool of empowerment and self-assertion for other feminists; it was a tool to challenge the patriarchy, not the "sisterhood." But Muriel Miguel had been swimming "upstream" (M. Miguel, *Muriel Miguel: A Retrospective*) for far too long to change course. She refused to conform to the lie that only males are capable of inflicting pain or humiliation: "We did everything like that, we just put our big feet in the middle of feminism and went plop, plop, plop" (M. Miguel qtd. in Canning 123).

> As the evening unfolds, more revelations will occur, and Spiderwoman's audience will be unceremoniously ushered, by a ragtag bunch of clowns, into a hostile universe peopled with "dirty mashers," big bad wolves, abusive husbands, violent siblings, betrayers, suicides and mass murderers. Each performer's clown embodies the "poor bare fork'd animal" beneath the quotidian mask, which conceals and protects every human actor as s/he goes about the business of living. These include a glittering Chameleon in constant pursuit of herself; a Nun whose mission it is to clean the world and the other women in it; the unruly Bag Lady; a magnificent leonine Trickster who wears a second face on her tail and who both uses and blames this marvelous appendage for all tricks and offending actions against others; and finally, a Perfect Woman – a "chocolate-box blonde" – whose final act in the piece is to strip off wig, gloves and makeup and publicly "come out" as someone other than she first appears. (Carter, "Processual" 263–65)

If certain critics and practitioners (trained in European or Euro-American traditions) were dismissive of the work, even as they were forced to acknowledge the profound ways in which it worked on them, these dismissals, more often than not, emerged from their reception of Spiderwoman's aesthetic and the distinct world view that underpins this aesthetic as "alien" and "inaccessible" (Mojica, "Ethnostress" 21). And while this is slowly changing, this troubling and dangerous trend has continued to persist in these first decades of the twenty-first century. Indeed, Monique Mojica (who has been intensively trained by her aunt Muriel Miguel in Spiderwoman's Storyweaving process) observed more than one generation after the premiere of *Women in Violence* that those works, which veer away from the "euro-centric aesthetic" are unlikely to receive positive reviews. If the Western viewer is not familiar with the rhythms, signifiers, cosmological underpinnings, or historical context that underpin a theatrical offering, this work "*must be* 'bad' or (even worse) 'inaccessible'" (Mojica, "Ethnostress" 21, emphasis mine).

Certainly, failures to appreciate Spiderwoman's distinctive dramaturgical structure or symbolic interlay seem to have been engendered by an utter lack of recognition and a lack of understanding that accompanies that recognition. By way of example, in 1978, the *London Times*' critic Ned Chaillet condemned *Women in Violence* for, what he perceived as, structural "incoherence" and "fragmentation," "chaotic" and "manic" performances, and dearth of "artistic effects" (12). Despite his realization that the troupe presented an embodiment of a "lively sense of community" ; despite the visual signifiers, which included the first layers of the mola that would become the signature backdrop of Spiderwoman Theater; and despite the final, powerful moments of self-revelation as the performers pared away the layers of their clown personas to reveal the women beneath, Chaillet remained largely uncomprehending and unappreciative of the aesthetic and philosophical precepts that governed Spiderwoman's exploration of women in violence.[7]

7 It is not my primary intent in this project to critique the scholars or the critics who have commented on the works of Spiderwoman Theater throughout its tenure. However, observations around critical reception of the troupe's productions do help to clarify and re-right misunderstandings and oversimplification, which stem from a serious gap in knowledge around the histories, cosmologies, languages, symbols, and aesthetic practices of Indigenous Peoples across this continent.

Admittedly, a "bad" review is not the sole indicator of a reviewer's inability to appreciate the aesthetics that govern the works of many cultural Others. Indeed, this lack of appreciation often shows itself more prominently in "good" reviews – and to more dangerous effect. Again, as Mojica has observed, such positive publicity may be pat and patronizing. In such instances, because the reviewers have failed to understand a work, they blithely praise it (fearing either to reveal their confusion or to be called to account for political incorrectness) without offering any serious, constructive critique. In such instances, "the community suffers and the art is not nurtured" (Mojica, "Ethnostress" 21).

This aesthetic, which is characterized by story fragments whose connections are often initially imperceptible; widely variegated playing styles; and the deliberate integration of flaws into the production design and performative execution is an aesthetic that binds the lifeblood of the company – in the persons of the Miguel sisters – to the body of knowledge they have inherited from their Guna father and uncles. Furthermore, the artists' fearless excavation of and descent into the layers of human experience in search of truthful revelation, which speaks to the very best or very worst of the human doing, invites (and perhaps requires) the ministrations and interventions of a Transformative Agent (an "inner clown," a Trickster) who has always negotiated those layers for and with Indigenous Peoples and whose prime function has always been to teach who we are and who we can be. To understand just how s/he negotiates those layers and reveals, within the chaos, the design that manifests the connections between spirit and material, potentiality and actuality, ancestor and descendant, and creation and destruction in *Women in Violence* and other Spiderwoman productions, we must first begin to chart those layers and come to know the decorative and performative "metaphors" that inhabit Spiderwoman's stages – not as metaphors but as patently literal manifestations of Guna world view and tradition.

Dramaturging the Mola: Mola Aesthetics

Since 1976, every Spiderwoman production has included the troupe's signature backdrop – a multi-layered quilt (or mola), which has continued to expand in breadth, depth, and intricacy over the company's life, as many of those who have worked with or been touched by Spiderwoman Theater have contributed their own material artefacts to the company's mola (see fig. 3.1). It is important to recognize that this signature backdrop is not only a signifier of the Miguel sisters' connection to their Guna ancestry but also a material representation of the dramaturgical and performative processes, which may be seen to evolve from the Guna mola-makers' aesthetic. As Monique Mojica, who is an artistic and genealogical inheritor of Spiderwoman's legacy, has reminded me, "Everything is based upon the mola in Gunayala" (Personal Communication 2007).

Molas are an important component of traditional female dress for the Guna woman, and the art of mola-making belongs strictly in the female arena. In earlier times, traditional adornments for the Guna body included tattoos, piercings, and intricate designs painted on the body. But in the late nineteenth century, Guna women began transferring

Figure 3.1. Muriel Miguel in front of the signature backdrop during a production of *Women in Violence*. The top right panel in the backdrop is the mola that Gloria Miguel brought back from Gunayala. Courtesy of the Walter Havighurst Special Collections and University Archives, Miami University Libraries, Oxford, OH.

the designs once used in body painting to hand-woven cloth. From there, they began to experiment with appliqué; and eventually they developed a layering process that is an integral component of Guna philosophy and aesthetics belonging not only to the mola but also to music composition, oratory, healing practices, origin stories, etc. The process involves layering fabrics of variegated colours, one on top of the other, cutting away the upper layers to reveal the colour(s) beneath out of which a complex design will emerge, and finally stitching each layer to the base layer with minute deftness to render the connections between the layers invisible (DeLeón Fernandez and Oswaldo DeLeón Kantule, 2007).

In 1919, the Panamanian government passed a law designed to forcibly assimilate the Guna people. In the years that followed, representatives of the colonial government including local leaders, religious leaders, and police personnel escalated their attempts to suppress the expression of Guna identity by prohibiting puberty and Curing Ceremonies, communal attendance at the Gathering House, and the traditional style of female dress. Women who dared to wear their molas out of doors (and many did) were beaten, sexually assaulted, jailed, or even killed by the police. In February of 1925, the people had been pushed past the point of endurance. Rising up in violent protest during the Carnival celebrations (which had been imposed upon the Indigenous population) and appealing to the United States for mediation, the people of Gunayala were finally able to negotiate a treaty, which is foundational to their status as a sovereign people within Panama today (Howe 146). Since this historic moment, Guna resistance and victory is performatively re-enacted by the people on the streets annually during public celebrations to commemorate the *Revolutión Tule* (the Guna Revolution). And amid the dramatized re-creations of oppression and civil disobedience, the "granddaughters of the revolution" proudly wear their finest molas for all to see. So, the mola – a dense riot of texture, design, and colour (whether it is being crafted, worn, or displayed) – is a celebratory marker of Guna identity, of Guna resistance, of Guna survival. Indeed, as I have come to understand it, the mola is a crucial signifier of Guna survivance. Is this, I wonder, what Ned Chaillet saw when he viewed *Women in Violence*, or did he see a homespun craft hanging suspended upstage – for him, a poor and unreadable replacement for the "artistic effects" he so craved?

Layering as a Dramaturgical Tool

> We begin our work (in "Women in Violence") by finding our own personal clowns. Together we sit on the floor and talk about a theme – "The Clown in Us" – and discuss all different aspects of it, good and bad, sad and happy, etc. Then we isolate a particular aspect which we want to make fun of and keep that as a basis for a clown persona. Using the buffoonery of clowns, we weave our personal stories of violence, fear, anger and frustration into the piece, juxtaposing the reality of our own lives with bawdy humor [...]
>
> We usually begin with a theme, someone tells a story, another repeats it, and we work together to transform it into movement or reduce it to

> its essence. Muriel Miguel, as director, has the final say as to what works or doesn't, and watches the pieces with an eye to the whole, pacing, etc. *but everyone in the group has a voice and doesn't hesitate to use it to suggest or express herself.* ("Spiderwoman Papers," emphasis mine)

Each story – each fragment of experience – selected for inclusion in a Spiderwoman project becomes a layer in the performative mola. As the company sifts through each, reducing it to its kernel or gwage (heart), the collective mola-maker is cutting away inconsequential details, revealing the shape and colour of truthful experience. The "fragmentation" that so mystified critics like Ned Chaillet was, I surmise, the multi-vocal perspective that resists privileging the easy answers provided by a singular author(ity), pushing against the positivist course to an absolute truth. This is not, however, to suggest that the presentation of a multiplicity of perspectives constitutes an implication that the truth is "relative" or that there is no truth. Rather, this process is a contemporary manifestation of a process common to many, if not all, Indigenous nations. This process mandates the preservation of a people's history as a communal responsibility wherein each tribal member is expected to learn and retain fragments (layers) of the greater communal story and is expected to participate in the transmission of that history, weaving into the grand design the details, shapes, colours, and fragments engendered by his/her memories, reception, and interpretations.

As Laguna Pueblo writer Leslie Marmon Silko has explained about the process, which underpins Pueblo Oral Tradition, it is process that has been engendered by an "inclusive" vision of the world, which acknowledges that all levels of human experience are relevant and crucial. Therefore, all interpretations (emerging from various levels of human experience) are voiced and duly considered. Each interpretive recounting of communal or personal history may contain a fragment of information, unique to its teller. Each constitutes a level/layer of knowledge, and the community understands that somewhere within those levels/layers, material and metaphysical truths may be preserved and recovered (Silko, 30–1). Silko is addressing Pueblo experience here, but her explication of objective and process speaks to a foundational principle that directs the aesthetic of bead workers, carvers, Wampum Belt artisans, and mola-makers throughout the Americas as much as it does that of Pueblo weavers and workers in clay.

Once, she tells us, all citizens of her own Laguna Pueblo from youngest to eldest were called upon to listen to the nation's stories and to remember and recount a portion – even if only fragmentary – of the story they had heard. The responsibility to hold knowledge and to ensure the knowledge would be passed down through the generations was a communal one; it was not simply reserved for the tribal specialist or Knowledge Keeper. With this system, communal knowledge could be retained even in the wake of unanticipated tragedy, such as the unexpected death of a crucial Knowledge Holder (Silko 31–2. Silko goes on to note that such a process, demanding communal responsibility and constant collective focus is a "self-correcting" one. In this arena of history-keeping everybody who holds some memory of the story being told is invited to insert their piece. Differing versions and conflicting interpretations are not dismissed in favour of a singular, authorized version of events: "The ancient Pueblo people sought a communal truth, not an absolute truth. For them, this truth lived somewhere within a web of differing versions, disputes over minor points, and outright contradictions tangling with old feuds and village rivalries" (Silko 31–2).

Likewise, Spiderwoman's founder and director Muriel Miguel was (and continues to be) very aware that no one person can lay claim to absolute truth. Even in speaking about the history of Spiderwoman Theater, she has been very careful to emphasize that her version constitutes only a fragment or layer of the truth, which cannot be discovered until all possible fragments are presented, explored, and sifted through (Canning 20).

It is undeniable that Spiderwoman Theater was neither the only nor the first theatre collective with a mandate to produce and present collaborative creations built upon the stories and improvisations of its members. But it is important to remember that there exists a profound difference between Spiderwoman Theater and The Open Theater with which Muriel Miguel began her professional career as an actor, or the Living Theater within which The Open's architect had come to embrace the collaborative process. The elements of their working methodologies may bear compelling similarities when considered, each for itself, as points on a map. But when these points are connected to represent the path of the artist in its entirety and when the destination (product) is finally revealed, the disparity in journeys and destinations – the processual differences between these seemingly similar companies – prove to be even more compelling.

The works of the Living and Open Theaters were directed by a singular authority who sought to reconfigure the fragments and process the layers that they might conform to a singular vision. At the end of the day, the works produced by these companies were "Joseph Chaikin productions" or "Beck/Malina productions," or they evolved into scripts "authored by" Jean Claude van Itallie or Megan Terry in which a multiplicity of perspectives was ultimately filtered through one lens.

By contrast, since its very inception, although the members of Spiderwoman Theater agree to defer to the judgment of Muriel Miguel as director with reference to what will work most effectively on stage, every voice is included; every perspective, honoured. And as further examination of their later works will demonstrate, stories that may not work for one piece are not discarded; they are preserved and often engender the central questions to be explored in future shows.

As the American-born Yoruba director Chuck Mike would say, "No *one* owns the story" (2002).[8] Everybody – performer, stage manager, designer, audience member – is recognized as a *co-author* of the communal story; everybody is enlisted as co-captain on a communitist mission to discover human truth and heal human brokenness. The late

---

8 In October 2002, I was accepted as a participant in a workshop facilitated by visiting director Chuck Mike at the Centre for Indigenous Theatre in Toronto, ON. Several months later, I performed under Mike's direction in Chinua Achebe's *Things Fall Apart*, which ran at the Robert Gill Theatre, University of Toronto, 26–30 March 2003. Yoruba-trained director Chuck Mike has developed his own series of culturally specific "Storyweaving" etudes, which he employed in the rehearsal studio and during auditions. One such exercise (to facilitate the development of artist as individual into artist as ensemble member and to facilitate the devising process) was called the "Improv Circle." At first glance, the first of these etudes resembles a familiar children's activity. Sit in a circle; begin a story; let the next person pick it up; etc. However, Mike had devised a set of restrictions, which speak directly to his pronouncement that "no one owns the story." Physically, participants in the improv circle were not permitted to simply adopt a seated position that conformed with their own body type and comfort. The integrity of the circle (dictated by the position of those seated within) had to be maintained. We were instructed to conform the positioning of our bodies to the group. All, for instance, might sit cross-legged. If, however, a member of the circle could not easily sit cross-legged, then all other participants would conform to the position that best suited that individual. Further, during the improvisation of story, participants were instructed not to take ownership of the story by recounting it in first person: It was no one person's story; it was to be a group creation. Therefore, it would be recounted in third person. No one person was to hold the story for too long – however talented and inventive they might be. The story had to move quickly through the circle with each member contributing a fragment, a detail, an action, or a character. Each contribution had to be received and taken up by the circle. It had to be held within the story and permitted to develop or to alter the course of the story as the tellers followed the tale to its natural ending.

I offer here a fleeting picture of my experience of an early exercise developed by Chuck Mike in an attempt to bring his philosophy around communal ownership and ensemble-building into clearer focus. While I perceive some marked similarities in intent and philosophy within the working practices of Spiderwoman and Chuck Mike, I am quite aware that their nation-specific aesthetic underpinnings, artistic objectives, and methodologies differ markedly.

Sandy Crimmins,[9] a former stage manager of Spiderwoman Theater, has testified:

> I was involved in the creation of many pieces. My own stories, my words are spoken by actresses, made real by them. Choreography first tried with my body is performed with much more grace by actors. Sound tapes I assembled and home movies I researched as if they were archival footage are part of the mise-en-scene of several shows. Props and costumes I created bring substance to the action on stage. Because I made brocade "armchairs" out of folding chairs and some material I found on the street in Brooklyn; because I hung and gelled lights and made a movie scene from old sheets; because I knew where in the script the actresses would start fighting with each other; because we toured everywhere from Vancouver, B.C., to Rovaniemi, Finland; because I saw audiences from an old age home in Baltimore to a woman's theatre festival in Boston interact with these performers, this group is part of me and always will be. These things keep me forever linked to Spiderwoman, as linked as I am to my family, to my children. (Crimmins 49)

Certainly, this philosophy of inclusiveness realized itself in Nancy, France, where the story of one female audience member became part of *Women in Violence*, transforming a "cultural experience" into a ritual undertaking that transformed spectators into actors. The troupe had been approached by a woman who had been attacked and severely beaten by an inebriated man on the streets. She reported the attack, and when the police finally acted upon her complaint, they forced her to identify her attacker without granting her any protection or anonymity. She made the identification, and the police released the man with only a warning. Fearing repeated attacks from this individual, the woman approached Spiderwoman's artists who told her story each night at the end of *Women in Violence* (Canning 96). Now that this woman's story was out there in the world, what was to be done? Passive reception on the part of French audiences was not enough for Spiderwoman Theater: "After each show we would tell the story and say 'If you want to do something about it, we're going to do something this Saturday, what do you suggest?'" (M. Miguel qtd. in Canning 96).

The troupe organized post-show discussions and organized a protest that brought French feminist activists from many towns in France

9 Sandy Crimmins passed away at the age of 55 of an apparent heart attack in July 2007. At the time of her death, she was an established poet in the Philadelphia area and a member of *Philadelphia Stories*'s editorial board.

together. On these post-show "stages," erstwhile audience members became "actors," weaving their own stories, perspectives, and solutions into those of the larger collective of feminists seeking change. Together, they sifted through the layers of the story-quilt they were creating, finding the narrative thread-lines that connected them. In this way, they were able to mobilize as a strong community and collectively dramaturg the performative intervention (a protest) that would eventually effect concrete changes in French *herstory*.

In publication, too, Spiderwoman's works assert themselves as community-authored creations; hence, the troupe is represented by a collective face, rather than by one singular personality. Tellingly, the artistic split that led to the inception of Spiderwoman Theater (as we know it today) and Split Britches Theater in 1981 occurred within the context of a struggle for directorial control and communal identity. But again, I get ahead of myself.

Layering as a Performative Tool

Women in Violence undoubtedly dealt with difficult and powerful truths; and as Muriel Miguel has noted, the danger of alienating the audience with heavy-hitting didacticism was something the troupe wished to avoid at all costs ("Performance Lecture"). To remediate the blunt-force trauma of the truth communicated in *Women in Violence*, each actress created a clown character (see Appendix 3), which found its basis in the personal, idiosyncratic flaws of its creatrix. This riotous, performative self-confession realized an aesthetic model that is specifically tribal and specifically Guna at two crucial levels: First, the integration of *flaws* into the fabric of Spiderwoman's performative mola is a key element of the mandate of the company with regards to its processual aesthetics. This mandate has been built upon the legacy of Josephine Mofsie-Tarrant, the Hopi storyteller and finger weaver, whose work provided the inspiration for the company's name. As Spiderwoman Theater's earliest publicity materials assert, "We take our name from Spiderwoman, the Hopi goddess of Creation who was the first to create designs and teach her people to weave. In her designs a flaw was always woven in to allow her spirit to find its way out and be free" ("Spiderwoman Papers"). It is only when we can locate, face, and learn to embrace our brokenness that it becomes possible to transcend that brokenness and finally to free our spirits (see Canning 94). Incidentally, it may be of worth noting that in accordance with Guna aesthetic criteria, while patterns and motifs are generally repeated within a mola, subtle asymmetry in the finished creation is a prime requisite of excellence. The "flaws" that some assiduously avoid for fear of compromising artistic excellence and marring their creation are painstakingly sought and wrought by Others to effect artistic excellence by weaving into their creations the potential for transcendence and transformation. Further, the layering of a clown persona afforded the troupe an opportunity to corporeally inhabit the mola – peeling away each layer piece by piece until the woman beneath and her connection to the stories were explicitly and powerfully revealed.

> Created by each of Spiderwoman's performers to safely (if not, comfortably) convey performer and spectator through difficult stories, these clowns embody archetypes of contemporary feminine humanity. And these, like all such archetypes, are vehicles of discovery and revelation. Through their ministrations and interventions, performer and spectator alike are unceremoniously forced into confrontation with themselves and publicly called into account. The chaotic combat zones, where violence plays itself out upon women and where women play out their own violence upon themselves and each other, are transformed into healing spaces wherein human accountability, responsibility, possibility, value and dignity may be realized, reclaimed and celebrated.
>
> Like Nanabozho, Weesageechak, Raven or Coyote, Br'er Rabbit, Homer Simpson,[10] the Zany of the Italian Commedia, or the low-born European booby who gets the girl, the gold and the Kingdom, these vehicles of

10 I do not mean to posit, imply, fabricate, or explore an outright parallelism here between the transformative agents (Tricksters/culture heroes) of Indigenous traditions and the clownish culture heroes of European nations or Western pop culture. However, it is worth noting that even those Western culture heroes – particularly those disseminated through popular media – fulfil a pedagogical function for their viewers, which (however, one-dimensional) bears some similarity of objective and affect to the functioning of the Trickster/Transformer figures in Indigenous discourse. In their immoderate appetites and behaviours and gratuitous acts of creative generosity or self-destruction, denizens of the societies to which they are contemporary see themselves reflected in all their beauty and ugliness and learn something of what it is to be a "human doing" in their world – the world they have created, the world they are creating. And it is important to remember that we (as colonized peoples), along with our children, often gaze into these "mirrors" that mainstream society holds up to itself and are often subtly and profoundly affected by the "reflections" that gaze back at us. It is particularly important to consider this when we consider the lessons they carry. The contemporary clown may be bumbling, stupid, greedy, and destructive, but he is never more so than the community that surrounds him: Generally, he is a stupid, ugly being surrounded by a community of even stupider and uglier beings. Laughter at his antics is most often a signifier of audience approbation – as if to say, "Yes, that is exactly what I have done/would do/wish I had the courage to

> primordial human impulse tease, shock, rage and bumble and stumble, as they audaciously confront us with outrageous and uncomfortable truths about who we have become as they learn for themselves and teach us through example what we were born to be. (Carter, "Processual" 263–65)

Muriel Miguel's process to "find" her clown anima for *Women in Violence* began with a headlong dive into an inchoate space of remembered abuse and impotent confusion. In rehearsals, she gave herself over to a story of one person calling another person an animal. As she *did* this story, Miguel took corporeal possession of all its characters shifting moment-to-moment from abuser to abused to witness and back again. Eventually, as the story settled into her body and she began to settle on its shape, the story began with the words, "Animal! Animal! Nothing but an animal" (M. Miguel, Interview 2007) as her abused and abased "animal" crawled rapidly across the floor growling a rhythmic score to her physical movements. From this story, Miguel's inner clown began her outward manifestation: The abused and abased was transformed into a personal allegory of contemporary *Revenge*.

Like the Koshares (sacred clowns) in the Pueblo Corn Dances who often hurl abuse (and/or refuse) at Caucasian spectators, this one delighted in settling old scores and "getting people back" (M. Miguel, Interview 2007). She sprouted a tail bearing its own face with which she would whack fellow cast members upside the head or tickle the private places of other characters. And since the offending appendage had a face of its own, Muriel Miguel's clown could also ascribe to it a will of its own and hence assign to it all blame, declaring with picaresque sincerity, "I wouldn't do a thing like that."

---

do." Such laughter is born of a different spirit than the laughter that denotes teasing (albeit, unmistakable) disapproval with which Indigenous observers greet inappropriate behaviour in either culture heroes, children who have not yet learned better, or contrary adults. And this points to the significant differences between cultures that glorify the individual and the assertion of individual identity apart from all others and cultures in which individual identity is unrealizable if it is not sought from within the community of which the seeker is an integral part.

Part of the work that belongs to the sovereign reclamation of the Indigenous *self* is bound up in our engagement with these reflections, particularly with those that seem at first glance to be the most removed from us (or from which we feel ourselves to be at the greatest remove). And these reflections along with Spiderwoman's strategies towards countering and/or reversing their ill effects will be explored throughout this work.

Gloria Miguel's clown persona was a fabulous creation protected by a hard hat and mirrors, which covered her entire costume. Her reflective armour shielded her by projecting back, to all onlookers, images of themselves, thereby deflecting any negative judgement back to its issuers. At once creatrix and creation, Gloria/clown wielded a flashlight with which she searched the mirrored layers of her costume, sifting through the layers of herstory to find her "*self*" and so discover the connections between personhood and personation: "When they call me beautiful, I say, 'Oh yes, I'm beautiful.' When they call me exotic, I say, 'Oh yes, I'm exotic.' When they call me powerful, 'Oh yes, I'm *powerful*.' So, I'm all those things but I don't know who I am. I am whatever I reflect and I have to find my *self*" (G. Miguel qtd. in France and Corso 180–1).

The discovery of Lisa Mayo beneath the blond ringlets and form-fitting, formal black dress of the "perfect woman" shocked audiences – particularly, as they were suddenly able to make hitherto unperceived connections. The fabric of violence and the composition of the feminist critique thereupon were suddenly thickened – made more complex – with the discovery of the hitherto unacknowledged "race layer." To illustrate, reviewer Diane Cartwright has written of the experience:

> Matching each performer with her clown *I realized that some of the stories told by American Indian women had involved violence encountered in personal relationships with men.* The incidents of male-inflicted violence acted out by the other women had occurred on the street or subway, in their dreams and fantasies. (5, emphasis mine)

For Lisa Mayo, this final "reveal" allowed her to "come out […] to the world as an Indian," just as the process of creating *Women in Violence* had allowed her to *come into* herself, forcing her into an honest acknowledgement of and reckoning with the "tremendous" violence that she had "completely put out of [her] mind" (Mayo qtd. in Burns and Hurlbutt 169). The "perfect woman" who had denied *herstory*, denied her family, and denied her Indian-ness to breach the gates of middle-class "Elysium" completed her transformation by shoving a pie into her own face, as the other women on stage pelted each other with pies. Throughout her life, Elizabeth Miguel would never discard the "mask" of glamour – of privileged perfection. Indeed, throughout her eighth decade, almost to the end of her time on this earth, she carried herself with the insouciant grace of an eternally ageless diva. At the same time, in true Trickster fashion, Elizabeth Miguel's glamorous façade was always cut with a healthy dose of irony, a "little wink" as it were, as if to remind us not to be too overwhelmed by the mask, which was as "phony" as the name with which she had identified herself to her public (Mayo qtd. in France and Corso 182).

But the slapstick humour of *Women in Violence* was not simply a sugary palate-pleaser to cut the bite of the troupe's anger – to please and entertain even as it educated and enlightened. Nor was it simply a "weapon" with which to surreptitiously attack the audience as *The Times*'s critic has suggested (Chaillet 12). Rather, in seeking the threads with which to connect the layers of a dense and complex show, the troupe hit upon the idea of weaving the (sadly) ubiquitous racist and sexist jokes they had overheard, been told, or of which they had been the subject on the streets, in places of business, or in social gatherings. As the show progressed and the layers peeled away to unearth increasingly ugly truths, so the jokes intensified in brutality and ugliness, sharpening the edges of the design, tightening the weave and pulling audiences into the fabric as they revealed their own complicity (through laughter) and were finally locked into a face-to-face encounter with their own brokenness, the flaws that marred their design (see Carter, "Processual" 281).

> It started with "Why do Puerto Ricans wear pointy shoes? To kill cockroaches in corners." "How can you tell an Arab at the airport? He's feeding bread to the plane." Finally, as the audience was still laughing … "What's the difference between a Jew and a pizza? The pizza doesn't scream when you put it in the oven." We kept smiling, it got worse, we slaughtered them. (M. Miguel qtd. in Canning 168)

When audiences expressed shocked disapproval at its more "unacceptable" jokes, Spiderwoman answered their objections with loud, juicy raspberries. With such lewd articulations, the unapologetic Zanies spit into a collective mask of removed disdain with like disdain: Spiderwoman's spectators collectively disavowed their participation in the creation, dissemination, or encouragement of verbal atrocities by shouting down the "more offensive" jokes they heard at each performance. So, Spiderwoman "slaughtered them" by adding layers of direct accusation and pointed (albeit scatological) demands for personal accountability because, as Muriel puts it, "people who behave this way pull back and tell you that they are kidding" ("Performance Lecture"). Threading the connections between these incidents of absurd, **anti-social** *gest* (the "raspberry") and the more "civilized," social gest of Muriel's contrary, which manifested itself in her repeated protestation, "It wasn't me, it was my tail," the troupe challenged the fabricated I-dentity of its spectators by shattering the illusions upon which collective, complacent assertions of the "civilized" self had so comfortably rested.

To those who might characterize Spiderwoman's attitude here as too harsh, too cynical, or unfairly judgmental, I offer this reminder: *The troupe had not authored these jokes* (see Pearson). Spiderwoman merely performed the "scripts" it had collected. Tellingly, some audience members could not or would not recognize or acknowledge their position – *our* position – in the deadly design that emerged from beneath *Women in Violence*'s layers of "humour," racism, and violence. Illustrative of this sad truth is the response of a prominent American female theatre practitioner who, after seeing the show, suggested to Muriel Miguel that she substitute the climactic Jew/pizza joke with a *Polish* joke (Canning 168). Apparently, for this culture worker racial epithets against Poles were less harmful and hence more "acceptable" than anti-Semitic humour.

Women in Violence became the catalyst that united the Miguel sisters in a lifelong enterprise of communal artistry and self-discovery. The questions for which they had sought answers spoke to their location in the Miguel family as sisters; to their location in the families they were creating as wives and mothers; to their location in urban America as women and as American Indian women; to their location in the American Indian Movement as female activists; to their location in the feminist movement as wives and mothers who wore makeup when "radical feminists were not doing that" (M. Miguel qtd. in Haugo, "Weaving a Legacy" 228), who identified as heterosexual, and who (despite past efforts) were neither white nor middle class; and to their location within the cycle of damage that they had helped to sustain even as it had constrained, contained, and grievously wounded them. The answers they found during these initial investigations led to further questions, which also demanded answers, and which compelled them to continue their work together in pursuit of new answers. As Spiderwoman Theater began to work on its second project, a processual pattern was being established that would continue to weave these self-proclaimed "myth-breakers" (France and Corso 115) firmly into the aesthetic and philosophical traditions that inform the construction of Mythos from within their family and nations: "Storytelling begins there, about who you are … Then it continues from there about who you are in the family; of where you are as a tribal member, as part of that particular nation; then where that nation is in the community; and where that community belongs in the world. There's always circles upon circles upon circles" (M. Miguel qtd. in Haugo, "Weaving" 225).

Spiderwoman Does a "Numbah" on Aristophanes: The Circle Widens

During the European tour[11] of *Women in Violence*, the Miguel sisters had endured questions from sceptical feminists who disapproved of Lisa's "traditional" domestic arrangements, Gloria's soft romanticism and her desire to find lasting love, and the outer signifiers they donned to showcase their femininity (e.g., lipstick), deeming these to be "out-of-step" with the movement.[12] In 1977, the sisters were still either married or in heterosexual relationships (Beaucage 7). But they were beginning to question their own agency as it related to sex, power, and control within these relationships. Through the process of sharing *Women in Violence* with audiences over two continents, the women of Spider-woman Theater were beginning to apprehend the potent effect of their work on audiences inside the theatre and to recognize it as a catalyst for change in the larger world. Their performances of *Women in Violence* in Nancy, France, attracted such large audiences that spectators were obliged to sit in the rafters of the theatre. And in the wake of these performances, women's groups from across the nation had mobilized to challenge French systems and legislative policy that had encouraged and perpetuated violence against women. Before this, they had been unaware of that power. As Muriel Miguel has explained, "Even though our material was so important to us, we still could not get it through our heads that it was important to other people" (qtd. in France and Corso 24). Their stories were important. The provocative call Spider-woman Theater had sent out into the world was a call to which their audiences responded – a speech act with the power to evoke personal

11 After its New York City run, *Women in Violence* was first performed in Le Festival Mondiale du Theatre (Nancy, France), The Fool's Festival (Amsterdam), Berlin, Rome, Florence, and Lausanne. In 1978, *Women in Violence* played in London and toured throughout, Italy, Germany, and Switzerland.

12 It seemed that no matter what they did, none of the sisters ever felt totally embraced by the movement. Within the troupe, the more radical feminists had rejected men outright and committed themselves to same-sex partnerships. As will be discussed later, the heterosexual lifestyle embraced by Gloria and Lisa disrupted relations within Spiderwoman Theater, creating a split between the heterosexual women and their gay colleagues. Outside the troupe, the mainstream feminists, Muriel has explained to me, did not readily accept gay (or poor or racialized) women into the movement. She and her colleagues within Spiderwoman felt that they were not welcomed by the feminists with whom they had been trying to establish solidarity (Interview 2007). Similarly, Gloria and Lisa (although self-proclaimed feminists) were challenged outside of the troupe because they refused to condemn outright the male gender: They had uncles, lovers, husbands, and sons whom they loved and respected and whose manhood they sought to nurture.

and socio-political transformation. As Spiderwoman's artists were beginning to apprehend their own power and the responsibilities that come with that power, there were so many *questions* ...

Did they or had they given over their power to the males in their lives? How did that feel? Were they indeed "out of control"? Were they who they wanted to be within these relationships? Who did they want to be? Again, the troupe began to explore these questions through story – personal anecdotes, family legends, and origin stories. Where nasty racist and sexist jokes had been utilized as the through-line that connected the variegated strata of *Women in Violence*, the text of Aristophanes' subversive comedy *Lysistrata* was adopted as the thread-line that connected the layers of their *Lysistrata Numbah!* (1977).

Aristophanes' anti-war comedy was presented at the Lenaia of 411 BC in the 20th year of the Peloponnesian war. Seven years later, this war would finally end. So, too, would Athens – as a naval power, an empire, and a democratic *polis*. Lysistrata, who bears a common women's name meaning "Disbander of Armies," mobilizes a general strike of Athenian and Spartan wives and mothers against their warring men. These women refuse to perform their domestic and caretaking duties; more importantly for the purposes of this comedy, they withhold sex from their husbands and/or lovers. All lovemaking ceases in the war zone. Athenian women, beyond their childbearing years, freeze the city's assets and cut off military funding by occupying the Acropolis, in which Athens' treasury was housed. Aristophanes pits the creative, life-bearing force of the matriarchy against the destructive impulse of patriarchal forces, and the armies, which threaten the continuance of the *polis*, are overwhelmed by the force of frustrated sexual desire. Life, love, and desire defeat the forces of hatred and destruction.[13]

As a rollicking, irrepressible embodiment of feminine (pro)creative power, Spiderwoman's Lysistrata (played by Lisa Mayo) was a belly dancer, decked out in a bright red wig, purple brassiere, and diaphanous skirt. Resisting the myth-borne expectation of American Indian women in "feathers and beads," the Miguel sisters and their troupe, in the words of one reviewer, "attack[ed] feminine stereotypes by simply parading them in all their lurid, tit-shaking ugliness" (Shewey). They

13 Muriel Miguel is still in possession of a notebook, in which is written the signed "oath" taken by all the cast members at the beginning of the rehearsal period for *Lysistrata Numbah!* As director, Muriel had insisted that the members of her creative team begin the project of taking back the power they had given over to the men in their lives by abstaining from all sexual contact until the completion of the rehearsal period (M. Miguel, Personal Communication, 7 July 2007).

exercised their personal power with their *Numbah!* by writing *who they wanted to be* on their bodies from the stories that contained their genealogical, spiritual, political, and social lives – stories that spoke to their Guna essence, their female essence, to their lives as daughters, as wives, and as women in post-modern America. The intersections between Attic origin stories, interlaid within the foundations of the West; feminine creative power, interlaid within the foundations of the world; and feminine resistance to patriarchal impulses that have long worked to control, suppress, or destroy that power were made manifest through the exploration and retelling of the origin stories that had been passed down to the sisters by their Guna father and uncles. These manifested themselves with unshakeable authority as the performers found new ways to embody these stories, re-creating the "beginning of the beginning of the beginning" through the *present first person* of an eternal and enduring feminine voice.

> 1st Voice: I woke up. *[Yawning, stretching, childbirth-crying noises.]* Out of me came blood, running down my legs and on my hand. *[More cries.]* Out came a head, then a body, and it ran away. *[Cries. One woman emerges from between the legs of another.]* Another head, another body, and it ran away. Another one, another one, another one, – *[Repeated throughout speech of 2nd Voice.]*
>
> 2nd Voice: A great tree rolled around on its axis, and from its branches flows woman, man, bird, beast, and the great tree rolls around on its axis, and from its branches flows woman, man, bird, beast –
>
> *[The serious ritual dissolves into the "Indian Love Call"]* (Spiderwoman qtd. in France and Corso 115–16)[14]

Ultimately, this searing social commentary, peppered with peanut-shaped dildoes that "sang" Sparta's national anthem, painful testimonials of humiliations visited upon the female artists by men, narrated

14 The second voice here recounts a fragment of the Guna origin story of the baluwala tree. I first heard this story recounted by Oswaldo DeLéon Kantule (Guna artist and Knowledge Keeper) in November 2007 during a developmental workshop for Monique Mojica's *Chocolate Woman Dreams the Milky Way*. While the baluwala does not exist as an actual tree on this earth, it held in its imagined branches all that is needed to sustain life – sunlight, salt water, sweet water, fish, birds, animals, soil, vegetation, etc. Conceptualized as the holder of abundance and fecundity, the baluwala (Tree of Salt) is also understood as the seat of gluttony, greed, and oppression, holding, as it did, a "fat man" who lived at its very top and who hoarded all the gifts the baluwala held, leaving the children of earth to starve. Eventually, the Guna people decided to chop down the tree and to release these life-sustaining gifts over all the earth (Kantule 2007).

advertisements for Oil of Olay and country western parodies ("Stand by your man. Give him two arms to fracture / And something warm to punch on.") pushed Aristophanes' script beyond his comic restoration of a patriarchal – albeit, peaceful – status quo towards a more logical – albeit subversive – lesbian conclusion. And within this company that they had formed with Naja Beye, Pam Verge, and Lois Weaver, the Miguel sisters continued, with this project, to thicken the layers of I-dentity – asserting themselves not only as actresses, writers, and American Indian feminists but also as Guna women written into and writing *onto* the Guna stories to which they had listened as they sat upon the laps of their father and uncles at a kitchen table in Red Hook, Brooklyn. It was within this project, also, that Muriel, who had previously identified herself as the troupe's "final eye," claimed her rightful title: "In the beginning, I didn't want to be called a director, so I was called a "final eye" and I realized *I'm a director. I'm directing this*" (Miguel qtd. in Beaucage 7, emphasis mine). It is here, I imagine, that Muriel began to more rigorously traverse the layers of her sexual identity as she followed the stories, which connected her to her own female power and to the possibility of tapping into that power by walking away from the men who had abused her and finding love and companionship with other women.

Collective Identity

From 1977–80, the six-member troupe continued to perform and tour *Women in Violence* and *Lysistrata Numbah!* throughout North America and across Europe. At home in New York City, the core members (Elizabeth, Gloria, and Muriel with Naja Beye, Pam Verge, and Lois Weaver) continued to develop shows for their touring repertoire that would identify the group in no uncertain terms as an inclusive, Feminist (with a capital "F") collective largely informed by and strongly allied with a lesbian feminist agenda. In 1978, Spiderwoman presented its *Trilogy*, which included *Friday Night*, *Jealousy*, and *And My Sister Ate Dirt* for New York City's Theater for the New City. Even at this early stage in the formation and development of Spiderwoman Theater, I suspect, issues around identity, around story, and around communitism (seeking one's *self* through the discovery of one's relationships within a specific community) were already manifesting themselves and creating subtle divisions within the group, leaving Muriel to sift through their differences and to uncover and sustain the connections that would weave Spiderwoman's members into a tight community of artful activists.

As is characteristic of every Spiderwoman production, *Trilogy* was built upon the collective efforts of Spiderwoman's six member-artists, but it relied less on the intensely active collaboration between all six than preceding and subsequent productions. Lisa Mayo and Gloria Miguel each created and performed her own solo piece, while Verge, Weaver, and Beye created and performed *Friday Night*. All three pieces were produced under Muriel's direction. And with the multi-dimensional clarity that characterizes an examination of things past, the isolation of Gloria and Lisa from the others (with Muriel running interference in between) seems (at least, coincidentally) portentous: Within three years, just such a split would again occur, pitting the stories, concerns, and objectives of Gloria and Lisa as American Indian women against their white feminist colleagues. Once again, Muriel would be set betwixt and between. No longer would it suffice for her to "run interference." She would be called upon to *make a choice that would rest upon her identity, to make a choice upon which her identity would come to rest.* Muriel's choice in that delicate moment rests (as does her I-dentity), finally, upon the community/ies into which she had been born and to which she felt herself most urgently drawn to serve.

Described by one critic as a "trio sonata" (Sainer 99), *Friday Night* was an interdisciplinary presentation that interwove the inner lives of three women just trying to get through one night. With *Jealousy*, Gloria Miguel presented a "narrative portrait" (Sainer 99) of a woman working her way through episodes of jealous, blinding rage, which threaten to unhinge and/or consume her as she imagines herself as a "face like a fist" and as she strategizes the ways in which she might gain absolute power over her lover; at one point, she even considers imprisoning him. But as she works her way through this all-consuming rage, she begins to realize that she does not need to fantasize about her power: She *is* powerful, and the most efficacious expression of this power emerges from self-mastery. It is one thing to control another; it is quite another thing to control one's *self*. With *And My Sister Ate Dirt*,[15] Lisa Mayo shared an image of her life as a "cabaret" through a potent but charming cycle of songs and monologues. She had very lately come out to her public as an American Indian; she had publicly ridiculed the artful façade of

15 Does "dirt" in this title refer to the snails, given to them by Italian neighbours, which Lisa so loved? Her grandmother abhorred the idea of eating snails because snails consume the "filth of the sea." Eating dirt, of course, will most likely hearken back to the hungry years of her childhood. Children who eat actual dirt do so because they are lacking an essential mineral in their diet (often iron), and now in her ninth decade, Gloria ("my sister," here) requires regular treatment for pernicious anemia.

perfection she had constructed for herself; and she had claimed and embraced the cause of feminism (in the face of those who questioned her alliance because of her sexual identity, her role as mother, and her mask of glamorous femininity). Chronicling her personal struggles as a young, Native woman growing up in Brooklyn, Mayo wrestled and came to terms with parental rejection, with her need to be admitted to and accepted by white middle-class society and with her sexual identity.

Their *Trilogy* differed markedly from Spiderwoman's other shows, focusing itself as it did upon the isolation and loneliness that characterize the quotidian existence of contemporary women. And while the three pieces of which *Trilogy* was comprised externalized the inner lives of the women who created and performed them, it would be Gloria Miguel's *Jealousy* and Mayo's *And My Sister Ate Dirt* that brought its artists into a more comfortable communion with their isolate selves in preparation for the day when Spiderwoman Theater would become a company of three Guna-Rappahannock sisters, journeying together through the difficult psycho-spiritual spaces that had divided and isolated each from the other and forging the connections within and between these spaces to create bonds deeper than skin and thicker than blood.

In 1979, Spiderwoman's ranks swelled to ten with its *Cabaret: An Evening of Disgusting Songs and Pukey Images*, which they first produced for Theater for the New City. Muriel Miguel had originally conceived of *Cabaret* as a one-woman show, but after seeing the gay performance group Hot Peaches while touring in Amsterdam earlier that year, Miguel decided to expand the production and invited four other performers (including Peggy Shaw of Hot Peaches) to collectively interrogate the illusory, impermanent mystique of heterosexual romance, layering saccharine Hollywood imagery atop the sweet decay of the cabaret. And it was during their work with this production that Lois Weaver and Peggy Shaw, who would eventually form Split Britches Theater in 1981, began to explore the idea of working on a piece around Weaver's (Blue Ridge Mountain) family history. This piece would become the inaugural production from which Split Britches would take its name.

Unsettling changes were afoot. While on tour in Amsterdam that year, Muriel had come out publicly and to her sisters as a lesbian. And tragically, during the New York City run of *Cabaret*, Elmira Miguel had passed away. Although a married professional with children of her own, as the youngest girl of the Miguel family, Muriel had been precast into the role of caregiver to her mother. As Muriel reads the situation, by her very presence, Gloria and Lisa had been emancipated: They had been free to pursue the lives of which they dreamed, knowing that there would be one Miguel child to care for her parents and to carry on their legacy:

> My sisters left and *they became people*, White people, and they married, and I was the youngest and I was left at home. We were still dealing with drunks in the family, and at the same time, my sisters were giving messages to me that I had to improve myself. But at the same time, I had to be Indian. *There had to be someone left behind that was Indian*. (M. Miguel qtd. in France and Corso 182, emphasis added)

Each discrete life event surrounding Spiderwoman's acid indictment of the conventions of romantic love comprises an isolate layer requiring a narrative "thread-line" that will connect one to the other and so reveal the larger design and the impact of its inlay upon the identity of the individual and the collective artist.

By 1979, the layers of Muriel Miguel's "design" revealed themselves in a riot of vivid hues that sometimes clashed. She was an Indigenous woman with intimate knowledge of and connection to tribal tradition who sought, through her own artistic creations, to break with convention and challenge tradition. As Muriel was growing up, her older sisters had directed her artistic journey; now, she was their director. She was a feminist who had married and borne children, who wore lipstick, and who wondered if abortion is "genocide." She had felt herself to be "motherless" as a child; and as an adult, she served as the primary caregiver to the mother who had not mothered her. Informed by these experiences, Muriel had set out to form an American Indian theater company with her sisters and intimate friends – a "poor theatre" that would give voice to the poorest women in America (M. Miguel, Interview 2007). And this American Indian company would eventually include women of all ethnicities, world views, and sexual persuasions (wherein American Indian performers represented only 50 per cent or less – depending on the size of each cast – of the company).

Suddenly, her mother was dead. And who she had been (or felt she should aspire to be) in the maternal gaze had died with those eyes. Muriel had been released from the role of caregiver to a woman who had been unable to care for her. And while still and forever a mother, she was no longer a wife. She had been able to embrace her sexual identity on a continent far from the one on which she had been born, and which had contained and defined her as a woman and as an American Indian. When she was finally able to come out to her sisters – to reveal to them this layer of her identity – the impact of Muriel's revelation was considerable. Indeed, it is something that has been addressed and revisited by the troupe in testimonials from *Sun, Moon, and Feather* to the three sisters' final collaboration *Persistence of Memory*.[16] From 1979 onwards, Muriel Miguel would be an American Indian woman, a feminist, and a lesbian.

Likewise, through her work with Spiderwoman Theater, each of Muriel's elder sisters had also begun to connect the layers/strata of personal, sociological, political, and familial histories to reveal the hues and shapes of her own unique design: Each had committed herself through her life and art to her role as an Indigenous woman in the project of survivance and as a feminist in the struggle against patriarchal oppression. Initially shocked by their younger sister's Sapphic alliances, Lisa and Gloria wrestled with their doubts and struggled to accept their "baby" sister's choices. So too they struggled to remain open and cooperative members of a community whose interests and preoccupations increasingly subsumed their own, threatening to divert their energies away from the pathways they had chosen to follow in their own quest to identify and explore the questions that would lead them to themselves as artists and as human beings.

Before 1979, Spiderwoman Theater had identified and been regarded by its public as a "Feminist" theatre troupe, which included many voices and perspectives, three American Indian sisters, and *lesbian representation*. With *Cabaret: An Evening of Disgusting Songs and Pukey Images* and thereafter until its reformation in 1981, Spiderwoman Theater would be identified by critics, publicists, and reviewers, from North America and abroad, explicitly or implicitly as a *lesbian Feminist* troupe and often cited for "push[ing] the gay side of femininity" (Holliday). These issues around individual and collective identities had already begun to engender a struggle, which would lead to the 1981 dissolution and subsequent reformation of Spiderwoman Theater, and which would force Muriel Miguel to choose between allying herself with her biological sisters and her American Indian identity or to subjugate that identity in the interest of allying herself with her political "sisters" in the queer, feminist cause.

16 *Persistence of Memory* premiered in 2002. When I first saw the show at Miami University in Oxford, Ohio, on 20 February 2007, I had no suspicion that this would be the last time all three sisters would devise and perform together. This iteration of *Persistence of Memory* will be discussed in the final chapter of this book.

The Split

"We would never choose to live with one another. We're all so different," Lois says sweetly.

"No one is perfect," Gloria says.

"Not even Gloria," the others say. Muriel leans forward into the circle and says confidentially: "I really hate all of them." They all laugh. (Kafer 2B)

In 1980, the nine-woman troupe (including seven performers and two support staff) conducted a lively interview with journalist Kathy Kafer to publicize their New York run of *The Fittin' Room* and the troupe's legal skirmish with the Marvel Group. The tone of the piece was playful and redolent with Kafer's admiration, capturing the quirky, intimate banter between seven earthy artists and reflecting their quick-witted, body/bawdy-centred improvisational virtuosity: "The women write all their own material. Or as Gloria says, 'We throw ideas around.' (Lisa Mayo, Lois and Peggy Shaw pitch invisible ideas into the middle of the circle)" (Kafer 2B). But beneath the off-centre ribaldry that seemed to characterize relations between the members of this theatre family, subtextual tensions among the women were cheekily asserting themselves, belying the spirit of breezy camaraderie that the troupe was trying to convey to its public.

Issues around identity insert themselves with telltale frequency within the chatty performance of group solidarity that so delighted Kafer in 1980. In one instance, Lisa Mayo redirects a sequence of childhood reminiscences offered by Weaver, Shaw, and Eva Bouman in answer to Kafer's opening question, "What are they all about?" (2B). Amid pithy anecdotes about "imprisonment" with a pack of pigs, bombs falling in Amsterdam, and mind-numbing maternal platitudes of middle-class America, Lisa Mayo announces, "I'm Lisa and I'm a heterosexual" (Kafer 2B). This deceptively innocuous non-sequitur would certainly have been read by *News American* readers back in 1980 as a flippant one liner, perhaps carrying with it a dash of self-parody. But Mayo's casually flippant interruption carries a more portentous *edge*. Indeed, the power struggle that would tear the group apart was already well underway.

Lois Weaver, Peggy Shaw, Pam Verge, and Eva Bouman were growing increasingly dissatisfied with the heterogeneity of Spiderwoman Theater. The stories they wanted to explore and the community they wished to serve were lesbian. Muriel Miguel had recently come out and had encouraged, facilitated, and lately participated in the layering and revelation of a gay feminine essence within the group's creations.

For Weaver, Shaw, Verge, and Bouman, it must have seemed eminently logical: More of Spiderwoman's core members than not were lesbians; hence, it was only fitting that the troupe identify itself through its works and through public declarations as a lesbian, feminist theatre company. Matters pertaining to race became increasingly inconsequential to these women – inconsequential to the focus of the company's work. The Indigenous origins of the troupe's founding members, it seems, were only important insofar as they legitimized the troupe's use of its distinctive name and allowed it to "legitimately" capitalize upon the "exotic" identities of its "three American Indian sisters."

But in the realm of story, wherein the isolate artist wove herself into the community through, for, and by which she would be identified, a line was being drawn in the sand. On the one side stood those who adjudged that the lifestyle choices through which they declared their individuality should define Spiderwoman's works. On the other, stood Lisa Mayo and Gloria Miguel, both of whom have repeatedly stated that although they had come to terms with their youngest sister's homosexuality, they were not (nor could they ever be) lesbians. They had not signed on to a gay theater company: They were artists, American Indians, and they were feminists. These were the communities that claimed their allegiance. These were the stories they wanted to tell. And "Baby" Muriel was left standing in the middle: Muriel's task has always been to locate and fabricate the connections, drawing isolate stories into a larger design. Now, in her own *person*, she constituted the "thread-line" that wove these disparate artists with their disparate preoccupations into a singular female creatrix – Spiderwoman. Suddenly, she was being pulled from both sides; the fabric was unravelling.

If there was ever any doubt as to which of the warring factions with which Muriel would eventually ally herself, her eventual choice is evident here in Kafer's interview, peeking through the overt façade of a united, collective sisterhood; it is woven into the clear dialogical groupings that manifest themselves as the group responds to Kafer's questions and that mark a clear division between the Miguel sisters and the others. It roots itself in the story the sisters choose to share – the story that demands recognition and solicits public acknowledgement of the container of their individual and collective past, present, and future – belonging to those three alone and requiring the participation of all three in its telling. What are they all about?

> Three of the women are sisters, Cuna-Rappahonock [sic] Indians, born (literally) on the floor of their grandmother's house in Brooklyn.

"It's the Indian way," says Lisa Mayo, the oldest sister. "My grandmother put my mother on the floor on her hands and knees. She didn't call a doctor, because doctors are only for sick people, and she wasn't sick."

"My father buried the placenta [note that Gloria is speaking of *Muriel's* placenta here, and she helped to bury it] in the backyard. The doctor came to cut it," says Gloria, the middle sister.

"We sound alike, we look alike," sings Muriel, the youngest sister.

"I taught her everything she knows," says Lisa, sister number one. "I'm the most intelligent and the most beautiful," Lisa says. "I've been married three times. I would have been married five times, but two got away."

A grandmother, Gloria needs no prodding before she produces pictures of her grandchildren, children, sons-in-law and other assorted relatives. "This is Aaron," and so on. (Kafer 2B)

At first glance, this interview may be regarded by some readers as a colourful anecdote that asserts the "individual" quirkiness of each Miguel sister and that celebrates the heterogeneity of the troupe by highlighting eccentricities particular to each member. I read this, however, as a testament to the potency of Storyweaving as a process for both art and life and as a declaration of community, allegiance, and identity rooted in the disparate and common histories of the artists. The life of each Miguel sister is contained within one or more layers, separating each from the other: They are alternately heterosexual, homosexual, mother, grandmother, eldest, middle, youngest. One is separated from the others by half a generation; they have enjoyed/endured differing expressions of relationship with their parents and extended family; they have followed differing artistic paths; they have forged lives separate from the others with husbands, lovers, children, and grandchildren; they have followed differing spiritual paths at different times; their understandings and interpretations of past events, of current events, and even of each other separate them, also.

In 1980, for Kafer's readers and for themselves, they were performing their creation of *the* narrative thread-line that connects the disparate strata containing their lives. All three sisters were born on a kitchen floor. The umbilical cord of each sister is buried behind the home, still occupied by Muriel Miguel today. These cords bind the siblings – one to the other – rooting those connections deep into the earth, weaving them into their history, into a larger design. In their account of personal histories for Kafer's article, each Miguel sister followed a narrative thread-line, which had already begun to direct her personal questions, her processual approach, and her journey back to *self in community*.

Already accomplished "storyweavers," Weaver, Shaw, and Bouman performed their own narrative thread-line in this edgy conversation with Kafer. As latter-day twentieth-century women in America and as feminists, they cohabited these socio-political strata with all the Miguel sisters. Like Muriel, they lived openly as lesbians.[17] They had accepted and adopted the aesthetic methodology that defined (and continues to define) Spiderwoman Theater. They were committed to the exploration of the female condition and to effecting the social changes that would abolish female oppression. Likewise, they shared motherhood, marginalization, material impoverishment, and the courage to speak out with unabashed honesty and outrageous humour. In 1980, who and what Weaver, Shaw, and Bouman presented themselves to be seems, at first glance, to have emanated from the distinct spaces of communally shared strata. And yet, as each of these woman recounts the story of her beginnings, a pattern that differs markedly from the one crafted by the Miguel sisters emerges: Lois Weaver speaks of being raised "with a pack of pigs," likens her rural upbringing to being "held hostage," and characterizes her move to New York City as an "escape." Eva Bouman speaks of a traumatic childhood in Amsterdam during World War II, characterized by privation and falling bombs. Peggy Shaw wants "to get married," but her girlfriend will not comply (Kafer 2B)

Tellingly, the thread-line that connects these Euro-American artists is a mutual life theme of escape from intolerable circumstances. The bonds they have forged in the present moment of 1980 find their roots in each woman's rejection of her own history. Refusing to be contained within or defined by the communities that engendered them, Weaver, Shaw, and Bouman have chosen to find themselves within layers deliberately constructed by contemporary humans[18] and to weave themselves into a community of their own choosing and making. Ironically, this escape

---

17 Lois Weaver and Peggy Shaw fell in love early. It is not clear when Pam Verge and Eva Bouman came out (M. Miguel, Interview 2007). Muriel Miguel is no longer certain if Verge and Bouman had come out before the split or shortly afterwards.

18 For instance, while lifestyle choices and behaviours are regarded by many, in this time, as markers of an essential characteristic imparted to the human in the womb (e.g., one is "born this way," to quote Lady Gaga), European and North American individuals have for decades constructed "communities" within which a homosexual individual might safely live, work, and express him/herself in accordance with his/her essence. By contrast, Indigenous individuals who exhibited traits that differed from the gendered-heterosexual construct remained within the community of origin. They often played key roles within the social fabric, serving their communities as medicine people, visionaries, or nurturing intermediaries who balanced male and female energies within a society. Rather than being defined by lifestyle choices and behaviours, they forged identity and made meaning via service to and within their communities.

narrative was the common cord/chord that had drawn these artists into an artistic community, which was governed by a process that required its artists to revisit the very sites from which they had fled. But the act of following the dictates of this process (even within the limited context of Kafer's 1980 interview) revealed essential differences that speak to irreconcilable issues of identity. That which had brought Spiderwoman's artists together would tear them apart.

The Miguel sisters were not simply united by a common past; indeed, their troubled history had created *divisions* between them. And it had provided the motivation for each to separate herself from the others to transcend this past. Ultimately, the need (conscious or unconscious) to return *(together)* to this troubled history, to root themselves within it and to fabricate the narrative thread-lines necessary to situate individual within family, the family within community the community within nation and the nation(s) within the larger matrix of earthly existence would weave the sisters more tightly together, even as it separated them from the other members of their troupe.

In the months following Kafer's interview, tensions within the company had escalated to such a degree that the troupe embarked upon a "trial separation." As previously noted, a power struggle was erupting around the essential identity of the company, the community/ties for which it laboured, and the questions around which subsequent shows would be generated. As the troupe's founder and director and as a woman who strongly identified with the American Indian, feminist, and queer communities, Muriel Miguel grew increasingly aware that her concerns and those of her sisters (as American Indian women) were being pushed to the fringes of company consciousness.

Harkening back to this time, Muriel has noted that the working and personal relations within the group were characterized by racism and classism and that the racialized members of Spiderwoman (the Miguel sisters and Naja Beye) were outnumbered by the (seven) white members, the business manager, and production personnel. She had founded Spiderwoman Theater to explore very specific questions around race and class; now, it seemed this majority – the artists she had brought into her troupe and trained in her methods – were pushing against the very mandate of her company: "Everybody was White. And they were saying, 'It's not fair.' And finally I was saying, 'I don't give a shit if something is not fair.' Then I was a bad woman" (Haugo, "Weaving" 228–9).

The identity of the company and its mandate was not the only point of contention. Adding fuel to the fire, Lois Weaver had begun to challenge Muriel's identity/role as Spiderwoman's director/dramaturg. Weaver had her own questions and concerns, and she was pushing for the opportunity to take the helm, shift Spiderwoman's course, and to redirect the company's resources and energies into the pursuit of the answers she sought (see Jenkins 299).

Trial Separation

In the summer of 1980, Weaver received her opportunity. Spiderwoman Theater had been granted substantial funding to develop a new show. By this point, however, relations were so fraught that the company decided to divide the grant and develop two separate shows. Lois Weaver would finally be able to direct an exploration of her own family history, enlisting Pam Verge and Peggy Shaw to afford voice and body to her Blue Ridge Mountain ancestors. *Split Britches: A True Story* mythologizes the daily grinding existence of three female relations, who have been cut off from their other relatives – indeed, from the rest of the world – living as impoverished, marginalized eccentrics in a crumbling family homestead. In performance, live bodies frozen in photographic tableaux were layered atop projected family photographs. The narrative thread-line that (initially) connected ancestor to descendant was fabricated from the taped voices of living family members – each contributing fragmented stories coloured by their own interpretations of the lives and doings of these ancestors. In this way, *Split Britches* was able to weave layers of myth and meaning into the silent isolation of forgotten existence. As a queer descendant of those queer mountain women whose arduous struggle to survive is memorialized in the "split" of their under garments – thus allowing them to urinate while they stood and worked in the fields – Weaver (with her colleagues) would be able to utilize the layers she had discovered or created and weave them into the fabric of her own marginalized existence as an artist, a feminist, and a lesbian in post-modern America.

The performative layering utilized in *Split Britches: A True Story* remained faithful to the aesthetic methodology of Spiderwoman Theater. However, under the direction of Muriel Miguel, the stripping away of protective layers and camouflage in performance had *allowed* witnesses of earlier shows to make and interpret their own discoveries around the true nature of these layers and the nature of the core that lay beneath. Under Weaver's direction, by contrast, the essence of each layer was *explicated* for the audience, leaving neither space nor incentive for investigative engagement or opportunity for discovery.[19]

> Della: I got to have my protection. I didn't always dress like this. I didn't always live like this, you know. I got to have my protection. This here (*takes off her coat*) is for the North Wind (*throws it down stage*). This here (*removes apron, throws downstage*) is for the fog that comes in over the mountain. (*starts unbuttoning her dress*) This is for all the mothers that thought I was after their little girls. (*takes off dress*) This is for all the little girls my Mother broke me up with because they was … Catholic! (*throws dress at EMMA's chair, starts removing next layer*) This is for the time in church my brother was embarrassed because he said I looked like a boy. (*finishing removal*) And this is for the 25 dollars I saved up to go to the prostitute and I walked back and forth all day trying to get up the nerve. (Shaw, Margolin, and Weaver 82–3)

Here, Weaver's aunt, played by Peggy Shaw, continues in this vein to remove layer upon layer of clothing until she has stripped down to her underwear, revealing a vulnerable, abandoned, lovelorn, "butch" woman, slugging whisky and singing the blues. But while we have learned a great deal about the nature of and need for Della's protective layers, her ultimate "reveal" does not surprise (as Lisa Mayo's "reveal"

19 Cherokee author and scholar Thomas King reminds us in his 2003 Massey Lectures of the profound structural differences that exist between Indigenous and Western narratives. Here, in this early work by Split Britches, we see those differences quite clearly despite the non-Indigenous troupe's deployment of Spiderwoman's methodology in the creation of their work. Where the Indigenous storyteller refrains from inserting an authoritative interpretation ("this means this") and instead, invites auditors to make what they will of the story, the Western teller is often careful to dictate meaning and communicate the "moral" to a passive, accepting audience. While neither mode is aesthetically superior to the other, the latter strategy strips the auditor of her responsibility to wrestle with the story, to sift through its layers and to discover its meaning for herself. (I would add, also, that while such tellings often do afford great pleasure, the neatly packaged moral robs the auditor of the opportunity to earn and experience her own "eureka moment" and the rush of joy that moment brings). She has not had to work for the teaching, and so it may be easily forgotten or discarded. She feels no obligation to take this teaching out into the world, to act upon it, and to *own* the consequences of her actions (King 29). Muriel Miguel articulates these differences this way: The stories Spiderwoman Theater tells can be told from any point; their structure lies in the questions with which witnesses and auditors are invited to actively engage in collaboration with the storyteller and for which the storyteller provides no answer (Personal Communication 2023).

in *Women in Violence* did). Here Della's layers do not conceal the truth as much as they contain and repress what has been ever apparent to all.

In 1981, Pam Verge left the production and Deborah Margolin joined Weaver and Shaw to re-invent the character of Emma, drawing upon memories of an eccentric, unmarried, "scandalous" great-aunt to personalize the character (Patraka 58–9). The addition of Margolin and the subsequent success of *Split Britches: A True Story* encouraged its performers to transform what had begun as a "trial separation" into an outright divorce from Spiderwoman Theater. Naming themselves in accordance with the production through which they had come to terms with their own social and sexual identities by engaging with the lives of their queer foremothers and through which Weaver had been able to exercise her talents as director, Weaver, Shaw, and Margolin became "Split Britches" – a white, feminist, lesbian theatre troupe.

For their part, the Miguel sisters had utilized their half of the grant monies and their time during this period of trial separation to develop a show around the questions that had preoccupied them. With *Sun, Moon, and Feather* they worked through their childhood relationships with their parents, extended family, and with each other; interrogated their early socio-economic positioning as American Indian children growing up in Red Hook, Brooklyn; and worked to reconcile their individual remembrances of things past with their collective work in the present and their communitist struggle that would take them into the future.

While *Sun, Moon, and Feather* will be discussed at length in chapter 5, it warrants some brief introduction here because it archives a defining moment in the development of Spiderwoman Theater: Indeed, it marks the *historical moment when Spiderwoman Theater stepped away from its identity as a mainstream "feminist" or "lesbian feminist" theatre company and declared itself an American Indian theatre company* comprised of contemporary, urban American Indian feminists speaking with, to, and for Indigenous *people*, Indigenous ancestors, and those yet to come (see Haugo, "Circles" 238). Like their estranged sisters in art, the Miguel sisters developed their 1980–81 project around identity; unlike Weaver and her company, they embarked upon this exploration while playing themselves that they might *recover* themselves. The play's title signals this act of *recovery* as the Miguel sisters assume and assert their Rappahannock names – the names with which they had been introduced and announced to their family and community. "Sun" (Muriel), "Moon" (Gloria), and "Feather" (Lisa) are fragments of these names bestowed upon them by their Rappahannock relations. And while the primary question around which their creative investigations spiralled begins as an intensely personal conundrum ("How did we survive?"), it is a question that ultimately speaks to entire communities of Indigenous Peoples, whether these communities remain intact and relatively insular or whether these communities are composed of dislocated, dispossessed Indigenous individuals living together in isolation from their communities of origin in modern cities constructed by and for the dominant society.

4 Towards a Poetics of Re-Worlding: Becoming (and Then Staging) the New Human Being

I was very close to my father and my uncles and the men who came from Kuna Yala, and how they made me feel, because when they would come to the house, they would say (I was a little girl), "there's a little Tule girl; there's a little Tule girl; there's a little Tule girl." And I would say to myself, *"Geez, I belong somewhere."*

– Gloria Miguel, Interview 2007

"That Place that Indians Talk About" is No Performative Utopia

Contemporary Euro-American scholarship, by and large, posits the experience (and creation) of live theatre as a *liminoid* phenomenon – that is, as a "voluntary" experience, during which a pleasurable but *fleeting* moment of communitas may be experienced in a border interstice (a no man's land, as it were) that can only be imagined, and from which a rite of disengagement is required to prepare audiences to re-enter the actual (real) place where day-to-day existence unfolds (see Schechner, *Performance* 169 and Dolan, "Performance" 455–9). There is something profoundly passive, sadly ineffective, and highly discouraging in this vision of theatre as either a tool of re-visioning or of resistance. Liminal events, unfolding in non-Western cultures, are, by contrast, "socially required." They are understood to effect the permanent transformation of the communities in which they unfold. So, while the contemporary performative event may be invested with liminality (e.g., audiences may find themselves suddenly overwhelmed by an intense sense of communitas), the impermanence of its effect on space, performer, or spectator render it, in essence, a liminoid event.

As scholars and ethno-dramaturgs, Richard Schechner and Victor Turner scrupulously set the liminal apart from the liminoid (see

Schechner, *Between* 4). Performance theorist Schechner and anthropologist Turner characterize liminal events as "sacred" rituals involving personal or collective rites of passage belonging to and taking place in remote, exotic communities where bloodlines remain "pure," and tradition remains static and intact. In their estimation, the liminal event is neither socially required by contemporary theatre audiences; nor has it any place on the urban stage. The British cultural anthropologist Turner, whose research has significantly impacted the field of drama, theatre and performance studies, believed that liminal phenomena offer little to satisfy the developed palettes and passions of individuals living in "total" societies – societies, which are characterized by technological and socio-economic advances, that afford their citizens increased time and opportunity to pursue personal and creative development. Where the "less developed" society can only *experience* "collective liminal symbols," the more advanced society (governed by technology and industrial growth) has produced individual *creators* of "liminoid phenomena" to replace the outmoded, less "play[ful]" liminal event belonging to those disappeared or disappearing societies governed by "organic processes of maturation and decay" (Turner qtd. in Schechner, *Performance* 144).

However, even within these "total" societies operating within the urban superstructures imagined into being by the settlers of North America, the liminal event *is* fervently desired and desperately required by contemporary Indigenous Peoples who have been permanently transformed by the experience of colonization (Little Bear 84–5). We are perforce a *liminal* people, occupying the threshold between what was and what is. And in this historical moment, Indigenous Peoples have surged forward in the project to reclaim and re-operationalize the ceremonies that remember and recreate creation and the cycles of life and death, ancestral connections, kinship ties, Indigenous languages and Knowledge Systems, traditional dietary practices, stories and lifeways, and traditional territories, even as we remember and mourn what has been stolen, despoiled, or lost. The Miguel sisters are no exception. As women of mixed heritage, they are at once indigenous to Gunayala (an oceanic culture) and to an inland Anishinaabe culture from Virginia.[1] Growing up in an Italian neighbourhood in Brooklyn, New York, with

1 I use the term Anishinaabe here to refer to linguistically related peoples of the Eastern Woodlands. The Rappahannock are Eastern Woodlands Peoples. Their language is an Algonquian language and, hence, closely related to Anishinaabemowin. For further reference, see Paula Gunn Allen's *Pocahontas: Medicine Woman, Spy, Entrepreneur, Diplomat*. HarperCollins, 2003.

dreams of escape to Manhattan, they began their negotiation of cultural limens when they were children. In their adult years and throughout the early stages of Spiderwoman Theater, these negotiations continued until they reached a definitive impasse in 1981 when it seems all negotiations ceased, and a definitive path towards personal reclamation and the facilitation of collective re-worlding was forged.

To characterize the works of Spiderwoman Theater and of the many other Indigenous artists and thinkers who inform this study as "liminal" is to acknowledge that these works negotiate the interstices between pre-colonization and colonization in order that they might affect *permanent* decolonial re-worlding. Each Spiderwoman production reveals itself upon examination not as an ephemeral moment to be captured and preserved in memory only. These works are not dusty archives to be retrieved and celebrated as poignant signifiers of loss; they are living *cells* of a timeless body, which will continue to grow and change and to effect growth and transformation long after the individual founders of Spiderwoman Theater have completed their walk on this earth. The struggle to decolonize, as Hawaiian scholar Poka Laenui reminds us, is ultimately bound up in the struggle to re-form human identity – to create a community of *new human beings* (150). Hence, the creation of art that contributes to and facilitates this project of re-worlding cannot simply constitute the construction of "performative utopias" in which a social group may briefly retreat from itself to pretend to enact an ideal future (see Schaer qtd. in Dolan 457). Such a retreat into an indeterminate non-place, fleeting as it may be, could only undermine the Indigenous struggle to advance into our *selves* in "that place that Indians talk about."[2] And "that place" is an actual place. It is rooted in the traditional lands of the people and in the lands to which many were forcibly relocated or compelled to flee, as are the peoples' Traditional Knowledge Systems, histories, languages, cosmovisions, and spiritual practices. As scholar and activist Andrea Smith asserts, the struggle of Indigenous Peoples for the recovery of cultural knowledge and expression is always a struggle to recover the land and to restore harmonious relations between human beings and their biotas (121). Inarguably, the

2 I borrow this expression from Acoma Pueblo poet Simon Ortiz who uses the concept of "place" to map both physical geography and spiritual geography in his writings (Ortiz, "That's the Place" 46). He explains: "[T] hat place that Indians talk about" has sustained us and will always sustain us if we cherish and honor it. As a poet, it is important for me to strive to have my poems reestablish and reaffirm relationships among ourselves as a community of people and that community to know itself in relationship to all other forms of life, especially the land." (Ortiz, "That's the Place" 48)

phases of the colonial project, which include the destruction of Indigenous material culture and sacred sites; the denigration of the people and their belief systems; the belittling of their knowledge systems; the prohibition of their spiritual praxis; the exploitation of the people and the reduction of their material culture to a commercialized "fetish," effected the dehumanization of Indigenous Peoples to justify the misappropriation of lands (which could be regarded as *Terra Nullius* since the peoples to whom they belonged were no longer classified as human beings). The recovery of Indigenous humanity, which is bound up in all that has been denigrated, suppressed, and exploited, necessitates the recovery of relationship with place. Fleeting feel-good moments, temporary retreats from self, trips to no place, and representations of a hopeful future, which both audience and artist agree to be patently unachievable, may be powerful opiates in which the privileged (albeit disaffected) elites of the West can afford to indulge, but they are too rich for Indigenous blood. In the struggle to permanently recover the Indigenous *self* in right relationship, a timeless body of liminal works is required. And to mould this body, contemporary Indigenous culture workers need only look back to their nations' knowledge systems and the processual models that have sprung from these to discover the way forward, the path on which the human being advances to self.

Hawaiian scholar Poka Laenui and Gregory Cajete (Tewa Pueblo) have each provided us with a multi-layered programme intended to form character and to facilitate self-actualization. Each step they carve out for us on the path to self finds its foundation in something that has come before. Each of these models occupies its own layer in the fabric of Spiderwoman's collective works because each of these speaks to a specific human need. Gregory Cajete's educational model bases itself on traditional pedagogical praxis and so affords the opportunity to re-operationalize ancestral processes devised to affect the healthy development of Indigenous humans in right relationship with the human and other-than-human beings within their families, communities, nations, and biotas. Likewise, Poka Laenui's model turns its focus to the past that he might offer a vision for a future untainted by the depredations of the colonial project. Retracing and analysing each phase of colonization, Laenui presents us with a sociological model that prescribes a series of movements to be executed by the colonized body (individual and collective) in the struggle to actualize transformation in the formation of new human beings for a newly transformed world.

In his seminal work *Look to the Mountain*, Gregory Cajete consults and compares Traditional Stories from various nations to discover common archetypes, moral objectives, and structural frameworks from which to hypothesize didactic objectives and pedagogical processes belonging to pre-colonized Indigenous societies in North America. Although he does not use the following narrative in his study, I have chosen to offer a fragment of a familiar Anishinaabe teaching to illustrate and disseminate his findings. During a 1986 Drum Workshop on Birch Island, Ontario, Anishinaabe Elder Eddie Benton-Banai provided an eloquent teaching about the dream out of which the heart of Anishinaabe ceremony has emerged. When this dream is *performed* through its retelling (the drum teaching, which must precede the actual making) and through the drum's construction (in accordance with the original dream), it constitutes a *core ritual*, which generates all other ceremonial enactments of the Anishinaabeg.

The story begins in a chaotic time of violent warfare. One woman ventures out alone onto a hilltop. She abstains from food and water for many days as she seeks the solution to bloodshed and inhumanity, and she prays that the men will remember themselves – that they will *come back into their humanity* – and conduct themselves in peace and honour. So great is her faith; so urgent her prayer that Creator comes down to her, listens to her, pities her, and answers her. The answer delivered is a vision of the drum "suspended" above the earth, just as it is always to be suspended above the ground in ceremony. Creator communicates instructions around its fabrication and use – instructions that must be assiduously followed if this gift is to symbolize and to *affect* the communal transformation for which she has prayed: "Anishnabekwe in turn gave it to us with these instructions. And one of those commandments was that we, as Anishnabe men, should sit around that circle, that we should circle that circle, and that it should be a circle of peace ..." (Benton-Banai qtd. in Diamond 37).

At its core, this story reads, quite simply, as an instructional manual for the care and maintenance of the essential components that are the building blocks of our humanity. Structurally it adheres to the traditional pedagogical model outlined by Cajete: (i) Ask; (ii) Seek; (iii) Create; (iv) Have / Take Ownership of; (v) Share; (vi) Transform; (vii) Celebrate (*Look* 71).[3] The female intercessor, whose function it is to carry, bear, and train-up the next generation of humans *doing*, starts by interrogating a serious problem; she undertakes a journey to seek answers through fasting and prayer; makes the vision material; takes ownership

3 There is an eighth step in Cajete's model, which is "Being." I understand "being" or discovering the nature of our being (essence/identity) as the goal of this pedagogical journey.

of her responsibility to faithfully communicate the instructions she has been given; and shares everything she has been given. In so doing, she effects profound and enduring transformation within her community through the celebration of ceremony that has continued throughout the generations. Like the tribal culture heroes enumerated by Cajete, this Anishinaabekwe is a "hunter of a good heart." As such, she is one representative of a community's desperate search on "one path of human meaning" (Cajete, *Look* 59). As such, she inhabits only one of myriad tribal stories that teach us how to become the humans *doing* as we were meant to do.

Similarly, Poka Laenui's model of decolonization calls for (and facilitates the creation of) a community of new human beings. Although Laenui's stated objective is to create a model that speaks to the governance of a nation (as opposed to one that devotes itself to the development of individuals), he remains ever mindful that political reform is contingent upon social reform and that changes in political governance can come into being "only after the people themselves have sufficiently changed" (150). Drawing from a model of colonization set forth by the late Filipino scholar Virgilio Enriques, Laenui addresses each processual step towards the successful colonization of a people by proposing its alternative to effect a successful reversal of the process.

As Enriques has mapped it (see Laenui 150–2), the road to colonization begins with (1) Denial and Withdrawal whereby the colonial body denies the existence of a pre-existing Indigenous culture and some Indigenous individuals begin to remove themselves from their community and its cultural practices. The Destruction (2) of material artefacts belonging to the Indigenous culture (sacred sites, codices, art, etc.) quickly follows, and this lays fertile ground for the Denigration (3) of that culture (as a construct void of history, meaning, artistry, etc.). If, after this onslaught, any material artefacts or cultural praxis belonging to the Indigenous people have survived, these things are now held up as "Tokens" (4) and "tolerated" as folk art, which is ultimately co-opted by the colonizing body as part of its own history and/or Exploited (5) by colonizing institutions to solicit the cooperation of and exercise control over surviving Indigenous communities (Laenui 151).

Laenui's proposed model counteracts each of colonization's stages and charts the way back home for Indigenous Peoples. To answer the Denial/Withdrawal phase of colonization, Laenui offers (1) Recovery/Rediscovery; to answer Destruction, Laenui proposes (2) Mourning; to address Denigration, Laenui prescribes (3) Dreaming; to counteract Tokenism, Laenui calls for (4) Commitment (to a carefully and collaboratively crafted vision for the future); and to resist Exploitation, Laenui calls upon Indigenous Peoples to transform that commitment into (5) Action (152–9).

But where Cajete's model of traditional pedagogy is demonstrably applicable as a dramaturgical tool, which a close examination of Spiderwoman's *Winnetou's Snake Oil Show from Wigwam City* and its structure will later reveal, Laenui's model of decolonization applies itself less to one work and more readily to an entire canon, spanning several generations. It is a model for both Indigenous life and art, which are both characterized by the selfsame objective. It is important to note that Laenui stresses that the phases of decolonization do not adhere to a linear, ordered model. They overlap each other and repeat themselves again and again and again. Even as we dream, we may be momentarily overwhelmed by an unexpected onslaught of mourning; even as we commit to that dream, we may be momentarily paralysed by poignant reminders of loss; even as we begin to act on that commitment, our initial acts may be acts of recovery as we reclaim family ties; learn ancestral languages; learn our stories (or hear them with new ears); or devote our energies and talents to the recovery of Treaty Rights, self-governance, and tribal lands. Themes, phases, memories and actions, trauma and loss, joy and recovery may reverberate throughout the lives of individuals or their communities time over time. And this is important to think about in terms of Spiderwoman's work and the legacy of its artists as evidenced in the works of their daughters, their students, and their daughters' colleagues.

It is likely that Laenui never dreamed of applying his model of decolonization (which he has designed to facilitate Indigenous statehood) to theatre (Indigenous or otherwise); but it is intriguing and, indeed, instructive to vision his model as a communitist model of dramaturgy, which finds no parallel in Western dramaturgical practice. As it remains to be shown, this model applies to an entire project comprising the life and works of several generations; *these works are intentionally liminal* (as opposed to liminoid). And the "dreams" belonging to and reverberating throughout these works have nothing to do with "utopias" and everything to do with that actual "place that Indians talk about" – a place, rooted in both patent and spiritual realms.

Already, it is apparent that Laenui's model (constructed more than one generation after the formation of Spiderwoman Theater) traces itself throughout the map of the Miguel sisters' journey back to self. The early years of Spiderwoman Theater, as we have seen in the previous chapters, were years of Recovery and Rediscovery, precipitated by a profound, multi-layered experience of Mourning experienced collectively by all three sisters. Family stories, memories, and an intense, quotidian sibling relationship (which had dissipated in early adulthood as the women married, relocated, and started families of their own) were recovered in rehearsal halls as the Miguel sisters painstakingly remembered, rearticulated, and worked through personal stories and family history together. In this, they effected the relocation of this intensely personal site where they had first come to know themselves from Red Hook, Brooklyn, to mid-town Manhattan, and ultimately out to spaces of public performance across the globe.

The Kitchen Table: That Place that Indian Women Talk About

> In the house of mirrors there was a really big table. Around it could fit all our blood relatives and all our extended family, sometimes the neighbours upstairs or whatever Indian family was passing through the house of mirrors waiting to get back home after being stranded in New York by the outfits they performed with; rodeos, circuses, exhibitions. They brought with them the sounds of Winnebago, Kanawake, Rosebud, Hopi land and they would all tell stories about "Mrs. Mofsie, Mrs. Martin, Mrs. Deer, Douglas Grant, Blow Snake, Big Mountain, Red Wing." Stories that my eyes never saw but that I know. (Mojica, "Stories" 18)

If, as Spokane writer Gloria Bird and Muscogee poet Joy Harjo assert, the family hearth is the place of our spiritual and intellectual beginnings – the place where we first "actively listen through the membrane of the womb wall to the drama of our families' lives" (Harjo and Bird 19) – then it must also be regarded as a key site to be recovered and to effect recovery. It, too, is "that place that Indians talk about." Certainly, it is that place that Indian *women* talk about. It is that place that Gloria speaks about—that place around which her Guna relatives gathered, that place from which they saw her as a "little Tule girl" and that place from which she first began to recognize herself as a Guna person who "belong[s] somewhere" (Interview 2007). It has been recognized and reclaimed by Indigenous female artists as a vital site of our spiritual geography, which is thankfully laden with a movable feast that spans the generations and resists the relocations.

The kitchen table is also a site wherein the body and mind are engaged. Unlike the stolid, more formal dining room table, it is a place that invites physical action. Admittedly, at both tables, we ingest food, and as our bodies begin to integrate that food, our enzymes flow and a series of complex internal movements begin. However, in contrast with the more formal dining site, where roles are prescribed and action is restricted in accordance with those roles, the kitchen solicits physical interaction and communal participation at a much deeper level. Here, roles are more fluid. Guests often take on the role of host or helper, alternatively serving and being served with easy alacrity. Here, we can wave our arms, jump up to help with the pouring of the tea, the stirring of the pot, the clearing of the table, or the washing of the dishes and still remain a part of the circle (in ways we would not if we engaged in such behaviours in the dining room, where the server serves and the diner dines).[4]

As Indigenous creatrices (i.e., Lee Maracle, Gloria Bird, Joy Harjo, Monique Mojica, and the Miguel sisters) reclaim this space of day-to-day experience, of warmth, of nurturance, and of action as a hub of creative endeavour, the works and words conceived therein distinguish themselves in several specific ways. First, the words that are born at the kitchen table are borne on action. They require kinetic effort and physical articulation to achieve their efficacy. Second, the words, works, concepts, and stories that emerge from this site (such as Harjo and Bird's *Reinventing the Enemy's Language*) are *communitarian* projects in that they are collective creations, which include all voices from the circle. And they are perforce communitist. As they have been created within a complex web of interrelationships, they reflect and communicate those relationships and the responsibilities these entail. Third, although a precedent seems to have been set whereby it is the women who occupy and create from this space, the kitchen is a site of community for the whole family. Male voices and male perspectives are not excluded from the endeavour.

The male presence in Spiderwoman's works, for instance, manifests itself quite distinctly in the Miguel sisters' utilization of Guna language, Guna linguistic patterns, and Guna aesthetic expression, which they inherited from their father and uncles. These Guna men are also given voice throughout the Miguel canon. Uncle Joe's "Now, I telling you," which ends *Winnetou's Snake Oil Show*, and home movies of their father's sideshow productions or of his boat project, which are layered into *Sun, Moon, and Feather*, are only a few instances of many. These will be discussed in the subsequent chapter, which interrogates the published works of the Miguel sisters. For now, it is enough to consider that if we take all of these defining characteristics together, it seems that

4 Of course, the "server" who is often the host/ess may remove her apron and set down her serving platters to assume the role of fellow diner after a "liminoid" event, which accompanies her/his entrance into the space in this alternate role. S/he takes a place and becomes one with the other diners during a ritual of toasting, thanksgiving and/or both.

works produced within that place that Indian women "talk about" are *womanist* works rather than feminist works.

I recognize and honour the Miguel sisters' identification of themselves as feminists and of their troupe as a feminist troupe; at the same time, I hearken back to their testimony about the conflict that existed between themselves as women of colour and the feminists with whom they worked. Certainly, in their view, the feminist agenda during the troupe's early years did not align itself to the concerns of working-class women or of racialized women. Where whitestream feminists of the educated middle classes struggled to achieve political and material gains for themselves and for women like them, racialized women struggled for the "optimization of well-being for *all members* of [their communities]" (Phillips xxv, emphasis mine). Womanism was developed by African and African American artists and social activists (including Alice Walker, Chikwenye Okonjo Ogunyemi and Clenora Hudson-Weems); it remains today a communitarian initiative with communitist goals, and it speaks ultimately to a project of re-worlding in which the oppressive superstructures wrought by colonial agency might be dismantled. After many conversations with the Miguel sisters and much reflection, I have come to suspect that the term "womanism," which was not (and still is not) widely discussed in mainstream academic and whitestream activist circles, may not have been part of the Miguel sisters' vocabulary. "Feminism" may have been the only word they had to articulate the container that framed their struggles. But regardless of the words through which that struggle was articulated, the Spiderwoman process of Storyweaving and the womanist process of activism bear startling parallels.

Indeed, the processual steps employed by womanists to achieve social transformation bear remarkable similarities to the processual stages that go into the making of Spiderwoman's work. These steps include:

1. **Harmonizing and Coordinating** to reconcile seemingly disparate elements by finding and manifesting the connections between them;
2. **Engaging in Communal Dialogue** around a site of nurturance (such as the kitchen table), where all voices are heard, and all perspectives are integrated;
3. Engaging in **Arbitration and Mediation** to restore right relations and harmony. Disagreements are resolved for the sake of the general good (rather than to establish an individual's "moral right" or supremacy);

4. Engaging in **Spiritual Activities** to facilitate communication between spirit and material realms – again, with the goal of establishing right relations between these interlaid layers of existence;
5. Practising **Hospitality** to foster relationships between individuals and helps to build community;
6. Facilitating **Mutual Aid and Self-Help** by coming together at a grassroots level to share tools, wisdom, and strategies solve problems. For instance, Spiderwoman's visits to reserve communities to teach the troupe's methodology to the people were carried out with precisely this objective;
7. Committing to **Motherhood** by consciously adopting specific behaviours whether one has borne children or not. These behaviours root themselves in the maternal responsibilities of caregiving, nurturing, and mediation for the maintenance of a healthy and unified family; and
8. Practising physical (and spiritual) **Healing** with the understanding that when individuals are sick, families and communities cannot function optimally. This step involves self-care and caregiving. The womanist works to restore balance in the individual (herself or another) to restore and maintain balance in the greater community. (Phillips xxvi–xxx)

As African American scholar Layli Phillips observes, womanist methodologies have been employed and applied by Indigenous artist and scholars of all genders across the globe far "more frequently that [they have] been written about" (xxi).

Rooted in the struggle for social transformation, womanism is the anti-whitestream woman's answer to the feminist movement. Rooted in the everyday and commonplace, womanism requires a commitment to the restoration of right relations between human beings, between communities, between human and environment and between material and spirit (Phillips xx). And it is the kitchen table that has been identified as "a key metaphor for understanding the womanist perspective on dialogue" (xxvii). This understanding may help us to identify and comprehend the subtle instances of misunderstanding and/or dismissal of womanist works, which emerge from this material and metaphorical site, by early feminist commentators. Despite their commitment to CR and repeated avowals of the importance and value of personal story to the struggle, such commentators strove to remove women from "the kitchen," viewing it merely as a site of female containment and oppression, rather than a site of healing and liberation for entire communities.

As well, it may bear repeating (an earlier *caveat*) that the cultural specifics that underpin Spiderwoman's processual journey and the signifiers that manifest themselves in their performances have often been ignored or misinterpreted by commentators. Whereas a pre-eminent feminist scholar (who is among the earliest and most prolific commentators on Spiderwoman Theater) has seen "a patched quilt of multi-cultural images" as the backdrop to Spiderwoman productions and instructs us to associate this motley signifier with "poor theatre" (Dolan, *Presence* 168), she has failed to see (or to communicate) that Spiderwoman's signature mola, which has appeared in its every production since *Women in Violence*, should be recognized as a material annunciation of the Miguel sisters' recovery and celebration of Guna aesthetic expression. Such (ubiquitous) over-simplifications are misleading and dangerous, especially when they presume to explicate Spiderwoman's dramaturgical structure(s) and to interpret their distinctly Indigenous objectives and resultant product. Jill Dolan, for instance, has characterized Spiderwoman's productions as collages – a series of "pieces that are loosely compiled around various themes." And this structure, she informs us, "allows the troupe to explore and celebrate its gender and ethnic heritage" ("*Winnetou's*" 364).[5] She is one of many non-Indigenous commentators who have failed to apprehend that *it is the troupe's "ethnic heritage" that has engendered its process and the resultant dramaturgical structure*. As "loose" as the structure may appear to the outside eye, its "pieces" are not vaguely arranged around "various [random] themes." Rather, each production recreates a journey that has begun with one or more distinct question(s). And this journey does not simply "celebrate" the human being: It is, rather, an exercise of nation-specific pedagogical practices designed to facilitate the formation of tribal identity through the discovery of interconnection and interrelationship:

> Up north – years far away from the house of mirrors – I meet two brothers from the Deer family. "I know who you are!" one brother says. "When my grandparents died, there were photographs of your grandparents in their things." "I know who you are!" I say. "Your uncle is my godfather!" "My children know who you are!" says the other brother; "I tell them, 'that's your cousin on TV' [...] "I know – ." We knew. We are connected over three, four generations of Indian performers – from way back. (Mojica, "Stories" 18)

5 In her 1990 review of *Winnetou's Snake Oil Show from Wigwam City*, Dolan infers that other commentators "dismiss" Spiderwoman's productions for being "incoherent and diffuse" ("*Winnetou's*" 364). However, she herself declares in a later publication that the troupe's works "are often incoherent and diffuse" (*Presence* 60). Has she also decided to "dismiss" their work?

The pieces/stories/layers, which began around the Miguel kitchen table, and which now make up each performance, are not simply or "loosely" arranged around a theme or a question; they *emerge* from that question, and their efficacy within the whole rests upon the way they make, mark, or manifest the connections and relationships that determine one's place in the warp and weft of creation and hence one's identity within community.

It is not my intent with these reflections to imply that womanist methodologies, Cajete's pedagogical model, Laenui's socio-political model, or Spiderwoman's Storyweaving process (practised severally or in combination) constitute, in and of themselves, comprehensive blueprints on which to map a poetics of re-worlding that will speak to and for all Indigenous Peoples on this continent or across the globe. Neither should it be inferred from this discussion that the artists of Spiderwoman Theater *consciously* engaged with the models proposed by Cajete, Laenui, or other Indigenous artists and theorists in the creation of their works or in the development of their process. But the fact remains that from the example of the Miguel sisters' lives and works, we have acquired an invaluable legacy that affords us a clear, nation-specific referential point. From this point, the exploration and concentrated interrogation of and experimentation around the formation, applicability, and efficacy of artistic models within a larger project of re-worlding have already begun to occur.

The web here is complex. And what is wonderful to contemplate is how these models interlap and work together within Spiderwoman's performative mola, which constitutes the creation and staging of the "new" human being. As we have already begun to see, each of Spiderwoman's productions has been engendered by an urgent question (the initial "ask" step of the paradigm posited by Cajete). And as we shall begin to see, Spiderwoman's dramaturgical process evolves to accommodate that initial query. The Miguel sisters (and those who follow their process) do not take the floor (stage) to communicate answers; *they have been driven to each other, to the rehearsal hall, to the stage by their questions*. Indeed, each Spiderwoman production becomes a microcosm of Indigenous life (mapped out in traditional pedagogies) as it repeatedly retraces specific steps in the sociological process of re-worlding: Each production constitutes an act of recovery/rediscovery; each production contains an element of mourning; each production opens a window to collective dreaming and each show articulates commitment, translating that commitment into action.

Equally wonderful to contemplate is the geographical breadth of that "kitchen table," which extends far beyond the circle of light cast by the central hearth. I am speaking here of the connection with land, which constitutes a key layer of the Spiderwoman process, a process born around that circle of light and authored and developed in the studios and rehearsal halls of New York City by artists separated by one (on their father's side) and two (on their mother's side) generations from the traditional territories to which they are indigenous. Within this stratus of the Storyweaving process, connection and relationship are made manifest, as the new human being finds her *self* and the language to articulate that self within a remembered landscape.

Although, in this, the Miguel sisters have not consciously embraced and adopted aesthetic models such as those put forth by Kiowa scholar N. Scott Momaday or Chickasaw writer Linda Hogan, one aspect of their work, in essence, tests the ideas and claims of Hogan and Momaday "on their feet." Hence, within the processual web out of which Spiderwoman's artists weave the stories in which they make, unmake, and remake themselves, we may discern and will here unravel yet another thread, which is integral to the formation of the new human being.

Organic Dramaturgical Praxis Rooted in *Topos*: "A Different Yield"

> We are looking for a tongue that speaks with reverence for life, searching for an ecology of mind. Without it, we have no home, have no place of our own within the creation. It is not only the vocabulary of science that we desire. We also want a language of that different yield. A yield rich as the harvests of the earth, a yield that returns to us our own sacredness, to a self-love and respect that will carry out to others. (Hogan, "A Different" 124)

Many contemporary Indigenous performative storytellers have (as have the Miguel sisters) received much of our "professional" theatrical training in Western schools, specializing in variations of Stanislavski's Method or of Brecht's Epic Theatre, in European systems of dance, or in conservatories of Western music. Indigenous artistry, by contrast, has been traditionally understood as a *lifeway* – a spiritually mandated duty within the commonplace – and training becomes a lifelong apprenticeship for one who lives within or maintains close connections with his/her community. As theatre students, some of us have been subjected to "shamanic journeys" and inaccurate Medicine Wheel teachings, embedded into the curriculum by non-Indigenous teachers. In the Western conservatories, we have been taught that it is we (the human creatures) who invest meaning and significance on the objects that surround us – on "props" that carry our story.

David Smukler, for instance, is a renowned Canadian vocal coach who points to a prevailing philosophy that underpins much of the pedagogical praxis of contemporary actor training in North America: "Other societies that have produced great art have had a strong mythological and spiritual base from which to draw. We do not. Therefore, it seems logical that we exploit available sources from other cultures to make up for this lack in our own" (qtd. in Forsythe 70). In 2003, I participated in a workshop with Stewart Pearce[6] who was (at that time) the vocal coach for the Globe Theatre in London, England. Here, he enjoined us (regardless of our own spiritual beliefs and praxis) to get in touch with Wakan Tanka (Lakota for "Great Spirit"), so I was fairly certain that he had some familiarity with the Oglala prophet Black Elk or with the American poet John G. Neihardt who wrote *Black Elk Speaks*. Acting instructor John Paul Fishback offers students of the craft a "Shamanic meditative journey" wherein the actor's body is imaged as a "medicine wheel," and movement coach Jo Lesly "begins and ends each of her classes with a ritual action patterned on a medicine wheel" (Forsythe 75–6).

While the teachings of the Medicine Wheel (*and they differ subtly according to the terrain inhabited by each nation*) do inform a more profound understanding about the maintenance of a healthy, balanced life and healthy, balanced relationships between all interacting life forms, I harbour much doubt about the healthiness or efficacy of imaging one's form as this graphic representation of a complex and multi-dimensional concept. I am discomfited by the implementation of a *generic* Medicine Wheel (disconnected from the teachings of a specific territory) to be utilized in such a self-reflexive manner. While I can claim no specialist's knowledge in the teachings of the Medicine Wheel, I have come to understand it as a *lens through which we look outward* (as opposed to inward), seeing ourselves in relationship to the whole, and orienting ourselves directionally from our starting place along a *lifeway* that will maintain the integrity of the web and the survival of all. To adopt, piecemeal, many and diverse spiritual practices, which are not sufficiently understood, for the sole purpose of developing the actor's instrument – e.g., to "open the body" (Forsythe 75) – is exploitative and dangerous.

I was personally awakened to the dangers during the late spring of 2000. At this time, I met a young actor who was participating with me

6 Mr. Pearce offered this voice workshop in January 2003 during his visit to Toronto. While I was fascinated by his elucidation of the "sacred geometry" of the New Globe Theatre, I was confused and discomfited by his "authoritative" clarification of Lakota cosmology and his attempt to fuse the world view of the sixteenth century British adventurers with that of the Indigenous Peoples they eventually subjugated.

in a vocal workshop at Equity Showcase in Toronto. The instructor had been taking us (as per usual) through a series of exercises based in Yoga and in Alexander technique to open frequently ignored cavities in the body as repositories for breath and to relax muscular tensions so that overall resonance through the body would be achieved.

Before class one day, my talented young colleague sat with me in the sunshine and confessed an overwhelming urge to end his life. As our conversation progressed, he revealed that he had no idea why he had this urge. Life had been going very well; there were no interpersonal difficulties with family, lovers, or friends; his finances were in order, and his career was progressing nicely; he was in excellent health and just beginning to reach the pinnacle of his talents; he was not using drugs or alcohol; in short, life was good. He then went on to discuss a recent trip to Thailand, from whence he had just returned, and during which he had attached himself to a monastery and participated in various ritual observances. As he spoke, I remembered how he had discussed some of the meditation and relaxation techniques he had learned during this trip in several classes. And I remembered, too, that I had felt vaguely envious of him because of the exquisite quality of his vocal instrument. He, apparently, had learned the secret of opening deeply and filling those spaces with breath, and his entire corporal being resonated with great power. In class, while discussing his discoveries, he had seemed absolutely elated. Now the elation had dramatically dissipated. And suddenly his home (Toronto), his friends, family, colleagues, and the people with whom he came into daily contact seemed alien and/or hostile. He saw no purpose to his life – no efficacy to his endeavours.

I asked him about his spiritual beliefs, and his answers were vague. He had grown up as a non-practising Christian in a non-practising household. He had not really thought much about what he believed (if anything). His activities in the Thai monastery had been undertaken solely for "the experience." These "others" had interested him: They were quaint, exotic, mysterious. Their techniques had interested him: Perhaps they would (and did for a time) aid him in perfecting his actor's instrument. He had returned to Toronto feeling "light," "focused," and full of purpose. Less than one month later, his purpose fled, and he felt that he could "not face one more day."

I claim no expertise in psychology, Eastern philosophy, and ritual practice, or even in the Traditional Knowledge of my own peoples. But from the little that I have learned, this is what I have come to believe. This young man stepped over a threshold (limen) he had no business crossing. *For the sake of his artistry, he had engaged his being in a story he did not fully understand, to which he was not absolutely committed and for which he had not been prepared.* Westerners have a naively "democratic" understanding of the Oral Traditions and age-old ritual practices that emerge from Indigenous cultures. All tribal knowledge does *not* belong to all; all performative ritual acts are "not the province of the folk" (Allen 55). Dance, song, curing rituals, Chantways, and the specialized knowledge and story behind these things are fully known only by *specialists* – those individuals who have been chosen and intensively trained to carry the philosophical, cosmological and literary wealth of their nations. If even members, born and raised within the cosmology of a certain nation, know themselves to be ill-equipped for the acquisition of certain knowledge or of engagement in certain acts, it is indeed an act of profound hubris or naïve foolhardiness on the part of a tourist (even an educated one) to so engage himself ...

I believe that the sense of alienation and purposelessness that this young man began to experience upon his return had little to do with spiritual confusion: In this regard, he had, in his conversation with me, posed no serious questions. Nor do I suspect that he was being tormented by some malevolent force he had unwittingly unleashed. I surmise that the ritual practices in which he had engaged his being effectively "fused" him, for a short time, to the cosmic force governing the land and the community to which he was a stranger. He had experienced a *liminoid* transformation: For a brief time, he had become, perforce, part of a *whole* bound into the fabric of a foreign biota.

When he returned to his home, he was still (for a time) governed by a different set of cosmic forces. Severed from the biota out of which these forces emerged, he began to apprehend organically (although not then intellectually) that while he still practised the rites, the tie had unravelled. *He had engaged in a series of ritual actions he did not fully understand, locating himself (his instrument/his consciousness/his ability to focus) at its centre. And he had done this with one objective in mind – his personal development as an artist.* This young man had experienced the efficacy of his labours because he had been only part of the celebratory circle, centred in sacred space (land). And then he lost the centre. And when he lost the centre, he lost himself: "For without such a ritual fixing of a centre there can be no circumference. And with neither circumference nor center where does a person stand?" (Huntsman 85).

Misappropriative practices, undertaken for self-aggrandizement and profiteering, are not only offensive and dangerous; they are confusing! Brandon University professor and acting instructor James Forsythe posits that "in these times of increasing demands for accountability ... we need to appropriate the spirituality of other cultures to inform our actor training" (68). Just who is accountable, and to whom? Are the appropriators not accountable to those from whom they appropriate? Are they not accountable to the metaphysical forces they might invoke in the service of (even) a secular enterprise? Are they not accountable to those they teach, but to whom they will not "preach" (Forsythe 69)? Do they not bear a responsibility to disclose *all* – to inform their students of the significance of the acts they are called upon to perform, and of the original objectives behind and possible consequences of such acts? Is there not a responsibility to seek out and fix upon a *truth*? The same artists and thinkers who expound mightily upon the responsibility of the artist to reveal truth – whether it be in the revelation of emotional truth, psychological truth, and "scientific" truth in the penetration of the social mask or in the revelation of the economic and social machineries that govern human life – blithely discard the idea of a metaphysical truth, all the while selling myriad and widely varying spiritual practices to "complement actor training" and to facilitate a "search for structure" (see Forsythe 71). If this contemporary North American society does not invest spirit with any significance, if such spirit requires no real respect, and if this society, as David Smukler has asserted, has no spiritual base, why is such a base – and a misappropriated base, at that – required for the training of its actors? If contemporary Western society requires a secular story, should not the storytellers who serve this society develop a secular technique?

Indigenous artists within the Western conservatories are also taught that the ground upon which we "stand and deliver" is inconsequential: The human story is carried within, and the land upon which we set our feet is a mute, insentient vessel to support the storyteller or to enhance the telling with its sounds, its light, its colour. Never are we invited to consider the notion that the task of the human teller might be to serve as a vessel for the land's story. And yet, those who survive the training go on to rediscover their initial creative objective and to alter the processual lessons they have learned. Indigenous artists across Turtle Island are developing their own methodologies through which to create contemporary, urban theatre that is funny and mundane, rooting itself within the commonplace even as it invokes healing and transformation. In short, through a recovery of our own processes, we forge a path to that elusive place "that Indians talk about" wherein the commonplace is sacred and the limen between ritual and daily life has been dissolved.

> Once in his life a man ought to concentrate his mind upon the remembered earth, I believe. *He ought to give himself up to a particular landscape,* to look at it from as many angles as he can, to wonder about it, to dwell upon it. He ought to imagine that he touches it with his hands at every season

> and listens to the sounds that are made upon it. He ought to imagine the creatures that are there and all the faintest motions in the wind. He ought to recollect the glare of noon and all the colors of the dawn and dusk. (Momaday 99, emphasis mine)

In 1970, the Kiowa poet, novelist, and orator Dr. N. Scott Momaday introduced his "land ethic"[7] to a Princeton audience at The First Convocation of American Indian Scholars. His famous oration "The Man Made of Words" constitutes an explicit outline of the process, which he employs as a storyteller, and which, itself, serves as a structural model of the aesthetic literary form that it engenders. It is not a process he created himself; nor is it to be evidenced in Western models and teachings. It is a process, as Momaday himself testifies, which lies in "living memory [...] and the verbal tradition which transcends it" (97). It is a legacy passed down through the generations of the First Peoples of this continent, and it is the process that continues to inform our creative acts – be they on the page, on the stage, cut in stone, wrought in metal, woven in fabric, or danced upon sacred ground. This ancient process of Storycreation and its realization in performance continue to grow and adapt in accordance with the base realities of quotidian existence and the contemporary social and political constructs, which govern almost every facet of that existence. But its foundational core remains unchanging.

The Spiderwoman tradition is more than a rich exercise in Storyweaving. And it certainly did not begin with the theatre company that bears its name. It is a tradition, which pre-dates written history. It points the direction and mandates each step along the artist's path towards discovery, creation, and structural realization. Through it, the artist is able to aesthetically realize what Paula Gunn Allen has termed a "seamless web of human and nonhuman life, which is simultaneously the oral tradition and the thought of Old Spider Woman, [which] is neither causal nor sequential, [which] is achronological and ahistorical and [which] is simultaneously general and highly specific" (*Sacred Hoop*100). Further, as Gunn Allen reminds us, the primary function of this processual legacy inherited from all those cosmic figures who wove, beaded, sculpted, or plaited the world into being (even as it is being recovered

---

7 Here, "ethic" is used in the philosophical sense. That is, it connotes *a rule of natural law*, by which humans must live. The ethical action as it is understood here is the right action, the correct action. The Attic playwrights expressed this idea as "necessity," and it is expressed by Indigenous communities as alternatively "lifeway," "the Red Road," "the Good Rainbow Road," "walking in beauty," "balance," or, in Anishinaabemowin, as "Minobimaatisiiwin" – the way of living well.

and employed by contemporary Indigenous culture workers) is to provide the gateway to ritual through Oral Tradition (*Sacred Hoop*100) and thereby to manifest the interconnections between all life forms and the inextricable connection of all creatures to the lands they inhabit.

With mounting urgency over the past two decades, contemporary Indigenous theatre practitioners have been turning to and working with the lands that contain their histories. In 1997, Cree playwright/director Floyd Favel concluded, "I should bury deep into Mother Earth into the soil that has my ancestors [sic] remains, my work and theatrical experience. From here the earth and the ancestors, spirits of this land will inform the style, methodology of what the work shall be, how it shall define itself" (qtd. in Mojica, "Ethnostress" 22). But Earth and all her inhabitants, animate and inanimate, spirit and material, ancestor and descendant, life and art are not viewed as independent of or particularly distinct from each other. Indigenous artists do not simply look at something "other" for analogies that will inspire, adorn, or enliven their works. When one is a vital, functioning part of the whole, there is no "other." All is a part of self, and self is a part of all. The other is understood, then, as a vital "limb" – as inextricably bound to the human shell and as urgently vital to its existence as blood, heart, lungs, or liver.

In 1999, during a whimsical and evocative talk to precipitate dialogue around Native American dramaturgical theory, playwright Diane Glancy remembered herself airborne, looking down onto a frozen lake, its pristine, glacial surface clouded and etched over by snowmobile and truck tracks. To the many descriptions she offered to express the essence of a Native play, she added this: "A snowmobile on a frozen lake which is only sometimes frozen" (Glancy, "Further" 128). These tracks, notating the recent migratory history of humans on the landscape, are etched on to a transitory base. As Glancy notes later, the ice will melt. But it is compelling to consider that these notations remain forever a part of the waters that flow through the region.

Equally compelling is Glancy's later assertion that Native plays are "often orbiculate" ("Further" 130). That is to say that they are spherical, rounded. And this might be immediately recognized in the circular structure of many Native plays (and stories). However, this descriptor also infers the existence of spherical igneous inclusions, like the rings contained within a tree or a rock. Like the crisscrossed hatchings on frozen water that mark the migratory histories of Earth's youngest "children," these rings are historical etchings, recording the years and mapping the movements of Earth's eldest. And as "circles upon circles" contain the lives of the trees and mineral foundations of this earth, so the stories in which human life is contained and around which human identity forms itself have been discovered by the Indigenous teller to require the application of a narrative structure that expresses this sacred geometry. If the structures of the stories themselves are orbiculate, what of the lifeways contained/remembered therein? After all, "you can't fit a square peg into a round hole." Those igneous inclusions cannot be contained in a four-cornered structure and retain their integrity. As Indigenous Peoples throw themselves with renewed vigour into the project of recovering and reinstituting traditional forms of governance, jurisprudence, and social structures, many are remembering those traditional systems of governance and political organization, which by their own orbiculate configurations demonstrate the extent to which the people of each nation once adapted their own movements (physical, intellectual, social, and political) to the lands they occupied, rather than blasting those lands to adapt them in accordance with human will(fullness).

To illustrate, I share some fragmentary reflections of a teaching offered by Jan Derrick, Métis Kanien'kehá:ka therapist and educator,[8] during a governance workshop she facilitated in March 2005 at the University of Toronto. Derrick carefully explained the extent to which the traditional Kanien'kehá:ka socio-political system mirrors the orbiculate geographies of creation's oldest beings (rocks and trees) and how the identity of each Kanien'kehá:ka individual defines and expresses itself within the same sacred geometry. For this workshop, she did not rely on the efficacy of charts, diagrams, or even her words to clearly impart how the concentricity of the circle facilitates the support of all community members within this governance structure and the degree to which everyone's role was valued and held sacred within that circle. She utilized these tools to great effect but added to these a somatic requirement: If her teachings were to cut to the bone and live in the heart as well as the mind, we would have to experience them at all levels of being. Corporeal engagement would have to be part of the process of witnessing. I offer two rough sketches (see fig. 4.1) – visual and textual – to communicate both my intellectual and my corporeal apprehension of the governance structure about which Jan Derrick was speaking:

During the workshop, Derrick assigned the roles (outlined above) to each workshop participant. We were in a very large room, and 60–75 learners were in attendance. Derrick then positioned us within the circle, so that we would occupy the ring to which our "role" corresponded. The

8 Jan Derrick speaking at the Ontario Institute for Studies in Education (OISE), University of Toronto. 30 March 2005

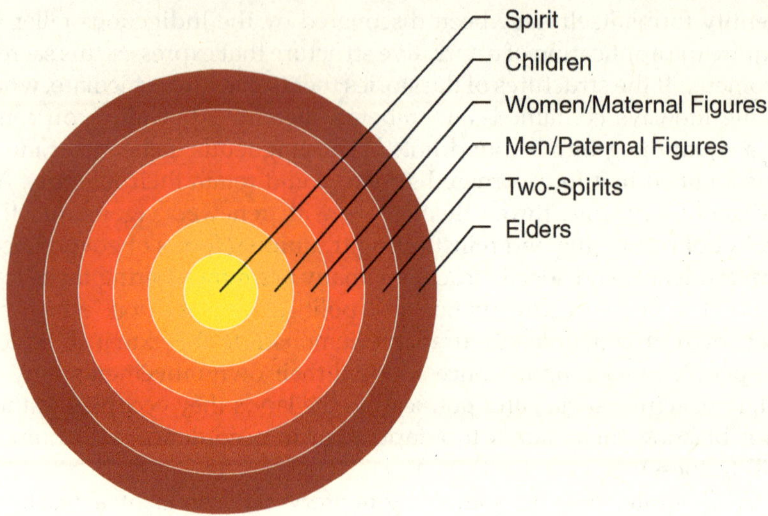

Figure 4.1. A rendering of Jan Derrick's teaching model of a traditional Haudenosaunee community. Courtesy Jill Carter.

innermost ring of our structure was occupied by the governing spirit around which the created world revolves. Surrounding the spirit ring were the children – the nation's future – closer to spirit than the adults as their emergence from that realm to this is more recent. Surrounding the children were those who assumed the maternal roles. Their task was to listen to the children (the future) and ensure that all provisions would be made to ensure health and continuance of the nation. The mothers of the community could then turn to and direct the actions of those who formed a ring of protection around them – those who assumed the role of father, husband, or provider. Medicine people (who were often Two-Spirit)[9] formed their own circle of protection and care around the others. And finally, the Elders in the outermost circle guarded and guided all. Established in our roles and positioned within the structure, we were asked to respond to Derrick's inquiries. What were we able to see? We could see everybody; we could see the community we had formed. Where, specifically, were our eyes trained? Every one of us was looking forward at the children – towards the nation's future.

As the exercise progressed, my body as well as my mind apprehended the degree to which this model expresses a dynamic geography where

9 Within this structure, it is the role (with its requisite actions) that one assumes, which determines one's position within the circle, not one's gender.

identities present themselves as naturally fluid. Derrick inscribed upon our minds and imprinted within our bodies the understanding that personal identity, defined by one's relationship to the whole, is realized through the enactment of one's role towards the furtherance of the community's long-term vision. We experienced how identity shifts over time, moving the "actor" through each ring of the circle as child grows into adult, grows into Elder, and finally passes on to become spirit.

I share this fragment of Jan Derrick's teaching here, as the effect of her 2005 somatic workshop constituted the genesis of an experiential understanding of the dramatic difference between a traditional Indigenous governance structure and the linear governance structure imposed by colonial agency. Moreover, to an (admittedly) limited degree, participants (many of whom were non-Indigenous) began to develop an embodied understanding of the deleterious impact this imposition had exerted upon Indigenous communities (human and other-than-human) across Turtle Island.

The teaching I carry from Derrick's workshop into this discussion is this: The landscapes, which were the first teachers of Indigenous Peoples, carrying the people's languages, histories, and ethical precepts and marking the moments to plant, harvest, build, hunt, travel, conceive and pray, remain the primary texts in which their "readers" can remember and recover ancient relationships to forge new identities. Perhaps, it would then be helpful to consider narrative structures, which express themselves as "circles upon circles," neither as exotic artefacts nor as self-conscious constructions designed to express cultural difference but as necessary processual containers (directed by and encoded within the earth) in and through which her human children might remember, write, and re-member the relationships in which the human *self* comes to be.

As culture workers who are each devising a poetics of re-worlding that is based in Traditional Knowledge Systems and land-based learning, Monique Mojica and Cree director Floyd Favel began, in 2007, to gather a team of collaborators to develop a specifically Guna dramaturgical structure based upon the pictographs, which notate Guna medicine chants. Their investigations have contributed an additional layer to the processual mola, which Mojica has inherited from her mother and aunties (see Carter, "*Chocolate Woman*"; Carter, "The Physics"). As Mojica has observed, artists from all nations might in a like manner turn to the birch bark scroll, petroglyph, or inuksuk – histories written on the land – to create their own dramaturgical structures (Personal Communication 2008). To this end, in the summer of 2008 Mojica and Favel assisted emerging Mushkego (Swampy Cree) playwright/performer

Candace Brunette,[10] as she returned to the community of her birth to create a foundation of land-based imagery around which her *Omushkego Water Stories* was to structure itself (Brunette, Personal Communication 2008).

Upon her return to Toronto, I had the opportunity to speak with Brunette about her experiences. With her collaborator Erika Iserhoff, Brunette had visited the land to listen and respond under the guidance of Favel and Mojica. They also visited relatives, community Knowledge Holders and Elders to learn about their own personal histories, stories of their human family, and stories about the greater family of non-human relatives that inhabit the biota into which they had been born. Brunette and Iserhoff then curated a performance through which to gift the community with their own retelling of the stories they had been given. As Brunette discussed the performance with me and her community's response to it, I was suddenly picturing a collaborative session in mola-making. It was as if Brunette and Iserhoff had presented the community with several fine layers of a mola in progress. As Elders watched and admired the skill with which these young artists had woven their stories into this work, they began to remember fine details and suggest additional colours. Where a medicine was discussed with reference to one or two of its healing properties, more properties were remembered, recounted, and offered as "layers" to thicken the story (Brunette, Personal Communication 2008).

Brunette's physical instrument (itself, an archive) not only carried and disseminated texts transferred to it by other bodies (human and non-human); it also facilitated (through the reverberations generated by its "playback" of the original texts to those other bodies) the recovery of vital, momentarily forgotten "texts." Suddenly, witnesses to their own stories were prompted by the scenes played out before them to recall additional fragments of knowledge that had been omitted in their original accounts. These fragments may now be added to the communal canon to be transmitted to and carried into the future by still other bodies. Chapter 6 of this work will explore this exciting phenomenon, the possibilities it holds, and the challenges it offers to Native artists and scholars who are committed to the project of personal and communal re-worlding. An Indigenous play, like an Indigenous life, like a community lifeway, cannot be contained by a single circle; these works are as a stone cast upon the waters; they are "circles upon circles"; they

10 Brunette studied with Muriel Miguel at the Centre for Indigenous Theatre in Toronto. In a 2014 developmental workshop of *Omushkego Water Stories* in Toronto, I served as the workshop's director, while Mojica served as dramaturg.

are many lives contained within the one and one life contained within the many.

Euro-American theatrical training also devotes attention to the sensory re-creation of land, life forms, and objects that exist outside the self. But such explorations are undertaken to discover how "the thing outside" feeds the artist's creative self – how it serves the artist's story. Hence, a theatre worker may invoke and re-create a geographical feature to enhance mood, inspire belief in the "given circumstances," or provide the solid ground in which to root the story. The Spiderwoman storyteller, by contrast, engages her being completely in the sensory re-creation. She "gives her *self* over," to become the empty vessel through which the land speaks. She dwells upon terrain that is intimately known to her in all its incarnations, through all its seasonal changes, in relationship to all its inhabitants. And the stories that emerge from her being after such an exercise are authored and directed by the image she has internalized. The land, then, does not become a convenient backdrop to the human story; the land is author and protagonist of many stories, and the human becomes the vessel through which these are communicated.

Techniques employed by both Euro-American and Indigenous storytellers to facilitate such sensory re-creations may bear structural similarities. Indeed, to some eyes, they may seem virtually indistinguishable. But the objectives, which fuel them, are diametrically opposed, as are the resultant presentations in both aesthetic form and efficacy. The Indigenous artist journeys outward, giving her *self* over to something greater than she. She allows it to work on her, to shape the story she tells, and to *reshape her* in the telling. Her technique becomes the vehicle through which the land can shape the individual in accordance with the content of its story and the aesthetic demanded in its transmission. These techniques, as the Euro-American artist generally utilizes them, afford no such transformation. The artist engages himself in finding the setting (and appropriate accoutrements) that will service his story; if necessary, he will reshape the landscape or re-imagine it to suit the story and facilitate its telling. Western story is born in and of the artist; and these – story and teller – are generally isolate, independent, and inviolate.

By way of example, I will refer here to my own experience in the professional world of theatre: I have worked with many collectives outside the Spiderwoman tradition wherein the storytellers connect with an image to create and develop an isolated story. Other members of the company observe its evolution, comment upon it, make suggestions, and ultimately find a place for it within the whole. The finished product, then, unfolds as a collage of isolated experiences, which may bear similarities in theme or shape. But each of these stories is *owned* by its teller. Even within the process that Richard Schechner has developed wherein actors are encouraged to try out various roles and to tell the story from different angles, ownership is established as the actor moves "from the 'not me' (the blueprinted role) to the 'not-not-me' (the realized role)" (Turner, *From Ritual* 93). The actor moves *inward,* utilizing the story as a vehicle to self, *rather than utilizing the self as a vehicle to a greater story outside himself.*

The storyweaver, by contrast, connects with an image, explores and internalizes it, and allows it to lead her without any attempt at accurate mimesis or literal transformation. She does not "become" a rock, a tree, or a wooden bust of an "Indian maiden." She does not look to "find herself" (or to hook herself into her own story) within these things (as Strasberg's sense- and affective-memory exercises train actors to do). Nor does she hold as her primary objective the search for truth in the "accurate" re-creation of what has already been created. These things exist apart from her. And although she understands that her existence is tied into theirs, she understands that, as the last and least element of all that has been created, she cannot presume that her story carries more importance than the stories of those others for which she has consciously prepared herself to become the vessel. Rather than looking within to discover herself, she seeks to discover and express the *cord* that connects the human self with all other elements of creation. She does not place undue emphasis upon her mood, her psychological truth, or her physiological reactions. She is concerned with the mechanics of existence, how each member of the greater community works upon her, how she works upon it, how balance is destroyed or maintained, and the ways in which she must adapt her being and its creative expression to fit the terrain and to maintain balance. When we apply ourselves fully to organic dramaturgies rooted in "that place that Indians talk about" (even in the exploration and revelation of highly personal and painful incidents), we begin to understand that no story is ours alone; all story belongs to the biota in which it unfolds. The act of re-worlding is a shared responsibility between teller and auditor alike. And this, too, is reflected within the Spiderwoman process.

Organic Dramaturgy in Action: Workshop One

On 22 January 2002, Muriel Miguel facilitated a Storyweaving Intensive at the Native Canadian Centre of Toronto. Although this workshop is not characteristic of all of Miguel's workshops where layers of the collective "performative mola" may be spun from dreams, true events, witnessed events, fantasies, or overheard conversations, it provides a lucid demonstration of organic dramaturgy as a facilitator of interconnection in action.

As it does in every Miguel workshop (and in the rehearsal studio), this workshop's warm-up focused itself on discovering and tapping into personal energy and utilizing that energy to connect the organic being with sky and Earth. Drawing upon her training in modern dance, Miguel led participants through a series of Laban exercises designed to facilitate connection (with energy from above), grounding (to Earth), and protection (from inner or outer interference and judgment).

After preparing the physical and vocal instrument, Miguel concentrated on ensemble-building through her own version of (Chaikin's) "Transformations": Participants each received a sound from another, replicated that sound (giving it back to its author), allowed that sound to transform itself within them, and finally passed a newly created sound on. The same exercise was repeated with movement, and finally participants formed two lines flanking a central aisle. Each participant was moved down this aisle propelled by a sound and movement that emanated from and drove her being. She allowed it to work upon and transform itself within her until she was ready to pass both sound and movement onto one of the colleagues who flanked her. This colleague would pick up the original sound and movement, replicate it, and give it back to its author. When the originator was satisfied with her colleague's kinetic, rhythmic, and oral replication, she would fill her colleague's position in one of the flanking lines, while this colleague allowed the original expression to work upon and to transform itself within her own being. When the transformation was complete, she would pass on her sound and movement, and so the exercise progressed until each participant had received, given back, re-created, and passed on a sound and movement. "Transformations," as utilized by Chaikin's Open Theater, privileged the "unconscious resources" of the actor and exercised the actor's "ability to handle a wide range of situations, acting styles and emotions" (Pasolli 20). And although frequent practice also fostered receptivity and cooperation between ensemble members (and was intended to do such), the development of the individual remained the paramount objective of the exercise. Ironically, this exercise, developed to free Open Theater members from the "grip of the Method" (Pasolli 21), was ultimately seen by its original practitioners as a tool to "[free] the actor to *be* the child {now *I'm* the grass, now *I'm* the queen, now *I'm* the king of the mountain, now *I'm* the cloud}" (Pasolli 21, emphasis mine). Chaikin's actor was ultimately trained to understand himself as "the king of the mountain," wielding the power to author and transform time, place, relationship, and personal identity.

The Indigenous storytellers in Miguel's 2002 workshop were also freed as we worked through the primary "Transformations" exercises, but this was freedom of a very different stripe. We were compelled to closely observe and actively listen to each other. Relationship and interconnections were privileged over self-conscious self-development: After all, it is in the connections to place and in the development of relationships to other selves that the Indigenous human establishes and develops his/her identity. Miguel's version of "Transformations" did not free the storytellers to work transformations; rather, it facilitated the transformation of our physical instruments (our material selves) into "vessels" of which another's stories could take possession and through which these stories would be expressed. The connection between self and other manifested itself as personal expression (that is, the personal story to be communicated), which emerged directly out of the relationship between the vessel (belonging to self) and the story (sound and movement belonging to an *Other*). And frequent repetition of this exercise, as it has been adopted and adapted by Miguel, comprises a crucial, preparatory stage in the craft of Storyweaving.

Before stories are woven, however, they must be created, recovered, or discovered. Whereas in rehearsals, senior students or experienced performers might bring in stories to work through with the ensemble and to ultimately weave into the final work, participants in Miguel's 2002 workshop first *created* stories and then worked through them using Miguel's Storyweaving Practice. Instead of a theme or concept, we were asked to work with a remembered tree. Utilizing sense-memory exercises, Miguel guided each of us into a potent encounter with this inhabitant of a personal landscape. Such an exercise would manifest itself as an "object exercise" in the studios of Uta Hagen or Lee Strasberg where a potent evocation of the "object" (the tree) would serve to strengthen the actor's belief in the given circumstances or to engender the evocation of a remembered story in which the actor is the "subject" – indeed, the protagonist – and the tree (as object) is merely a backdrop or a prop. In Miguel's workshop, by contrast, once the storyteller could see, feel, hear, and smell the tree, it did not remain outside and apart, acting as a catalyst to stimulate and inspire. Rather, Miguel's storyteller allowed the tree to enter and *take possession of her*. She did not *become* her tree; nor, did she *represent* this tree; she allowed the tree to express itself through her organism. The difference between seemingly similar exercises undertaken by Western Method practitioners and by the Indigenous Storyweaver is subtle, but it would be a grave error to dismiss it or to deny that such a difference exists. It is bound up in the opposing understandings of self and identity and in the clash of Western and Indigenous attitudes towards place and biota. And it produces strikingly dissimilar aesthetic approaches and strikingly dissimilar aesthetic expressions. Where the Western artist (like the Western explorer, discoverer, or landowner) possesses the landscape,[11] the Indigenous artist (like her ancestors) *allows it to possess her,* to direct her physical movement and her tellings.

Notes from a Kitchen: A "Processual Encounter" That Became a Story

> Behind my eyes my grandmother was stepping into my head
> I was still Muriel
> The sound of wind whistling through gauze
> The sound of my heart
> My heart
> My heart thumping
> The sound of wind whistling through my ears
> My head split open and fell to the floor
> My head split open and fell to the floor
> My grandmother stepped into my head and behind my eyes
> The voice
> *I was still Muriel*
> *The contour of my face changed*
> *Behind my eyes were* [sic] *my grandmother*
> *I was still Muriel*
> The voice, the voice, the voice
> The voice that went through the gauze and the blood and the heart thumping
> The sound of my heart through the gauze
> The voice, the voice the voice I heard from behind my eyes changed
> This voice changed
> My head split open and fell to the floor
> My head split open and fell to the floor
> My whole face became another face
> My voice became different
> I changed. (Spiderwoman, *Reverb-ber-ber-rations* 125–6, emphasis mine)

11 "Landscape," here does not just connote a topographical feature (such as the "tree"). I am speaking of an entire biota here, composed of all beings – human and non-human, living, dead, and yet to be born.

This fragment from Muriel Miguel's "Grandma" story of *Reverb-ber-ber-rations* does not recount the storyteller's deliberate engagement of and with her process. It remembers an actual and *involuntary* moment in 1988 when Miguel was visited (and literally *inhabited)* by an ancestor. Nonetheless, it provides us with valuable insights into the workings of Miguel's process. The storyteller may allow herself to be inhabited by something other, but she is not utterly subsumed by otherness. As Miguel testifies in "Grandma," throughout the experience of her grandmother's unsolicited visitation, Muriel Miguel remained Muriel Miguel – altered, perhaps, but nonetheless herself – looking through another's eyes. During the 1990 rehearsals for *Reverb-ber-ber-rations*, Miguel distinguished this experience from the experience of "channelling" in discussion with her older sisters. Her niece Monique Mojica had witnessed the visitation, which took place in the kitchen of a home where Muriel was a visitor. Muriel understood from Mojica that, during this event, her own voice and face had altered significantly. Later, she could never quite recall what she had uttered in this altered voice, but she always remembered that she, Muriel, had for a moment seen the world through her grandmother's eyes (Spiderwoman, *Reverb* Rehearsals 1990 Tape 6).[12] The lived ontological event manifested an unmistakable connection between the youngest Miguel sister and her maternal grandmother. Moved (literally, propelled) by an element of her spiritual landscape, Miguel's body (as a vessel of ancestral vision and voice, reverberating within) became the fleshly bridge between the generations, momentarily linking, her mother's mother with her mother's daughter's daughter (Monique Mojica) in a time and place this grandmother had never inhabited during her mortal existence. When, in 1990, Miguel remembered her experience to her sisters during rehearsals at the American Indian Community House in New York City, this foundational story of generational reverberation became a catalyst, which extended the original reach of the lived experience (bringing all three sisters into the connective web) and which produced further reverberations and infinite concatenations.

---

12 I am indebted to Gloria Miguel for providing me with the rehearsal cassettes in her possession for this production. As of this writing, I have been provided with rehearsal tapes 6–9 for *Reverb-ber-ber-rations* (1990). Upon completion of this project, these tapes will be digitized. All copies (digital and cassette) will be returned to Ms. Miguel who will donate/distribute them to the archive of her choosing.

"Processual Encounters" in the Studio

Moved (literally, propelled) by our remembered trees, we began to find our stories and give them voice in Miguel's 2002 workshop: Some emerged from personal memory (re-seen through the storyteller's eyes); others emerged as if they were memories of the tree itself (now bearing witness through the human vessel); others manifested themselves quite distinctly as fragments of ancestral memory (perhaps stories heard long ago; perhaps knowledge buried in the very earth – tangled up in the roots of a centuries-old tree who once bore silent witness – or woven into the DNA of a living descendant through whose veins flows ancestral blood and whose flesh has been composed of the same earth on which her predecessors lived and died). Some incredibly powerful stories came out of this process, but as a fellow student, I was bound (and remain beholden) to a community of trust. It was not my place to record these stories. Nor would it be proper for me to share them here. Instead, to more clearly disseminate this process and its possibilities (as I have come to understand them), I share a brief excerpt of *my* first experience as a workshop facilitator in Storyweaving with young professionals during December 2002 and January 2003:[13]

> After a group warm-up, I dim the lights and ask the actors to lie down on the floor. As they begin to relax into the space, I ask them to focus on a personal, remembered landscape. I ask them to explore it with their hands, to feel it beneath their backs, to smell and taste it in the back of their throats, to describe each minute detail in breath carried on sound, and finally to begin to adjust their bodies to the remembered land beneath them. Eventually, they begin to take in one feature of that landscape – a rock, a tree, a root, a vine, a stone, a blade of grass, a creature or insect. They take it into their bellies, like a coiled snake, breathing into it and speaking to me with sound on breath. The snake begins to uncoil within them, and as they feel it stirring, they allow it to move them through the space – to carry them through the story. They do not imitate the image; nor do they "become" the image: they simply allow the image in and allow it to lead them through the story. The space throbs with inarticulate sounds, snatches of song, repeated phrases.

13 This series of workshops conducted at the University of Toronto's Graduate Centre for Study of Drama (now the Centre for Drama, Theatre, and Performance Studies) was carefully and collectively transcribed. The work described here emerged from the exploration of a central question: "What happens to the children of Earth when covenants are broken and relationships to the 'mother' have been violated?" To protect the anonymity of the storytellers, no names are given here.

Bodies move through space, winding serpentine on the floor, kneeling, rocking, climbing on tables, basking in the light coming through the windows, cowering in shadows, skipping, dancing, punching walls …

Afterwards, I ask them to present their stories to the group. "S" (a non-Indigenous participant) begins, and I am fascinated as I watch her move through the space to recount her story. She takes us with her into a rainy, cold night after a long day of tree planting. Her feet test the frozen mud beneath them as she maneuvers her way around bushes and under ropes and tarps, wending her weary way back to her tent for the night. She shudders as icy rain droplets spill down on her neck and slide beneath her clothing. And for a moment, I can hear the same rain she hears as it beats down on the tarps in her camp and the whisper of the poplars swaying in the wind. She has entered the bowels of the "beast," and she has carried us with her.

Throughout this etude, "S" remains herself – a young woman doing what she can to "give back something that has been taken away" by eschewing a "real job" and dedicating her time and strength to reseeding the earth. Time and place conflate as we shiver with "S's" younger self, sharing the discomforts of exposure to relentless rain and penetrating cold. I hear the wind shriek and the "tarps [that constitute her shelter] rattle." My nose wrinkles catching the acrid smells of "diesel" and "scorched earth" that assail her nostrils. I catch myself repeatedly wiping my hands on my pant-legs, feeling the "ooze of life" squelch between my fingers.

"S" remembers a human story – the story of her younger self. And yet, even here – through the vessel that is her body, Earth speaks through and remembers itself: "This earth – this scorched earth – is written into my body." It has imprinted itself upon the "lines of [her] hand." It has imbedded itself under her nails. And as this human articulates her own human memories, a faint whisper of other-than-human lingers in the silences between her words like an echo. The stripped, scorched body of Earth – a body to which she has ministered – has gifted her with memories of what was and what could be again: "I plant trees and dream my dreams of a lush vertical."

It has been a long afternoon, and we are all exhausted. Before we leave, I ask them, "Why do we tell stories? Why is story important? Why is this story important?" I want to hear them say it. I want to know what this means to them. "G" (an Indigenous participant) tells me that we must keep the circle strong to keep story alive. She points to the many who have stepped (or have been dragged) out of the circle; to the many who have been ripped from their families, torn away from ancestral languages, pushed out of their lands … She mourns the links in our Oral Tradition that have been broken, allowing for the loss of ancestral knowledge. Our Elders were betrayed – manipulated into signing treaties written in a language that wasn't their own; they were told lies about what they were signing: "Once you sign your 'X,' that's it; everything's lost." She talks about the powwow circuit; the dance tradition seems to be alive and well there, but many dancing in powwow dance competitively for cash prizes. "Where are the young ones in Ceremony?" she asks. Traditionally, she reminds us, dance was an offering for someone. "When we Sundanced for healing we kept our eyes only on the central tree, 'the tree of life.' Nowadays, people host Sundances for money. They are selling our spirituality, and the 'tree of life' has no meaning anymore." "G" is an Indigenous woman, responding to the work she has witnessed by a non-Indigenous colleague. In her reading of the testimony inscribed upon and communicated by the corporeal archive that is "S," "G" has already identified a narrative thread-line that binds a layer of her own story to the layer offered by "S."

I hang onto this potential narrative thread-line: "the tree of life," the Sun Dance tree. I recognize it as part of the covenant we have come together to address – *trees and betrayal*. We are a multi-ethnic group of individuals who identify (at this moment) as women. We are Indigenous and non-Indigenous inhabiting variegated experiential realms but sharing geographical proximity in this historical moment. The integration of storytellers with the land and with each other is unmistakable, as is the intersection of their images.

"But what is the betrayal?" I ask at our next meeting. "Does it begin with lies? And what is the lie?" I want to know. "What engenders it?" In the Judeo-Christian story, evil is personified in and engendered by "The Father of Lies." In Anishinaabe tradition, the first gift of life is the gift of breath. To utter untruth is to corrupt that first gift – to corrupt life, itself. To lie is an abomination. What leads to this abomination? What feeds it? What fuels it? "I believe," I tell them, "if you look to the root of every lie, every betrayal, you will find fear. Go with the land. Follow the story. But this time, look out for the fear; find the fear beneath the betrayal, if you can."

"A" (a non-Indigenous participant) begins describing a woman walking barefoot in the darkness on a public sidewalk. She is bleeding from the head; she is disoriented; she is in pain. "She's trying to get away" from a person with whom she lives, a person with whom she sleeps, "a person who hurts her every day." As she walks down a dark and dangerous street with no destination, other than escape, in mind, her feet betray her and carry her back to the site of her wounding. "She walks IN HER OWN HOUSE" and wonders hopelessly why she cannot free herself from the violent story that has been roughly etched on her body, her mind, and her soul.

What are the thread-lines that connect "S's" story with "A's"? While it is readily apparent that "S's" story (previously recounted) has emerged from a remembered encounter with the land, we cannot be certain from whence or from what perspective "A's" story has emerged. Is "A" speaking from her own experience as witness? Has an "other-than-human" witness entrusted her with this story? Is "A" simultaneously remembering her own experience of partner violence and disassociating herself from it? Is she "I," or is "I" she? "S" has carried us with her on a journey of discovery. With her, the witness begins to apprehend and experience the complex and profound connections that exist between "S," a landscape to which she is not indigenous and its inhabitants, the (all too familiar) economic landscape in which she has been raised, and her relations who inhabit it. She emerges from this experience a child of two mothers – the human mother who tells her to "get serious" and to "get a real job" and the nurturing Earth who tells her that her "real job is to give back what has been taken."

"A's" story is a story of violation, of profound disconnection. The violated body of "A's" recollection dreams only of escape, and no helper appears to minister to its brokenness. Yet, between the two, a thread-line manifests itself, connecting a multiplicity of seemingly disparate experiences. "A" has presented a portrait of experience shared by women of all backgrounds in all times and places. Her emphasis on the violence that has been inflicted "IN HER OWN HOUSE" recalls "S's" testimony of violence that has been perpetrated on Earth – regarded as Mother by Indigenous Peoples on every continent. And it, further, strikes at the heart of Indigenous human experience.

As I revisit my experience of this workshop series, 20 years have passed. I write now in the wake of the Final Report of the Truth and Reconciliation Commission of Canada (2015), in the wake of the Final Report on the National Inquiry into the Missing and Murdered Indigenous Women and Girls (2019), and in the wake of the discovery of more than one thousand unmarked graves on the grounds of only three (and counting) residential schools in Canada (2021). I reel from the marks of violence perpetrated upon Indigenous mothers and their children "in [their] own house" as temperatures in Canada's western provinces soar to record highs, as their infrastructures melt in the heat, and as more than 170 wildfires rage throughout British Colombia (Jung). I think of the falling trees, the scorched earth, of violence, betrayals, and covenants broken.

"G" has worked with Muriel Miguel many times. She is well versed in the art of Storyweaving. So, it comes as no surprise that her experience and the evolution of her story within the process most apparently mirror Miguel's. Her first encounter with a remembered landscape connects her almost immediately with a fatally wounded bear, as she articulates its experience of dying. "G's" body contorts: It is as if this mukwa (bear) is "writing" the story of its death upon her body. Crying out from the pain and pulling back against the forces, which are drawing her/mukwa away from earthly existence, "G" rigorously enumerates each stage of the dying process. She is at once mukwa in his death throes and "G" recounting flashes of thought and sensation: "My body begins to twitch [...] The coil of my being tightens [...] Choking [...] Taken to a place I do not want to go [...] I have no voice."

"G" later tells us that while she began with the image of the wounded bear, she could not focus on anything beyond the entrance wound of the bullet that has ended this revered creature's life. The "bullet hole" became the biggest part of her being, and she felt herself being "invaded." This hole and the subsequent intrusion into "G's" being bear significant resemblance to Muriel Miguel's experience with the spirit of her grandmother who steps into her "split" head and settles behind her eyes.[14] Mukwa, we would do well to remember, is teacher and protector of the Anishinaabeg. And it is most wonderful and terrible to consider that the fatally wounded creature remembered through "G" carries her through a series of profoundly fatal transformations, which remember the profoundly fatal transformations wrought within her own family – within all Indigenous families – by an invading force. The "hole" in "G" through which the bear has entered becomes the hole through which an instrument of death (bullet) has been able to penetrate the teacher/protector of our ancestors. And it ultimately reveals itself as the "hole" through which the instruments of cultural genocide entered those ancestors. In death,

14 It bears repeating that this is not the same thing as "channeling." And it is not meant to be. Those who channel spirits experience a trance state during which they (as self-conscious beings) are not aware of what their physical instruments are experiencing, thinking, or articulating. They are utterly possessed by a foreign consciousness, and their own interior identity (consciousness of self and other) has been entirely subsumed. This is not the experience of the Storyweaver. A foreign consciousness may enter her, but interior space and exterior stimuli are shared and experienced by both the self that is indigenous to the body and by the entity that has momentarily settled in that body.

"G's" mukwa opens a portal into a story about the residential schools: "Being taken from your home, being forced to pray in a language you don't know, trying to pray in a language that's been taken from you." Through each session, "G" has allowed her body to completely lead her; her story requires almost no vocal explanation, but the voices that emerge from her during each phase of her journey are distinct and accord with each transformation of body, mind, spirit, and emotion that her "character" undergoes. I am convinced that her connection with this remembered landscape has tapped into information, which has been passed down through her blood and stored in the marrow of her bones. "G" has, thankfully, not had to endure residential school. I feel quite certain that although "G" has not planned this, she, like Muriel before her, has invoked an ancestor and that this ancestor speaks through her.

"G"
I don't want to go!
What? Why? Geygwya? Danagey?
Namoya!!! Moyspwatay!! Moyspaytay!!
Not me not me myneya MOYNEYA!![15]

What we have been reflecting upon here is the extent to which Miguel's process (as it is applied to the creation/recovery/discovery of story) facilitates and strengthens the connections between the storyteller and her biota. But it is in the weaving of disparate stories that the storyteller establishes and deepens her connections to her immediate community of "fellows." Through it, she develops an organic sensitivity to the imperceptible cords that bind one story to another and a profound appreciation for the impossibly intricate web that contains life entire.

Making Molas/Spinning Webs: Weaving the One into Many

During Miguel's 2002 workshop, the first phase of Storycreation connected the isolate individual to something outside of herself. Here, the storyteller consciously engaged in processual exercises to open her being/instrument and to facilitate this connection, whereas Miguel's personal encounter and ultimate connection with her grandmother during a visit to Canada came unbidden and unsolicited. This isolate experience was witnessed by her niece who remembered details that Miguel had forgotten and recounted those details, along with her own experience as

15 I have transcribed the nêhiyawmowin (Cree language) words and phrases here as their creator/performer originally transcribed them.

witness back to Miguel, thus weaving herself into this metaphysical fabric, connecting four generations of women. Two years later, when Miguel brought this story into the rehearsal studio with her sisters, this "fabric" became denser and more ornate as her sisters wove in their own stories. And later, this fabric would achieve even greater density and become even more ornate, as witnesses in the public space wove their own stories into these or wove these into their own stories by recounting their experience of the theatrical event to family, friends, readers, or students.

Even amongst theorists, this phenomenon is apparent.

For instance, in *The Explicit Body in Performance*, feminist scholar Rebecca Schneider credits Spiderwoman's *Reverb-ber-ber-rations* with tapping into and releasing her own "counter-memories" (157), the reverberations of which Schneider then "performs" on the page. Schneider reads Spiderwoman's *Reverb-ber-ber-rations* as a site of resistance wherein the newly re-membered, colonized body can subvert the colonial gaze through a series of counter-mimetic performative interventions by means of which the colonial construct of "primitive authenticity" is turned on its head. And as she thinks through this reading (on the page), Schneider remembers herself. She shares with her readers a late-night visitation by the disembodied spectre of a hitherto unknown "American Indian" great-grandmother (156–7). And she says of this experience:

> The presence of the absence of my forgotten great-grandparent underscored for me the notion that implicit in the visibility of my "whiteness" and Spiderwoman's "color" is a host of invisible bodies – a host of counter-memories that reverberate between us. And yet it is very important to emphasize that those counter-memories would reverberate *regardless of a Cherokee grandmother*. (Schneider 159)

Compelling as it may be, Schneider's testimonial here is problematic in several instances and warrants some interrogation. She tells us that it is dangerous to theorize about the body because such theorizing ultimately constructs a containment unit in which the articulated/explicated body has been "made appropriate, congealed, accessible and therefore safe." And she acknowledges Audre Lorde's indictment of feminist scholars who refuse to acknowledge difference or who deal with that difference by appropriating it (and hence the strengths that emerge from that difference) for themselves (Schneider 156). Schneider, then, finds a convenient way around these problematic issues without seriously addressing herself to the task of answering either Lorde's indictment or her own misgivings about her methodological framework. Instead, she divests herself of all responsibility by discovering a bridge – a long-lost Indigenous ancestor – between her and the bodies of colour with which she wishes to engage. Once this ethereal "bridge" has been located, however, Schneider immediately dismisses her as irrelevant and unnecessary: Although she is no longer just another white feminist scholar trying to write about, erase, or appropriate difference, it would not matter if she were. With or without her disembodied great-grandmother, "a host of counter-memories" would "reverberate" between her and the women of whom she writes (159).

Further, Schneider also seems to dismiss as irrelevant any cultural knowledge that may be necessary to properly read and interpret the "signs" that cause those reverberations to occur. For instance, what Schneider identifies as "a tape of Indian singing and Coyote calling" (153) is actually Paul Ortega's rendition of the "Trail Song," which was sung by travellers on the trails at night as a courteous alarum to warn those who might be ahead of them of their location and of their approach from behind. Spiderwoman uses Ortega's "Trail Song" in *Power Pipes*, as well as in *Reverb-ber-ber-rations*. It is a polyvalent signifier, which is as profoundly exciting as it is poignant. Spiderwoman Theater tells us that the spirits talk to us through ambient/incidental sounds (*Reverb* 102), and this play is about communication with the spirits and the resonance of their messages. Just as spirits alert mortals of their presence on the earthly plane with sound, so the Miguel sisters, in this performance, alert the next generation that they not only walk ahead to blaze a trail but will also someday follow from behind to support and guide the sojourner. What Spiderwoman is recuperating from the past is for the use of those in the future. It is their legacy.

Finally, it is troubling to note that while Schneider lauds Spiderwoman's "searing critique" of stereotypes and metonyms, her own "authentic" ancestral apparition could be seen in just such a light. Schneider's cryptic ancestor (cryptic to the point of invisibility) certainly talks like a metonyndian! With her catalogue of "certain Indian diseases" and her sensible injunction to "keep working," no Indian grandmother (who signs her name with an "X") could have been more ably constructed (156–7). Despite such misgivings, Schneider's assertion that the 1990 production of *Reverb-ber-ber-rations* somehow tapped into and released counter-memories that had lain dormant inside her body and Schneider's "performance" of "doubling back" onto the production the story of her own "remembered self" help to illustrate how this process facilitates the interweaving of individuals and communities through the stories they tell, the metamorphosis of passive receptor into "actor" and communicator, and the transformation of a secular site of entertainment into a space of remembrance, healing, and communitas.

In Miguel's studio, weaving is a painstaking process that requires intense focus, immense patience, and an unconditional willingness to offer one's physical instrument as a vessel of containment and conveyance for another's story. This is one aspect of "generosity," as Miguel's students and colleagues understand it. Generosity is generally not understood in the same sense by the Western performer who evaluates this quality in fellow performers in accordance with how much they "give" (the histrionic conveyance of emotion) and how "available" they are (how open they are to receive another's conveyance and how profoundly they react to what they have received). Miguel's performer includes these manifestations of generosity in her process, but she has deepened these by two layers. The first, we have already discussed. The second layer of generosity is, perhaps, more personally challenging. Miguel speaks of this as "the feeling of a generous heart, because [in this process] you give the story, and it's no longer yours" ("Performance Lecture").

In studio, the teller tells her story. Perhaps it is one that she has created in earlier studio sessions; perhaps, it is one she brings to the table (a lived event, a dream, a witnessed event, etc.). She utilizes her entire body and her entire vocal range in the process of the telling. Indeed, as Muriel Miguel has cautioned her colleagues and students time and time again, at this stage in the process, it does not work just to "sit and talk." The words really come when stories are put on their feet; action is privileged over talking (Spiderwoman Theater, *Reverb* Rehearsals 1990 Tape 9). The other performers witness. They must fully concentrate, as they listen and watch. Then the witnesses – each in their own turn – retell the teller's story (mimicking physical expression, tempo, rhythm, tonal changes, etc.). Hence, the original teller can readily see how her story has been received. She has stepped back and thus been able to view her (rendition of the) story *translated* by another. In her turn, she receives the translation, and she is offered the opportunity to adjust or fine-tune that translation. As each witness performs her reception of the teller's story, not only does the teller perceive how much has been absorbed and what parts of her telling have resonated with her witnesses, each witness is gifted with the opportunity to see what has resonated with the others (that may not have resonated with her) and what information may have slipped by her. Herein, a door is opened for rigorous self-reflection; so, too, is a portal carrying each witness into a more acute awareness of the sensibilities of her fellows, and hence, into a deeper intimacy with a circle of fellow creatrices.

As the process continues, the ensemble members offer themselves up in service of the story. Eventually, each takes on responsibility for one "bit" of the story, just as the flautist, the drummer, the cellist, and the bass player each bear responsibility for their musical parts. Like players in a symphony, each "bit" is orchestrated into the whole, and the original teller can add or omit them from the weave she creates. As this stage of the process unfolds, the kernel of story is located, and, here too, both teller and witness are drawn into a more profound awareness of *self* in the larger fabric of creation and their connections to the whole. By way of illustration, I offer up my own experience within a Storyweaving workshop facilitated by Monique Mojica in July 2006 at the University of Toronto.

Here, an Oji-Cree student told a profoundly compelling story about his two grandmothers (one Ojibwa and one Cree) to explore and to, perhaps, find some resolution for a conflict that had been plaguing him since he had made his home in Toronto. One grandmother, he told us, had retained her traditional ways and was trying to pass them on to her grandchildren. The other grandmother had adopted a more "Western" lifestyle, which was destroying her. She cut and permed her hair; she wore makeup; she flaunted her sexuality; she drank; and finally, she drank excessively. And she had (perhaps, without intending it) passed on her love of parties and her excessive lifestyle to her children and grandchildren.

This young man, attracted by the lifestyle of the less traditional grandmother, had left his reserve, hoping to immerse himself in the "glamour" and good life he thought Toronto held for him. But the "glamorous life" had taken its toll on him. He was battling addiction. He had encountered frequent incidents of racism and abuse from both strangers and intimate partners. This gentle soul had become increasingly angry, and he longed to lash out. Indeed, he stopped in his tracks at one point during the telling, planted his feet and strongly declared his right to walk unquestioned and unmolested on his own land!

Mojica had him repeat his story several times pushing him to punctuate each new thought or image with physical action and pushing him to inflate and broaden the physical score he was developing. Then, she asked each of the students to get up and replay his story, recreating text and action with as much accuracy as possible. The original storyteller watched carefully, noting what had been omitted (e.g., what had not been fully received) and what had most powerfully resonated with each of his colleagues.[16] I was one of those who witnessed and retold this story. And I was deeply conscious of my responsibility to this story – that is, my responsibility to receive and retell the story accurately without

16 Notice how this first stage in the practice of Storyweaving has evolved from Miguel's adaptation of the "Transformations" exercise.

adding to, omitting from, "improving" upon, or altering it in accordance with my aesthetic leanings. Nonetheless, in perceiving the connections between my own story and his and in perceiving what had been omitted, forgotten, or reconfigured by other re-tellers (many of whom were non-Indigenous), I had selected particular instances to highlight in my own retelling. For *me*, this story was about his right to walk unquestioned and unmolested on Indigenous lands, and it was about the reclamation and assertion of Indigenous languages. So, while I strove to recreate the story as completely as I could, I instinctively highlighted those things that had most powerfully resonated with me. After each witness retold the original story (in sound and movement), the original teller took the floor; informed by our reception, he re-worked the story to speak back to his witnesses by heightening moments that may have been lost in our retellings or to adopt the instances of heightened emphasis that he had witnessed. Thus, the teller teaches his witnesses who learn by opening themselves up to become vessels for his story. In turn, they teach him; they connect him more deeply to his story, perhaps by demonstrating the significance of incidents/actions that he had heretofore taken for granted.

Next, we sought to identify the kernel of the story. This kernel becomes the cornerstone to which all other stories may be linked and through which the connections between all may be perceived. This processual stage takes the form of a "jam session" – an orchestral improvisation, as it were – in which the original teller holds the melody line while his colleagues fill out the score with bass lines, counterpoints, and brief "wind," "string," or "brass" solos, alternatively playing by instinct and trying to blend with the whole and then, at times, following a "conductor," who in this case was Mojica. Each witness selects and becomes responsible for one beat in the story – that is, one action articulated by one (or a brief series of) sound(s) and movement(s) provided by the original teller. I chose, for instance, the very first beat in the young man's story: "Waaciye!" This is a Nêhiyaw (Cree) greeting, which had been so joyfully articulated by the teller with firmly planted feet and arms spread wide in an all-encompassing embrace.

Once the "musical parts" have been assigned, the teller begins the melody line. His orchestra may be on or off stage. If they are on stage, one or more may be instructed to begin an "overture," that builds to the telling. Alternatively, they may remain still and muted until they receive a signal from the conductor to begin their section. If they are off stage, the conductor will signal them to take a particular spot on the floor and articulate their section. All ears are attuned the teller and the other members of the "orchestra." All eyes are on the conductor and the teller at once. The teller continues the melody unchecked; the orchestra continues to play behind, around, above, or beneath the teller, working diligently to integrate each beat into a harmonious whole. From time to time, the conductor may call for the cessation of one or more beats during the "song." She may call for the cessation of all beats in moments, leaving the melody line to carry the story alone for some moments. At other moments, she may stop the melody line, allowing for an interval to be filled by one or several or all of the accompanying beats. Eventually, as the story nears its conclusion, she will begin to "fade out" the accompaniment. One by one, the performers leave the stage. The story may end on the melody line, but it may just as easily end on one reverberating beat or a harmonious blend of two. It is through this process – the separation and isolation of each beat and its reintegration (via orchestration) into the whole – that the kernel of the story is located.

As I have already mentioned, I had instinctively selected what, *for me*, was the kernel of the story (as had all my colleagues and, perhaps, even our conductor). And herein lies an activation of Jeannette Armstrong's "Enow'kin Principle" (see Armstrong 283). In a courageous and generous act, the teller has relinquished sole authority over the story, has made space for a multiplicity of perspectives, and has opened himself to multiple ways of seeing. Again, from my perspective the heart of this story lay in recovery (history and language) and in the assertion of Indigenous language and Indigenous Title. But while my perception ultimately was bound up within and integral to the whole, our "jam session" had revealed something else. *Through the ministrations of our conductor Mojica, the kernel was finally located and identified by the original teller as the particular beat that spoke directly to his traditional (and oft-ignored, oft-dismissed) grandmother: "My grandmother gathered the medicines."* Ultimately, I came to see (as I had somehow not seen so clearly) that this, indeed, was the cornerstone upon which recovery, conflict resolution, and reclamatory action rested. Through this process, we participants came to understand more intimately something about our colleagues – some essence we had not previously apprehended. We had been afforded an opportunity to see through the others' eyes, to witness what reverberated through the bodies of our fellows, and to reflect upon those resonances in light of what had resonated with ourselves: Enow'kin![17] Such a discovery might go far to restore relationships that have been damaged by misunderstanding, miscommunication, forgetfulness, or misinterpretation.

17 As previously discussed, Siylx author and educator Jeanette Armstrong named her creative writing school "Enow'kin." I understand this term as a reciprocal invitation – an offer to open the self to another way of seeing, and an invitation to another to share the speaker's way of seeing. It constitutes a gift to self and others of a multiplicity of perspectives (Armstrong 283).

In the rehearsal studio, each story goes through the same corrective process until its kernel is located. Then the jam sessions become more complex as two or more stories (with accompanying bits) are layered together in an orchestral movement until the kernel that binds all stories together has been identified. Tellingly, when we watch productions that have been orchestrated by Muriel Miguel, a central story emerges, which is either constantly before our eyes on stage or which repeats itself (or slivers of itself) cyclically throughout the piece. And it is to this centre – this base layer of the performative mola – that all other layers (stories) are subtly and often imperceptibly connected.

More often than not, that foundational kernel takes the form of a question, which must be answered with more stories. And these produce more questions, requiring the generation of more stories to generate answers, or "if not answers," then, "explanations and contexts" (Haugo, "Weaving" 222). The artist follows the kernel, "like following the pain" (M. Miguel qtd. in Haugo, "Weaving" 226). She does this to seek its solution, not to relive it or wallow in it. The emergent piece maps a path towards healing, and the fabric becomes denser, richer, takes on more colours. Circles form themselves around circles, around circles, around circles in a project that extends beyond one play, one performer, or one troupe; that extends, moreover, beyond the works emerging from one lifetime or one community, into a *liminal* phenomenon that tracks the spiritual geography of communities upon communities and of generations upon generations.

"Two Blonde Indian Sisters" Follow the Pain and Find Common Ground

I am in Paris.
I am in a garret.
I am standing in front of a vanity.
I am standing in front of a creamy-white vanity with a big, round mirror.
I have long, blonde hair.
I have beautiful, long blonde hair.
It is sooooo long.
It is soooo beautiful.
I am beautiful.
My skin is peaches and cream. I am soooo beautiful!
Then she comes in.
What is she doing in my Paris garret!?!
She is small and dark.
She loves me with a terrible love.
She hates me.

She is a malignant bitch.
She screams with fury.
She lowers her head and rushes at me.
She bites me.
She bites me in the stomach.
She bites and bites.
She bites and rips and tears.
Then I am running, running, running.
I am running on the *Champs-Élysées*
My shining, blonde hair streams out behind me.
My creamy cheeks are flushed.
My diaphanous, white shift floats around me.
"A pretty girl is like a melody."
I run and run and run.
No matter how fast I run, I know that she will catch me.
I hear her screaming in my head.
AAAARGGGGH!
"A pretty girl is like a melody."
I feel her behind me.
I feel her behind me, closing in.
I feel her behind me.
Her hate.
Her terrible love.
I run and run – long, blonde hair streaming behind me, diaphanous, white shift swirling around me.
"A pretty girl is like a melody."
I feel her closing in.
As she gets closer, the pains that rip through my belly intensify.
I feel her teeth.
I can't run any more.
At the wall – the stone railing – looking down, down, down – down into the water below.
I climb onto the wall, careful not to expose too much (*hikes shift down*).
I take a breath and think, "I can die now, or wait for that malignant bitch to catch me.
And when she does, I will die screaming."

The preceding fragment recounts a troubling dream I experienced many years ago and which I brought to the final phase of Muriel Miguel's 2006 Storyweaving Workshop at the University of Toronto. Miguel had asked us to bring in a dream to performatively distil and eventually weave into the dreams of others for a final performance. The dreams that were recounted were rich and variegated; there were nightmares, absurd incidences, and even the ubiquitous "naked in public" dream. Certainly, the images that emerged from almost every other dream connected these dreams at some level with my own. But within the workshop was Hindu playwright-performer whom I will call "Dhriti," which I am told means "Courage."

In the dream, Dhriti Dhiriti recounted to our group, she, like I, had long, flowing blonde hair. She combed her long, shining hair, which was "soooo long" that it stretched all the way out the door of our studio and into tomorrow; that was "sooo shiny," it lit up the world like a sun. Dream Dhriti was very sedate, sensual, and content – content to comb and comb and to admire her cascading, golden mane. Towards the end of the dream, without any emotional shift, Dhriti began to feel hungry; she tasted all sorts of delicacies to assuage her cravings. But her hunger grew. Finally, with the same sensual contentment with which she had revelled in her dream hair, Dhriti began to chew on her own arm.

Haunted, as I was by the violence of my own dream, violence perpetrated by outside agency (or so I thought), I assumed that the easiest and most logical course of action would be to weave my dream with other dreams of being attacked by outside forces (of which there were several) or with dreams of running (there were also several of these). But Muriel Miguel saw a thread-line that connected a common kernel that I was not seeing. She chose to weave my dream with Dhriti's, and we became, for the course of the workshop, the "two blonde, Indian sisters." Through this weaving and the subsequent rehearsals and discussions between Dhriti and myself, I came finally to discover the link that Miguel had initially perceived and pursued. My discussions with Dhriti (conducted at our own makeshift "kitchen table") began to concern themselves more and more with the stories of our mothers and grandmothers and with our own experiences as survivors of the colonial project. Through the stories, two passing acquaintances – born a half a world away from each other – identified the deeply buried shame we were carrying (symptoms of our internal colonization) and the self-destructive impulses (and acts) precipitated within us, against which we were obliged to fight if we were to survive. As our dreams were interwoven, a Hindu woman and an Anishinaabekwe discovered the threads and fragments within their stories that connected them as "sisters" and that linked their communities.

"Re-inventing the Enemy's Language": Making Molas Out of Words

Even within the context of this abbreviated introduction to the craft of Storyweaving, the Guna Gathering House Tradition, which has informed the narrative artistry of the Miguel sisters' father and uncles, manifested a powerful and unmistakable presence in the downtown rehearsal studio that housed Miguel's Toronto workshop series. It subtly insinuated itself in Miguel's attention to specific metaphors, which she drove participants to push orally and kinetically, to elongate and to repeatedly duplicate with slight changes in each "panel" of our narrative molas. Not coincidentally, linguist Joel Sherzer has observed that Guna linguistic patterns (emerging from the narrative traditions of the Gathering House) resemble the patterns that occur in Guna visual arts – particularly molas (118). The Guna people have long regarded the length of a narrative as a marker of its quality, just as they assess the quality of a mola by its thickness. Linguistically, extreme attention to fine detail, repetition, and parallelism have long been the favoured devices for thickening the narrative – for creating the "layers" that lengthen its telling (Sherzer 112). The most skilled orators in Guna Gathering Houses easily send their auditors into fits of laughter by inflating the most pedestrian experiences with exaggerated detail and painful repetition (Sherzer 113). Hence in this workshop, under Miguel's prodding, the long, blonde hair of which Dhriti had dreamed became soooo long that it stretched first across our downtown rehearsal studio, then out the door, down a long passageway, and into the neighbouring theatre, and finally "into tomorrow." Nor was the hair of Dhriti's dream simply "blonde." As she combed and combed and combed it out, it became progressively more golden; it shone like the sun; it lit up the world! As Dhriti explored what had begun quite simply as "long, blonde hair," repeating its life through her body and repeatedly sounding its life on her breath, she stretched a lovely (but pedestrian) detail into a glorious metaphor, and this metaphor commanded wholehearted celebration in the absolute dedication of the performer's entire instrument.

American anthropologist Mari Lyn Salvador has located the point of connection between the mola and Guna narrative arts (Gathering House Tradition) in the place of their making – the communal "kitchen table": in Gunayala, women often sew their molas at the Gathering House while listening to a visiting Sagla (Chief) "chant about the history of mola making" or while listening to "a discussion centered around some aspect of women and their arts" (170–1). I do not conclude from Salvador's observation, however, that the mola-maker somehow takes her inspiration and guidance from the narrative soundscapes that sweeten her labours – that is, I do not suggest that the mola is formed in and by the language. Instead, I have come to regard the complex relation between textile and text as a reciprocal affair grounded in mutual interdependency. Whether the Guna artisan shapes text or textile, his/her labours are guided by the same principles; after all, in Guna cosmology all life plays itself out within and betwixt intricately connected layers of patent and metaphysical existence. And the Guna lifeway, at every level of expression (narrative expression, ceremony, artisanship, social and political interaction) configures itself to negotiate those layers with the utmost grace and respect.[18] Just as the mola is characterized by the repetition of visual motifs, which are subtly altered with each manifestation (so that with a mola shirt, which consists of near-identical front and back panels, the same motif may manifest itself four to eight times on the body of its wearer), "motifs in Guna narratives are presented in units of four and ritual activities are repeated four or eight times" (Salvador 187).

In Spiderwoman's *Reverb-ber-ber-rations*, for instance, which constitutes the Miguel sisters' reclamation and assertion of their spiritual inheritance, both the "tea scene" and the "noise band" are each repeated four times throughout the play with subtle variations. And we would be remiss in dismissing these as merely "happy accidents." Chapter 5 will explore with greater rigour how Guna ceremonial life, narrative, and aesthetic conventions and curing tradition intersect with and inform Spiderwoman's *Reverb-ber-ber-rations* and *Power Pipes*. For now, however, it is exciting to consider the possibility that the Guna-Rappahannock founders of Spiderwoman Theater first began to adopt Guna linguistic devices and aesthetic patterns organically – without conscious intent. Perhaps, the Miguel sisters began by instinctively imitating the narrative stylings of their Guna relatives. But it was certainly a conscious choice to bring the *kitchen table* into the rehearsal studio, just as their father and uncles had brought the Gathering House of Nargana to that kitchen table in Red Hook, Brooklyn.[19]

---

18 To illustrate, the intricate system of curing rituals practised by Guna specialists is the cornerstone of Guna culture (Chapin 219). This system is predicated upon the understanding that the material world, which we occupy, is only one layer – and a secondary layer, at that – of a multi-layered spirit world that underlies the tangible world and animates it with its life force (Chapin 219). During rehearsals for the first workshop of Monique Mojica's *Chocolate Woman Dreams the Milky Way* (November 2007), Oswaldo DeLeón Kantule recited medicine chants to the company and carefully showed and explained various pictographic symbols denoting illness, medicine plants (cacao, tobacco), Baba Nana (the fe/male deity), and cosmological layers. Later, he shared a pictographic notation of a medicine chant, which clearly revealed the depth of specialized knowledge required to gather botanical medicines (seemingly from this terrestrial stratus). Readers interested in exploring such notations might refer to the *Acualel* (see Severi 264).

Immense courage and skill are required to harvest medicine from the earth – medicine that emerges from the fourth layer of the cosmos. "To effect healing, [the Guna specialist] must be prepared to dig deeply and to negotiate the densely complex layers of patent and metaphysical existence" (Carter, "*Chocolate*" 7).

19 Nargana is the island in Gunayala on which Antonio Miguel was born.

Negotiating the Textual Archive: The Road Ahead ...

> Each story is an idea in which we are embodied and when that idea is realized in language – I use this word in its broadest sense – then it becomes the vehicle by means of which we can "take possession" of ourselves. (Momaday 104)

In the chapter that follows we shall, at last, undertake an examination of Spiderwoman's published plays. These are the only publicly accessible textual archives, which constitute more or less complete transcriptions of the troupe's performative events.[20] As such, they differ from many other instances of dramatic literature, which have been first "performed" by characters on the page and then bodily transcribed by the living archive. Spiderwoman's texts "embody," as it were, the Miguel sisters' kinetic and linguistic realization of the ideas that embodied – or more often, disembodied, distorted, or dis-eased – them. They document each stage of a specific journey, undertaken by specific individuals towards personal and communal decolonization in that each transcription charts the mechanics of a "vehicle," which conveys its artists yet another step closer to self.

Sun, Moon, and Feather (1981) marks the rebirth of Spiderwoman Theater as an Indigenous theatre company and constitutes a definitive and conscious act of *recovery*. In this piece the Miguel sisters, re-member and declare the Rappahannock names they received at birth as they recover, deconstruct, and then reconstruct (through Storyweaving) personal and family histories. I imagine it as the vehicle through which the Miguel sisters began to take possession of themselves as American Indian women and to take possession of the ties that inextricably bind them to each other, to their family of origin, to their communities of origin, to the communities in which they have lived, and to the communities to which they hold themselves responsible.

Sun, Moon, and Feather also marks the beginnings of an intense engagement with a blend of specifically Indigenous aesthetic and pedagogical processes that enable the individual to take possession of her identity even as the greater community (immediate family, clan, community, nation, biota) takes possession of her. The following chapter will continue to engage with these processes and to specifically identify the connections between the performance transcriptions and the

---

20 As this book goes to press, *Material Witness* has just been published in a third anthology of *Staging Coyote's Dream* (Playwrights Canada, 2024).

processual stages towards decolonization (re-worlding), as Poka Laenui has mapped them out.

While the Miguel sisters' first explicitly "Indian" play may be viewed as an act of *personal* recovery, their next published play, *Winnetou's Snake Oil Show from Wigwam City*, is emblematic of a *communal* recovery. This piece they created at the specific behest of the Circle of Elders in 1988. In this year, Elders and invited participants had set themselves the task of confronting and neutralizing a growing circle of "plastic shamans" who were publishing "authoritative" accounts of Native spirituality; conducting workshops; and organizing and leading "authentic" Native ceremonies – curated rituals, which purported to purify, heal, or enlighten the individuals who paid enormous sums to attend. The Circle of Elders challenged Spiderwoman Theater by asking its members what they, as artists, were going to do about the problem of "plastic shamanism." Although they were outraged by what they had already witnessed in their own lives and what they were hearing at the Circle of Elders, the Miguel sisters had not specifically planned to *do* anything about this phenomenon. But answering the call of the Elders who spoke for hundreds of Indigenous nations across Turtle Island, they set to work and created one of the most potent and influential pieces in the troupe's history – *Winnetou's Snake Oil Show from Wigwam City*.

Mining the roots and exploring the sites and consequences of misappropriation in their *Snake Oil Show*, the Miguel sisters *remind us to remember* a more authentic Indigenous spirituality, as they recover the woman's place in the circle, the community, and in spiritual praxis. No less compelling is that in devising this piece, the troupe has recovered elements of traditional Indigenous pedagogical praxis and explicitly unlocked new possibilities for this learning paradigm – a paradigm, which extend beyond the "classroom" to transform all sites in which human existence is contained into "lifeway classrooms" in their own right. Indeed, this pedagogical model (upon which Gregory Cajete has based his recommendations for contemporary classroom practices that will best serve today's Indigenous learner) is demonstrably applicable to the formation of dramaturgical frameworks around which contemporary Indigenous storytellers might shape their narratives to meet communitist objectives, perhaps, with the greatest efficacy. And, as this framework was originally employed to effect, such projects, which initially turn our focus outward into our communities, eventually lead us back to self.

As *Winnetou's Snake Oil Show from Wigwam City* moves the troupe to investigate questions around cultural misappropriation and its devastating effect on Indigenous communities, Spiderwoman Theater begins to revisit and recover sites of authentic spirituality in the person of the Miguel matriarch. In subsuming individual artistic preoccupations to fully dedicate their energies to a communitist project, the Miguel sisters have laid the groundwork for the intensely personal *Reverb-ber-ber-rations* (1990) – a mourning song for their mother Elmira Miguel.[21] Just as several stages within the process of re-worlding may occur simultaneously or unexpectedly and repeatedly reoccur, so *Reverb-ber-ber-rations* winds its way through the stages of recovery, mourning, dreaming, commitment, and action – simultaneously looking back to remember and mourn, even as its creatrices look forward to proclaim and celebrate "the persistence of memory across the generations" (Mojica and Knowles 101). Remembering the spiritual legacy left to them by their mother and mourning their separation from their father's community, the Miguel sisters reclaim, deploy, and embody all the gifts that constitute their inheritance (including spirituality; aestheticism; linguistic patterns; and personal, familial, and community narratives) – not for themselves but to be passed on to future generations. Each Spiderwoman play constitutes a discrete mola, which is being layered into a larger mola. As fleshly archives that cradle memory, culture, and spirituality (Mojica and Knowles 101), the Miguel sisters have worked to layer themselves (and the generations that precede them) onto the coming generations by passing on their works, their signature backdrop, and their gifts to those whose task it will be to continue to thicken the mola they have inherited.

---

21 Unlike *Winnetou's Snake Oil Show*, which precedes it, or *Power Pipes* (1991), which follows it, *Reverb-ber-ber-rations* was created and performed solely by the three Miguel sisters. It is, I argue, a container for a personal rite of mourning as opposed to a consciously communitist project. For *Winnetou's Snake Oil Show*, the Miguel sisters invited Hortencia and Elvira Colorado (Coatlicue/Las Colorado Theater) to collaborate with them as co-creators and co-performers. The Colorado sisters also collaborated on Spiderwoman's *Power Pipes* (1991) along with Gloria Miguel's daughter Monique Mojica and Muriel Miguel's daughter Murielle Borst-Tarrant.

Reverb-ber-ber-rations is certainly a highly personal project, but it has been engendered within a communitist project. Ultimately, it opened the door to a collective (intergenerational and inter–First National) recovery and implementation of Indigenous spirituality in 1991. And the collaborative relationship that was built between the Miguel sisters and the Colorado sisters (who had been taught and mentored within Spiderwoman Theater) carved out spaces for a *rite of collective mourning* in 1992 as Indigenous nations across North America performatively intervened upon the celebrations that marked Columbus's arrival to these shores five hundred years before. Coatlicue Theater's *1492: Blood Speaks* is a collaborative project undertaken by the Colorado sisters with performers Pura Fe Crescioni and Soni C. Caballero under the direction (and formed within the process) of Muriel Miguel.

Just as the repetition of motifs and metaphors (albeit "consciously varied") is integral to the design of the mola (Salvador 178), so themes, issues, and motifs reoccur not only within the individual performative molas that make up Spiderwoman's canon but also within the greater narrative mola, which is the canon itself. Hence, the personal reclamation and embodiment of the spiritual gifts, which reverberate throughout the Miguel family, undertaken in 1990 with *Reverb-ber-ber-rations* is revisited and developed as a communitist enterprise in 1991 with *Power Pipes*.

Power Pipes, I argue, performatively charts the evolution of recovery, mourning and dreaming into dreaming commitment and action. If *Reverb-ber-ber-rations* first dreamed the past alive, first dreamed the gift back into being, first dreamed the acceptance of the gift, first dreamed of healing for the mourner, and first dreamed a legacy with which to gift the coming generations, *Power Pipes* dreams the spiritual empowerment of women and shows us how, through commitment and action, Indigenous women might utilize their spiritual gifts to recover their rightful social and political positioning within the circle.

As one rapidly discovers through the examination of each Spiderwoman production, "way leads on to way" (see Frost): Questions lead on to answers, which lead to more questions, which in their turn lead the work back and forth, around and around, weaving one play into another and yet another, deepening the layers and thickening the fabric of an ornately patterned design crafted with invisible seams. And these invisible seams preserve the integrity of a deceptively simple whole.

The Miguel sisters' collaborative works, considered first severally and then in their totality, speak to the timelessness of the project that is their life's work. This study, it is hoped, will map *a* way for others who seek to take possession of themselves as Indigenous Peoples in community. Perhaps, the example provided by the Miguel sisters can teach us how to first affect and then to transform the communitist project of survivance into meaningful life projects in which individuals and their communities need no longer occupy themselves with the struggles of self-protection and resistance to oppression but have the space, security, and freedom to engage wholeheartedly in the business of joyful participation in an ongoing process of re-worlding.

5 The Published Texts

> This is a project of recovery, of reinvention, neither a nostalgic return, nor a naïve optimism. It is a bringing forward of what is not broken, of who we were and are prior to and outside of the disconnect that is colonization. It is not nostalgic because it moves forward; it is not naïve optimism but a first step because it is a provision of something solid to stand on while building for a future. It's not a nostalgic return because it is outwardly directed, it is active, it's a revitalization of things that have always been there.
>
> – Monique Mojica and Ric Knowles, "Creation Story" 2–3

The project of recovery and reinvention to which Monique Mojica and Ric Knowles refer here is Monique Mojica's *Chocolate Woman Dreams the Milky Way* (then under development), but their words could very easily apply to the entire canon of published and unpublished play texts by Spiderwoman Theater. Indeed, *Chocolate Woman Dreams the Milky Way* is a "first step," just as each new step on an arduous journey towards the fulfilment of a dream is again and again a first step. And truly, this new work will provide a solid processual framework that gestures towards an inter–First National poetics of re-worlding. But the framework Mojica continues to develop and perfect rests upon the solid methodological base authored by Muriel Miguel and developed by Spiderwoman over a lifetime of theatrical praxis. And their praxis has been built upon the stories told around a kitchen table in the house of mirrors, upon a "family business" of snake oil and spectacle and upon ancient communal narratives, aesthetic principles, and performative traditions.

The five published play texts that document collectively created and performed works by Spiderwoman Theater stand as representatives of 21 years (1981–2002) of an artistic career that now spans almost half a century;[1] nonetheless, they offer a rich and finely detailed portrait of the Miguel sisters' progression through the temporal and spatial "steppes" of the seen and unseen worlds. I read these texts – on page and stage – as abstracted notations of a contemporary medicine chant, in which an entire poetics of re-worlding is remembered and preserved for those who may wish to carry on Spiderwoman's work.

Sun, Moon, and Feather (1981) maps a journey of personal healing – a journey back to self. *Winnetou's Snake Oil Show from Wigwam City* (1989) extends that map and carries the sojourner into the greater community to continue the healing work on a socio-political level. *Reverb-ber-berations* (1990) returns its artists to the realm of the highly personal, as they pose and answer questions around the repair of the fragmented connections between flesh and spirit, between ancestor and descendant, and between Earth and her children. With this work, the Miguel sisters look outward from the world of flesh to the spirit world, re-membering and creating anew what Diane Glancy has called the "intertextual facings" and the "interfactual textings" that repair the lines of communication between the isolate human and the metaphysical sources of power, which direct and animate the material world (127).

Power Pipes (1991),[2] the final text under discussion in this chapter, looks from the spiritual realm back to the material realm to reinforce our understandings of the interdependencies between flesh and spirit. It presents, too, a sombre warning: The spirit guides may send direction, but if the messages go unheeded, dis-ease will ultimately possess the inhabitants of all realms of existence. This multi-generational, inter–First National project heightens the manifestation of these interdependencies by stitching the layers of existence together and so binding temporal, spatial, and substantive realms into a tight weave. It challenges its witnesses to decide for themselves just "which [world] is which? Is the shadow world the spirit world and the real world the physical world we live in? Or is the shadow world the real, and the real world we live in the shadow?" (Glancy 127).

---

1 *Persistence of Memory* (2002) is the last production, collaboratively devised and performed by Lisa Mayo, Gloria Miguel, and Muriel Miguel. It was published in 2009 and will be discussed in the final chapter of this work.

2 In *Seventh Generation: An Anthology of Native American Plays*, editor Mimi Gisolfi D'Aponte places the first production of *Power Pipes* at Chicago's Randolph Street Gallery in 1993 (153). However, the official website for Spiderwoman Theater indicates that *Power Pipes* premiered in 1992.

Sun, Moon, and Feather: First Steps Towards Self-Recovery

In Performance, we are dying together.

– Jill Dolan, "Performance, Utopia" 459

We are not supposed to be alive now if the people who came here had their way.

– Lisa Mayo qtd. in Abbott 175

Spiderwoman Theater's 1981 split marked the covenant between the three Miguel sisters to address their familial past and to negotiate their current relationships with each other (as sisters and co-creatrices) and with their communities (as American Indian mothers, lovers, grandmothers, and artists). In that year, they created and performed their first published act of recovery *Sun, Moon, and Feather*. The following year, they produced *The Three Sisters from Here to There* (unpublished), adapting Chekhov's famous masterpiece to tell their story of three Indian sisters who dream of escaping their Brooklyn neighbourhood to find fame and fortune in Greenwich Village, Manhattan. Although it might be inferred (from the chronological performance history) that *The Three Sisters from Here to There* evolved out of *Sun, Moon, and Feather*, Lisa Mayo remembered things differently. She has testified that as the Miguel sisters researched Chekhov and his final play to find themselves within and to arrive at their own answers to his work's central question, "[they] discovered that [they] had a lot of personal information and that [they] could create another show, [their] show" (Mayo qtd. in Abbott 175). Perhaps, what they discovered was that their questions and their struggles differed somewhat from those belonging to Chekhov and the decaying world of which he wrote. Perhaps, his personal fears that permeate his *Three Sisters* – that we all die and are ultimately forgotten, that our struggles are meaningless and absurd – proposed little that fell into line with their personal experiences or cosmology.

The Three Sisters was written in 1900 by one who knew that he had a very short time to live: As a medical doctor, Anton Chekhov surely understood that the tuberculosis from which he was convalescing in Yalta (far from his friends, his artistic collaborators, and his wife in Moscow) was worsening and would soon kill him. This anguished cry at the dawn of a new century (albeit, not Chekhov's last word on the matter) addresses urgent questions about the human condition, about why we live, why we suffer, and what is the meaning behind it all. The central problematic condition from which all suffering represented in this play stems (malaise, entrapment, disappointed hopes, thwarted and unrequited love, love that disappoints, thwarted communication and hopelessness) is the universal condition of individual loneliness. There is a hole in the human heart, which nothing in this world – the world of Chekhov's play – can fill. In this world where merchants eat themselves to death in enormous, anonymous restaurants (Chekhov 218), where a cuckolded husband gambles away his family home and his son's future and where we "snatch happiness in fits and starts" only to be "shattered" in the end (Chekhov 264), this weeping wound is most vividly expressed in terms of hunger and thirst. The morose, volatile Solyony eats up the sweets that had been put out for the entire household and its guests even as he maliciously tells his hostess that if her little Bobik were his child, he "would put him in a frying pan and eat him" (Chekhov 228). Later, as Solyony declares his love to Irina, he describes her eyes as "sumptuous" (234). But his avowed "love" is a desire to possess that he might consume. And at the end of the day, Solyony's hunger consumes him; he reveals himself to be a destroyer – a rapacious assassin. Similarly, a destructive thirst takes hold of Chebutykin. After losing a female patient, he becomes inebriated, breaking a two-year period of abstinence. His answer to the fire that devastates his town, to Masha's agonized confidence and to the pointless duel in which Irina's affianced will die is detached and deadly: "It doesn't matter" (Chekhov 265).

The loneliness here does not stem simply from the conditions of being alone or feeling misunderstood; nor is it born of unrequited love. These things, which we lose or lack, are not solutions to the loneliness. And this, Chekhov makes abundantly clear. Love disappoints; humans disappoint; we do not live up to our own ideals; we are cruel and petty and weak and foolish despite our best intentions; we die and are forgotten; neither work nor knowledge can invest us with a sustained belief that our lives have meaning; Moscow, at the end of the day, is just a dirty, cold, lonely city. What, then, will fill the hole? What will give these things meaning? Is there meaning? Can we ever know? Is there a plan? Is there a planner? Do I fit into the plan at all? Do I matter?

Olga, as the eldest of the three sisters, is the keeper of family memory. Masha has forgotten her mother's face; Vershinin has forgotten the faces of the general's three little girls: he only remembers that there were three of them; Irina, the youngest sister, thinks only of a future of glorious work. But Olga who knows that we die and are forgotten strives to counter the despair born of such knowledge, and as a token of her faith, she has made it her task to remember and to remind. Of course, by the end of the play, the eldest sister has let go of the past and forsaken memory to concentrate on "knowing." Although Chekhov offers no pat solutions to the questions he has posed, he has left us with a processual map. Before we can know (our purpose, our meaning, our place in the larger design), we must remember. It is, then, reasonable to assume that during their quest to find the answers to a larger riddle around place and meaning within the entire fabric of Creation, the Miguel sisters discovered that first they must find "[their] own 'three sisters'" (Mayo qtd. in Abbott 175) and embark upon an act of recovery on the brink of a new millennium.

"How Did We Survive?"

No act of recovery is possible without an initial *asking* and the without the act of *seeking*, which perforce must follow the question. The processual investigations underpinning *Sun, Moon, and Feather* have emerged from the question, "How did we survive?" and the answers they yield map a personal journey that speaks directly to the larger, communitist project of survivance – a survivance that eschews any simulation. This is an intensely personal piece; indeed, it is the first of several Spiderwoman productions that dedicates itself solely to the Miguel family autohistory, and it is the first of several signature Spiderwoman productions that features a homogeneous collective at all levels – familial, genetic, communal, and political.

It is telling that the Miguel sisters had temporarily abandoned their less homogeneous and less specifically personal *The Three Sisters from Here to There* to "revisit" their childhood home and to replay the struggles, rivalries, and moments of joyous affection that belong to that time and that directed their adult attitudes and behaviours towards each other and others with whom they shared their lives. They had to first land *Here* before setting out for *There*. *The Three Sisters from Here to There* was produced in March 1982 at The Theatre for the New City, but it was not received with the same degree of enthusiasm as *Sun, Moon, and Feather* had been.

Where, as Birgit Däwes observes, in the 1981 production of *Sun, Moon, and Feather* "the characters' identity is conflated with that of the performers through the English names of Lisa, Gloria, and Muriel," (216) *The Three Sisters from Here to There* utilized Chekhov's characters to carry and explore seemingly larger political questions around the suppression of female agency in contemporary America (Gussow). Certainly, this show, which must have first been conceived prior to the 1981 split, could not frame itself around the profoundly personal questions that drove *Sun, Moon, and Feather*. Its creative team consisted not only of Lisa Mayo, Gloria Miguel, and Muriel Miguel (who each took on multiple roles, including Olga, Masha, and Irina respectively) but also of Eva Bouman (Fedotik-Roday, Anfisa, and Ferapont), Elvira Colorado (Vershinin and Kulygin) and Pam Verge (Natasha, Tusenbach, and Andrey). In performance, the male characters (transplanted from

Chekhov's world) were represented by life-sized puppets and given voice by the female puppet masters (see ch. 2, fig. 2.2).[3]

Characterized as "aimless" and "top-heavy with artlessness" in *The New York Times* (Gussow), *The Three Sisters from Here to There* did not enjoy a long run. At the end of the day, I suspect, it served neither as a vehicle to self for the Miguel sisters nor as an assertion of Indigenous survivance, which might serve the American Indian community. At the same time, it provided no discernable rallying site for the heterogeneous feminist audiences whose concerns it had been created to address. Presumably, there are several reasons for this. First, the acting was uneven, and while the Miguel trio was praised for its "earthy vitality" and its musical performances, their colleagues were castigated for their "amateurishness," their "inept[itude]" and their "overacting" (Gussow). Most damning of all, this show was criticized for its polarizing didacticism. As Mel Gussow received *The Three Sisters from Here to There*, Chekhov's play had, in this instance, been co-opted to make a political statement, rather than to explore questions that had concerned Anton Chekhov himself or that might concern those separated by almost one century and a vast expanse of water and sky from the tortured playwright who had sent up his anguished cry. Indeed, as Jill Dolan reading the production from a materialist perspective receives it, Spiderwoman's "ironic attitude" towards Chekhov and his "angst" is the engine that drives this piece (*Feminist Spectator* 113). She identifies the central problem of *The Three Sisters from Here to There* as a very human problem: males oppress females and prevent them from getting "from here to there." Metaphysical questions around meaning and existence are, for such a reading, redundant and absurd. With their return to and completion of *The Three Sisters from Here to There*, the Miguel sisters were widening their circle of care – stepping away for a time from the urgent, personal questions around meaning and identity, which they had just explored in *Sun, Moon, and Feather*. Now, they were ready to dive into philosophical and political questions, which, perhaps, they presumed would interest a larger and more diverse audience. Ultimately, it seems that (production and publication) history has come to show that the more personal and specific production resonated (and continues to resonate) much more powerfully with audiences than its more overtly political counterpart.

3 The effigy of Andrey was animated alternatively by all three Miguel sisters, Vira Colorado, and Pam Verge (see Gussow). These puppets, as Jill Dolan informs us, would be manipulated to create a series of "gests" that spoke to the "structure of gendered relationships." For instance, Muriel Miguel, playing Irina, manipulates the Tusenbach doll at one point to fondle Irina's (her own) breasts (Dolan, *Feminist Spectator* 112).

The Three Sisters from Here to There was never published; little scholarly commentary has been devoted to it, and it is not a show that the Miguel sisters themselves speak about often or at any great length. It has become a footnote in the performative history of Spiderwoman Theater. Nonetheless, its importance within the overall project of discovering and recovering personal identity and relationship within community should not be overlooked. Indeed, Muriel Miguel has noted that *The Three Sisters from Here to There* raised the stakes and perhaps deepened the commitments of the Miguel sisters. If they had harboured any prior doubts about a permanent split from the Euro-American members of the core company, it was now "definite." "Now, all of [their] pieces [would address] racism" (qtd. in Haugo, "Weaving" 229). And it is from this interrupted and ultimately less efficacious work that the Miguel sisters' first chapter of a performative autohistory that has spanned nearly five decades has emerged. The Miguel sisters' first family project achieves its universal significance in its exploration of the domestic, the personal, and the specific. Their *Sun, Moon, and Feather* demonstrates that the commitment to pursue the most intensely self-reflexive questions (kernels) may lead the seeker not only to recovery and personal healing but also to political achievements of the utmost efficacy.

Bringing the Gathering House to the Stage

> LISA: So, we were talking about that layer of worthlessness, selflessness, coming out of being poor, being dirty, not having enough to eat.
>
> GLORIA: There wasn't much hope. When you came home after school to a cold house, no food, a drunken father, a depressed mother, a neighbourhood that's very hostile to you.
>
> LISA: What is there? It's horrible. How did we make it? (Spiderwoman, *Sun* 291)

On a still, dimly lit stage, it begins. As the "Poverty Tape" plays, disembodied – at times, indistinguishable – voices remember specific moments in the Miguel sisters' childhood and the general conditions, which governed it. Behind the human conversation, Mozart's *K. 546 Adagio and Fugue in C Minor* interweaves itself between and behind the words adding resonance to each syllable and punctuating moments of silence. It is as if two pianos and a string quartet have struck up a conversation with the human beings who are grasping at the "kernel" (the reason for their survival) as they follow the pain. Within this aural mola, time and space are conflated, as child converses with her adult counterpart and as "some godawful neighbourhood," a local laundromat and the sisters' childhood home are invoked on the public stage.[4] At times, the human voices reflect upon the past: "You *were* only 13. [...] I *was* [...]. I *looked* [...]. That *was* really terrible" (Spiderwoman, *Sun* 290, emphasis mine). But these are entwined with voices that speak directly from the past as if it were the present: "Hello pretty one you have 10 cents for me?" (Spiderwoman, *Sun* 290).

Onto this aural tapestry of dirt, privation, violence, and humiliation a contrapuntal visual layer is added. "Uncle Joe's" home movies, featuring the "[b]eautiful Indian faces" of Antonio Miguel, his brothers, and the idyllic San Blas Islands (Gunayala) where they grew up thicken the narrative and introduce the central question to the audience: "The juxtaposition of that sad tape and the lovely islands where they come from. The worry about money in the city against a coconut culture. The wonderment: How did they get here? How did they survive?" (Spiderwoman, *Sun* 292). And onto this aural and visual background, the living performers layer themselves and their stories interweaving these with Chekhovian dialogue, as if to test out the efficacy of his *Sisters'* strategies of survivance and the relevance of these to the lives of three Indigenous women from Brooklyn.[5] As sibling rivalries, childhood games (i.e., Elizabeth Miguel's tea parties) and old hurts are remembered and re-enacted, declarations of personal identity begin to emerge.

---

4 The Miguel sisters brought their childhood home onto the public stage in their 1981 production, but in the 1989 film version of *Sun, Moon, and Feather*, their childhood home (in which Muriel Miguel still lives) becomes the public stage. As the film begins, we do not hear the "Poverty Tape," which opens the stage production. Instead, as the camera travels through the home's empty rooms focusing at moments on pictures or furnishings that carry emotional resonance, we hear fragments of ancestral conversation. Uncle Joe, Aunt Lizzie, Antonio and Elmira Miguel are remembered and voiced into being as if something of their spirit still resonated within the walls of the rooms that once contained their mortal existence.

5 It may bear repeating that Anton Chekhov sought within his plays to affect a revelation of the human spirit beneath the layers of mundane, quotidian existence. Hence, the Miguel sisters' attraction to his work seems, to me, quite logical, as they also work to reveal the spiritual essence/kernel within the material. It is also worth noting that Chekhov's polyvalent dramaturgical structure might well put us in mind of a performative mola (or perhaps a matryoshka doll). And this resemblance was not lost upon Spiderwoman's artists. Portions of his work, therefore, might quite effortlessly be woven into the fabric of a Spiderwoman project. As Gloria Miguel has remarked about her early encounters with Chekhov's works during her training at Oberlin:

> [T]he scene is set up where something is going on way back there. And something is going on outside. And something is going on here. And that's life. And it's all connected. You know? Chekhov has a scene going on back there – although they're not talking; they're not in the forefront. But you see people talking like that, people on the outside just sitting if you look out the window. All that is set up on the stage. All that just fascinated me, you know. (Interview 2007)

Gloria remembers with gladness how her father's relations claimed her as their own. In so doing, she remembers, lays claim to an ancestral language and brings the Gathering House of her father's island of Nargana onto the New York stage: *"Ige benuga,Igi, be nuga be a beni be agbanaed. E be nueti.* They called me *Tuli* [Dule] girl. (Sings.) *Tage. Tage.* [Degii, Degii]" (295).

"Tage" [Degii], a chanted affirmation meaning "it is so" or "indeed," is a familiar response in the dialogic form of storytelling in the Gathering House Tradition. In this tradition, there are generally two "performers." The Chanting Chief is the main storyteller, and he directs the narrative. The Responding Chief may simply affirm each of the chanter's utterances ("Tage"/Degii) or he may perform a "reformulation, translation, and recasting" of these utterances to complicate the rhythms and/or enhance the performance (Sherzer 122). Gloria, by adding her breath to sound, not only affirms her identity as a "Tuli [Dule] girl" but also casts herself as a respondent in the Gathering House Tradition. *How did her father's relations survive financial hardship, oppression, and racism in their new home?* They transplanted the Guna Gathering House (which housed the stories that had made them) to a kitchen table in Red Hook, Brooklyn. They told and retold stories. They lived new stories and added those to the communal canon. In the stories that had made them, they remembered who they were. And in the stories that had made her relatives, in the stories that have gone into making her and in the community that has kept those stories alive, Gloria Miguel remembers herself and declares her place.

Lisa, by contrast, remembers herself in relation to her mother's community, naming and claiming her Rappahannock relations and their gifts:

> I am the granddaughter of Elizabeth Ashton Mourn,[6] a beautiful Rappahannock Indian woman from West Moreland [sic] County, Virginia. My great-grandmother Felecia was a midwife and she taught my grandmother how to deliver babies. My grandmother delivered me and both my sisters […]
>
> My mother gave me to the witch. (Spiderwoman, *Sun* 295)[7]

6 Elizabeth Ashton Moore.

7 In chapter 2, I discuss this period in the elder sisters' lives and its emotional repercussions. Gloria was born while her sister was still a toddler. Feeling herself unable to cope with caring for both a newborn and a toddler, Elmira and her own mother agreed that Elizabeth (for whom Lisa Mayo was named) would care for her in her home next door. As Gloria saw it, her elder sister was loved and pampered by the extended family, while she was left out. As Elizabeth saw it, she had been displaced from her family home with the arrival of Gloria.

Her grandmother was, at times, undoubtedly cruel, but it is through her ministrations that all three Miguel sisters came into this world. It is from her that Elmira inherited her medicine and her gift of prophecy, and it is from her that Elmira's daughters inherited their own acute intuitions and paranormal gifts. Pain and privation threaten survival, but these are key components in our making, and we risk our own unmaking if we try to forget or deny those things that seem negative or shameful – those things that cause us pain. Pain, too, may be a great gift. Indeed, it serves as a physiological alarum that warns us of oft-times less apparent dangers, which threaten our lives. It teaches us humility, compassion, and empathy. And at the very least, it reminds us that we are alive.

Elmira Miguel had completely withdrawn by the time her youngest daughter was born. Hence, the adult Muriel (speaking after her mother's death) declares herself to be "the only child of [her] two sisters" (Spiderwoman, *Sun* 295) who ultimately took on the task of raising her. And counter-intuitively, although she is "very lonely" and although her mother never talks to her, she understands that she has been "covered with love" (295). Throughout the piece, Muriel sifts through story fragments to work through the complexities of a fraught sibling relationship and to understand herself in relation to and independent of the women who raised her.

By the same token, as they replay their desire to mother and nurture their baby sister, Lisa and Gloria come more fully into recognition of themselves. Lisa has struggled to teach Muriel the traditions of the family, so that she herself would be free to leave. Gloria wanted to extend that same freedom to their young charge by making sure she was educated, cultured, and worldly. In her turn, the "baby" of the family has outgrown their dreams for her: She has achieved greater professional success than her mentors ("how does it feel when your baby sister steals the limelight?") (*Sun* 296); she comforts and advises Lisa after her divorce (*Sun* 296); and she comes out to her shocked sisters as a lesbian (*Sun* 301). Despite the fears, resentments, fierce disapproval, or bitter rivalries that punctuate the sibling relationship, each Miguel sister continues to assert her love for the others, and each remains the "soft place" for her sisters to fall in times of crisis: "Jerry. Jerry. The car turned over and over. I felt his body shake against me. Elizabeth, Gloria, he's dead, he's dead!!!" (*Sun* 297).

Much has been made of the musical send-up during which Gloria Miguel and Lisa Mayo re-enact the famous "Indian Love Call" duet of the 1936 classic film *Rose-Marie*. So much, indeed, that those unfamiliar with *Sun, Moon, and Feather* could not be blamed for harbouring the impression that apart from a brief allusion to a drunken father, some home movies, and an anecdote about the Miguel family's boat (which

I will discuss later), this musical moment of resistance is the heart and soul and substance of the work entire.

The duet concludes a brief but poignant "dreaming sequence" throughout which all three sisters articulate their desires to escape the hostility that surrounds them in the Brooklyn neighbourhood of their youth and the ennui that their poverty has produced (see Spiderwoman, *Sun* 308). Beginning with dreams of physical escape (rich husbands who will take them away or the apartment that Muriel will acquire) and moving into dreams of artistic success (a tap chair dance number to "Give My Regards to Old Broadway"), the sequence concludes with the re-staging of an obviously old and beloved childhood game, which precedes dreams of marriage, escape, and/or professional success, and which precedes the youngest sister's participation in their games and contribution to the collective dream:

> LISA: Hey Gloria we have a captive audience – let's you and me play "Indian Love Call."
>
> GLORIA: Oh yeah.
>
> LISA: Okay? I'm Jeannette Macdonald and I've got this long red hair and big green eyes. (Spiderwoman, *Sun* 309–10)

Gloria and Lisa commence arguing about who will take the role of Jeannette Macdonald – she of the long red hair, big green eyes, and high, clear voice. Next, Muriel tries to insinuate herself into the game, offering to play Nelson Eddy's horse (Spiderwoman, *Sun* 309–10). But the elder sisters carry on as if she were not even there. Although one performer is shut out of the scene (either because she was too young to have participated in the original game or because she had not yet been born),[8] the "Indian Love Call" duet that follows carries within its polyvalent structure an origin story about the *trio*. It is precisely because the two elder sisters played such games – sang, danced, and dreamed – that all three sisters transcended the multiple oppressions, which defined their lives, to sing, dance, and weave the stories and dreams that eventually carried them out of Red Hook, Brooklyn, to public stages the world over. The "kernel" of the game – manifested in the stereotypes it references – gestures to a tightly woven filament belonging to an entire net of oppressions, which has threatened to choke off the lives of generations of Indigenous Peoples across the Americas. And yet, the game itself (as it has been curated and played out by

8 In the film version of *Sun, Moon, and Feather*, Muriel Miguel does not appear at all in this scene (Rosen and Zipp).

Gloria and Lisa) constitutes a tightly woven filament belonging to an intricate web of strategies, which speak to personal and political survivance.

The "Indian Love Call" duet has been celebrated by feminist scholars as a defining scene in Spiderwoman's post-split premiere (see, for example, Schneider 170–1 and Däwes 220–1). Rebecca Schneider has famously identified it as a single, perfect instance of "counter-mimicry" (170) through which the contemporary Native performer subverts and overturns the nostalgia upon which colonialism's nationalist mythologies have been constructed. This nostalgia has been borne upon the myriad colonial simulations of Native experience, which have saturated North American culture and influenced cultural consciousness to deadly effect. As Robyn Diner reminds us, the longings such simulations produce are not so much for what has been lost as they are for *what has never been*. This is the irony, which scholars (like Diner, Schneider, and Däwes) find so delicious; they use words like "unruly, "carnivalesque," "grotesque" (Diner) or "inappropriate" and "heavy" (Schneider 170) to communicate the corporeal presence of the Guna-Rappahannock sisters as they talk back to the Empire – or at least, back to Hollywood.

As these scholars read the scene, the "inappropriate" authentic re-appropriates and plays out a seemingly appropriate instance of nostalgia, thereby dis-covering it as a pretty but hollow simulation – a lifeless mask. While two zaftig, middle-aged American Indian ladies soulfully sing the song that "Indian maidens" hear when they dream of their lovers (Spiderwoman, *Sun* 311), grainy, celluloid shadows of the svelte, youthful onscreen lovers Jeanette MacDonald and Nelson Eddy mouth the song's lyrics behind them in bloodless, ethereal silence. Robbed of voice, lacking colour, and so glaringly out of place in the raucous, colourful, and unapologetically busy world of Spiderwoman's 1981 production, these shadows (of rustic lovers and dancing "brave") can in no way be mistaken by the audience as a fading archive of a disappearing people; rather, the positioning of life and colour over colourless non-life asserts the continuance of actual Indigenous Peoples in the persons of the three living performers. The "disappearing people," for whom the archive has been constructed to conjure up colonial nostalgia, *never existed*; the experience offered by white performers in "Red face"[9] proposes nothing. It is a non-experience.

9 This is not to suggest that either Nelson Eddie or Jeanette Macdonald appeared in actual "red face" in the 1936 film *Rose-Marie*. I use the term quite broadly here to refer not only to the white actors who were decked out to "play Indian" in such films but also to the effects adopted by Hollywood film studios to produce signifiers of Indigeneity (i.e., makeup, costume, props, music, and choreography). The couple's famous duet ought to be regarded as an instance of "red face" for its content (lyrics), arrangement, instrumentation in moments, and vocal opsis.

Such readings, of course, are appropriate, accurate, and important. But they fail to fully penetrate Spiderwoman's performative mola. And while these readings do not "archive" a non-life, they certainly document and catalogue a "half-life." They cast this performance as a *reaction* to the perverse metonyms, which have inhabited the colonial imagination for centuries now. As this fragment of autobiography has been critically imagined, a metonym born of colonial mimesis is cast as protagonist under attack by an antagonist in the person of three American Indian sisters. There is a dangerous irony here. Out of the wrack of the tribal simulations (which they decry while celebrating Spiderwoman's performative intervention) these cultural critics are weaving into the scholarly canon new (and perhaps equally damaging) tribal simulations of their own making.

Activations of struggle, resistance, defiance, and confrontation do *not always* activate survivance. Often born of dire necessity, such acts constitute *reactions against* a thing done that threatens *survival*. But human beings must exercise their capacity for action as well as for reaction to live in a whole, healthy, and balanced way. Action is a privilege reserved solely for the living; a corpse, after all, will still *react* to external stimuli and forces that exert themselves upon its composite elements. Survivance requires the threatened body (communal or individual) to articulate, facilitate, and embody a consciousness that partners reaction with *pro-action* – that balances that body's rejection (of the intolerable) with active aspiration (towards a desirable future). Gerald Vizenor has observed that when the static pose of the "tribal warrior" ceased, in the nineteenth century, to pose a threat to the occupying nation state, this imagined "Indian" suddenly became an expedient tool in the project of nation-building. Indigenous Peoples have since been rewarded for playing the part of the "radical" or "warrior" (Blaeser 53–4). The pages upon which Indigenous essence (human *being*) and action (human *doing*) are actualized have become, for Vizenor, the killing fields of the "cultural word wars," the outcome of which, shaped by "money and politics," has shaped us into one-dimensional relics carrying the label of either "victim" or "survivor" (Blaeser 39). These labels assume a twisted co-dependence between Indigenous Peoples and the colonizing powers: The human, being a victim or survivor, can only, in colonial imagination, *react* against the forces/conditions/agents that victimize or that threaten survival. Hence, the tribal individual's capacity for action is engendered by, fuelled by, and predicated upon the actions of the victimizer. The prisoner of this paradigm is stripped of agency, independence, and responsibility; the prisoner of this paradigm is no longer a human doing or a human being; the prisoner of this paradigm has become a puppet.[10]

One shortcoming of the "counter-mimicry" construct is that it isolates the "Indian Love Call" scene from the rest of the project and the question(s), which have engendered it. Over-investment in the political effect of Spiderwoman's whimsical musical number diverts us from the central question – from the *kernel* of the story. As Muriel Miguel explains, this kernel emerges from personal experience. She does not at first set out to disseminate an abstract political message. She begins by "going for the kernel" – by interrogating her personal "pain" and seeking its sources. The isolate human undertakes a journey that is specific to her and is transformed through that journey into a political actor with the capacity to affect change on the greater stage outside the theatre (M. Miguel qtd. in Haugo, "Weaving" 226).[11]

Sun, Moon, and Feather's kernel demands far more of its creatrices than reactionary counter measures. The answers that each of the Miguel sisters come up with as they pursue the core question – "How did we survive?" – explode with robust, autonomous *doings* and irrepressible, joyous life in the midst of chaos, privation, and despair. And this is certainly how Spiderwoman's audiences received and were affected by the 1981 performances, which critics have characterized as "life-enhancing,"

10 Ann Haugo concedes that there are significant dangers associated with limiting critical engagement with Indigenous women's theatrical interventions to a one-dimensional examination of the resistance they pose to the colonial project. Such readings (to the exclusion of all else) would ultimately contain Indigenous artistic expression within and define it in accordance with a colonial framework. "[B]y extension," she cautions, these readings "would encourage a latent ethnocentrism on the part of the critic" ("Colonial Audiences" 133). To forestall such developments, Haugo proposes that we attend to the nuances wherein multiple resistances are identified and Indigenous agency is assumed ("Colonial Audiences" 133). I would append to this the notion that stance – as opposed to counter stance – is often the most efficacious (and most nuanced) form of resistance we can execute. The simple refusal to "give face to" or to acknowledge the existence of the agents of oppression or their works coupled with the recovery of lifeways and knowledge systems, which predate their arrival, may go further to facilitate a project of re-worlding than it will if we continue to allow ourselves to be drawn into the trap of interminable debate.

11 The necessity of following that personal kernel to achieve greater political efficacy hit home with me during the 2019 rehearsals of *Encounters at the "Edge of the Woods,"* a production for which I was dramaturg, co-devisor, and director. Although I will be discussing this production at greater length in the concluding chapter, I feel compelled to share part of my experience during rehearsals to elaborate on the distinction between placing a larger political ideal at the centre of the creative investigation and the placement of personal experience at that centre. The show was

"full of grace," (Faber 92) or simultaneously as "an actual exposé of … inner life" and a "sylphlike dreamworld" (Haye). All this is not to suggest, however, that the political tones were absent or so muted as to be overlooked or ignored. Rather, the questions Spiderwoman pursued and the resultant celebratory "romp" the sisters presented (Faber 92) illuminated the political messaging, rendering it more palatable as it had "subtly insinuat[ed]" itself as a layer in their performative mola "without hectoring or rhetoric" (Faber 92). The Miguel sisters were initiating a new conversation – issuing a new call. This call required full investment in its audiences; it solicited heuristic response, not a fleeting, involuntary reaction to guilt, gesturing to white fragility. An answering "ow," from their audiences would not suffice.

---

devised as a container for conversation between Indigenous and non-Indigenous individuals – all of whom had some relationship with the University of Toronto (faculty, staff, students, alumni, and individuals living and working in the Greater Toronto Area) and the fraught histories contained within the walls and foundations of its buildings; in the buried waterways upon which those buildings rest; the works that have emerged from those buildings; and the attitudes and policies these works engendered. What futures might we, together, imagine? What violations need to be acknowledged and addressed? Acknowledged by whom? Addressed through what actions? How might we personally begin a process of righting fraught relations between ourselves (Indigenous and non-Indigenous) and between ourselves and this *"arm of the settler state"* (Grande "Refusing," 47)? Sharing circles and devising sessions throughout were conducted alternatively in separate spaces (Indigenous and non-Indigenous) and in communal spaces where we all came together to share the questions that most occupied us, the kernels we were following, and the work we had done. Where, from the very beginning, the Indigenous artists brought their most pressing and personal concerns to the table in oral and kinetic expression, too many of the non-Indigenous artists (all of whom had considerable training in voice and movement) engaged their intellect, while disassociating themselves from the matter at hand. They pointed outwards at political leaders; they decried (historical and contemporary) policies and events; they were of good heart and strong mind, but in their commitment to effect a macro-transformation, they had forgotten that the micro-transformation is a requisite first step. The project of re-worlding requires the formation of "new human beings." I began to understand here that these non-Indigenous collaborators were not intentionally disassociating themselves from the fraught relationship upon which we had gathered to intervene. Rather, they were holding back to make space for their Indigenous colleagues; theirs were the stories that needed to be privileged and heard.

Over time, they began to apprehend that their Indigenous collaborators were sounding a call – a call to which they were required, *personally*, to respond. Story needed to be answered with story. Before the kernels of our stories could be identified and connected, they had to be followed. Each of us had our own work to do before we could begin to work together. As their awareness grew, the non-Indigenous artists became more courageous. As they began to "follow [their own] pain," their physical instruments went with them. The conversation began.

To posit that the "Indian Love Call" scene of *Sun, Moon, and Feather* simply "doubles back upon white culture the problem of [the Miguel sisters'] own authentication" (Schneider 163) is to ignore the scene's relationship with the larger question around which the play has been constructed. Lest we forget, each layer of Spiderwoman's performative mola is not the thing itself. Each scene is not the answer; each scene, rather, plays out a process of discovery. This piece does not derive its value from its political stance or because it provides instruction and correction to non-Indigenous viewers. It derives its significant worth from the life lessons and urban survival strategies that it offers to its *Indigenous* audiences. And as the Miguel sisters play out "what they've spent their lives becoming" (Faber 92), it becomes apparent that while "counter-mimicry" is certainly a tool of political resistance, it can be effectively deployed as a tool of survival – indeed, of survivance. In her artistic statement, which precedes the published text of *Sun, Moon, and Feather* in *Contemporary Plays by Women of Colour*, Muriel Miguel reminds us of this fact:

> One time I found several postcards of very elegant white ladies. They were obviously rich. They were wearing long white lace dresses and had flowers in their hair. For fun, I cut up snapshots of my sisters and myself. *I pasted our faces on those ladies' faces.* It was difficult, I had to maneuver and squeeze the faces into place. The final image was funny, the postcards looked lopsided. I thought this is what my family is like. Struggling to fit in, we look lopsided. Where were our role models? *When you grow up in a hostile atmosphere where you are different, you try very hard* to *squeeze and push and smash yourself into some form that does not make waves.* (qtd. in Perkins and Uno 298, emphasis mine)

The dreaming aspect of survivance is very apparent here, as is the resonance of that dream in the history and development of Spiderwoman Theater (which was created to allow its performers to play outside "type"). In addition, there is, here, a less apparent layer, which may not have even entered the consciousness of Muriel Miguel at the time she told this story: During a performance of her one-woman show *Something Old, Something New, Something Borrowed, Something Blue* at the Robert Gill Theatre (University of Toronto) in October 2008, Gloria Miguel related a story about their maternal grandmother. During preparations for the wedding of Gloria's Aunt Lizzie, the family matriarch was dressing. According to Gloria, she looked stunning in a fine "maroon velvet dress trimmed with ecru lace and diamond buttons." Her long black hair was piled on top of her head and held in place with a "sparkling Spanish comb." Gloria and her older sister were playing in the room, and during their game, Elizabeth accidentally trod on her grandmother's toe. "Nana" picked up the pint-sized culprit by the neck and began throttling her. This regal beauty undoubtedly would have fit into Muriel's picture of the finely dressed white ladies; yet, her actions, in this instance, do not fit into our picture of a loving, nurturing grandmother. In retrospect (offered by Gloria Miguel's revelations of 2008), we begin to see more clearly something that Gloria Miguel and Lisa Mayo had learned as little girls: "passing" (e.g., surviving by mimicking colonial models) and survivance are not the same things.

How did the Miguel sisters survive? How did they maintain their will to survive? They survived by dreaming. They survived sometimes by trying to "squeeze and push and smash" themselves into forms that, for them, personified elegance, happiness, and success. About this, they are very clear and brutally honest. It may not have been the best way, but at the time it may have been the *only* way. Locating a role model who inspires one to aspire may often, for one who is born into seemingly "hopeless" circumstances, tip the balance in her life between hope and despair, between creating and destroying, between surviving and succumbing. It is a double-edged sword to be sure, and certainly, the irony has not escaped the sisters; nor should it escape their audiences. In the absence of visible and celebrated American Indian role models upon which to construct their aspirations, the Miguel sisters, here, reveal how they adopted and adapted non-Indigenous role models – perhaps, even metonyms and tribal simulations. Paradoxically, even as such "role models" embody a centuries-old campaign of cultural genocide, these simulations may have contributed to the survival of the Miguel sisters who are, themselves, authentic embodiments of Indigeneity and who would (and *did*) eventually grow into authentic Indigenous role models for those yet to be born. To wit, some years after its premiere, Spiderwoman Theater was touring *Sun, Moon, and Feather*. After one show, three little Anishinaabe sisters came backstage to meet the sisters who had inspired them: "They were proud of us! They wanted to be us! We were their role models" (M. Miguel qtd. in Perkins and Uno 298).[12] Despite an intense and long-standing colonial campaign of theft and suppression, Indigenous cultures and culture heroes still survive; recovery is possible.

---

12 These three little girls – Keitha, Polly, and Karen – are the daughters of Anishinaabe author, journalist and poet Lenore Keeshig Tobias (Mojica, Personal Communication 2022).

Gloria Miguel and Lisa Mayo do not simply mimic the Hollywood icons who introduced the "Indian Love Call" into the cultural lexicon and orientalist imaginary of North America. They publicly replay their younger *selves* who are training themselves for what they will become. They turn their gaze (and our gaze) upon the children that they were – young, beautiful, talented, creative dreamers. And these young artists-in-training were, at this time, playing out their own dreams of escape from Red Hook, Brooklyn, and from the metonyms that they themselves were being forced to play in the Miguel family business (clips of which are woven into the celluloid layer of home movies in front of which the actors perform).[13] Where the non-Indigenous viewer may require the

---

13 In the 1989 film version of *Sun, Moon, and Feather*, the Miguel sisters explicate one of the home movies, which has been layered into the stage production. In the film, we see a loin-clothed Antonio Miguel equipped with a bow, a quiver full of arrows, and a headdress dancing before a large group of picnickers seated on the grass under a blue sky. Shots of Aunt Lizzie, swathed in buckskin and sporting a flattering headband, are woven into Miguel's onstage performance, as are deliberately pedestrian shots of each Miguel sister who singly interprets a snippet of the action for us from the front stoop of the family home in Red Hook, Brooklyn. They explain that their father is performing a "hunting dance" during which his movements make us understand that he is getting into his canoe; he is "crossing the water"; he is stalking a wolf. He sees the wolf; he reaches behind him for an arrow; he draws upon the wolf.

Meanwhile, just offstage, Aunt Lizzie is winding up. At just the right moment, she throws a stuffed wolf with big glass eyes across Miguel's line of fire. She has carried this prop from Brooklyn to Manhattan on the subway, which is (as Muriel Miguel observes) a very "unusual" sight for even the most jaded NYC commuter. As Aunt Lizzie tosses her charge, Miguel lets go of the arrow. It hits the wolf, which falls "dead" at his feet. The audience is delighted. This stuffed wolf, in fact, is Miguel's "gimmick." It is what sets his hunting dance apart from those of other American Indian performers who perform their own versions of this popular crowd-pleaser. But "sometimes," we are told, "Aunt Lizzie missed." Sometimes she overshot her mark, and the wolf went "skittering across the stage" and right into the audience. What happened then, we are left to imagine (Rosen and Zipp).

My aim here is to communicate to us the considerable planning and effort it requires to construct and execute such spectacles. These are "show-biz Indians" playing "Indian" to survive tough economic times. They are industrious and sophisticated; they have done their "market research." They know what mainstream audiences expect, and they give it to them. Authentic liveness embodies the inauthentic shade – the mediatized tribal simulation – in an earnest effort to satisfy the paying customers who do not believe in his existence (despite his unmistakable presence beneath the faux trappings of romantic imagination) and who would not find it convenient if they did. In so doing, the live authentic thereby affects and ensures his survival and continuance. One wild toss may shatter the comfortable fantasy and reveal the corpse beneath the mask of life, but a living, pulsating reality of warm flesh and seeing eyes bursts out from behind the metonym and stares back at the disillusioned spectators offering a cure for diseased imaginations and destructive dreams.

easily accessible political lesson, which is imbedded in this scene, the Indigenous viewer may require a lesson in transcendence: This viewer may need to be reminded that while "[i]magination is a frequent casualty to the grinding plod of poverty," (Justice 45) it is necessary to the health and life of the human soul. As such, it should be cherished and nurtured amid even the harshest of material realities. In the absence of such nurturing (from either their withdrawn mother or their alcohol-dependent, volatile father), two little brown girls nurtured that imagination in themselves and in so doing, nurtured the artistic voices that would facilitate the escape of which they dreamed.

At the end of the day, Gloria Miguel and Lisa Mayo replay the story of two little girls who are finding their voices together: Despite the humorous arguing and the jockeying for position (both girls want to play the *ingénue*), they discover their individual instruments and how to make those instruments blend. Lisa Mayo is a mezzo-soprano, and her voice (now, as it probably was then) is best suited for the lower (Nelson Eddy's) part. Gloria Miguel is a natural coloratura soprano; her voice is best suited for the higher (Jeanette MacDonald's) part. Together, they harmonize beautifully, and we bear witness to the genesis of a choral community in which each voice fulfils its role, contributing beautifully to a larger whole. To focus on the Miguel sister's send-up of the white gaze (Schneider 163), is to privilege that gaze and to pass over a crucial lesson in survivance. Perhaps, also, it affects an obfuscation of a complex and inconvenient truth: As children, the elder Miguel sisters *enjoyed* watching Nelson Eddy and Jeanette MacDonald; they admired their musical abilities; they now credit these performers for being (along with the Marx Brothers and Laurel and Hardy) early artistic influences (see Mayo qtd. in Haugo, "Native Playwrights' Newsletter" 336). These performers and the movies in which they appeared are part of Spiderwoman's story and are honoured as such.

Be that as it may, Antonio Miguel's eldest daughters were never bound in "slavish imitation" to the flawed "originals." The children that they were may have admired certain aspects of the performers they imitated, but they also saw room for embellishment and *improvement*. In the clips of the original film, Jeanette MacDonald sports an elegant, short curly hairstyle (*de rigueur* for the fashionable American woman at the time) and a modest, sensible dress, designed to get past the censors and to garner the approval of any sensible housewife or office girl sitting in the audience. But Gloria *improves* upon the *ingénue* bestowing upon her "long red hair that comes down to there [past the waist]" and a "low-cut," frothy white gown (Spiderwoman, *Sun* 310). It is interesting to note that childhood pictures reveal that Gloria – unlike her mother and sisters –

wore her hair (usually plaited) at a comparable length. So, the "model" she creates bears more resemblance to herself (and her creative abilities) than the musical comedienne she seems to be emulating.

Similarly, young Elizabeth adds embellishments of her own to improve the original. Her Royal Canadian Mounted Police (RCMP) Officer Nelson Eddy quite sensibly wears a "leather thong" tied under his chin to keep his hat on as he gallops to the foot of the mountain on a *white* horse – perhaps chosen to compliment the leading lady's sensational gown (Spiderwoman, *Sun* 310). The film clips behind their scene clearly show that Nelson Eddy's steed was dun-coloured rather than white (perhaps to complement his leading lady's more sensible frock). And sadly, Eddy's broad-brimmed hat had not been sensibly furnished with any contraption to keep it from blowing off.

These embellishments and the adult artists' refusal to "correct" the details they altered as children when faced with the (film) archive of the authentic fantasy bespeak a commitment to the stuff of *their* reality – to a reality that resonates at much deeper levels than reactionary posturing. Those little details speak as much to who these women are and how it is that they have been able to survive as they do to the Hollywood iconography, which threatened that survival and worked towards their unmaking. Hence, the scene affects a more complex and deeply layered response than the dry, rueful chuckle of the politically "woke." This is a scene which touches the viewers' core and elicits therein tenderness, grief, joy and hope simultaneously: tenderness as we contemplate the innocent dreaming of children; grief as we contemplate the implications and potentially devastating effects of internal colonization (which often lurk just behind the role models we are taught to emulate); hope and joy as we witness the transcendence of familial love and solidarity over petty rivalries, domestic violence, crushing poverty and shame. As two aging sisters imitate the children they were, imitating two youthful onscreen lovers, they rediscover, through the exercise of their artistry, the ties that bind one to the other. They may be portly; they may be brown; they may be past their youth; they may be whimsically attired. Indeed, they may be (as Rebecca Schneider insists) "inappropriate" for the roles of the young *ingénue* and her rugged swain (170), but as Schneider herself concedes, they sing "beautifully" (170). And they lead us with a delicate grace (which often takes us by surprise when it is manifested within larger bodies) towards the central lesson of the scene when, with arms akimbo, they open themselves totally to each other and declare, "You belong to me / I belong to you" (Spiderwoman, *Sun* 312) (see fig. 5.1). Without missing a beat, Lisa (borrowing her words from Chekhov) next observes: "Oh how the music is playing/ so gaily,

Figure 5.1. Gloria Miguel in *Sun, Moon, and Feather*. Courtesy of the Walter Havighurst Special Collections and University Archives, Miami University Libraries, Oxford, OH.

so bravely and one wants to live" (Spiderwoman, *Sun* 312). In the midst of disrepair and chaos, in the midst of mourning, in the midst of all the damage that the agents of colonization have wrought on the lands, life-ways and personal psyches of the Indigenous Peoples, one seeks transcendence. *We are not supposed to be here. Nonetheless, one wants to live.*

How did they survive? They dreamed. They created. They hid the baby (Muriel) when their father came home drunk and agitated (Spiderwoman, *Sun* 304); they helped their mother to physically restrain this large man and so prevent him from harming himself or frightening others (Spiderwoman, *Sun* 305). They remembered who they were; they stuck together; they cooperated.

Just as the Miguel sisters' violence against one another is a learned behaviour – learned through years of observing the alcohol-fuelled domestic dramas initiated by their father and through their lived experiences outside the home – so, cooperation, hard work, optimism and endurance are learned behaviours, also communicated to the sisters by their parents. Indeed, Spiderwoman's famous "Boat Story" asserts these lessons in no uncertain terms. And its placement in the performance only emphasizes this assertion.

They begin by moving rapidly through a replay of a tea party that has started to turn ugly as the sisters jockey for position ("I am sister number one. You have to listen to me") and respect ("You always leave me out") (Spiderwoman, *Sun* 302–3). As momentum builds, the tea party begins to go further and further awry until it escalates into a physical fight during which Lisa cries out, "I hate you bitches. Hope you both die" (*Sun* 304). Immediately, the scene shifts as the memory of an earlier incident is layered in. Suddenly, the shadow of a drunken and distraught Antonio Miguel returning home insinuates itself over the story of sibling warfare. And as the warring sisters remember this terrifying moment, their anger at each other evaporates in their desire to protect their baby sister, their mother and the progenitor of the chaos: "Mama jumped up and pulled the window down. Mama grabbed Daddy by the waist, we grabbed Mama, and we pulled and pulled him down to the floor [off the windowsill from which he was threatening to jump]" (*Sun* 305).

The transformation into the "Boat Story" comes out of the physical act of cooperative *pulling*, which all three enact,[14] morphing out of the tableau, which concludes the story of Antonio Miguel's thwarted suicide attempt. Quite simply, the story is this: Antonio Miguel who loved the sea was able (after years of work) to either rent or buy a seaside bungalow on Cedar Beach in New Jersey. He also acquired a boat upon which he and his brother-in-law Joe lavished countless hours each summer to refurbish and make seaworthy:

MURIEL: And every summer, my father would paint it, caulk it, pet it, hose it down; then all our friends and family would come. *(All push very hard stage left.)* And we would –

ALL: Puuush it. To the other side of the yard.

GLORIA: Then we would pose by it, on it and under it. *(All strike a pose like being photographed by boat.)* And Daddy and Uncle Joe wold [sic] stand at the helm and pretend.

LISA: And then next summer … (Spiderwoman, *Sun* 306)

14 Muriel Miguel plays her mother in this scene.

Each summer, the same ritual takes place. Each summer, friends and family gather to consummate this ritual by pushing the boat from one side of the yard to the other. Finally, we are told, the boat is deemed seaworthy. This time, when friends and family gather, the generally depressed and withdrawn Elmira Miguel throws a party! "She made potato salad, punch and sandwiches" (307). And everybody in attendance pushes the beautifully refurbished boat into the water …

Where it sinks like a stone.

Several interesting things are happening with this scene. First, as this core lesson in cooperation begins, it carries a reverberation of the former rivalry (or jockeying for position) that the Miguel sisters have been addressing throughout *Sun, Moon, and Feather*. In this contemporary, urban "Gathering House," Muriel Miguel positions herself as the director and prime engineer of the scene – the "Chanting Chief," as it were. While her sisters do not contest her primary position in this regard, Gloria Miguel does object to her own physical positioning in the scene. As the middle sister, she contends, she should be positioned between the other two. Muriel (ever the director) overrides this assertion, placing herself in the centre, and thus temporarily privileges aesthetic concerns over identity (305). Although Gloria Miguel makes it apparent that this has angered her, she does assume her assigned position and cooperates in the telling of the story. Cooperation is possible even while old hurts are still raw and old arguments remain unresolved. Perhaps, it is through the exercise of such cooperation that healing and resolution can occur.

As respondents to the primary storyteller, Lisa Mayo and Gloria Miguel add multiple layers of perspective offering alternate ways to view specifics of the story, so that its kernel may become more readily apparent. Where Muriel Miguel remembers a "beautiful red and white bungalow on a beautiful beach by a beautiful bay" (Spiderwoman, *Sun* 305), Gloria Miguel remembers "[a] dilapidated old bungalow in New Jersey on a dirty beach off a dirty polluted bay" (306) from whence, Lisa Mayo adds, "a god-awful odor" rose to meet them twice daily (306). Behind all three, ghostly black-and-white shadows of their former selves, their family and the contested boat dance behind them, opening a portal into the past. Thus, we are granted an opportunity to see the young witnesses, to see through their eyes, and so form our own judgments. The boat, beach and bungalow are neither as impressive as they must have seemed to the young Muriel nor as pitifully dilapidated as they have been remembered by her elder sisters (306). But what the visual archive really adds to the performance of this story is the sheer fun, the hard work and the comfortable sense of community engendered by this summer ritual. And these comfortably layer themselves beneath the sheer fun, physical effort and comfortable sense of community, which characterize the trio's telling.

In the final analysis, the "Boat Story" of *Sun, Moon, and Feather* reveals another layer in a sumptuously palimpsestic performative-teaching about the power and necessity of dreaming. At the root of the sisters' dreams of tea with the Queen, of escape from their childhood home, of enough to eat, of artistic success, of attentive lovers and of unconditional love lies a powerful lesson in survivance: How did they survive? They dreamed. Despite the financial and personal sacrifices of Antonio Miguel and his brother, despite the continued support of family and friends and despite all the brothers' ministrations, Antonio Miguel's beloved boat takes on water and sinks. *The dream, however, stays securely afloat*. And this is the lesson we have come to learn. We are never told if that boat *ever* became seaworthy, but we do know that the Miguel patriarch did not give up his dream that it would. Harbouring a dream is more vital than realizing it. Harbouring dreams keeps individuals afloat; unites communities; and fosters optimism, discipline and endurance. At the end of the day, when survival is threatened, a leaky boat may just be enough to carry us through. How did they survive? They received and withstood every hardship, every disappointment, every humiliation as *one* body – "[m]y echo, my shadow and me" (Spiderwoman, *Sun* 197). When all is said and done, *Sun, Moon, and Feather* is Spiderwoman Theater's teaching about living together in "that place that Indians talk about," not "dying together" within some nostalgic celebration of non-existent inhabitants of a place that never was.

Survival is not survivance. What meaning does our survival – the fact that we once lived and laughed and struggled, made love and broke bread together – carry when we are gone? In the midst of mourning, we struggle to recover and rediscover meaning, and often, when we have lost those who gave us life – those who have struggled, suffered and sacrificed to ensure our survival – we are left to question the point of their existence and of our own. As *Sun, Moon, and Feather* nears its conclusion, the Miguel sisters borrow the words of Chekhov's three sisters to express the pain of loss and to articulate the terror of doubt inspired by their parents' deaths.

MURIEL: I'm crying. I'm crying.
GLORIA: Imagine. I'm already beginning to forget her face.
MURIEL: God grant it will all work out.

GLORIA: Just as *we won't be remembered either.*
MURIEL: Weather is beautiful today.
GLORIA: *They'll forget us.* (Spiderwoman, *Sun* 313, emphasis mine)[15]

But even as the Miguel sisters give voice to Chekhov's agonized doubts, they have already recovered a solution: The dead are not simply forgotten. Gloria, who has articulated Chekhov's greatest fear, answers it: "No. She'll go on in us, in me and my family" (*Sun* 313). The stories of individuals or nations do not end with death. There is no separation between the ancestors and the descendants. The descendants carry the ancestors, and their own lives are layered within an epic tapestry in which the dead, the living and the yet unborn dance together, speak together, remember and dream together in a liminal space fraught with colour, pattern and infinite meaning. *Infinite meaning*. After all, as Muriel Miguel has noted, "You're really responsible for six generations. Even if you die, you're responsible" (qtd. in Haugo, "Weaving" 222).

If *Sun, Moon, and Feather* finds its genesis in a question around survival – a question that necessitates the re/activation of recovery and mourning, it ends with a new question that calls upon the survivors to continue dreaming, to commit to their dreams and to act upon that commitment. Through this project, the Miguel sisters begin to recover their sibling relationships, their identities within family and nation, and the legacies that have been left for them (including the names bestowed upon them at birth). They mourn and lay to rest old hurts and devastating losses. They rediscover the potency of dreaming (e.g., its role in their survivance). And they come, finally, to an acknowledgement of their responsibility (the responsibility of "We Three") to share the answer to which their quest has led them, as they continue to dream the survivance of the coming generations:

MURIEL: Such wonderful thoughts thrilled through me. Such thoughts.
GLORIA: *I'm the only grandmother now, the only grandmother in the family.*
LISA: It's warm today. (Spiderwoman, *Sun* 313–14, emphasis mine)

15 In the film version of *Sun, Moon, and Feather,* this dialogue is preceded by Muriel's account of the moment at which she communicated her father's death to her uncles: Language breaks down here, as she flatly reproduces an eerie, guttural cry that is all the more painful to hear, because it carries no histrionic undertones. It does not (in her performance) express wounded emotion; it is, rather, the expression of pure spirit – a soul rent in two: "AAAAAAAAAAAAAAH" (Zipp and Rosen). Layered atop an image of a glorious sunset over Gunayala, it reverberates across the oceans, over space and through time – a primordial echo like the first note of Creation. But unlike the first note of Creation, it is a flat echo of the human being's inchoate, uncomprehending terror in the face of a great mystery.

Communitist Acts: Recovering the Sacred, Recovering Self

Winnetou's Snake Oil Show from Wigwam City (1988)[16] was created at the behest of the Traditional Circle of Indian Elders and Youth,[17] which has been meeting annually since 1977. The Elders, at this time, particularly wished to address an epidemic problem of New Age charlatans who were building corporate empires, which purported to offer Indigenous spiritual wisdom and healing secrets for large sums of money. The Circle of Elders invited Spiderwoman Theater to join with them in this intervention, telling the sisters, "We think you should do something about this" (M. Miguel qtd. in Haugo, "Weaving" 229). In answering this call, the Miguel sisters widened the orbiculate, narrative construct through which they had recovered personal, familial and tribal identities to perform their roles/responsibilities within the larger hoop of Indigenous nations.

Winnetou's Snake Oil Show from Wigwam City is a scathingly hilarious indictment of cultural theft. With this production, Spiderwoman Theater has crafted a dramaturgical vehicle through which to deconstruct colonial metonyms and resist the appropriation, bastardization and marketing of spiritual knowledge and Indigenous identity. But this vehicle does much more than shout down the oppressor:[18] it affects a recovery of self in its recovery of Indigenous Knowledge Systems, as it imagines and operationalizes anti-colonial pedagogical and narrative frameworks that not only challenge colonial representations of Indigeneity but also render them moot.

---

16 Spiderwoman Theater first presented *Winnetou's Snake Oil Show from Wigwam City* at the Stage Door Festival in Holland. In 1989, the show's American premiere took place at New York City's Theater for the New City. From 1990–2001, the show travelled extensively throughout the United States from coast to coast and was produced at Toronto's Native Earth Performing Arts in 1993.

17 Since its inaugural gathering in 1977, the Traditional Circle of Indian Elders and Youth has met yearly (hosted by a different nation each time) to discuss issues, which involve or affect Indigenous Peoples and to develop strategies to ensure the continuance of traditional lifeways and spiritual praxis ("The American Indian"). Communiqués and statements coming out of these gatherings and other materials may be accessed by visiting the website of the American Indian Institute (see "The American Indian").

18 Feminist scholar Jill Dolan reads *Winnetou's Snake Oil Show from Wigwam City* as an expression of "racial rage over the appropriation of American Indian culture" and detects within its use of "alternative" aesthetic devices and dramaturgical structure "the potential for feminist subjectivities" (*Presence* 49). Rebecca Schneider similarly detects and privileges the "searing critique" to which Spiderwoman Theater turns its "counter mimetic" effects (171). Both readings are inarguably legitimate and

The settler society may be in need of re-education (and *Winnetou's Snake Oil Show* certainly offers this), but this performative intervention was created with Indigenous audiences in mind (see Haugo, "Weaving" 229); its spiritual core, its good effects, its teachings and its processual map present themselves for reception by Indigenous communities. Recognition and acknowledgement of these good effects will, I believe, result in the more "nuanced reading of [...] resistance" for which Ann Haugo has called ("Colonial Audiences" 133).

Indigenous lifeways, which are inseparable from spiritual praxis, are less easily relocated than some mainstream religions such as Judaism, Christianity and Islam. Andrea Smith warns that when the expression of Indigenous cosmological understandings is disconnected from the traditional territories of the people, it renders praxis impossible and ultimately destroys the belief system out of which such praxis was born (122).[19] This works itself in two ways: Most obviously, original peoples have been removed from the traditional lands they once occupied and

---

important. However, as we have seen with regard to *Sun, Moon, and Feather*, such readings fail to address the more life-affirming and life-sustaining layers of this project, which include its scrupulous search for the roots of misappropriation, the scrupulous self-examination of its artists and its inherent mechanisms for healing. Indeed, such readings reveal a marked disinterest in how performative interventions by Indigenous artists might serve the people by and for and about whom they were created. Dolan, by way of example, concludes her performance analysis of *Winnetou's Snake Oil Show* by observing that Spiderwoman Theater and other artists like them will never have the "leisure to inhabit" the spaces of "dominant cultural privilege" (*Presence* 64), but she never imagines that they may have the opportunity to inhabit a much richer community, a community, in fact, that they have enriched and that carries privileges of its own. Nor does she imagine that this performative intervention might serve any greater purpose than to "transform feminist theater once again into a site of radical political action" (*Presence* 64).

19 Cherokee scholar Daniel Heath Justice has suggested (quite rightly) that the connections between land and ceremony might be unpacked with greater delicacy than they are laid out here. This discussion, informed by Andrea Smith, might lead the reader to conclude that those who have been removed from their traditional lands are no longer able to maintain the belief systems and ceremonial praxis once held by their ancestors. These belief systems, he points out, are engendered and nurtured in "significant, long-term, and ground[ed] relationships that require deep, reciprocal investments of time, energy and commitment" (Personal Communication, 15 January 2010). And relationship is alive and dynamic; its aspect and expression are altered as the parties who are bound therein are transformed by time and/or circumstance. Hence, new relationships between Indigenous peoples and the (new) biotas to which they have been removed may be established by those who are willing to commit themselves to a sustained, collective investment of time and energy. Among Peoples who cherish their relationships with and within the biotas that contain them and whose cosmological understandings reinforce the importance of those relationships, this commitment has been bred in

hence prevented from practising their ceremonies. But more insidiously, non-Indigenous Peoples have appropriated fragments of spiritual praxis, packaging these for sale in a global market. In packaging cultural materials and spiritual practices for distribution to mass markets, they deliver the assertion "that anyone can practice Indian spirituality anywhere, so there is no need to protect the specific Native communities and their lands that are the basis of these spiritual practices" (Smith 122–3). Spiritual appropriation, then, locks us into a "catch-22" situation: It shows itself as a tool of cultural genocide insofar as it helps to uphold the seemingly plausible justifications for continued colonial infringement on Indigenous lands, which results in the curtailment or outright cessation of Indigenous embodied expression of spiritual faith and then an erosion of the faith itself. And once the damage is perceived as an irreversible *fait accompli*, those who have sought to eradicate Indigenous presence or to co-opt Indigenous praxis defend themselves thusly: Indigenous people have forgotten themselves; hence, it is up to others to teach them who they are and who they have been (see Smith 123).

And this makes sense. In some awful, unconscionable way, this makes total sense because for Indigenous people, the land is not simply a "set" upon which to play out our lives or perform rites of worship. These lands house and *are* agential forces within the larger community in the context of which human beings come to know themselves, their roles, and their responsibilities. Hence, a recovery and re-righting of the collective's cosmological understandings and spiritual praxis is tightly woven into a recovery and re-righting of collective identity and individual selfhood. And this complex project of multiple recoveries necessitates the recovery and deployment of a pedagogical process through

---

the bone and passed through the blood. Certainly, with respect to his own Cherokee Nation, Justice points to the fact that "removed peoples still maintain [traditional belief] systems, as do those who stay behind." And while elements of praxis may change their shape, "full loss and destruction are rare" (Personal Communication, 2010).

Notwithstanding, a question remains: How rare? How much is lost to a people – indeed, how much is lost to the entire Creation – when once-crucial knowledge (rendered obsolete by removal) has been forgotten by its original holders? How much is lost to a people when the fabric of the body politic has been degraded by divisions between those who maintain the traditional belief systems, those who have adopted foreign systems and those who have ceased to believe in anything at all? What losses remain to be discovered? History has yet to render a full accounting. Justice places before us an exciting task: What are the processes we must adopt, recover, invent or adapt to forge these new relationships and the modes of their expression? Certainly, I believe, this is the question that Spiderwoman Theater and the aesthetic inheritors of its artists have begun to answer for themselves.

which Indigenous humans came to know themselves long before the European invaders pretended authority to tell them who they were. It is, I argue, through the lens of this pedagogical paradigm and its application as a dramaturgical model for the contemporary stage that *Winnetou's Snake Oil Show from Wigwam City* is viewed to best effect.

Pedagogy, Dramaturgy and Metaphysical Mimesis

Before any healer can activate the remediation of any dis-ease, that healer must first seek and identify its sites, its roots, its agents and its consequences to the "organism." *Winnetou's Snake Oil Show* ventures into several originary sites from which to conduct its performative intervention on the dis-ease that results from cultural appropriation. The piece opens with a parody of an early scene in Karl May's *Winnetou* during which a noble Teutonic hero who is still a stranger to America's "Wild West" has managed to kill an aggressive bear and so save the life of his noble Apache counterpart. On Spiderwoman's stage, May's learned Teuton makes short work of this bear with a "hit on the head, [a] shot in the eye, [and a] stab in the chest." For this admirable feat, May's fictional Apache Winnetou bestows upon him the name "Old Shatterhand." (Spiderwoman, *Winnetou's* 238). These two heroes of the "New World" eventually become blood brothers, as they recognize qualities in each other, which they have never been able to detect in anybody else (Indigenous or European). Of course, as Lisa Mayo observed in 1991, while Winnetou is "brave, courageous, has ethics [and is] very good looking [...] *he is never as good as the German*" ("Appropriation" 54, emphasis mine). Hence, he must die, leaving his European blood brother to remember and embody his noble spirit. And herein lies the terrible genius of the mechanism through which "white people establish themselves as the true inheritors of Indianness" (Smith 123): The "noble savage" is disappearing. Indeed, he must perforce disappear, as he is not equipped to compete with and within the "superior" settler society. However, to ameliorate this tragic denouement, the superior settler society will take it upon itself to salvage the cultural fragments it deems to be valuable or worthy of survival. Certainly, these are the sentiments with which Karl May introduced his *Winnetou* in 1892:

> What a proud, handsome figure he used to be as he flew over the wide savanna, the mane of his mustang fluttering in the wind! And how miserable and degenerate he has become [...] like a *mangy cur*, reduced to begging and stealing [...] What could this race have achieved had it been given the opportunity? *What characteristic cultural forms will forever be lost to mankind with the annihilation of this people?* (May xiii, emphasis mine)

It is with these words that generations of German nationals and their European neighbours have received their first introduction to Indigenous people in North America. And it is from such preposterous fictions that they formed lasting opinions about us. May's questions insinuated themselves into the hearts and minds of countless hobbyists and directed the philosophies and practices of thousands of Indian Clubs across Europe and North America: "What characteristic cultural forms will forever be lost to mankind with the annihilation of this People" *if we do not take it upon ourselves to preserve these things?*

Karl May had lived a hard and terrible life in Germany and had spent most of his life in debtors' prison. From there, he wrote 73 novels – every one of them an exotic potboiler set in a faraway land, peopled by "Turks," "Africans" and all manner of "exotics." His *Winnetou* with its heroic German protagonist and noble Apache sidekick captured the imaginations not only of May's compatriots but also of readers across Europe. We might well be tempted to underestimate the influence of this "outdated" and "obscure" work. But it is a matter of public record that May (for as much as his work has been dismissed by "serious" literary scholars) has been the one of the most read authors in his country and throughout Europe (Kimmelman). Indeed, May's "noble savage" has inhabited and profoundly affected the German imagination (and the imaginations of their Dutch, Swiss, Italian and Russian neighbours) throughout the twentieth century and into today. In 2006, journalist Dirk Kurbjuweit dubbed Germany "The Land of Winnetou" in *Der Spiegel*, a national news magazine. He observed with reference to the nation's soccer team:

> There are the German poets and thinkers, the German forest, the German "comfortableness," German efficiency, the German longing for Italy, and there is Winnetou [...] *Winnetou is the quintessential German national hero*, a paragon of virtue, a nature freak, a romantic, a pacifist at heart, but in a world at war he is the best warrior, alert, strong, sure [...] Eleven Winnetous and we would be world champions. (Kurbjuweit qtd. in Kimmelman, emphasis mine)

Certainly, there can be no mistaking the sentiment here! As inheritors of Karl May's literary legacy (most particularly, his epic *Winnetou*), the German people (and their neighbours into whose languages May's novels have been translated) have come to see themselves – reflected in the mirror (*Spiegel*) of the national *Zeitgeist* – as the heroic preservers and "rightful heirs" of Indigenous cultural wealth. It is not unreasonable to identify May's *Winnetou* as a critical site of misappropriation, along with the Wild West and Medicine Shows that toured Europe and the Americas throughout the nineteenth and early twentieth centuries, the contemporary commercialized pageants that celebrate the "Indian Princess" and the "noble savage," and the fraudulent spiritualists who purport to sell Indigenous teachings and ceremony. Nor is it unreasonable to position May's opus squarely within the psycho-spiritual heart of spiritual theft and cultural genocide.

Spiderwoman Theater frames its performative assault on this spiritual theft with key scenes from May's novel, restating and answering May's thesis with brutal succinctness. In so doing, the Miguel sisters also answer countless individuals (encountered during early European tours) who wondered if they were intimately acquainted with May's famous Apache, who claimed to have been transformed by ceremony into Sioux "sisters" or "brothers," and who refused to acknowledge the racist ideology that lay at the heart of their preconceptions about the tribal peoples they so admired or to abandon those preconceptions (see Mayo, "Appropriation" 54; Mayo qtd. in Burns and Hurlbutt 176–7; Spiderwoman, *Winnetou's* 234). Such pretenders are neither heroic preservers nor legitimate heirs; they are, quite simply, opportunistic carrion eaters – destroyers of the very cultures on which they perpetrate their "ministrations."

> MURIEL: She looked at me and smiled and said "I'm an Indian, too." Too [...]
>
> GLORIA: Thank you, thank you, thank you. For discovering me, for recognizing me, for saving me. Thank you for giving me the opportunity to exist. For knowing more about me than I do. Thank you for giving me spirituality. Thank you [...]
>
> MURIEL: That's nice. I smile. My rubbery lips stretch over my teeth. My eyes go blank. My shoulders go up. Sell out, sell out, sell out, sell out.
>
> GLORIA: Thank me, thank me, thank me. My spirit, my body, my wisdom. You feed on me, create on me, enjoy my remains. Thank me, thank me, thank me. (Spiderwoman, *Winnetou's* 258–9, stage directions omitted)

Woven into this indictment of cultural theft are crucial and far-reaching questions around the issue of complicity. Apart from colonial agency, Indigenous Peoples must also interrogate our own (at times, enforced or unwitting) complicity in the misappropriation of sacred knowledge and spiritual praxis. If one smiles and says nothing to those who flout falsified identities, is one a "sell out"? And how do we address the struggles of those authentic American Indians who participated in the popular dissemination of stereotypes by performing in the Wild West shows and other pageants of ersatz Indigeneity to avoid prison or to feed their families? What of the Guna showman and his Rappahannock wife who don Plains regalia to hunt stuffed wolves and sell homemade snake oil or turtle cock juice[20] in Central Park to advertise the latest Hollywood Western or to entertain Sunday picnickers? Are they, too, "sell outs"? What of those authentic Indigenous individuals who sell spirituality to the highest bidder or who abuse the authority and unquestioning trust invested upon them by the desperately trusting and spiritually needy?

These questions are layered into the performative mola as home movies of authentic powwows organized and attended by their family (1940s–70s) provide the backdrop for the live Snake Oil Show, during which the performers advertise a ceremonial retreat "all for the low, low price of $3000.00 for the weekend" (Spiderwoman, *Winnetou's* 255). And as these historic archives continue to be projected throughout the show, they manifest themselves as a potent contrapuntal underlay against which Muriel Miguel interprets the lyrics of the Hollywood ballad "Pale Moon (An Indian Love Song)" with a farcically ersatz version of Plains Indian sign language and against which Mother Moon Face (played by Hortencia Colorado) flirts shamelessly with a (white male) audience member who has volunteered to undergo Spiderwoman's plastic ceremony, which is guaranteed to transform him into an "authentic" Indian (*Winnetou's* 257).

Ceremony rests at the heart of this production. It manifests itself as a series of misbegotten rites as the "shamanesses" Mother Moon Face, Princess Pissy Willow (Lisa Mayo), Minnie Hall Runner (Gloria Miguel), and Ethel Christian Christiansen (Muriel Miguel) perform equestrian feats on mops instead of horses, execute bullwhip stunts and rope-tricks with "invisible" implements, channel "spirits" afflicted with hemorrhoids, and transform Caucasian acolytes into American Indians. Here, their pointed criticism of plastic spirituality could not be lost on their audiences. More crucially, however, with *Winnetou's Snake Oil Show*, Spiderwoman Theater has curated a ceremony of *recovery*,

20 Muriel Miguel told the story of her uncle Joe and his trade in "turtle cock juice," marketed as an antidote to impotence and prepared in his bathtub, at a workshop facilitated by James Luna in October 2005 at the Graduate Centre for Study of Drama (University of Toronto). This story has also been woven into several live Spiderwoman productions, although it has not yet been published.

which effects the transformation of both performer and witness. With Hortencia Colorado, the Miguel sisters have *made* for themselves a vehicle of authentic healing from the shameful detritus of falsehood. And their audiences (regardless of ethnicity) are invited to *share* – to participate at various key stages – in this rite of re-righting and to thereby be transformed. When Princess Pissy Willow demonstrates her "crack shot" with a toy rifle, a volunteer from the audience is selected to come up onto the stage and hold the balloons, which are her targets. This volunteer, however, becomes complicit in the fakery, as s/he has been armed with a straight pin and instructed to burst the targets s/he holds up as the rifle is "discharged." The volunteer's actions are *completely obvious* to the audience, which is enthusiastically encouraged by Muriel Miguel's "shamaness" to vigorously applaud the princess's skill. And this, it invariably does with like vigour and enthusiasm.

The revelation of the mechanics of the illusion is one key component of ceremonial praxis in many Indigenous communities. Across the nations, healers, ceremonial practitioners, and artists have, in key moments, traditionally revealed the sleights of hand behind the uncanny illusions they create.[21] One deliberately allows the observer to see the red clay he chews, "later to be spit out as his own 'blood'" (La Barre qtd. in Schechner, *Environmental* 174), just as the Yaqui deer dancer, who is understood to represent a visitant from another world to the world of men, makes no attempt to disguise his own humanity beneath the antlers he has donned for the ceremony. The non-Indigenous observer has been trained to regard such revelatory instances as evidentiary of failure – the failure of the deer dancer to completely transform (Schechner, *Between* 4) or the failure of the "magician-shaman-showman" to sustain an illusion (La Barre qtd. in Schechner, *Environmental* 174). This speaks to the Western propensity to privilege the *semblance of material*

21 Tsitsika, a Kwakiutl word that means "everything is not real," is the name bestowed upon the Winter Ceremonials of that nation (Norwell qtd. in Ford 198). During this time of Potlatches and clan initiations, dances depicting gory executions and "brutal" assaults by clan initiates on community members (during which their houses are ransacked, or their bodies are bitten and seem to bleed real blood) are enacted to the delight of all (but heretofore horrified outsiders and anthropologists). But all is not real. The victims of the Hamatsa initiate's rapacious attacks have become "actors" for the occasion. They conceal blood bags beneath their clothing to be broken at the appropriate moment, and they scream with convincing outrage as their houses are "ransacked" by the Hamatsa initiate even as his kinsman follows closely documenting all property damage (for which restitution will be made) and ensuring that the initiate does not damage chattel that has been designated off-limits for the purposes of the "play" (Norwell cited in Ford 198–208).

verisimilitude over spiritual reality. But the teaching communicated through such "flawed" and "failed" illusions is that the material world is somehow less real, less relevant, less potent than the world of spirit that lies beyond the veil. As such, it warrants far less attention than the interdependencies that link all with all. *Healing is what is required, not a magic show.* And the healer, himself, despite his showmanship is only a vessel through which the spirits work. Parlour tricks are only parlour tricks, and as it turns a blind eye to the slippages that reveal the banal impotence thereof, the audience plays its own part in the production: it understands and embraces the teaching.

Similarly, Spiderwoman's audiences, as informed and consenting participants in the sham rituals of *Winnetou's*, are lulled into revealing and enacting their own complicity in actual acts of cultural theft outside the theatre. As the sham reaches ludicrous heights in a climactic "ceremony" during which a Caucasian audience member will be transformed into an American Indian of perhaps the "Wishee Washee" or the "Rappa Hamburg" tribe and adopt – with the enthusiastic encouragement of the cast – the name "Two Dogs Fucking," the audience raises its collective voice to chant its approbation as Muriel Miguel conducts (Spiderwoman, *Winnetou's* 257).[22] In this moment of *sharing*, wherein all witnesses are invited to take their place in the performative mola *created* by Spiderwoman Theater, the opportunity to learn from and be transformed by the experience manifests itself: nobody is innocent here. To differing extents, we are all complicit in the crime of cultural theft, and it is important that all of us interrogate our *ownership* here if we are to end it. The flaws built into Spiderwoman's performance do not exist as an invitation to simply laugh ruefully at the more ludicrous aspects of cultural theft; rather, they contribute to a *metaphysical mimesis*, as it were – revealing the spiritual mechanisms of misappropriation and the extent of the damage caused by the "Great North American Medicine Show" in all its incarnations.

Internalized shame and personal despair are manifestations of that damage. And as the company tracks the movements of those who vandalized Indigenous cultures, each performer is led into an honest reckoning with that damage, which has to some extent directed her relationships and choices: Muriel Miguel, for instance, voices her youthful

22 When the initiate is deemed fully prepared, the "rite of transformation" is completed by sending him on his way armed with a brown paper "medicine pouch" (containing a Q-tip, a Band-aid and a condom) and a picture of a handsome American Indian male in full Plains regalia, which the "transformed" initiate is instructed to hold in front of his face for the rest of his natural life.

wish that her mother had been "taller" and "like every other mother in the neighborhood" (*Winnetou's* 252). While some (represented by Muriel Miguel's Ethel Christian Christiansen) sell false prophecy and may don a false identity along with faux buckskin and plastic beads, even as they fall into inauthentic "trances" (see *Winnetou's* 247), authentic American Indians have often been ashamed of their ethnicity, of the physical features they have inherited from their parents, and of their authentic gifts or spiritual power. Indeed, such power, when it is authentic, is never flamboyant, and it brings no monetary gain. The body of Elmira Miguel became the bridge, which linked spirit to material and across which the dead communicated with the living. And for this dedication of body, Elmira was never paid in money; instead, we are told, those who sought her services "brought crackers, buns, and tea" (*Winnetou's* 253) as tribute or payment while her youngest daughter flinched with (misplaced) shame, because her mother was not like "other mothers" in the neighbourhood (*Winnetou's* 252).

Pro-Action vs. Reaction: The Red Reading

Several years ago, one of my (non-Indigenous) students responded to this idea of misplaced shame by observing, "all children feel some shame with regards to their parents." Sadly, in North America (and perhaps throughout the industrialized world) this seems to be the case. But it is important to realize that the gap between youth and Elders in Indigenous cultures is not a natural occurrence. The West has come to accept – indeed, to nurture – this gap. Children in North America expect and are expected to leave home and to assert their independence. They are conditioned early in life to cultivate and celebrate their individuality; and quite often, the first manifestations of that individuality are expressed through impatient tolerance and/or long-suffering shame of their parents. These expressions, interestingly, are encouraged by peers, celebrated in the media, and met with approbation and acceptance throughout the culture.

For Indigenous Peoples, this generational gap is one consequence of the colonial project. Our children were removed from their parental homes and communities; their parents' language was quite literally beaten out of them; they were taught to speak, worship, eat, dress, and work in accordance with settler norms. They were taught to be ashamed of their parents, of ancestral traditions, of their languages, their belief systems and their lifeways. The shame that some of us have come to feel is not a natural phase of human development; it has been imposed upon us by those who sought to destroy Indigenous family and kinship structures; *it is not merely an aspect of the universal human condition*. Indeed, as I write in this historical moment, Indigenous people across Turtle Island are working purposefully to bridge the imposed lacunae between the generations, between Indigenous communities, and between the people themselves.

Within *Winnetou's Snake Oil* Show, Muriel Miguel takes the first steps to address the gap between herself and her mother. She publicly acknowledges the shame she felt in the face of her mother's authenticity. And this acknowledgement will lay the groundwork for Spiderwoman's next production *Reverb-ber-ber-rations*, which is a profoundly personal mourning song for Elmira Miguel and a celebration of the authentic spiritual gifts she left to her daughters. But this site of shame occupies only one layer of a subtly intricate matrix of damage caused by misappropriation. Another key site of the damage wrought by the corruption of Indigenous story, the misappropriation of Indigenous spiritual praxis, and the grossly constructed distortion of Indigenous image is the positioning of Indigenous women – or, rather, the *erasure* of position. The imposition of patriarchal governing structures has resulted in the glorification of the "chief" without recognition that this male authority figure was a servant of the people; he had learned his language, his position in the family, his responsibilities, and much of his history from his mother; he had inherited his clan membership from his mother, and in many nations, he was appointed and guided by a council of Clan Mothers. Across Turtle Island within many Indigenous communities (including Pueblo, Cherokee, and Haudenosaunee), women held the property, and they made the decisions that would affect the future of their nations. But when the settler came, he refused to deal with Indigenous women, preferring to negotiate with an autonomous male "sovereign." Eventually, as colonial agents took control of the land, they altered the political and economic structures of Indigenous societies, so that women no longer owned their property and had no say in decisions made on behalf of the whole nation. Hence, across Turtle Island, Indigenous communities have been working diligently to operationalize their understanding that the project of re-worlding is dependent upon the repositioning of the female to her former place in the social fabric.

As *Winnetou's* performers "model" European-designed costumes and characterizations of the American Indian ("Noble Savage"; Mangy "Hordes"; or flamboyant, crack shot, trick-riding "Princesses") and play out the settler narratives on their feet, the layers of faux hides and hideous lamé, macho posturing, razzle-dazzle quackery and sexually charged salesmanship begin to unravel. The shoddy patchwork reveals its flaws. And beneath these, the authentic originals – solidly designed, Indigenous female bodies – publicly dis-cover themselves as the sites in which authentic Indigenous gwage (essence) may be sought and found.

Birgit Däwes asserts that the troupe's "asymmetrical assignment of 21 characters to four actresses and the visible dissolve of various characters into others (e.g., when Gloria Miguel changes from the Bear into Klekepetra, "leaving the costume in the center of the stage" [57]) clearly undermine essentialist notions of cultural difference" (337). But such a reading diverts us from the kernel/gwage of the project and obfuscates an essential truth. As the Miguel sisters with Hortencia Colorado lend their physical and vocal instruments to play out European notions of cultural difference, they are accessing cellular memory. They are accessing a history that has been inscribed on and within the Indigenous body, which serves as the container/archive of that history and the site from which the "text" of that history may be both "read" and articulated. The published versions of Spiderwoman's works, then, should be understood as *archives of performance*, not "dramatic literature." Similarly, the family films, which are frequently projected onto the bodies of the performers during Spiderwoman shows, should not be read simply as texts or historical archives in and of themselves. Layered atop or behind the performing body, these celluloid shadows serve as a visual reminder that the *living flesh* across which they dance is a container for communal/ancestral memory. We embody all of those who came before. And as storytellers, we serve our communities by becoming the vessels through which they speak. Working within this aesthetic realm, the performing female body does not simply challenge "essentialist notions of cultural difference." Rather, she conducts a performative "Red Reading" on the settler narrative. In so doing, she weighs her own embodied knowledge (tradition/ancestral memory) against the distorted histories and deformed representations of Indigenous humanity that have been documented on countless pages to allow her "readers" to assess the value of those European-authored texts for themselves. As she embodies the "noble savage" Winnetou, the "mangy hordes," the "Princess" and the "Shamaness" and utters the words that have been scripted for them, the fantasy collapses and the murderous mechanics of the colonizing *Zeitgeist* are revealed.

No exaggeration is required here. The troupe's staged excerpts from May's novel adhere faithfully to his text. If they seem ridiculous, the troupe has not had to bastardize them to make them so. When the authentic Indigenous body revisits the sites of misappropriation to embody the inauthentic, the *faux* fabric of these constructed identities begins to disintegrate and the authentic Indigenous body (the authoritative text) bursts through its seams to share itself and to celebrate its unique gwage, clearly differentiating itself from those who are estranged from the lands they occupy and from the narratives these newcomers have constructed to justify their occupation: "Now *I* telling you. Watch *me. I'm alive. I'm* not defeated. *I* begin" (Spiderwoman, *Winnetou's* 262, emphasis mine).

The Play Text and the Pictograph: *Reverb-ber-ber-rations* as Curing Chant for the Contemporary Stage

> LISA: [...] Grandma said, "Your mother was born with a caul, so she has strong psychic powers. She can tell the future. She can see through anybody." (Spiderwoman, *Winnetou's* 252–3)
>
> MURIEL: [...] My mother's a witch I didn't say that (Spiderwoman, *Reverb* 106)
>
> GLORIA: Self-hatred can be a secret. Self denial can be a secret. My self-hatred came from the outside.
>
> LISA: It *all* does, Gloria. (Spiderwoman Theater, *Reverb* Rehearsals 1990 Tape 9)

Always, within this process, we begin again. Each cycle of asking, seeking, making, owning, sharing, and celebrating certainly generates answers, which inspire in the learner a deeper understanding of self in community. Then, it generates further questions, which require the learner to repeatedly re-engage with the process, discovering new answers and generating more questions for which answers will have to be found. Similarly, while Spiderwoman's published works could be read as isolated texts, we would lose something significant in isolating one from the whole. Each play text documents a *stage* in a process of becoming – a process, which is not linear and therefore requires that stages be revisited in subsequent works. Inspired by half-remembered fragments and generated by echoes, they reverberate, expanding the orbiculate construct in which they are contained. Each new question becomes yet another stone cast upon the waters, engendering more circles within circles within circles and alternately drawing the individual inward and then outward and then inward again on an eternally spiralling journey to the self.

If *Winnetou's Snake Oil Show from Wigwam City* was a communitist project designed to re-right the dominant society's bastardized "writing" of Indigenous identity in the political, mythological, and spiritual realms, it has led its creatrices back to the personal and familial realms by revealing glimpses of the authentic beneath the layers of ersatz farce. If, beneath the ephemeral posturing of the mighty-but-doomed "brave," the warm, brown flesh of female Indigeneity is revealed, what is her place in all of this? Where lies her power? How does it manifest itself? If, beside the glamorous and mercenary "shamaness" glowing in the refracted aura of her lamé gown, a tiny, unprepossessing mother becomes a source of shame for her children because she exercises the gifts with which she was born, how do those gifts reverberate throughout the lives of her children and grandchildren?

I receive *Winnetou's Snake Oil Show from Wigwam City* as a communal ceremony of healing (framed within a farcical, misaligned "ceremony"), which has been designed to peel back the layers of cultural appropriation to expose and treat the roots of communal *dis-ease*. And I suggest that through their curation of and participation in this communitist project, the Miguel sisters were carried back to the root of a very personal dis-ease – a dis-ease requiring immediate attention and redress. Spiderwoman's subsequent show *Reverb-ber-ber-rations* (1990) offers itself as an avenue of this redress. Here, the story, upon which this piece is based – "Mama's Caul" (see Mojica and Knowles 101–2) – and which was first articulated in *Winnetou's Snake Oil Show* by Lisa Mayo – is remembered word for word, claimed and retold by all three sisters as if it were in itself a medicine chant taught first to the eldest sister by her grandmother and mother and then taught by the eldest to her younger sisters. Like survivors sifting through the wreckage (of their childhood discomfort and shame), the Miguel sisters performatively deconstruct their legacy to find at its kernel the thing that will make them whole.

GLORIA: Grandma said
Your mother was born with a caul
So she has strong psychic powers
MURIEL: She can tell the future
She can see through anybody
She can tell the meaning of the symbols
Left by coffee grounds and tea leaves
In the bottom of cups
LISA: When Mama went into a trance
Mama said everything changed in the world
TUTTI: Mama said, Mama said, Mama said (Spiderwoman, *Reverb* 107)

In Gunayala, apprentices first learn medicine chants by rote. Working side by side with the healer, they labour to articulate and embody each lesson without error. Only after they have mastered this will they have earned the right to see the pictographic notations, which they then will study and interpret.[23] Let us, then, consider this play text as an annotation of embodied knowledge and impulse – a "cousin," as it were, of the pictographic notation. It is exciting to consider, then, that Spiderwoman Theater's scripts are first annotated upon and within the bodies of its performers. Their dense poetry and the lengthy mono-and-dialogic chants, which form the narrative base of *Reverb-ber-ber-rations*, are not evocative tellings as much as they are momentous *doings*. Like the Guna curing chants, which Mac Chapin likens to "scripts in which the events being described take place *simultaneously* in the world of spirit as the words come out of the chanter's mouth" (235, emphasis mine), Spiderwoman's "scripts" are not simply intended to be read or appreciated on page and stage as much as they are meant to be *experienced*. As audiences, we are invited to inhabit the worlds Spiderwoman articulates into being and to be, ourselves, inhabited by those worlds. This intersection of Guna tradition with Spiderwoman's performative praxis is fraught with compelling possibilities.

When contemporary Indigenous dramaturgical models are constructed upon nation-specific traditions, the potential for activation arising from a rigorous practice of remembering and re-*membering* is great indeed.[24] As storytellers work within these models, based in tradition, their bodies are remembering and being re-membered as they

---

23 Oswaldo DeLeón Kantule speaking in his role as cultural advisor and set designer at rehearsals during the first developmental workshop of Monique Mojica's *Chocolate Woman Dreams the Milky Way* (10 November 2007, Equity Showcase, Toronto, ON).

24 This convergence of traditional, land-based cultural and aesthetic praxis emerging from Gunayala with Spiderwoman Theater's development of a contemporary artistic practice in New York City, perhaps, owes itself more to (what Muriel Miguel has termed) "organic continuity" than it does to an intentional exercise in devising a nation-specific performance methodology that is explicitly beholden to the ceremonial praxis and aesthetic principles of a specific community or nation. However, the *frame* through which I have come to understand "organic continuity" and its mechanics has expanded, as I have witnessed the continuing development of Spiderwoman's Storyweaving Practice in the creative investigations and works of Monique Mojica.

Mojica's artistry finds its beginnings in a like "persistence of a known sense" (Personal Communication, 2022), but the dramaturgical and structural models that Mojica continues to develop emerge from her investigations of a "known sense" – from deliberate, rigorous study of the cosmological foundations and aesthetic principles belonging to the nations from which she has descended; from her inclusion of saglas, Elders, and Knowledge Keepers during all stages of the creative process; and from her deeply intentional engagement of the land as a creative partner, inspiritor, and somatic director in the creation of her work. *"Organic continuity," in this instance requires not only the unfettered flow of epigenetic memory and cultural legacy but also intention, rigour, and intimate engagement with shifting landscapes and evolving knowledge systems to affect survivors and effect their survivance.*

remember other "bodies" within the material and spiritual realms. Mama's caul (see Spiderwoman *Reverb* 106–8) for instance, is a fleshly artefact still retained by Muriel Miguel in the family home. This carefully preserved caul remembers the birth of Elmira Miguel to Elizabeth Ashton Moore. Like the pictographic notation, it functions as the mnemonic aid, which will link the generations to come with those who are now and those who came before through the stories of their coming and of the spiritual gift that reverberates through the blood – the gift that the Miguel sisters have come finally to accept and to celebrate:

> MURIEL: Grandma said you should be thankful
> GLORIA: You have a gifted Mother
> LISA: Grandma had the gift too
> And all of my mother's children have the gift
> *All begin to give the names of people in the family who have the Gift.*
> (Spiderwoman, *Reverb* 108)

When Elmira Miguel's gift manifested itself, "everything changed in the world" (*Reverb* 107). And everything changed in *her*. Her physical being – the house of an isolate soul – reconfigured itself to become a vessel for a multitude of spirits with whom she communicated (*Reverb* 108). In turn, as the gift manifests itself in Elmira Miguel's youngest daughter, her own body becomes a vessel for the ancestral spirits who have passed this gift down to her. And as Muriel's body opens itself to the gift, its cells rearrange themselves transforming the contours and structural supports of her outer being. As noted in the previous chapter, when the long-dead Elizabeth Ashton Moore ("Grandma") came unbidden to momentarily possess Muriel Miguel, everything changed – her internal voice, her eyes, and the sounds she heard from within and around her. Indeed, "[her] whole face became another face" (*Reverb* 108). It is exciting to speculate here that as the sites of contemporary performance are being internally reconfigured (e.g., the internal decolonization of its artists), so too may their outer structure (e.g., the architecture and administration of the sites upon which the story unfolds) begin to change shape.[25]

---

25 Indeed, when one visits the Native American Women Playwrights Archives at the Walter Havighurst Special Collections & University Archives (Miami University Libraries, Oxford, OH) to which Spiderwoman has donated its private papers, scripts, rehearsal notes, and production materials, the monumental difficulties an editor might encounter in trying to reassemble these works (without access to the performers' corporeal archives) are abundantly apparent. Hence, it is clear just why so few play texts (amid so extensive a body of work) have been published.

In Gunayala, physical illness has traditionally been regarded as an attack on the burba of an individual. Textile artist and scholar of the mola Herta Puls defines burba as the indicator of "a power or essence that is part of the human being but can also be the noise of the wind, the music of the flute, the heat of the sun, a mirror image or an echo" (46). Although burba is often translated as "soul" (a word, which will at times be used here), Puls differentiates the Guna concept of burba from the Judeo-Christian concept of soul by reminding us that in Guna cosmology, all things whether animate or inanimate possess burba – an essence that communicates with and that has the power to affect other essences outside of itself on multiple planes of existence.[26] The intricate system of curing (which is the cornerstone of Guna culture)

---

26 During her first visit to Gunayala in the fall of 2008, Monique Mojica and her party were taken on a medicine walk through the rainforest on one of the island communities. She was brought to the imposing sabbigarda tree, which is known as the medicine tree for artists (Personal communication 2008). During the equatorial summer season, an orbiculate pattern begins to appear on its drying leaves as the fungus that lives upon them begins to grow outward in radiating circles (Puls 47). Mojica was instructed to hug the sabbigarda and to ask it to invest her with the strength and vision to go on with her work. This, she has testified, was a powerful moment for her, as she had come to this ancestral home specifically to ask permission of the community's saglas to recount traditional Guna stories in her *Chocolate Woman Dreams the Milky Way* and to solicit the participation of other Guna artists in the project.

Traditionally, an Inaduled gathers the leaves of the sabbigarda and distills from these a liquid (invested with the tree's burba) with which to soak the eyes of mola-makers to enable them to create beautiful, intricate designs. The inspiration these artisans have derived from this medicine often manifests itself quite literally, as the patterns of the sabbigarda leaves are often a traditional feature of classic mola designs (Puls 47).

The concatenations between the aesthetic and dramaturgical structural models discussed throughout this work and the foundational principles and processual models of traditional medicine in Gunayala are compelling indeed. In Spiderwoman Theater's early work, these are evidenced in the ability to apprehend and the impulse to navigate the complex layers of the unseen world and in the oral molas (finely layered chants) they have crafted as their conveyance. It is important to note here, again, that the reverberations of Guna tradition, aesthetic, and structure in Spiderwoman Theater's work spring organically from somatically ingrained rhythms of daily life – from songs and stories and utterances of a Guna father and of Guna uncles that charged the air day upon day and year upon year within their Brooklyn home.

As we, later, explore the dramaturgical structure of *Chocolate Woman Dreams the Milky Way*, this "persistence of a known sense" continues. But it *evolves*, as Monique Mojica adds a layer of intentionality to this foundation of epigenetic memory and ingrained cultural knowledge. The dramaturgical and structural elements of her *Chocolate Woman* and subsequent works constitute a rigorously crafted methodology through which Mojica applies nation-specific Traditional Knowledge and aesthetic principles to the crafting of a contemporary performative event.

bases itself on the understanding that the material world is simply one layer of existence in which the fleshly element (in all its interactions) is a "secondary" reflection of the "world of spirit [or burba]" (Chapin 219). When the body becomes ill, in other words, it is understood as the physical manifestation of a violent disorder that has taken place in the metaphysical realm: dysfunction in the unseen (innermost) structure of being reconfigures the being's outer structure. Two primary ways in which the burba of a Guna individual may be adversely affected are (1) soul loss, which occurs when a piece of one's burba has been abducted by a malevolent spirit, and (2) the infiltration of an individual's body by the malevolent spirit, which then corrupts his/her burba (Chapin 220). Once the illness has been diagnosed by the Nele (the diagnostic specialist), the Inaduled (medicinal specialist) goes out to gather medicinal plants and then performs a series of chants designed to communicate with *their* burba and so confer with those medicinal spirits about the correct action to take to ensure effectiveness. Finally, the Igar Wisid (Knower of Chants)[27] sends his/her own burba to the fourth (of the eight levels) of the spirit world to defeat the malevolent spirit and to restore the violated burba (Chapin 220).

Reverb-ber-ber-rations is both a ceremony of mourning (literally, an honour song for Elmira Miguel) and a ceremony of personal healing, which draws upon aesthetic and cosmological principles specific to Guna curing practices around soul loss. It is, at once, a piece about spiritual reclamation through ceremony and a ceremonial act that effects the restoration of the afflicted, abducted, or fragmented human soul. In the realm of the personal and the familial, "This is a song for [their] mother / This is a song for [their] mothers / This is a song to release the *pain, the shame, the secrets*" (Spiderwoman, *Reverb* 130, emphasis mine). The "pain, the shame, the secrets" belong as much to personal identity as to an individual's youthful, misplaced shame over her unconventional parents. During rehearsals, as the Miguel sisters cut through the layers (that were their stories) seeking the invisible threads that would connect them, Muriel Miguel identified the essence of the piece – soul loss: "the secret and the shame … We were women of colour. That was the secret" (Spiderwoman Theater, *Reverb* 1990 Rehearsals Tape 9). She

27 Mac Chapin has translated "Igar Wisid" as "Knower of Chants" (220). This is likely not a literal translation. Monique Mojica informs me that "Igar" means "path or way" (Personal Communication 2022). To know the correct and appropriate chant, I surmise, is to know the correct and appropriate path that must be followed through the spirit world to effect a successful cure.

then went on to articulate its "cure": *"I am not ashamed of being a woman of color. It is not a secret ... This is our future ... This is our strength"* (Spiderwoman Theater, *Reverb* 1990 Rehearsals Tape 9). The cure, of course, is not just for her or for her sisters. The troupe's eye is squarely on the next generation here: To remain afflicted by the poison of self-denial, self-hatred, and shame is to pass those things on to one's children and grandchildren; it is a dark, destructive gift, which reverberates throughout the generations and which *denies* them. Hence, when the layers have finally been cut away to reveal the pattern of this performative mola,[28] all that remains is the kernel – the gwage – of this healing rite, which is its solution:

MURIEL: I am an Indian woman
I am proud of the women that came before me
I am claiming the wisdom of the woman in my family
I am a woman with two daughters, a granddaughter
I am a woman with a woman lover
I am here now
I am saying this now because to deny these events about me and my life
Would be to deny my children (*Reverb* 131–2)

Just as it is within the community that we come to realize personal identity, so it is within the community that the solution to the very personal problem of soul loss is to be found. It is within the realm of communal ceremonial praxis that the Miguel sisters have come to understand, accept, embrace, and be embraced by the knowledge that they are American Indian women. And so it is that a Lakota Sun Dance and a Taos Corn Dance are identified by the Miguel sisters as key sites of their own spiritual awakening and restoration of soul.

---

28 At this time, Spiderwoman Theater did not specifically refer to its process in quite this way, although Miguel's practice was always focused on locating the essence/kernel of each story and structuring the finished product by performatively and poetically manifesting the connection between one kernel and the others. The term "performative mola" emerges from the work I was privileged to do with Monique Mojica. And my apprehension of these elements in their work emerges not only from my participation in workshops facilitated by Muriel Miguel, Gloria Miguel, and Monique Mojica but also from Mojica's rigorous study and application of nation-specific aesthetic principles and cosmological praxis to her own creative process and to the impressive body of knowledge she has acquired and articulated around patterning (on the land and in material culture).

In the "Sundance" section (Spiderwoman, *Reverb* 112–17), three discrete experiences within two key ceremonies are interwoven to recreate a collective moment of reawakening. All three sisters had been invited to take part in a Lakota Sun Dance.[29] Muriel travelled to Crow Dog's Paradise on the Rosebud Reservation to dance (Mojica, Personal Communication 2022). And Gloria, who feared that she could not physically withstand the rigours of dancing, came to witness as Muriel fulfilled her Sun Dance vow (*Reverb* 113). Meanwhile Lisa Mayo chose not to join her sisters, because she could not obtain permission to bring her non-Indigenous husband and stepson. She opted, instead, to visit a Corn Dance in Taos, New Mexico, as an *outsider* – a "tourist" – with the family into which she had married. But as the Miguel sisters recall their individual experiences from a time before, they sound into being (through invocation and drumming) a ceremony for the here and now, which connects sister with sister, ancestor with descendant, and dancer with witness – body to body and burba to burba in a place where healing can begin.

These sites of ceremony are liminal spaces of permanent transformation where ants converse with humans (Spiderwoman, *Reverb* 114), where cloud fathers hold up their exhausted daughters (*Reverb* 116), where visions of the future and ethereal echoes from the past surge up from the earth to reverberate through contemporary bodies and where "[t]he dancers [who] came from long ago" welcome the dancers of today into the circle of nations (*Reverb* 116). Whether she is standing "behind a rope with the tourists" (*Reverb* 117) at the Taos corn dance (Mayo), whether she has wandered away from the Sun Dance circle to feast her eyes on all the colours of sacred landscapes (Gloria),[30] or whether she is dancing on sacred ground at the edge of exhaustion (Muriel), a revelation occurs, and she is restored to herself and to her "fellows":

MURIEL: And I said to myself
I'm really Indian
GLORIA: (*3 honour beats*)
LISA: The message was clear
GLORIA: Now I knew what I had to do (Spiderwoman, *Reverb* 117)

---

29 Monique Mojica was also present at this Sun Dance; this was the second time she participated in this ceremony as a dancer (Personal Communication 2022).

30 In *Reverb-ber-ber-rations*, Crow Dog's Paradise is represented as the sacred Black Hills.

Gloria's story of her first trip to Gunayala after her father's death to "heal open wounds / Rectify his guilt" (*Reverb* 121) carries weighty significance in light of the spiritual directives all three sisters have just received. She has been welcomed to the Sun Dance circle; she has returned to her husband and children at Oberlin "uplifted and happy" (*Reverb* 117); and this trip to her father's traditional lands is what she must do because his blood sings in her veins. She becomes, at once, the vessel through which Antonio Miguel's unfinished business will be accomplished; the intermediary through which her half-brother, abandoned by their late father, will be restored and welcomed into the Miguel family circle; the affected supplicant who has been directed to the place of her soul's healing; and the Inaduled[31] who will collect the medicines (stories, names, fragments of the Guna language and Traditional Knowledge, familial links, etc.) by means of which the curing can continue for both her and her sisters.

Metaphysical Mimesis: A Guna Curing Ceremony in Babylon

Reverb-ber-ber-rations recounts and effects a reordering of spiritual chaos. Like many of their shows and many a Creation Story, this piece begins on sound in darkness. But these disjointed sounds bump up against each other seemingly without rhyme or reason. They move uneasily from a traditional Grand Entry in the pre-set; to recorded Balinese music; to a live "Noise Band" featuring an aluminium garbage receptacle, a toy violin, and a heavy chain (Spiderwoman, *Reverb* 103); to fractured conversation as the lights come up; to Broadway show tunes. If, as Spiderwoman tells us, the incidental sounds that surround us daily are "spirits talking to [us]" (*Reverb* 102), the booming, clanging, beating, ticking and articulated epithets that assault our ears signal to us that there are some forceful, oppressive, and confusing spirits out there and that they are not just talking to us; they are *screaming*.

The first words we hear in that inchoate darkness are fraught with urgency and spoken at cross purposes. In that darkness, disembodied voices articulate fear ("What was that?"), suppressed need ("Can't you hold it?"), released frustration ("Oh shut up, you old fool!") and unheeded cries for help (*Reverb* 103). In a teeming, urban "no man's

31 Mac Chapin has observed that women in Gunayala always administer the medicines and care for the patients, although they are rarely medicine specialists themselves (220). However, he also notes that women who have been born with a foetal caul (and who can therefore peer into the world of spirits) are often trained to become Inaduled or Igar Wisid (226).

land" where spirits speak through the clanging of garbage cans, the roar of traffic, bells and whistles, disjointed snatches of music from across the globe, angry shouts, catcalls, and muted weeping, there is a risk of being swept away in the chaos – of losing connection with the ancestral spirits, because we can no longer hear them through the din. This inchoate metaphysical hysteria that expresses itself through the city's din has framed the lives of the Miguel sisters since birth. So too, Noise Band and their darkly nostalgic "tea party apropos of nothing" (*Reverb* 109) – a tea party, which I receive as a dis-eased reflection of the hitherto discussed kitchen table that was most definitely apropos of *something* – frame the stories of connection and power that make up *Reverb-ber-berrations*. This piece, however, is not simply a memorial to the soul's dis-ease It contains and utilizes the elements of the Guna Curing Ceremony with which to connect its participants (in the realm of spirit) to the physical and spiritual landscapes of their mother (Rappahannock), their father (Guna), and to the chaotic urban centre, which has always been their home.

The ceremonial elements of *Reverb-ber-ber-rations* are woven into the foundations of its visual, aural, and oral opsis. The hammock in which Gloria Miguel reclines to tell the story of her first trip to Gunayala (Spiderwoman, *Reverb* 121–2) sits at the centre of the Guna Curing Ceremony and at the centre of the Guna Gathering House. In the spirit of the Gathering House, Lisa Mayo and Muriel Miguel assume the roles of Responders in this scene, underscoring their sister's testimony with the affirmation "Tague" (Degii, "It is so"). In the spirit of the Curing Ceremony, the lead chanter (Gloria) re-calls that moment in the past when she bridged the limen between her late father and the son he had left behind in Gunayala. In so doing, she reinvents herself in the present moment as the thread that connects and binds all of Antonio Miguel's children and their families:

- They were all there, nieces, nephews, grand nieces, great grand nephew [sic] and my sister-in-law
- I spent the last day and evening in Panama City at the home of my brother with my family.
- Through me my brother was connected with his father.
- My father's blood, my blood, our blood (Spiderwoman, *Reverb* 122)

Spiderwoman Theater's laconic observation in the published text that "Guna people use them [hammocks]" (Spiderwoman, *Reverb* 102) *abstracts* the crucial presence of this key item to protect its sacredness and potency, even as it signals the dissolution of the limen between the sacred and the commonplace. The hammock is not only utilized to cradle the body of the sick in Curing Ceremonies; it is the very "heart of Guna culture." In Gunayala, one is born in a hammock; one sleeps in a hammock; children play in and on hammocks; the hammock sits at the centre of the Gathering House, and the saglas (spiritual and political leaders and ceremonial conductors) recline in it to recount communal and personal histories; and finally, in death, the Guna body is swaddled in its hammock and buried with it (Kantule, *Chocolate Woman* Panel). Indeed, Guna artist Oswaldo DeLeón Kantule asserts, "when the hammock disappears, Guna culture will disappear" (*Chocolate Woman* Panel).

Spiderwoman Theater's hammock here is far more than a material signifier of Guna ceremony; *it is a key site of spiritual restoration within an urban ceremony, conducted by three women of mixed-blood an ocean away from their father's homeland.* Hovering between Earth and sky, it positions its occupants in that liminal space of temporal and geographical conflation, which is the meeting place of flesh and spirit. And it securely positions them within their ancestral biota weaving them tightly within an unseen (but potently present) Guna community.

That the Miguel sisters have consciously dramaturged the vehicle of their own healing and that they seriously consider their responsibility to abstract elements of this publicly performed rite became blindingly apparent to me as I listened to some of the rehearsal tapes for *Reverb-ber-ber-rations*. During their discussion, for instance, of the "guardians" (e.g., the Nuchugana) that each sister places to the four directions near the top of the show, the issue of abstraction comes up. In the published text, we are told, "these are [their] protectors. They make the stage a safe place to tell [their] stories" (Spiderwoman, *Reverb* 104). And this is certainly what these small humanoid figures carved from wood have been intended to do. But more than this, the Nuchugana contain burba. They are helpers; the burba of one or all is called upon during Curing Ceremonies and enlisted to descend through the layers of existence into the metaphysical plane where it/they will engage in a cosmic battle to heal those afflicted on the physical plane (Chapin 223). The Nuchugana are key agents of soul recovery, and their presence here signals the reconfiguration of the site of public entertainment peopled by performers and audiences into a liminal space of healing populated by mortal celebrants and spirit beings.

During rehearsals for *Reverb-ber-ber-rations*, the Miguel sisters placed their guardians each morning and put them to rest each evening. After some discussion, they agreed that the guardians would be present in the theatre during the run of the show (*Reverb* 1990 Rehearsals, Tape 6). What remained undecided, however, was whether the audience would (or should) be aware of the presence of the guardians. Would the guardians distract the audience? Should the Miguel sisters *abstract* the guardians, as they had done in a previous show (*I'll Be Right Back*)? Ultimately, audiences are permitted to witness as each sister places her guardians. And although the Miguel sisters offer no direct references to or explication of these guardians in performance, they do nothing to deliberately obfuscate their purpose. The spiritual significance of their Nuchugana is made apparent during the introductory invocations, which situate us "on the rim of limitless dimensions" where messages from those who have passed on are carried in the blood of the living to be delivered to those yet unborn (Spiderwoman, *Reverb* 105). In essence, the significance of the Nuchugana, like that of the hammock, is acknowledged (and hence highlighted) for those who possess an organic understanding of ceremonial praxis (even if they are not intimately familiar with the specifics of Guna ceremony), while remaining "abstract" to others.

Nor is the significance of either the Cochiti Drum or the Bullroar obfuscated by abstraction in performance. As Muriel Miguel takes her place at the drum, Lisa Mayo informs the audience that she is an Elder (as are her sisters),[32] and they have brought the drum into this space to stay "in touch with the six directions" (Spiderwoman, *Reverb* 105). Although their audiences never see this, the Miguel sisters prepare the drum in ceremony *for* each evening's ceremony before the house begins to fill (Spiderwoman, *Reverb* 102). The drum, here, is not simply a prop or a culturally colourful instrument from which to generate a rhythmic soundscape. The Noise Band fulfils this function, and the garbage pail (which Lisa Mayo plays) provides a satisfactorily affective percussive backdrop. The drum around which these Elders sit, like the bullroar that Muriel Miguel swings before her "Grandma" story, are technologies by which human beings can directly and deliberately invoke the spirits. If the spirits speak to mortals through the ambient sounds of nature, through the tinkling of chimes or the discordant din of the inner city, so the flesh can answer them in kind. Each strike on the drum and each swing of the bullroar sends a thought (the impulse behind the actions of striking or swinging) reverberating past the "veil" and through the layers to inhabit and speak through antimatter, just as those who occupy the metaphysical realm shake the air of

32 In the notes on set in the play text, the Miguel sisters tell us, "The women of Spiderwoman are at an age where we feel we can sit at the drum" (*Reverb* 102). In many Indigenous communities, females, traditionally, have not sat at the drum. This is because, as life-givers, women carry powerful medicine, which may interfere with the healing properties of other medicines utilized in ceremony (including the drum). By 1990, the Miguel sisters had already passed their childbearing years; hence, they reasoned, their presence at the drum could pose no significant threat of interference or disruption.

the seen world with disembodied impulse to inhabit, reverberate, and speak through the bodies of their descendants.

However, we would do well to remember that the Cochiti Drum should not simply be understood a carrier of human impulse – an inanimate object serving human needs. Here, as it is in ceremony, the drum is an animate force; it is a fourth actor on Spiderwoman's stage. Do the Miguel sisters, as Rebecca Schneider asserts, "drum memories and counter-memories onto the stage" (153), or does the drum, which is layered under each story that is told, articulate its own remembered "text," eliciting reactions and responses from the actors who inhabit the physical and metaphysical realms it straddles? After all, the Miguel sisters not only sound the drum; they *listen* to that drum, which is "the heartbeat of all our communities" (Spiderwoman, *Reverb* 102).

Aftermath: "I am Here Now ... I Have to take the Past and Make it into a Positive Future"

> [I]t takes courage, and suspension of disbelief, to perform into existence a future that we cannot yet see. It is an urgent, ongoing project of the present.
>
> – Monique Mojica and Ric Knowles, "Creation Story" 2–3

In rehearsal, as she was crafting her final statement – "I am an Indian woman ..." (*Reverb* 131) – Muriel Miguel articulated this resolution: "I have to take the past and make it into a positive future" (Spiderwoman Theater, *Reverb* 1990 Rehearsals, Tape 9). On stage, an abstracted version of her declaration is articulated by Lisa Mayo who declares it to be the responsibility of the artist to go "back into the before to use for the future" (*Reverb* 129). Taken at face value, the kernel of this declaration (in either its literal or more abstract form) offers the possibilities of liberation and empowerment. But the manifestation of an unseen future fraught with these possibilities requires a leap of blind faith into the sources of our disconnection, our dismemberment, and our despair. It requires "cords that connect us to what is not broken" (Mojica and Knowles, "Creation Story" 5), and it requires cords plaited from faith, fortitude, and forbearance with which to hold gently on to those things that have been broken even as we free ourselves from the hold they exert on us:

> MURIEL: I have to take the past and make it into a positive future. That really makes me upset. That really makes me cry.
>
> LISA: Well, therein lies the thing. Why does it make you cry?
>
> MURIEL: It means that I have to forgive Mama. (Spiderwoman Theater, *Reverb* 1990 Rehearsals Tape 9)

To fully accept her birthright and to fully recover from a colonially imposed legacy of internalized shame, Muriel Miguel recognizes that a personal investment in the process of forgiveness is necessary.

Reverb-ber-ber-rations prescribes no easy solutions. It does not show us what forgiveness or atonement may look like; it does not show us how to successfully accomplish these; indeed, it does not even articulate the words. It does, however, begin to ask the questions, which Spiderwoman Theater more actively and explicitly explores in *Persistence of Memory* (2007). And it thickens Spiderwoman's weighty contribution to the global project of re-worlding by introducing another layer to the process of recovery/rediscovery, mourning, dreaming, commitment, and action. Where (if at all) does forgiveness – of ourselves, of those in our families and communities who have wounded us, or even of our oppressors and their descendants – fit into this paradigm? What does it look like? How dependent (if at all) is the realization of genuine liberation on the successful completion of this stage? The beginnings, at least, of an answer to these questions lie for me in a brief, interrupted exchange, which survives in the rehearsal tapes for *Reverb-ber-ber-rations*: Lisa Mayo asks her younger sister, "When did it come to you that this was a healing – that you had to forgive Mama?" And Muriel answers, "I transcribed a lot of this stuff [the stories she carried in her body]. I transcribed all the stuff that was mine" (Tape 9). It is during the process, then, of recovery/rediscovery and throughout, perhaps, the process of mourning that we begin to fathom the true cost of performing that unseen future into being.

In *Reverb-ber-ber-rations*, three human women (performing as themselves – Lisa, Gloria, and Muriel) reach out from within a broken material world into the world of spirit, the gateway to which is represented by a road leading upstage into an "infinite spiral" painted onto a large blue backdrop (102). Spiderwoman's ever-present mola hangs stage left, and a small table with three chairs sits in shadow before the troupe's signature emblem. The hammock to which chimes have been affixed swings gently in front of the spiral, while the Cochiti Drum sits upstage on a blanket straddling the space between the spiral backdrop and the signature mola (see Spiderwoman, *Reverb* 2008). This is a set of intricate simplicity wherein the tensions and the reciprocal dependencies between light and shadow play themselves out in uneasy harmony. It presents an unlaboured, yet somehow sumptuous, portrait of the multiple layers of existence, which finite humans in the shadowed, broken spaces of "the real" must negotiate to repair what is broken and effect healing.

When All Worlds Become One

With *Power Pipes* (1991), these uneasy layers are stitched together to form one perceivable realm in which all of existence plays itself out. Here, it is as if the (playing) space has contracted in on itself until it has become a single, perfect circle of light inscribed on a canyon floor, but (and this seems uncannily counter intuitive) this contracted world has significantly expanded and is far more inclusive than the worlds of Spiderwoman's previous plays.

Reverb-ber-ber-rations, as we have seen, plays itself out in a liminal space that looks simultaneously to the material world in which we (audience and actor) live and to the cosmos, occupied by the spirits of the dead and the unborn. *Power Pipes,* by contrast, immediately plunges performer and witness together into a shadowy, unformed world illuminated by a ceremonial circle and (in the final moments of the piece) the stars.[33] From a circle of light framed by shadow, the three mortal sisters who looked into the cosmos in *Reverb-ber-ber-rations* now look back at the human world *from* the cosmos as elemental female forces. And they have been joined by others: In *Power Pipes* the limen between the generations and between the nations has also been dissolved, as mothers and aunties dance with daughters and nieces and as Chichimec Otomi voices join in song with Guna and Rappahannock. This is a multi-generational, inter–First National project in which the Miguel sisters have been joined by Murielle Borst-Tarrant and the Colorado sisters Hortencia and Elvira as co-creatrices and performers.

---

33 Like *Reverb-ber-ber-rations* before it, this piece opens on sound in darkness. And as the light slowly begins to dawn, the inhabitants of this eerie realm gather; they "look out into the cosmos," which is occupied by the audience (Spiderwoman, *Power* 155). Then they begin to sound. They receive this sound – a "drone" – from the cosmos behind them, sending it out to the cosmos before them, sharing the breath, which the cosmos has shared with them, with the audience and linking all with all. This moment may be reminiscent of the drone (or "chord" exercise) developed by Joseph Chaikin for The Open Theater. And it is an exercise that Muriel Miguel utilizes in her Storyweaving workshops. As Pasolli articulates it, the purpose of this collective drone for Chaikin's company was to "affirm the Open Theatre as a collective," and to assimilate the individual into an "entity" greater than himself (33).

The opening "drone" of *Power Pipes* certainly serves a like function. But it carries this function further. The drone serves not only the company of performers but also those who witness. All are drawn into the greater "we." And as Monique Mojica has reminded me, the similarities between the collective drone that opens *Power Pipes* and the droning of the Guna pipes themselves or the vocalized drone that underscores Gathering House chants in Gunayala should not be overlooked (Personal Communication 2007).

Moreover, although her name does not appear in the published text, Gloria Miguel's daughter Monique Mojica inhabits this unified realm. She took part in the original creation of *Power Pipes*, and the stories remembered through her body during the play's development – specifically, "Gotcha" (Spiderwoman, *Power* 163) – have been inscribed on the published page and re-membered through her cousin's body in performance (Mojica, Personal Communication 2007).

Reverb-ber-ber-rations and *Power Pipes* might be read as two halves of the same whole. If *Reverb-ber-ber-rations* is the vehicle through which the Miguel sisters sought connection with the metaphysical sources of their power, *Power Pipes* presents the successful realization of those connections, and it reveals the sources of those things that stand between the human supplicant and her spiritual source. In *Reverb-ber-ber-rations* the human being looks into the abyss. In *Power Pipes*, the abyss returns the gaze. Indeed, as one watches *Power Pipes*, it is as if one were viewing a film negative or an X-ray, presenting a stark, unadorned image of the spiritual mechanics that govern the dis-ease of the colonized and direct its cure. There is little in the way of set, and no description of the set is provided in the published text. The excellent 1993 video archive, preserved from a performance at the American Indian Community House in New York City, features two backdrops, flanking an archway into nothingness (Spiderwoman, *Power* 1993). To the right (SR) of the archway hangs a night sky alight with stars; to its left, the signature mola. Most of the playing area is heavily shadowed except for the ceremonial circle, which is generally bathed in a warm, golden glow. And when the world of spirit peers into the world of flesh, it stares down through this circle of light, not out at the audience, which occupies the same realm as the spirits who dance on stage.

> What are the cords that connect us to what is not broken? One of the ways these connections are made is through the power of the word as invocation, through naming and honouring, the living and the dead who came before us. Another way is by bringing our deities and cultural heroes to the stage, being *inhabited* by them, and becoming their reflections and manifestations. (Mojica and Knowles, "Creation Story" 5)

Illumined in the interplay between golden light and velvet darkness, the female deities who "inhabit" the performing bodies appear as starkly outlined shadows etched in flesh. At times, the heavily painted performers resemble negatives or X-ray images. Which world is which? Which world is real? If the negative is the shadowy, celluloid image that offers us an *impression* of the reality it represents, and if the X-ray, by contrast, penetrates the layers of adornment, colour and flesh to dis-cover the essence of the thing itself, from what realm do these shadows emerge? Do they offer us impressions of reality or the reality itself? Is dwelling upon or upholding such distinctions at all valuable, or is it, in the face of all we are, irrelevant and perhaps even harmful?

Like the spirit of "Grandma" who once stepped into her youngest granddaughter's head, these deities change the contours of the human face, merging their identities with those of their human hosts so that the "I" becomes indistinguishable from the "we." Unlike the spirit of Grandma, however, elemental female powers of *Power Pipes step out* of the human performer, so positioning her flesh as the top layer of an impossibly intricate mola, which is itself only a single layer belonging to a much greater mola. As essence and story interlock, the well-being of the whole shows itself to be intimately related to and absolutely contingent upon the well-being of the individual.

Hence, Mesi Tuli Omai [Misi Dule Ome] whose moon headdress visibly articulates her identity as a moon goddess and whose "medicine is love" (Spiderwoman, *Power* 158) slips easily into the brokenness of the lovelorn human who performs her. Without relinquishing her power or position in this world of shadows, she articulates the stories of wounding that belong to Gloria Miguel on the mundane plane of material life on Earth. In the same vein, She Who Opens Hearts is "fed with the strength of creation" (Spiderwoman, *Power* 159). Yet she articulates the wounds inscribed upon the wounded person of Hortencia Colorado. Here, then, through the practice of Storyweaving, community is forged in an anti-liminal dimension where boundaries and otherness have become meaningless:

SHE WHO OPENS HEARTS: Shame. Shame. Shame. *(She crawls up on ramp)*
Eh, eh, eh.
India mecca mecca
No that's not me, that's not me
Yo no soy India mecca, mecca.
(Crawls into circle) Shame, shame, oh shame!
(Covers herself trying to hide)
Can't breathe
Can't breathe
Pieces, pieces, pedacitos, pedacitos.
You've broken me up in pieces, in pieces.
Can't breathe, can't breathe. *(She hides herself)*

MESI TULI OMAI: Squawk
SHE WHO OPENS HEARTS: India mecca mecca.
(*Mesi Tuli Omai crosses up to behind She Who Opens Hearts*)
MESA TULI OMAI: I hear them. Squawk. Squawk.
(*Slapping herself*)
She's dark.
She's dumb.
Don't let her in.
Don't look at her.
Throw her out.
She's black.
She has no talent.
Don't work with her.
She doesn't exist. (Spiderwoman, *Power* 181–2)

Mimi Gisolfi D'Aponte has discussed Spiderwoman Theater with reference to what she terms the "three significant keynotes of life." These keynotes, she asserts, thread themselves throughout the works of Indigenous playwrights and specifically throughout the works of artful Indigenous women whom she has come to view "as transmitters, as healers, and as transformers" (D'Aponte, "Native Women" 101). But Spiderwoman's point – communicated first from the human point of view (in *Reverb-ber-ber-rations*) and then from the point of view of the spirits (in *Power Pipes*) strips these keynotes of their mystery – their precious exclusivity. The women who comprise Spiderwoman Theater (on and offstage) are certainly transmitters, healers, and transformers, but the enduring power of their works lies in a central message: *we are all transmitters, healers and transformers*. We have all been gifted, but these gifts do not come without a price. In the paradigm that *Power Pipes* presents, our first duty is to be healers; we are to love and care for ourselves and, more importantly, to extend the same love and care to others in thought, word, and deed.

The "Subway Rape" of Scene 12, which occurs in a liminal space beneath the ground and between stations, powerfully lays out this paradigm in three tellings. In the first telling, we are confronted with the consequences of our choices either to ignore the "messages" that enjoin us to have a care for ourselves or to ignore the cries of those who require our aid. She Who Opens Hearts remains in a dangerous situation despite her internal alarums and is brutally gang-raped, while Mesi Tuli Omai (Misi Dule Ome) ignores a stranger's plight and leaves the unpleasant scene (Spiderwoman, *Power* 176). Then the story is played out for the second time. Now, we witness the healing power that accompanies the choice to risk personal well-being for the collective good. In this second reiteration, Mesi Tuli Omai (Misi Dule Ome) makes the choice to stand with She Who Opens Hearts against her attackers (Spiderwoman, *Power* 176); hence, the rape (the potential catalyst of a dehabilitating disease from which the victim might never recover) is prevented.

During the third telling, we learn that as transmitters, we must be vigilant so that we will recognize our spirit protectors; we must listen to the messages they communicate; and we must discipline ourselves to believe them:

WIND HORSE SPIRIT WARRIOR: Do you believe the warning?
OBSIDIAN WOMAN: Listen to your warning.
NAOMI FAST TRACKS: Who are your protectors?
OWL MESSENGER: Did you ignore the messages?
MESI TULI OMAI: Answer the voices. (Spiderwoman, *Power* 176–7)

As transformers, we must allow ourselves to be transformed in a good way and to transform others in an equally positive manner through active fellowship governed by good intentions. As the third telling of the "Subway Rape" plays out, its heroine hears, heeds, and acts upon the spirits' alarum. And she is transformed! The hapless victim of the first two scenarios has been transformed into a fierce resister, drawing strength and aid from her metaphysical guardians: "Oh no you don't, you motherfuckers! I'll crush your fucking balls. I'll kill you!!" (Spiderwoman, *Power* 177). Her guardians speak. She listens. And "there is a growling in [her] soul, now that [they've] met" (Spiderwoman, *Power* 164).[34]

The duties to heal, transmit, and transform are not carried solely by Indigenous artists and their communities. Non-Indigenous people who have settled on these lands have, by and large, severed their own connections by fabricating hierarchal notions of difference and have abandoned their responsibilities to the greater community of flesh and spirit. But while they may not yet recognize or acknowledge it, what happens to one happens to all; they too sicken and waste away in the carnage they have wrought. They too must take action to combat their own dis-ease and to contribute to the restoration of the biotas they have

34 This monologue was authored by Monique Mojica who performed in its first production (Personal Communication 2022).

despoiled. They too are called upon to engage in projects of healing and transformation because, as Métis playwright Maria Campbell has asserted, "the circle of grandmothers [has] no colour" (Griffiths and Campbell 17).

The world of spirit is formless and without colour: many may be called, but it seems that few *choose* to listen. With *Power Pipes*, Spiderwoman Theater adds its collective voice to the voices of the many Native women playwrights so fervently celebrated by D'Aponte to remind us to listen, because when we do, we are invested with the power to fulfil our responsibilities as transmitters, healers, and transformers, to mend the sacred hoop, to ease personal distress and to profoundly contribute to a collective effort to heal this broken world:

SHE WHO OPENS HEARTS: Yo soy, I am without shame
India mecca mecca
See my shame.
See my Indianness.
See it come out of here
Out of here.
This is Indian
And this
India mecca mecca
India mecca mecca
MESI TULI OMAI: Don't, don't.
Put the pieces back together
I love myself, I'll heal myself.
I don't need your love.
I love myself.
I'll heal myself.
I don't need your love.
I'll heal myself.
I love you. I love you.
I'll put the pieces back together.
I'll heal myself.
I love you.

(Spiderwoman, *Power* 184, emphasis added)

In this finely crafted moment of "intertextual facing," She Who Opens Hearts and Mesi Tuli Omai (Misi Dule Ome) speak through and to the human performers as they articulate their healing. In accordance with the mechanics of mola-making, as layers are cut away to reveal a piece of the larger design, their edges are folded in on themselves, and the facing that is created thereby is securely stitched onto the layers beneath. Here, the shapes and colours that belong to each "shame story" link the tellers experientially (e.g., they both suffer from the same dis-ease). And they "write" the tellers into a much larger text that documents the sad and shameful history of racism in this world and its devastation of the human spirit. In this story, no one is immune; no one is untouched. In this story, we have all played our parts. But this story does not end in brokenness. The mola thickens as more colours are revealed and facings are stitched to the layers of redress and healing.

The project to heal personal brokenness demands the active participation of the greater community. Owl Messenger who goes "to the place where everyone speaks the same language" to bring back messages for "all" (Spiderwoman, *Power* 159) and who speaks to and through Lisa Mayo intervenes on the "Shame Stories" weaving the women who have been socially isolated by their shame into a protective circle of living and dead. Here, a compelling phenomenon occurs: As Mayo invokes the spirits of her mother, her auntie, and her father, we are made to understand that they are carried within and manifest themselves through the bodies of their descendants. In Spiderwoman's earlier works, this idea was vividly communicated to audiences through the home movies, which often played across the performers' bodies. But in this piece, as in *Reverb-ber-ber-rations* before it, the troupe requires no digital archive. Here, as Owl Messenger/Lisa Mayo introduces each ancestor and proudly claims each as her own, "*All run across and [collectively] become [that] person*" (Spiderwoman, *Power* 182). Ancestral shadows no longer need to be projected onto living bodies from the outside; we understand that they are carried within. To underscore this idea, Mayo, speaking as the maternal grandparent who inhabits her very DNA, articulates a healing message for herself and her sisters: "You're light, you're pretty, you're smart. Beezebug, Beezebug. I gave you a wonderful grandmother. She's an Indian [and there is no shame in *that*]" (Spiderwoman, *Power* 183). The message could not be clearer. It is, in fact, the central message of the play. The cult of individuality has been built upon a lie. It is a virus, feeding on the divisions, which rupture the natural biota and tear each living organism apart. A life well lived is a life consciously lived within community. "We, we, we, we, we, we, we … ['We' in six directions. 'We' to the power of six …] We put the earth back together, we make the truth about ourselves" (Spiderwoman, *Power* 156).

Power Pipes connects us to one community of Indigenous women who shoulder the responsibility to help "put the earth back together." They play the pipes. They sit at the drum. In so doing, they not only open the channels of communication to the spirit world but also dissolve the limen between male and female here on Earth, as they consciously breach what has been generally understood as traditionally male territory in the space of ceremonial activity, restoring women (young and old) to their rightful place in the circle.

In 1992, Lisa Mayo told Jennifer Dunning that females in Gunayala had traditionally been prohibited from playing the pan pipes or sitting at the drum until they had gone through menopause.[35] Jennifer Dunning then observed that as the twentieth century neared its close, Guna "women, menstruating or not [were being] acknowledged as musicians" (Dunning). It might be inferred from this celebratory statement and from the general tenor of Dunning's interview that a purely feminist reading of Spiderwoman's work here is in order. Such a reading is problematic, because it implies that traditional Indigenous cultures are inherently inequitable and that women must elbow men out of the way to achieve the things they seek. Further, it widens the gulf between cultures rather than supporting the womanist project, which seeks to build bridges between individuals and communities through greater respect and understanding. It is not Lisa Mayo, but the article's author, who states that Guna "women, menstruating or not, are acknowledged as musicians." What is Dunning implying? And how does she know this? Women were always "musicians" in Gunayala. Indeed, according to their Creation Story, it was the "Youngest Daughter from the Stars" who taught *women* (specifically) to compose and perform the songs that ushered in new life (lullabies) and the songs to mourn the dead (Mojica, *Chocolate* 2011). This is a responsibility the women of Gunayala still carry out today.

---

35 There may have been some confusion or misinterpretation here on the part of the interviewer (or perhaps some inadvertent cultural conflation on the part of Mayo). Upon reviewing this manuscript, Monique Mojica informed me that in Guna culture, "there is NO drum and girls DO play the gammu, though it is more usual that they use rattles" (Personal Communication 2022). With reference to the drum, Mayo have been referring to some Indigenous nations across Turtle Island in which women have historically been prohibited from sitting at the Big Drum. Protocols around the Big Drum vary from nation to nation – community to community. Today, as I write, there are communities that accept women at the drum, while others remain adamant: "It's not putting down the women. It's putting them on a pedestal, because women have the ability to create life, and are very humble in their teachings and their ways. In our way of life, everything balances out. They may not be the so-called leaders or speakers of the people, or maybe the singers, but in a round-about way it is balanced, so that women actually have more power than men" (Elder Boye Ladd qtd. in Andrea Smith, "Men Only").

What does Dunning understand of how menstruation is regarded in Guna communities? Although she has watched *Power Pipes* and is reviewing it here, it appears that she has missed a significant "keynote" of Guna life (to borrow D'Aponte's apt and evocative phrasing). Indeed, as Gloria Miguel's "Cuna Story" and its juxtaposition with Hortencia Colorado's "Subway Rape" make clear, the dysfunction that characterizes the relationships between male and female did not manifest itself in traditional Indigenous societies. This is an affliction carried to these shores by the agents of colonization. Menstruation in Gunayala carries neither shame nor penalty. It is seen as a great gift. It is a blessing on the community. And it is celebrated as such. As Gloria Miguel remembers her 11-year-old self, a lonely, isolated child who had just lost her best friend and entered her time of womanhood, she remembers and re-invokes a powerful strategy of healing: She closes her eyes and travels in her mind's eye to her father's home community where she undergoes a puberty ceremony. The community ministers to her; they bathe her; they cut her hair; they paint her with the blue-black dye rendered from the "pollywalla" [baluwala] tree.[36] She is celebrated by men and women alike: "My father took me around the island, he blew a large conch shell. Ami Oma Sisquat [Ani Ome Sisgwa] 'Today my daughter is a woman'" (Spiderwoman, *Power* 174).

Here, the female body is imagined as a site of celebration, which unites men and women in Gunayala. Each member of the community plays his and her role. Always, a woman cuts the hair of the young initiate. Always, it is the men who visit the sabtur (jagua) tree and harvest its fruit to make the dye with which her body will be painted. And still

36 In earlier writings, I have stated that the baluwala tree was the source of the dye used in Guna puberty ceremonies. Since her return from Gunayala and through her own work with saglas and Knowledge Keepers, Monique Mojica's knowledge has deepened, and she has alerted me to my error (Personal Communication 2022). Here, the child Gloria who has not yet visited Gunayala has erred, confusing a symbolic concept (of hoarded bounty and oppression) with an actual tree, the fruits of which hold properties of protection for the young girl who is just entering womanhood (see footnote 82). The blue-black dye, with which young women undergoing their puberty ceremonies are painted, is rendered from the fruit of the sabtur (jagua/*genipa americana*) tree. In her conflation of the baluwala – a conceptual site of abundance and fecundity withheld – with the sabtur, a material site of sustenance (the fruit is said to taste like dried apples) and of ceremonial provision, the child Gloria has a way to organize and articulate an intuited awareness that her life and those of the children she will eventually bear are bound up in the life of her relations in Gunayala. These will not be fulsome lives, lived abundantly, so long as her access to the community of her father, to her relations and to the ceremonies that are her birthright continue to be withheld.

today, men, not women, play the pipes in this coming-of-age ceremony. Indeed, the entire matrix of Guna ceremony has been designed around the female: her birth, her naming, her coming of age (Mojica, *Chocolate Woman*). Her body, which is adorned with paint and gold and rich textiles, is the site of Guna continuance. It is, as it has always been, *honoured* because it is the gateway for the coming generations. By contrast, Hortencia Colorado's subsequent recollection of gang rape on a subway system makes clear the positioning of the female body in a modern, urban centre, built by and for progressive individuals who have chosen to forget history and discard all tradition. The female body (the gateway of life) has become a site of violence to be degraded, vandalized, and discarded in a dis-eased world where the connections between male and female have been irrevocably severed.

In and of itself, Gloria Miguel's "Cuna Story" offers us a wonderful model through which to consider Diane Glancy's concept of interfactual texting and its relationship to the larger project of intertextual facing. The child-Gloria remembered by the woman-Gloria (and perhaps invoked by Gloria's cosmic guide) had never been to Gunayala and had only the memories of her male relations to reference as she sent her mind into the puberty ceremony. But the woman-Gloria who remembers the child-Gloria has by this time visited Gunayala three times. She has sat in the Gathering House. She has witnessed the puberty ceremony. She has seen, heard, touched, smelled, and tasted it first-hand. The "facts" that direct the experience of the child are not the "facts" that direct the story of the adult. And both sets of facts – both stories – are woven together into an experience, which unfolds, as it were, for the first time, on the stage in 1991. Gloria the child understood that she needed to weave herself into the community of her father. Gloria the woman took the steps to achieve this. And an older Gloria on stage, responding to the direction of the elemental female who inhabits her, revisits the childhood realm of Brooklyn and her later introduction to Gunayala, weaving both into an anti-liminal site in which the healing sought first by the child and later by the woman is finally affected in the older self. Gloria's "Cuna Story" affects an intertextual facing because the interrelationships between the multiple texts belonging to multiple selves are made manifest. And it affects an interfactual texting in that these multiple texts – these multiple experiences – are interwoven to affect a new experience of the world for the present self – a moment of healing for which a new text in and of itself must be created.

Spiderwoman's lesson here is that if the borders of our lives stop at our front doors (see *Power* 170), we cannot live in a healthy way. And the women of Spiderwoman Theater respect this. They take their place at the drum, to be sure, and they play the pipes. But – *and this is a crucial point* – they claim this responsibility as grandmothers who have passed their childbearing years. It should not escape our notice that, in performance, Murielle Borst-Tarrant who is at this time a young mother does not take a place at the drum with the others (See Spiderwoman, *Power* 1993). As Wind Horse Spirit Warrior, she dances and sings, which are responsibilities specific to Murielle Borst-Tarrant in her offstage life. But always, in performance she remains just outside that circle around the big drum. This is after all a project of restoration and repair.

Whether we are laughing uproariously as two squabbling sisters refuse to break bread together and squirming in the silence between them (Spiderwoman, *Power* 160–3), listening tearfully to stories of bereavement (172, 173) or swaying in time with an uproarious 49'er about lost love and thwarted lust (165–7), we are witnessing the affliction of soul loss – a destructive keynote, which has reverberated powerfully through the generations of Indigenous families the world over since contact. In accordance with the teachings, which are their legacy, the Miguel sisters have with *Power Pipes* connected themselves, their afflicted witnesses, and their successors to that cosmic layer wherein fragmented souls and their human vessels are restored to wholeness. And they show us the way: "Make the offering. Remember. Homage Extended. Homage Received" (Spiderwoman, *Power* 195).[37]

Preparing a Legacy

It is significant that after *Power Pipes*, the Miguel sisters did not come together again as a trio to create and perform another show until 2002 when they presented *Persistence of Memory* at the Banff Centre for the Arts in Banff, Alberta. This piece recounts Spiderwoman Theater's 30-year journey (to 2002), re-membering countless connections and giving voice to the many, many people who have shared that long road with its core members. And it may well be a cornerstone of the legacy they have been preparing for their genealogical and aesthetic inheritors.

Although it is unfortunate that all the troupe's collective and solo works have not as of yet been published, the four published play texts to which we have access map a personal journey back to Indigenous selfhood, inextricably weaving its sojourners into the larger anti-colonial project of re-worlding. The final chapter of this book will, in

37 This fragment of text comes from Monique Mojica's writing during the development of this show (Personal Communication 2022).

part, explore the work of Monique Mojica, which builds on her inheritance from her mother and aunties. But I would like, here, to indulge in my own moment of interfactual texting – looking ahead, as it were, to inform my understanding of what has come before. During the second developmental workshop of Mojica's *Chocolate Woman Dreams the Milky Way* (March 2009), visual artist Oswaldo DeLeón Kantule identified significant links between the dramaturgical process through which *Chocolate Woman* had begun to take shape and the key principles of traditional Guna aesthetics. He explained that just as there are four supporting posts around which a Guna building is designed, so there are four supporting structures upon which Guna aesthetic expression stands. Kantule articulated these as: **Abstraction** (which includes the minimalization of elements, the removal of these elements from temporal to spatial realms, the encoding of these elements and the location of their kernel/gwage), **Metaphor**, **Duality & Repetition** (with subtle variations), and **Multidimensionality**. Through her work with Guna artists and cultural advisors, Mojica has long been developing a language through which to express what she does and its connection with her ancestral roots. And what she does in her work today is profoundly informed by what Spiderwoman has done before her. Her work, after all, is a new ripple on an ancient pool.

Four plays. Four "posts": the house that Spiderwoman built. Upon the first post are etched the key landmarks of a very personal journey back to self in which the seeker struggles to locate some meaning in suffering and find some way out of despair. The second post locates individual identity in community – specifically within communitist projects belonging to the political realm. The third post broadens the quest for identity, but narrows the "search terms," as it were, to the "personal" and the "familial." And upon the final post, the search for self has come to fruition. The fragmented, socially isolated, personally impotent "me" finds herself – Guna-Rappahannock granddaughter, daughter, sister, mother, lover, friend – in the "we." Connected to her ancestors and their nations by blood, history, memory, and ceremonial praxis, she is the memory keeper, the teacher and the gateway that locates her children and theirs and theirs in those circles upon circles upon circles.

Wholly Guna. Wholly Rappahannock. Wholly daughters of a Rappahannock wise woman and a Guna sailor with a "big light," they are wholly, unashamedly themselves in Brooklyn, Manhattan, Toronto, Paris, or Amsterdam. This is the legacy they have prepared. And it is a place from which to begin – not the conclusion of a journey.

6 The Three Sisters from *There* to Here: Spiderwoman's Issue and the Project of Re-Worlding

I see myself and my sisters acting as mentors for Native people [...] I want to keep this within myself, so I can work with the young Native people of this country and the Indigenous people of Central and South America and Mexico who want to study and do their own theater. You can do this when you're old. But I'm still going to act, I'm still going to sing, as long as I can carry a tune. I've only been working for the last forty years. What can you learn in forty years?

– Lisa Mayo qtd. in Abbott 180

Lest We Forget ...

On 20 February 2007, Spiderwoman Theater performed *Persistence of Memory* at the Honoring Spiderwoman Theatre Conference hosted by Miami University in Oxford, Ohio. Although nobody had realized it going in, this event turned out to be the Miguel trio's final collaborative performance. At the time, Lisa Mayo was unwell. It is likely that she was already suffering from the effects of Non-Hodgkin's Lymphoma with which she was later diagnosed. Also, unbeknownst to her collaborators and witnesses, her mind was already clouded by the (then) undiagnosed dementia from which she would eventually die. She had lost a great deal of weight; she was frail. And she carried her script on stage with her because she did not trust her memory. Backstage, she was mightily supported by her sister Muriel and by her nieces Murielle Borst-Tarrant and Monique Mojica. Onstage, however, Mayo rarely consulted the script in her hand. And while she did utilize the chair that had been provided for her, she certainly did not confine herself to it. She danced with her sisters and made it look effortless, charmed the audience with her easy glamour, and let loose a Broadway belt that galvanized her auditors. But the strain on all three sisters was not inconsiderable. And although Lisa Mayo later wrote and performed her solo show *Among the Living* under the direction of Muriel Miguel, the makeup of Spiderwoman Theater had forever altered.

During an historic night in February 2007, a privileged group of witnesses was woven into the story of three irrepressible grandmothers who had, against all odds, created a vehicle through which they could tell the stories they wanted to tell, who had drawn upon their Guna heritage to author and develop a workable poetics of re-worlding, and who had made a way for the generations of Indigenous performers and theatre practitioners who follow them. Creatrices. Teachers. Elders. They had indeed "acted as mentors for Native people," and they were still dancing!

As I watched them dancing on that knife's edge between forgetting and remembering, I was acutely aware of just what it is Indigenous theatre workers and audiences owe to these grandmothers. They were sharing themselves with us; they were weaving us into their story. That persistent struggle to "fight to remember who [they] are" (Spiderwoman, "Persistence" 42) is a struggle we all knew too well. Their courage emboldened us. Their dogged resolution strengthened our own. The legacy re-membered on stage that night was a legacy they had created for all of us. They had carved out a path in the wilderness and inspired us to follow.

Six months later (in late August 2007), I visited the Miguel sisters in New York City to chat individually with each about her process, her aesthetic objectives for Spiderwoman, and her assessment of her own life's work. I returned home from this trip with very mixed emotions. I was elated, to be sure. Each of these artists had let me into her creative process, and each discussion had revealed additional colours and layers to inform my understanding of the collective works that constitute Spiderwoman's canon. To the same degree, however, I was sad, angry, and frustrated; I kept replaying the final minutes of my interviews with Lisa Mayo and Gloria Miguel. I kept remembering a conversation I had had with Muriel Miguel months earlier, and my mind kept returning to her words: "I wish we had talked more about aging. I wish we had done a show about aging" (Personal Communication 2006). I felt that they had been betrayed and that I was somehow complicit in the betrayal. Now octogenarians, Gloria Miguel and Lisa Mayo were less elated by their accomplishments than I. After years of battling racism, after years of being pushed to the margins because of their brown skin, they had then to contend with ageism. They felt (acutely) that they were now being pushed to the margins and denied the chance to work because of their aging bodies. For Gloria Miguel, it was as if she "'took a breath but never got to say [her] last word' [...] What good is it? What good is Spiderwoman right now? Do I just have to live on the glory without money?" (Interview 2007).

How is it that these leading lights of Indigenous theatre in North America – Elders who had carved out the spaces within and "broke[n] open the doors" to an industry, which had previously shut out all of those who did not "fit" into its prevailing standards (Haugo, "Persistent" 70–1) – could not even get an audition with so many of the Indigenous theatre companies for which they had made a way? If we believe that "Elders are [the] repositories of cultural and philosophical knowledge and are the transmitters of such [vital] information" (Medicine qtd. in Archibald 37), was it not then (and is it not *now*) incumbent upon us to make the spaces of performance accessible to elderly bodies that we might read that knowledge from those fleshly archives?

Persistence of Memory was conceived by Muriel Miguel during Spiderwoman Theater's participation in the Persistence of Memory Conference, in Stockholm, Sweden, in 1998. This conference bore the same name as Salvador Dali's 1931 masterpiece – a painting, which depicts the decay/erosion of time (as conceptualized by humans) upon a stark landscape (that seems eternally immune to the processes of erosion or decay). It featured performances by Indigenous women from around the world – many of whom shared ancient stories of eternal relationships between their peoples and their traditional lands. These women remembered their relationships (and the obligations arising from these) as persistent and unchanging despite the temporal spaces that seemingly separate and differentiate one generation of humans from those that precede or follow it. During this conference, the Miguel sisters were struck by the common threads that wafted through the stories they witnessed. Nation-specific memory persisted through the very manner of its expression (e.g., the circularity of each performance and the honouring of the four directions by every performer). Herein, a commonality of legacy discovered itself as a thread, which bound one Indigenous woman to the others in all four directions (Haugo, "Persistent" 64–5).

After the 1998 conference, Muriel Miguel began to turn over questions around legacy (or "persistence of memory") in her own head. As she notes, "[It] doesn't necessarily have to be great, you know. It could be awful" (qtd. in Haugo, "Persistent" 65). But it is something we always carry with us and something we will invariably pass on. And that makes us responsible. Miguel had already directed Monique Mojica's *Princess Pocahontas and the Blue Spots*, which premiered at Toronto's Theatre Passe Muraille in 1990. In 1995, she had directed Murielle Borst-Tarrant's one-woman play *More Than Feathers and Beads*, which premiered at the New World Theatre in Massachusetts. She had been watching Borst-Tarrant's daughter Henu Josephine Tarrant develop her abilities as a traditional singer and dancer under the tutelage of her daughter, her son-in-law (Kevin Tarrant) and herself. And she was preparing for her role as director of the 2000 developmental workshop of *The Scrubbing Project* by Turtle Gals Performance Ensemble of which Monique Mojica was a co-founder and co-artistic director. As a primary facilitator of the artistic development of her daughter, niece, and granddaughter, Miguel had already begun, she realized, to shape and pass on her legacy to her issue (Haugo, "Persistent" 65).

Persistence of Memory is Muriel Miguel's vision; it is a tribute to the work that has been accomplished, to the work that is yet to come and to the inheritors who will accomplish that work. Its inception differs subtly from Spiderwoman's earlier works *because it rests less on the efforts of the core ensemble and more upon the energies of a much larger ensemble than may be initially apparent* (G. Miguel, Interview 2007). As its opening dedication alerts us, *Persistence of Memory* extends itself far beyond the realm of the personal or the specifically familial; it is a liminal event, collaboratively prepared over three decades by myriad individuals from many families, many nations, and all temporal realms.

Ingrid Washinawatok El-Issa, Flying Eagle Woman, is listed as the first individual to whom *Persistence of Memory* is dedicated (Spiderwoman, "Persistence" 42). And this dedication is poignantly apt at multiple levels. Flying Eagle Woman, a Menominee activist, exercised her talents as an orator, activist, and organizer to serve Indigenous communities around the world. At the age of 41, she answered the call of the U'wa and set off for Colombia where she, Hawaiian activist Lahe'ena'e Gay, and American environmental activist Terence Freitas laboured to help the U'wa protect their language and culture by setting up a school and by aiding in the defence of U'wa lands against oil exploration by Occidental Petroleum. On 25 February 1999, Flying Eagle Woman and her colleagues disappeared. They had been kidnapped by members of the Revolutionary Armed Forces of Colombia (FARC); days later, on 4 March, their bullet-ridden bodies were discovered just over the border in Venezuela. Those who abducted, tortured, and executed them have never been brought to justice.

With *Persistence of Memory*, Spiderwoman's lifelong project of *survivance* is remembered and celebrated. The process of its creation – the stitching together of multiple layers of experience and existence – declares itself in this act of remembrance as a key process, which exerts itself in *all* areas of Indigenous endeavour. The very invocation of Flying Eagle Woman conjures up her story and binds it to Spiderwoman's, manifesting the very threads that meld her breath with Spiderwoman's breath, her struggle with its struggle with our struggle and the solution to our humanity. In one of her final public addresses, Ingrid Washinawatok El-Issa reminded her listeners of the original instructions, which have been remembered and honoured by Indigenous nations from time immemorial. It is to these instructions that Indigenous people may return to find meaning and identity – amid even siege, disorder, dis-ease, and despair. Gratitude, responsibility, respect, ceremonial observance, mindful connection, and the maintenance thereof through creative acts – these are originary directives that direct individual and communal lifeways. And within these original instructions, Flying Eagle Woman reminded us, lies the key to re-worlding. Within these instructions lies an eternal possibility for human beings to create themselves anew.

> Since the time that human beings offered thanks for the first sunrise, sovereignty has been an integral part of Indigenous peoples' daily existence. With the original instructions from the Creator, we realize our responsibilities. Those are the laws that lay the foundation of our society. These responsibilities manifest through our ceremonies ... Sovereignty[1] is that wafting thread securing the components that make a society. *Without that wafting thread, you cannot make a rug. Without that wafting thread, all you have are un-joined, isolated components of a society*. Sovereignty runs through the vertical strands and secures the entire pattern. That is the fabric of Native society. (El-Issa qtd. in "The Dark Side," emphasis mine)

Flying Eagle Woman's words are not voiced in *Persistence of Memory*. Nor does this piece offer any explicit exposition of her story. But her spirit inhabits *Persistence of Memory* because the very kernel of her struggle and the essence, which underpins its expression, reveal themselves to be identical to the foundational structures upon which Spiderwoman's canon has been constructed. Remember who you are, Flying Eagle Woman has told us. And find the "wafting thread," the "vertical strands," the cords that connect us to each other and that weave us into the larger fabric of Creation.

1 I do not read the word "sovereignty" here in the Western sense of the word; that is, for me, it does not denote absolute authority or social hierarchy. I read this term as a translation of a concept that speaks to the inherent sovereignty bestowed at birth to all individuals and nations – the right to discover one's purpose within the fabric of Creation and to be free to act in accord with that purpose.

Legacies Upon Legacies: Flying Eagle Woman and *The Scrubbing Project*

Flying Eagle Woman's spirit and story more explicitly inhabit another piece, which owes much of its development to its director and "midwife" Muriel Miguel:

> Winged Victory: This Winged Warrior Woman wore a tattoo of a flying eagle on her arm: an identifying mark. Flying Eagle Woman put on her twenty league boots and took twenty league steps into La Selva.
>
> *(sings) Sequestrada! Kidnapped! Alla en Colombia, en la selva!* Two women and one man – Flying Eagle Woman. (Turtle Gals 340)[2]

Turtle Gals Performance Ensemble's *The Scrubbing Project* is a key cornerstone of Indigenous performance and its development on the public stages of contemporary North America. The troupe was established in Toronto in 1999 as a vehicle that would "bring Native women's voices and experiences to the stage" (Mojica and Knowles, "Staging II" 325). Originating as a quartet with Sandra Laronde, Jani Lauzon, Monique Mojica, and Michelle St. John, Turtle Gals (like its predecessor) eventually realized itself as a core-trio when Laronde left the company prior to the 2002 premiere of *The Scrubbing Project*.[3] In form and affect this piece set the bar at the turn of the century as a profoundly effective manifestation of what playwright director Floyd Favel (Poundmaker Cree) terms "Native Performance Culture."

Native Performance Culture (NPC) constitutes an artistic inheritance built upon the persistence of memory. Since 1991, Favel has been working with Indigenous theatre practitioners around the world

---

2 The Winged Victory speeches have been written by Monique Mojica (Personal Communication 2022).

3 Turtle Gals Performance Ensemble remained a professionally active troupe for nine years. In this time, Lauzon, Mojica and St. John developed and performed *The Scrubbing Project* (under the direction of Muriel Miguel); *The Triple Truth,* an educational piece first developed for Mayworks, which chronicles the contributions of Indigenous workers to the North American economy, diet, infrastructure, medical advancement, and scientific discovery; and *The Only Good Indian,* which chronicles the history of Indigenous performers in North America. In 2006, Monique Mojica resigned as co-artistic director and performer, and the ensemble continued to develop and perform *The Triple Truth* and *The Only Good Indian* with artistic associates Falen Johnson and Cheri Maracle until its dissolution in 2008.

(including Muriel Miguel and Monique Mojica) to test and develop a series of nation-specific "indigenous creative structures" (Favel Starr, "The Artificial" 70) through which Indigenous artists might construct "doors, which will open into ourselves and into the universe" (Favel Starr, "The Artificial" 71). These "doors" Favel locates in the temporal and experiential interstices between the exercise and experience of the contemporary theatrical event and the exercise and experience of the traditional ceremonial life, which precedes it (Favel, "Theatre: Younger Brother" 30). Favel and his collaborators are concerned with developing a process specific to Indigenous artists – a process that weaves those artists, their works, and their audiences into the lands out of which their nations' ceremonial praxis and traditional lifeways organically emerge. To do this, Favel tells us, one must "isolate the basic building blocks of [traditional aesthetic and ceremonial expression], and these become the starting points for a creative and vital action" (Favel Starr, "The Artificial" 69–70). This is a slow and painstaking process, but it mitigates any danger of cultural appropriation. It forestalls the insinuation of what Favel terms, the "artificial tree" into Indigenous work. The "artificial tree," as Favel explains, is a dead thing. When living aspects of a nation's ceremonial praxis (i.e., songs, dances, regalia, ceremonial paraphernalia, medicines, etc.) have been transplanted from the spaces in which they were meant to unfold to the contemporary stage, they cannot thrive. Such wholesale transplantation is dangerous, as the resulting ersatz *flora* curated for public display "has no roots, and no animating spirit" (Favel Starr, "The Artificial" 71). Rather than degrade those forces that spiritually sustain their nations, artists who work in the tradition of Spiderwoman, Favel, or Mojica are devising methodologies through which to immerse themselves in traditional and ceremonial praxis, to isolate core elements (through which to affect their witnesses), to then abstract those core elements, and finally to integrate these abstractions into the contemporary performance. Performative works engendered within this process are thus invested with the potent affectivity of their forbears. Like Muriel Miguel, Favel privileges the process over the product. For him, the journey – the navigation of the spaces between the social (theatre) and the spiritual (ceremonial praxis) – is more crucial than the end product that will emerge from the investigations (Favel, "Theatre: Younger Brother" 31–2). While the final product may (and has been curated to) transform many lives, the process that underlies its creation may transform many more. This is legacy.

As I have argued elsewhere, with *The Scrubbing Project* Spiderwoman's signature methodology, informed by latter-day investigations into

NPC, has expanded in potency and extended its affective reach as a "chapter" in the larger poetics of re-worlding (see Carter, "Writing"). Its complex weave of classic comedy routines, hit-television iconography, popular music, and survivors' testimony is corporeally navigated by "three raggedy-ass half-breeds" (Turtle Gals 331) who struggle to locate and isolate the source of the dysfunction that threatens their survival. The dis-ease that Turtle Gals seek to remediate here is a dis-ease that has impacted the lives of many contemporary Indigenous people – particularly, those of mixed-blood who (through legislation, relocation, re-education, adoption, etc.) have been disconnected from the traditional territories of their ancestors. Left unchecked, this dis-ease isolates and enervates the spirit of its host, often driving that host into desperation and self-destructive acts. To affect spiritual repair, each troupe member shows us how she navigates the dense historic weave of state-sanctioned genocide to locate the source of her dysfunction. But the work does not end here. With each "gal," we travel further into the depths, beyond colonial fabrication, as she locates and abstracts a remedial core of traditional praxis with which to meet and treat this dysfunction and through which to embody the agent of her own healing.

This complex attack on two fronts might be examined to best effect in the Turtle Gals' revisitation (and revision) of the tradition of Minstrelsy[4]

4 The Minstrel Show was a popular entertainment during which, for the most part, white performers blackened their faces and presented demeaning stereotypes of African American people. In later years, Black performers were contracted to perform as "minstrels," and they too donned blackface and assumed stereotypical speech patterns and accents associated with the stock characters they played. Soon, however, caricatures of Indigenous and other non-white peoples appeared in these shows. The white performers who represented Indigenous characters generally appeared in blackface and could be distinguished from the "Black" characters by their unaccented speech. These figures, first depicted sympathetically (as innocents), soon became associated in public imagination with savagery and alcoholism. Key elements of Minstrelsy emerge from the traditions of circus – the display of "exotics" – and became foundational elements in cinema, popular song, cartoons, and parodic variety shows throughout the twentieth century. Burlesque performances were entwined within this genre and began to emerge as entertainments outside of and apart from the Minstrel Show. One example of a popular burlesque emerging from this tradition is a piece that has been all but forgotten today.

By the mid-nineteenth century, the North American public had grown weary of representations of the "Noble Savage" and lost its taste for the more serious dramas (also performed in redface) that attempted a sympathetic depiction of the "inevitable" disappearance of Indigenous Peoples. Hence, in 1847, John Augustus Stone's much admired melodrama *Metamora; or, the Last of the Wampanoags* was rewritten as the burlesque *Metamora; or, the Last of the Pollywogs* by John Brougham. Interestingly, the American tragedian Edwin Forrest played the title role in both productions within a performative container they dub "The Scrubbing Portal" (Turtle Gals 337). Here, the "gals" embody a multiplicity of archetypes emerging from the history of Minstrelsy and redface performance, as they re-appropriate a historic site of cultural appropriation and shameful fabrication to scrub it clean and prepare it for ceremony (337). Thus, the spectacles upon which the settler myths were built – spectacles devised to dehumanize racialized peoples with their grotesque distortions of burnt cork and redface buffoonery – are converted into performative memorial. Within this newly cleansed memorial site, Turtle Gals Performance Ensemble re-writes and re-rights distortion, articulates its consequences, and redirects the misplaced shame visited upon the racialized towards the actual agents of shameful acts. Here, a two-dimensional shadow (the Minstrel Show) that once presented itself as an authentic representation of the stasis, degradation, and inevitable disappearance of Indigenous Peoples is embodied and articulated in three living, vibrant, and visibly present dimensions (living Indigenous women). Here, in the tradition of Spiderwoman Theater, Turtle Gals Performance Ensemble layers shadow atop flesh and flesh atop shadow, revealing the intertextual facing of its own "performative mola" and charging its witnesses to penetrate the layers and so discover a kernel of truth.

As the "gals" throw themselves into a vaudevillian slapstick routine of scrubbing the stage, they are serenaded by the scratchy, disembodied voice of Al Jolson singing "Who Played Poker with Pocahontas When John Smith Was Away?" And they answer in kind, lustily singing back the bawdy fiction of a crafty Indian maiden who has deceived her European "lover" and cheated him out of all his money (337). The action of scrubbing juxtaposed with a degraded (scratched) aural archive of bygone pop culture signals to its witnesses – the heirs and conservators

---

(Stanciu 45). In 1849, this parody was followed by a yet another popular sketch *Metaroarer* (writer unknown), and in 1855, Brougham's *PO-CA-HON-TAS; or, The Gentle Savage* opened to immense success and remained a favourite with American audiences for three decades (Wilmeth 135).

Birthed in the nineteenth century, Minstrelsy continues today in various forms and incarnations: From a thrice elected Canadian prime minister who has been photographed in blackface and brownface, to generations of American sports fans and team mascots, to celebrities in headdresses …

To readers who are interested in learning more about the long, complicated history of redface performance and Minstrelsy, I recommend Philip J. Deloria's *Playing Indian*; Douglas S. Harvey's *The Theatre of Empire*; Helen Gilbert's "Black and White and Re(a)d All over Again: Indigenous Minstrelsy in Contemporary Canadian and Australian Theatre"; and Donald L. Kaufmann's "The Indian as Media Hand-Me-Down."

of a damaging fiction[5] – that an accounting must be made; pretty lies must be "scrubbed down" to reveal their rotting core. This (con) textual layer is paired with a contemporary "vaudevillian" layer, as the gals offer a backhanded *homage* to Mr. Bones and Interlocutor while they speculate over a collection of abandoned shoes – the silent, unimpeachable witness to wholesale slaughter and genocidal policy:

OPHELIA: Did they jump straight up out of those shoes?
ESPERANZA: I wonder.
BRANDA: Did they have time to bend to untie them?
ESPERANZA: Did they struggle to squirm a foot out over the back of the shoe with a desperate heel?
OPHELIA: Did they step on glass as they ran?
ALL: as they fell (Turtle Gals 337–8)[6]

As the agents of soul loss are thrown into confrontation with the agents of remembrance, recovery, and re-righting, the site of public spectacle transfigures itself into that layer of existence wherein the drama of soul recovery and physical healing unfolds. Here, sacred acts are rendered appropriate for the public stage without distortion of their original purpose or degradation of their efficacy. Here, at every ontological level, the innumerable "wafting threads" that link this *Project* and its creatrices to innumerable human and non-human agents transform the performance of memory (and memory's less comfortable twin, *memorial*) into a legacy of survivance.

The Scrubbing Project constitutes a movable feast for the dead – a memorial dedicated to the countless victims and grievously wounded survivors of genocidal projects set into motion across the Americas (of which

---

5 Pocahontas was still a child when she encountered John Smith; she was never his lover. John Smith, like most European adventurers and settlers, entered into relationship with the Indigenous people he encountered to ensure his own survival and the survival of the Virginia colony that he was helping to establish. When his own compatriots turned upon him and tried to kill him, he fled Virginia, breaking his alliance with the Powhatan people, leaving them open to attack from the colonists. Pocahontas's subsequent relationship with tobacco baron John Rolfe began after she had been taken hostage by the English who used her as a "bargaining chip" with which to extort the Powhatan Peoples during negotiations over control of the fertile lands of what is now Virginia. Contrary to popular American fantasy, in their dealings with Indigenous Peoples, the light-skinned newcomers proved themselves to be covetous, crafty, thieving, utterly unprincipled.

6 This fragment comes from a monologue written by ensemble member Monique Mojica (Personal Communication 2022).

Indigenous Peoples were the targets) and in Europe (of which Jews, Roma, Christians, homosexuals, and all those who either opposed or did not comfortably fit into Adolf Hitler's National Socialist agenda were the targets).[7] At the centre of this movable feast is a material representation of the Winged Warrior Women – the mothers of our nations who continue their fight against an ongoing colonial project to eradicate Indigenous presence on "new-found" lands. These abandoned wings assert their spiritual presence even as they remember the physical absence of those who have fallen in the fight. Their mute splendour calls up, for me, an articulation of Ingrid Washinawatok El-Issa's teachings to remind the survivors of such projects to remember our responsibilities and to enjoin us to act upon them. Their very presence at the centre of a site of public spectacle, newly transformed into a space of ceremonial observance, fathoms the unfathomable, remembers what has been forgotten, and connects survivor to the fallen through legacy – wings with which to fly, boots with which to stride boldly, and purpose to fuel these mythic actions:

> OPHELIA: Grandmother sing
> Your song to me
> ALL: Sing your songs
> Of love and freedom
> Teach us who
> We are to be [...]
> BRANDA: Anna Mae Aquash
> OPHELIA: Helen Betty Osborne
> ESPERANZA: Ingrid Washinawatok El-Issa
> *Overlapping*
> *Presente, presente, presente*
> (Turtle Gals 364–5)

---

7 The crimes against humanity of the National Socialist Party of Germany and their international supporters 1939–45 were devised and perpetrated with the express objective of eradicating Jewish people in Europe (and perhaps, worldwide). This is not the first or sole instance of genocidal actions perpetrated on this people. The Jews worldwide have endured centuries of attack. So, too, have Indigenous Peoples on every continent. And with her every manifestation, in every era, within her every campaign, the "face" of genocide shifts, and her features rearrange themselves, as she acquires new strategies and finds new justifications and new modes of rhetoric to garner popular support for her crimes or to suppress any whisper of dissent. *The Scrubbing Project* makes no attempt to conflate the Inquisition, the Pogroms of Eastern Europe, or the Holocaust with the ongoing campaign against Indigenous Peoples on these shores. Nevertheless, the trauma wrought by *two* faces of genocide swims in

We are here (*presente*) because they were. We are able to exercise agency because they *acted* even as forces outside themselves exerted themselves to contain their lives and suppress their agency. *The Scrubbing Project* reminds us to remember this and to remember those forbears, even as it extends the process of Storyweaving *beyond the autobiographical*, weaving disparate individuals, nations, and doings undertaken in disparate temporal and geographical realms to bind the "us" in the here and now with those others in the "there and then." *The Scrubbing Project* rests on the foundations of the work that has come before. It is bound to its aesthetic legacy through the process it has employed, through the blood ties of Monique Mojica, and through the ministrations of its director Muriel Miguel. As director, Miguel mapped the processual journey and curated the *Project*'s public presentation, as three mixed-blood women[8] explored their bloodlines, navigated epigenetic trauma, and created medicine to heal the scars wrought by that trauma. Further, *The Scrubbing Project* remains anchored to the larger realm of Indigenous survivance through its spiritual centre – made manifest by the ever-present wings of the physically absent Flying Eagle Woman, a visual reminder to catch hold of those invisible, "wafting" threads that will bind us to our sovereign selves. *The Scrubbing Project*, as a crucial item in the bundle that is Spiderwoman's legacy, testifies to the reach of Spiderwoman Theater – a reach that will extend itself far beyond the mortal existence of the company's founders. It is a project that simultaneously reaches backwards, re-presences its ancestors in the here and now, and directly addresses Indigenous futurity.

Memory and Survivance

Lest we forget, Spiderwoman Theater and the process through which it created owe their genesis to the contributions of yet another American Indian woman whose earthly existence did not extend into its fourth decade: Josephine Mofsie-Tarrant is remembered as the inspirator of

---

the blood and nests in the bone of two of its creator performers. Both Michelle St. John and Monique Mojica are direct descendants of Holocaust survivors from Europe and Indigenous survivors of Turtle Island. All three "winged warrior women" of this performative offering survive in the face of genocide. And their *Scrubbing Project* has been created to draw performer and witness, alike, into a reckoning with this legacy.

8 Monique Mojica is Guna-Rappahannock and Ashkenazi; Michelle St. John is Wampanoag-Carib and Ashkenazi; Jani Lauzon identifies as a "Findian"--Métis and Finnish.

Spiderwoman Theater and listed as the second individual to whom *Persistence of Memory* is dedicated. And fittingly, this dedication binds this paternal grandmother to her grandchild Henu Josephine Tarrant (42) whom she did not live to see. Tarrant, now a young woman, has grown into a powerhouse performer. She is a member of Safe Harbors Indigenous Collective (NYC) and of Spiderwoman Theater. A triple threat, who is also proficient in traditional dance and music, she is a fleshly manifestation of the future of which her grandmothers (Mofsie-Tarrant and Miguel) dreamed. This grandchild has become the "catch-basin" at which multiple rivers, brooks, and tributaries – Hopi, Ho-Chunk, Guna, Rappahannock – have come together, "mix[ed] in strength" and "foam[ed] up" (Spiderwoman, "Persistence" 50). Like her grandmothers and great aunts before her, she will carve her own riverbed out of the stony places of existence and "travel on" ("Persistence" 50) into the future, carrying them and their teachings with her.

The image of the river (or of rivers converging) is a metaphor that I have chosen quite deliberately to pursue. This waterway is part of the genesis of Spiderwoman Theater. Visually manifested through projection on the floor of the stage during Spiderwoman's first public workshop (discussed in ch. 2), it functioned as a visual limen (threshold), physically separating the performers (Miguel, Mofsie-Tarrant, and Weaver) from each other. At the same time, it reflected the connections between the performers and the Creation stories they told. In moments, the stories were told discretely; in other moments, the stories came together: "So it was like the running of the river, this brook, but at the same time there were creation stories all happening at the same time" (M. Miguel qtd. in Haugo, "Persistent" 62). Three decades after that 1975 workshop, a river still ran through the consciousness of the Miguel sisters and was articulated as a key element of the process through which they effect their self-authored poetics on both the public and private stages. In *Persistence of Memory*, Muriel remembers and articulates the tension between being "one" and being "one of three" (see Spiderwoman, "Persistence" 48–9). Gloria, then, offers the solution to this ontological puzzle: How is it that "one" can be simultaneously a "whole" and a fraction of the whole?

– Three rivers, one rough, one calm, one
– winding.
– They meet at the bottom of a waterfall,
– they join.
– They mix in strength, they foam up, they
– travel on. (Spiderwoman, "Persistence" 50)

Survivance is bound up in the unfailing and unassailable soft power of water: Water is the first home; water sustains all life; living water must move; water allows herself to expand and contract as she mingles with other elements and life forms; water conforms to the shape of her container. Simultaneously, water seeps in, through, and around rock and sediment to filter out impurities and to thereby retain her singularity; water slowly wears down rock and ultimately carves out her own course through the landscape; waters come together to "mix in strength," and they drift away again to express the singular nature with which they were endowed at Creation. As it is with water, so it is with humans. We ourselves – at once, wholly isolate and fragmented limbs of a larger body – are contributors within the greater community of Creation.

This understanding is most poignantly illustrated in *Persistence of Memory* through the layering of multiple iterations Becky Thunderbird's song "Persistence of Memory." Lisa Mayo first sings the song as she takes us through the ritual of cleaning her home. Indeed, as she testifies, it is during these times, when she is sweeping her floors, that Elmira Miguel visits her ("Persistence" 45). As the eldest Miguel sister kinetically remembers the act of sweeping and wields the broom that connects her to her mother, she vocally remembers a song her mother sang for her: "My family, my nation. My Creator, my life. I sing for the next generation ..." (Spiderwoman, "Persistence" 45). Minutes later, a digital Murielle Borst-Tarrant as "Crystal," a fancy shawl dancer from Oklahoma, carefully demonstrates her prowess in this art form and explains just how she achieves it (Spiderwoman, "Persistence" 52). In response, Borst-Tarrant's mother and aunties are again moved to respond to her in song – to sing "for the next generation." This time, Borst-Tarrant's mother Muriel Miguel begins the song and is joined, in turn, by her sisters Gloria and Lisa. Finally, Borst-Tarrant's daughter Henu Josephine (then, seven years old) is layered into the performance. Borst-Tarrant owes her own proficiency in traditional aesthetic expression to the tutelage and training grounds provided her by her grandparents, parents, and extended family. And she has nurtured this legacy for her own daughter. Henu Josephine and her cousins will carry this legacy on to the children and grandchildren whom they engender. Memory is persistent, only when it is persistently passed on.

Like the generations that precede the live performers (the Miguel sisters), the generations who follow them (represented by Monique Mojica, Murielle Borst-Tarrant, Raphael Szykowski, Bear (Witness) Thomas, Frank Harris, and Henu Josephine Tarrant) occupy electronic layers of this performative mola. They sing, dance, speak, or simply watch over the proceedings in mute stillness. Here, in *Persistence of Memory*, these "actors," occupying disparate temporal realms (in the material world) are drawn together in a charged site of contemporary ceremony wherein the limen between the generations has been dissolved and wherein great-grandmother is linked to her descendants by ties thicker than blood and more enduring than flesh. On stage, three grandmothers who occupy three dimensions remember themselves as the fleshly bridge between the generations, transmitters of memory. But in performance, the veil between the two-dimensional and three-dimensional worlds has been penetrated; the limen between the ancestor and descendant has dissolved, as has the "bridge" itself. In this space, all times become one. In this space, the realms of flesh and spirit are drawn into immediate encounter, as the fleshly performers of the present moment subside into stasis to project themselves as mute shadows onto a scrim. In these moments when shadows speak, living flesh presences itself as a flat, indistinguishable witness to the living memory that dances on the screens before us all.

As *Persistence of Memory* concludes, the living performers subside again into shadowy stasis to witness their own active transmission of ancestral memory. This moment differs markedly from earlier shows in which the loud, vibrant, unapologetically bawdy body of the present was layered atop (or at times, beneath) the two-dimensional shadow of former times. Here, flesh and blood in three dimensions and in all its immediacy casts a mute, two-dimensional shadow onto a flat screen, as a digital future plays itself out in living colour and full voice. Now, a digitally captured seven-year-old (Henu Josephine) lights up the screen and sings a song her great-grandmother once sang to her own daughter. Under the tutelage of her maternal grandmother, she sings, now, not only "for the next generation" but also for *all* the generations – those who have been, those who remain, and those yet to come (Spiderwoman, "Persistence" 54). The commitment of the little singer to her song, her scrupulous effort to sing it well and her obvious enjoyment of the song and of her maternal grandmother's seal of approbation – "Very good, Josie" ("Persistence" 54) – bespeak the child's appreciation of and solicitude for ancestral legacy. She apprehends its importance, just as she profoundly understands that the bundle that is her inheritance is filled with ugliness as well as beauty. And perhaps she is coming to understand, more profoundly even than the previous generation, that a rejection of any portion of that bundle will by no means protect her from the oppression that has been visited on her ancestors; nor will it immunize her from the dis-ease of the colonized and the internalized shame so many of us have carried for generations. Open-armed acceptance of this bundle and all it contains, however, will surely equip her with the medicine to counter this dis-ease and afford her the endurance and the sense of purpose to resist current and potential oppressive conditions. And that the granddaughter of Josephine Mofsie-Tarrant and Muriel Miguel does, indeed, "understand" (where others did not) is most explicitly shown and told.

Young Henu Josephine's digitized vocal performance is connected to Spiderwoman's performance of Becky Thunderbird's "Persistence of Memory" via a dense intertextual weave, which begins as each Miguel sister wrestles with her own understanding of her legacy and of the beneficiary's relationship with and responsibility to that legacy:

> GLORIA: I didn't understand. I understood. She understands now.
> LISA: I understand now, but I didn't understand then.
> MURIEL: I understand. No, I don't understand. (Spiderwoman, "Persistence" 52)

Within this intertextual facing, Lisa contemplates her ancestral connections with the lands that now comprise New York City and its boroughs. Once home to Algonquian Peoples, relations of her mother's Rappahannock people, the Botanical Gardens in the Bronx, and the city that surrounds those gardens have become for Lisa an "available" site of timeless spiritual connection and replenishment (Spiderwoman, "Persistence" 53). This is strength and comfort. This is "that place that Indians talk about." This is legacy. Muriel, by contrast, remembers shame: "Are you ashamed of me? Are you? Are you embarrassed by your mother, your grandmother?" (Spiderwoman, "Persistence" 53). She is, here, Muriel-the-mother speaking to her own daughters. She is the one of whom her daughters are ashamed. Pain and shame – these too are legacy: "I understand. I was ashamed of my mother. My mother was ashamed of her mother. Are you embarrassed? Don't be" (Spiderwoman, "Persistence" 53).

Gloria's story, then, is woven in to negotiate the uncomfortable distance between the disparate legacies imagined by her sisters. It resolves the tensions between the wellspring of strength and connection offered by Lisa's vision of legacy and a congenital dis-ease that disconnects the afflicted from the generations that precede and follow them. As Gloria tells it:

> On a bookcase in my apartment, there is a very old photograph, tattered and torn. The photo is of me and my third-grade class. I'm sitting in the middle surrounded by thirty other children, the only dark one. I'm

> wearing a brown fur trimmed coat, my hair is in long braids. There is a faint smile on my face. (Spiderwoman, "Persistence" 53)

Over the course of her adult life, Gloria has preserved this material artefact that externally documents in two dimensions a complex and multi-dimensional interiority. Her sisters may not have always understood; those with whom she shared her life may not have always understood. And this knowledge may have served to exacerbate her sense of isolation and difference. But Henu Josephine, her grandniece, requires no explanation. She sees the picture and diagnoses Gloria's dis-ease, locating herself within the experience and empathically aligning herself with her great-aunt:

> "Is that you, Aunt Gloria?" "Yes, that's me." Looking up at me she said, "Then you know how I feel." Our eyes met for a moment. "Yes, Josie, I know how you feel." Three generations, three generations, and that knowing feeling is still present. (Spiderwoman, "Persistence" 54)

Young Josephine understands her great-aunt, and her great-aunt understands her. But this grandchild also understands survivance. She is a primary beneficiary of her grandmothers' struggle to remember and re-member themselves. And so, she sings the song Muriel Miguel taught her as if in jubilant assent to her grandmother's assertion that "We go back eons. Where you place your hand, your foot is padded with generations of us" (Spiderwoman, "Persistence" 54). Young Josephine sings in the present, padding the feet of future generations as she manifests her (and their) connections to the teachers and Elders who have come before. And as she sings, she completes a circle: *student becomes teacher as she reminds her Elders to remember that between the layers of the legacy they are preparing, the healing nests along with the dis-ease.*

Whose Memory? Whose Legacy?

> Working with a group like Spiderwoman can become all-consuming. The personal melds with the professional and life's stories. What I thought of as my own quite personal past and present concerns become part of a collective work. With Spiderwoman, because of the intimate use of storytelling, the blending of personal life and the professional life, and the intimacy required to make it successful, *one begins to function within a realm that explores memory at the same time as fostering together new, now collective memories.* (Spiderwoman, "Persistence" 43, emphasis added)

Persistence of Memory opens with this declaration by the late poet/author Sandy Crimmins who served as Spiderwoman Theater's stage manager during the early years. As with the other artists who are celebrated within this production (including the Colorado sisters, Brandy Penn, Pam Verge, Jan Robyn, Naja Beye, Lois Weaver, Ginny Mayer, Donna Couteau, Eduardo and Bonnie Duran, etc.), her connections to the Miguel sisters, their ancestors, and descendants have been made manifest within and by means of the process to which she gave herself. She with all the artists who have worked with the troupe are "Spiderwoman's issue." And Crimmins's acknowledgement alerts us to the fact that despite initial appearances, *Persistence of Memory* is not just a personal retrospective or an "auto-tribute." Nor is it simply an attempt to locate and explicate the legacy that Spiderwoman Theater has prepared for a chosen few. *Persistence of Memory* is more ambitious and further reaching than this: it explores the essential nature of legacy – the individuals' *responsibility* to the world we are writing for our children. The bundles we carry direct our lives and direct this task of re-worlding even after we have inadvertently forgotten how it is that we have come to be carrying those bundles. So too, the bundles we leave for our children will direct their lives and their own projects of re-worlding even after they have come to forget the exact nature – the discrete elements – of just what it is they may find themselves carrying.

Re-worlding is a project that requires reciprocity; so, too, the construction of legacy requires active engagement from all parties – the donor and the heir presumptive. As we have seen, Gloria's burden of internalized shame and isolation is reconfigured through the discovery of mutual understanding and empathic connection (through shared experience) with her grandniece. Young Henu Josephine not only lightens Gloria's burden (by sharing it); she has found a solution to its crippling weight. She may be acutely conscious of being Other in her own classroom, but the shame this consciousness once brought to former generations is performatively tempered with fierce pride and a sense of responsibility to the coming generations.

Offstage, this intergenerational project of collectively reframing legacy is an ongoing process that ultimately informs the works of Spiderwoman's issue. During an interview, which followed the company's performance of *Persistence of Memory*, Lisa Mayo and Gloria Miguel poignantly addressed the shame that they have long felt for their participation in their father's Medicine Shows (Haugo, "Persistent" 67). Then Monique Mojica spoke, answering their articulation of dis-ease by prescribing its solution: Antonio Miguel's Medicine Shows made survival possible. They "made Spiderwoman Theater possible." And this made

Mojica's work, her cousin's work, and her son Bear (Witness) Thomas's[9] work possible. The legacy of Antonio Miguel's Medicine Show is "not a shameful thing for us [the descendants], because it's in us, and it keeps transforming" (Mojica qtd. in Haugo, "Persistent" 69)

Mojica's words here reverberate powerfully, as I consider her 2018 exercise in "skating on razor blades" (Personal Communication 2017). From 2014–18, Mojica's Chocolate Woman Collective began work on the development of a performative intervention that would explore the history of Indigenous Peoples on display in sideshows, Wild West shows, circuses, and even in lunatic asylums. *Sideshow Freaks and Circus Injuns* was imagined as a remedial intervention, which would "dislodge" the dis-ease of the colonial subject by performatively "dislodg[ing]" and "revers[ing]" the "pornographic gaze" of the North American settler (Mojica, Personal Communication 2017). Mojica's *Izzie M: The Alchemy of Enfreakment*[10] (2018) is the production that emerged from the investigations originally undertaken for *Sideshow Freaks and Circus Injuns*. This is a project that at once, invites the hungry gaze of the voyeur, shrinks from that gaze, and turns its own gaze upon the audience to demand, "Have you come here as voyeur or as witness?"

Exploring the history of Indigenous people on display in colonial sideshows, Mojica enters this project with her own personal and familial history, embodying a Rappahannock ancestor. Izzie M is a Medicine Woman who has been routed from her home by her settler neighbours and committed to an Asylum for Insane Indians. She has learned to disappear – fading into the walls of her prison, performing in accordance with her captors' expectations of the "good [Indian] girl," as she "serves tea in the nuthouse" to the Matron and the wealthy donors for whom a visit to the asylum is an amusing diversion (Chocolate Woman Collective). Under her cloak of invisibility, Izzie watches those who have come to watch her. From their conversations, she gathers important information pertaining to the location of the local train station and the schedule of the trains. Eventually, Izzie is able to activate her plans

9 Bear Witness (Thomas) is a founding member of The Halluci Nation (formerly, A Tribe Called Red.)

10 *Enfreakment* is a term coined by David Hevey to describe a series of dramaturgical practices comprising **narrative strategies** (scientific treatises and fantastic hyperbole), **costuming techniques**, **set design**, **framing**, **publicity materials**, and **souvenirs** that work to excite in spectators a heightened sense of the distance between themselves (as representatives of the "normal") and the cast of different bodies performing as "freaks" (Thomson 10).

for escape, boarding a train bound for the 1904 St. Louis World's Fair only to find herself stranded within the wreckage of an historic collision.[11] Amid piles of baggage, bodies, and twisted metal, Izzie encounters FlimFlam Sam (performed by Métis actor Barry Bilinsky). Izzie's new acquaintance convinces her to capitalize on her talent for disappearing by building a sideshow act for the fair. Where else is she to go? Back to the Asylum for Insane Indians? Back to her expropriated home to be once again driven out by her neighbours? Where is she – indigent and alone – to shield herself from colonial violence? Skating the edge between hypervisibility and invisibility, Izzie M. becomes Izzie the Invisible Woman and decides to clothe herself in the gawdy glare of sideshow spotlights hiding in the direct line of sight of thousands of holiday makers. Together, then, FlimFlam Sam and Izzie M. make their way to the fairgrounds where they join a cast of historic Indigenous performers (including Edouard Beaupré who was billed as Eduardo the Métis giant and prisoner of war Apache leader and healer Geronimo).

The piece ends powerfully with a digital Gloria Miguel recounting the childhood humiliation of joining her family as a performer in her father's Medicine Shows. In these moments, *Izzie M.*'s audience sits shrouded in gloom, its collective eye pulled towards a sole source of light – the digital archive that contains Gloria Miguel. Our eyes pin her image, as she remembers the painful rush of shame that overtook her, as she was being pinned by the predatory stare of American circus/movie/ sideshow patrons seeking titillation. Who are we in these moments of intense watching? How do we watch? Do we watch as witnesses who are cognizant of our responsibility to properly carry and care for the testimony Gloria is offering? Do we watch as voyeurs seeking an ephemeral experience of *Schadenfreude*? Lulled by the breathing of our neighbours, by the close darkness that surrounds us, and by the rich, sonorous tones that carry Gloria's testimony, we may have forgotten these questions. But a familiar script has been flipped. Gloria Miguel turns her own gaze on those who gaze on her, challenging the members of *Izzie M.*'s audience to assess ourselves, our motivations, our behaviours, and our complicity in this historical moment: the enfreakment of her body, her daughter's body, or any Indigenous body could never happen in today's world, she surmises. *Could it*?

---

11 Izzie M.'s vehicle of escape turns out to be an eastbound Missouri-Pacific train, carrying passengers to the St. Louis World's Fair. In the early morning hours of 10 October 1904, this train was telescoped by a westbound train as a result of a head-on collision (Tanner).

With *Persistence of Memory* a decade earlier, it is Miguel's grandniece who soothes the sting of shame, acknowledging a shared legacy and articulating the profound connection that binds Elder with child in a space of reciprocal condolence. Here, too, Miguel's daughter Monique articulated her own grateful and proud acceptance of the "Medicine Show bundle" – a bundle, which, Mojica asserts, carries no shame. Now, with *Izzie M.*, such remedial ministrations have developed into a potent "exorcism" through which misplaced shame is cast away from the spectacularized Indigenous body and redirected back to those who have engineered such spectacles and infused them with shame.

Unashamed acceptance of the "Medicine Show bundle" is not a transformative phenomenon that belongs solely to Spiderwoman's issue; it is affected in collusion, and its benefits effect all. As if in response to Mojica's declarative embrace of this bundle (see Haugo, "Persistent" 69), Muriel Miguel has offered yet another lens through which to view Antonio Miguel's Medicine Shows: Times were hard in the years following the Great Depression. And where other families may have begged or stood in bread lines, the Miguel family chose "to perform instead" (M. Miguel qtd. in Haugo, "Persistent" 69). Shameful spectacle has been re-visioned as proud survivance. The "victim," through the act of remembrance transforms herself into the "victor." This portion of Spiderwoman's legacy – this Medicine Show bundle – carries a crucial reminder: "Whatever you do, you have the power. You have the power to change it" (Mayo qtd. in Haugo, "Persistent" 69). And when it becomes necessary, you enter the fray with every weapon you possess: "You gotta fight […] you need to fight" (Borst qtd. in Haugo, "Persistent" 70).

"Somebody Else Will Remember": *Chapan*

> The Cree word for great-grandparent is "chapan," which means "wagon." And it also relates to the verb, "to pull." From what I was told about this word, a long time ago, the old people would sit on a toboggan and the younger people would pull them through the snow as they moved camp. The word means that we as younger people are pulling our ancestors forward, with effort, compassion and duty. This is what an old elder from Northern Manitoba told me when I asked him about that word *chapan*. (Favel, "Poetry" 32)

Individual memory or even the collective memory of an entire generation is *not* consistently persistent. To be human is to be unfailingly fallible. Ultimately, as we age and decay our faculties fail us, and throughout our lives we are always teetering precariously on that edge between retention and loss:

> GLORIA: Do you remember?
> LISA: No.
> MURIEL: No.
> GLORIA: Neither do I. (Spiderwoman, "Persistence" 43)

But there is a remedy. As Gloria observes in this scene, just a few lines later, "Somebody else will remember" ("Persistence" 43) *if*, of course, we have begun the process of transmitting our knowledge. Hence, it is incumbent upon those to whom we pass memory to act as a bridge between the generations, passing back even as they pass it forward – to remind us to remember or to help us to reframe memory thereby reconfiguring dis-ease into empowered wholeness. Indeed, the process of "fostering new, collective memory" (see Crimmins qtd. in Spiderwoman, "Persistence" 43) or of birthing the new human being is a reciprocal one, which is neither solely self-reflexive nor unidirectional. The power of *legacy* here (whether it is passed intra- or inter-generationally) is that it is a gift that keeps on giving and *giving back*. This multidirectional flow – this reciprocity – is perhaps the most compelling aspect of all when we consider the employment of aesthetic, socio-political, or pedagogical processes to facilitate the anti-colonial project of re-worlding.

Lest we forget, Floyd Favel collaborated with the Miguel sisters and Monique Mojica (artists with whom he had worked) on the development of theatrical principles based on nation-specific legacies at the turn of the twentieh century. Within a few years, Favel had begun to express dissatisfaction with the initially unidirectional formula he had developed to articulate his concept of Native Performance Culture: Tr + Me = Th(2)[12] or "tradition plus method equals theatre doubled" (Favel,

12 It is interesting to note the similarity between Favel's "formula" and Muriel Miguel's formulaic expression for the craft of Storyweaving. Miguel, like Favel, insists upon the development of a method through which to distill traditional praxis to render it both appropriate and efficacious on the contemporary stage. She expresses this requisite distillation process thusly: "Storytelling [e.g., tradition] x Acting [e.g., process] = theatre" (qtd. in Borst, "Spiderwoman ... Legacy" 77). Theatre, for Miguel, is first and foremost a vehicle of (what she terms) "organic continuity": It carries the source of the people's ontological, epistemological, cosmological, and processual understandings, and it carries the mechanistic core of their affective transmission.

"Poetry" 34). Rejecting the term "method," because of the rigidity it infers, and replacing that with the more fluid term, "process," Favel has reconceptualized the relationship between the three elements of his equation. "[T]radition, process and theatre," he posits, "are all in equal relationship with each other, and they work together and influence each other." To express this reciprocal inter-dynamic, Favel developed this formula: "Tr/Pr/Th" (Favel, "Poetry" 34).[13] Elsewhere, Favel has identified theatre as "the younger brother of tradition" (Favel, "Theatre" 30). Hence, as Favel has come to conceptualize it, *the antecedent (traditional and ritual praxis) is simultaneously transforming and being transformed by the descendant (contemporary performance), as both transform the process, which facilitates this reciprocal affectivity.*

In chapter 4, we began some examination of this exciting inter-dynamic in the work of Omushkego-Cree artists Candace Brunette and Erika Iserhoff. Dr. Brunette belongs to a third generation of Spiderwoman Theater's aesthetic inheritors. She began her artistic journey as a student in my Indigenous Theatre class at the University of Toronto. From there, she travelled to Trent University to work with Muriel Miguel in a summer intensive, which the Centre for Indigenous Theatre runs each summer. A student and practitioner of Storyweaving, she had, since 2007, been visiting her own community to develop her *Omushkego Water Stories.* And with this project, Brunette and visual artist/costume designer Erika Iserhoff, under the direction of Floyd Favel and Monique Mojica, embarked upon an intensive partnership with several of those James Bay Cree trappers and hunters who, displaced from their traditional lands by the flooding and devastation caused by the hydro-electric projects, had been relocated to Cochrane, Ontario.

These Elders (holders of communal memory) shared their memories with Brunette and her creative team – "stories of starvation, supernatural stories and also hand-shadow storytelling and stories of the mysterious string game, which was traditionally used to invoke magic for hunting" (Favel, "Poetry" 34). Adopting and adapting some of these traditional aesthetic elements, the team wove these memories together. While they had been introduced to hand-shadow storytelling, Brunette

13 Commenting upon an earlier draft of this chapter, Monique Mojica reminded me of Favel's earliest formula for NPC (Native Performance Culture): Tr **x** Me = Th^2. Favel's earliest articulation of the evolution of this formula into a more multidirectional, fluid expression of the process he has been developing is the articulation Mojica prefers. This formula expresses itself as Tr ⇔ Pr ⇔ Th (Personal Communication 2010).

and Iserhoff adapted this technique to identify distinct historical moments and to locate themselves in the historical continuum of their community. They also utilized shadow work for visual emphasis in their storytelling, but the shadows they cast were full-bodied shadows, and these shadows were cast upon the canvas Bell tent that trappers began to use when they were introduced to the community in the early twentieth century. The choice to use the European canvas Bell tent as a site for story (rather than a traditionally crafted shelter) foregrounded a distinct historical layer. The history of the fur trade and its consequences to the Omushkego and the catastrophic history of displacement (e.g., of Indigenous humans, of water, of game) provides a base layer to which the stories that preceded that historical moment and the later stories (personal, familial, and communal) might be connected.

The performed work was not offered for public consumption; instead, it was a private affair within which the community could witness the distillation and abstraction of tradition (storytelling) through the theatrical methods that had been developed by Favel and Mojica. It was left to the original storytellers, their families, and the community to decide whether Brunette and Iserhoff had fully absorbed the teachings they had been offered and had earned the right to carry and communicate these stories. As I have previously noted, the aftermath of this very early stage in the work was an exciting surprise to all: "*Reading*" their own stories from the archives that are the bodies of Brunette and Iserhoff, the Elders began to remember long-forgotten remedies (this for tapeworm, that for lungs, this for burns, that for ...). Galvanized by these newly retrieved memories, they began to "riff off" of the duo's performance and to weave these lately recovered texts into the experience of the theatrical event they had witnessed (Brunette, Personal Communication 2008). Precious fragments of Omushkego knowledge were re-membered, reclaimed, and woven into legacy that may be operationalized in the present moment, carried onto the biota to which the people were relocated, carried back to the lands from which they were displaced, and carried onwards into the future. Within a short space of time, the first key stage in the process of anti-colonial re-worlding had begun to manifest itself in this community of heretofore "exiled" Elders.

In 2014, a second stage of this process began with a developmental workshop for which I served as director and Mojica as dramaturg. Here, our investigations plunged us more deeply into a structural exploration. As we have seen, the Guna mola (in design, aesthetic, and in the process of its construction) provides the structure upon which Spiderwoman's works and Monique Mojica's *Chocolate Woman Dreams the Milky Way* hang. By now, *Omushkego Water Stories* was part of a larger SSHRC-funded project (Traditional Knowledge, Contemporary Performance) within which Mojica, LeAnne Howe, Ric Knowles, Brenda Farnell, and I sought to investigate other, appropriate nation-specific sites of tradition through which to structure contemporary performative works. Ancient earthworks (specifically, mounds and mound complexes) across Turtle Island were identified as the *dramaturgical framework* upon which to create *Sideshow Freaks and Circus Injuns* (see Mojica, "In Plain"). For this project, which later premiered as *Izzie M.: The Alchemy of Enfreakment*, the team visited mounds and mound complexes across Turtle Island, declared our intentions, conferred with Elders from each community we visited, researched the construction of the mounds, attempted to understand them in conversation with each other, and considered their specific functions: Were these burial mounds, food caches, sites of ceremony, or effigy mounds?[14] What processes had been employed to "write" these enduring texts upon the land? What manner of "text" was Mojica constructing? How might the Indigenous Mound Builders' techniques be adapted within the construction of Mojica's performative intervention? Would the land, its ancient "texts," and its contemporary stewards grant Mojica permission to adopt and adapt this ancient knowledge to facilitate her project?

Similarly, in the 2014 developmental workshop of *Omushkego Water Stories*, we undertook to identify the land-directed Omushkego principles around structure (traditional narrative structures, the structuring of ceremony and lifeway around the seasons, string games, etc.). As this developmental phase neared its conclusion, Brunette and Iserhoff parsed out each structural stage of the traditional moose hunt (from preparation for the hunt to the return home and distribution of the kill). And this became the frame upon which to hang the *Water Stories* of their community. Not only would the content of communal life be brought forward for future remembrance but also an efficacious, originary structure of a community's life and art. Hence, while poetry – in content and in form and in all its manifestations – may be, as Favel asserts, "constructed out of remnants found in ruins" ("Poetry" 34), its power

14 Mojica had been riding her intuition, as she initiated the team's exploration of the structural patterns of Indigenous earthworks. At times, she herself wondered what connections she would find between these ancestral inscriptions of lifeway and knowledge and the sites in which the Indigenous body was displayed to sate settler-scopophilia. In the summer of 2014, those connections were made manifest when consultant Chadwick Allen informed the team that 16 mounds had been destroyed in St. Louis, Missouri, to make way for the temporary structures that would be constructed for the 1904 World's Fair.

lies in its ability repair the breakage, to transform those ruins into functional, life-sustaining worlds and to carry the denizens of those ruins into these worlds: chapan.

The potent alchemy of this exchange is compelling indeed. The possibilities and openings created by the multidirectional flow of intergenerational *processual* legacy afford a clear way forward in this fraught historical moment. Murielle Borst-Tarrant, for instance, is an erstwhile student of and apprentice to her mother. By 2007, Borst-Tarrant was already dramaturging and directing Muriel Miguel's one-woman show *Red Mother*. This piece carries us through the war-torn landscape (both geographical and psycho-spiritual) of Muriel Miguel's Indigenous incarnation of *Mother Courage* **without** her children. As Borst-Tarrant midwived the production and guided its articulation, she edited her mother's text and "taught back" to her first teacher. Borst-Tarrant, here, is one "somebody" who has remembered, scrupulously reminding the Elder of the lessons she – by virtue of being human – may have forgotten. Indeed, we see this dynamic playing itself out during the following exchange that occurred at the panel discussion, which followed the February 2007 performance of *Persistence of Memory* at Miami University in Oxford, Ohio:

MURIEL MIGUEL: Just doing *Red Mother* with Murielle here and my daughter says to me, "Oh, it's really nice, Mom. It's very beautifully written. We're going to have to do something about that (*audience laughter*). It's so well written, I can't do anything with this." I was going through the same process before she came in – all these beautiful words, but how do you act them? What did I write? It wasn't the actor informing. I was just writing, and so what happened? I stopped myself, and so when I gave it to her and I gave it to the director, it was like it's there. So she got out her pencil and she went zip zip zip zip zip. I had to start fighting for a couple of months there for something that I wanted to hold on to […]

GLORIA MIGUEL: [speaking of her early experiences with Spiderwoman moments later] … It's very difficult if you have an idea in mind and someone comes in and takes a word out that changes the whole idea of the story.

MURIEL: That's not true.

GLORIA: You have to fight to keep that idea […]

MURIEL: And so what happens when somebody says that they have this idea? You look at the idea and they say they want to do this and this with it. You say, "Fine," and then my job is to take it and make it part of the whole, because I am the final eye. You see it from far away, that it's *this*, so sometimes this has to be altered. And when this is altered, it's not the individual we're talking about. It's that all of this adds up to *this*. (Haugo, "Persistent" 72–3)

Throughout the development of *Red Mother*, Borst-Tarrant occupied the position her mother occupied throughout the decades of Spider-woman Theater's development, while Muriel Miguel occupied the position of her sisters within the relational dynamic of actor to director. First, a witness to the turbulent, relational dynamic that is an inescapable part of the experience of collective creation and then a student (through active engagement with Miguel) of the Storyweaving Practice itself, Borst-Tarrant ascended, in moments, to the position of "teacher" in the *Red Mother* endeavour, reminding Muriel Miguel to privilege the sum over its composite parts (however attractive those parts may be) and of just how powerful the swell of resistance to that lesson can be. At the same time, Borst-Tarrant continued to learn from her mother and to watch key lessons in the practice of Storyweaving evolve, transform, and extend their influence in other areas of contemporary artistic endeavour.

Indeed, Borst-Tarrant's award-winning one-woman show *More Than Feathers and Beads* emerges straight out of the Storyweaving Practice under the direction of Muriel Miguel (Mojica and Knowles, *Staging Vol. II* 113). As Borst-Tarrant herself asserts, the production's use of music and light as vehicles of storytelling have been directly influenced by her aunts Lisa and Gloria respectively (Borst, "Spiderwoman ... Legacy" 78–9). And this speaks to a profound and complex intergenerational exchange. Interestingly, however, Borst-Tarrant has identified her *cousin* Monique Mojica as a key inspirator of *More Than Feathers and Beads*. And this speaks to a powerful instance of *intra-generational* exchange.

In 1990, Mojica performatively intervened upon the "authorized" history of encounters between the Indigenous Peoples of Turtle Island and European newcomers. Her *Princess Pocahontas and the Blue Spots* articulates the claims and plays out the characterizations immortalized in travel accounts, originally crafted to titillate European audiences or to attract continued financial support for European exploration of and expansion across Indigenous lands. Utilizing her own physical being as the vessel through which the much-maligned grandmothers of mixed-blood peoples might express themselves, Mojica called to account the manufactured stories of Pocahontas (Powhatan), Malinche (Nahuatl), the Quechua women of the Puna, and the mothers of the Métis Nation. Weaving their stories with those of several contemporary Indigenous "everywomen," Anna Mae Aquash and one female Trickster, Mojica affected a potent re-visioning of history through which to re-educate contemporary audiences and, as I have argued elsewhere, facilitated active and actual transformation in the realms of both flesh and spirit (Carter, "Blind Faith" 9–10).

The processual link between Mojica's work and that of her mother and aunties manifests itself not only in the dramaturgical framework of her plays (Storyweaving) but also in the extension of the corporeal process into what I have previously termed the Red Reading. With *Princess Pocahontas and the Blue Spots*, Mojica took up the work Spiderwoman began in *Winnetou's Snake Oil Show from Wigwam City* in her sly re-animation of the dead fictions that pretend to represent Indigenous humanity and experience. Like the bodies of her mother and aunties before her, her own body became the archive in which to read a colonially authored literary artefact. In Mojica's body, two texts were juxtaposed – that belonging to the authentic descendant informed by the "persistence of memory" and the pervasive (and erstwhile persuasive) colonial fabrication. Through her body, we were invited to scrutinize this intertextual facing for ourselves, to assess two inconsonant narratives (interfactual texting) and to decide for ourselves which story would govern our own attitudes towards ourselves and/or towards others. Within the vessel that is Mojica's body, Pocahontas, Malinche, and the grandmothers offered us fresh eyes through which to view the European "text" and held up an Indigenous lens through which witnesses could interpret these texts to arrive at a more profound understanding of the fears and fantasies that drove the colonizing body and that inspired its documentation of Indigenous histories.

As if she were exploring a costume outlet, Mojica tried on and tried out literary constructs that had been imposed upon Pocahontas, Malinche, and the grandmothers of the mixed-blood peoples to expose their cheap plasticity, poor design, and flimsy construction. She vocally *and kinetically* articulated the words written about or attributed to these ancestors, revealing garbled translations and misconstrued meaning. As Spiderwoman Theater had originally intended their own intervention to do, Mojica's Red Reading affectively reconfigured the public stage into a space of transformation and healing and offered its witnesses the opportunity to experience a transformational shift from a state of ignorance to a more profound and truthful intimacy with their own ancestors and the ancestors of the Others who sat beside them (see Carter, "Blind Faith").

What so struck Borst-Tarrant about *Princess Pocahontas and the Blue Spots* is that Mojica had utilized their processual legacy to step outside of herself and to expand the orbiculate structure to which this process lends itself: She "didn't use her personal stories; she took characterizations of different women and she performed them on stage using the method of storyweaving" (Borst, "Spiderwoman's ...

Legacy" 79). Mojica's work, then, realizes itself within a subtle *evolution* of Spiderwoman's technique. This is not to say that Mojica's performative mola is devoid of any autobiographical strands. For instance, Mojica did recall her own brief encounter with Anna Mae Aquash at Rosebud, South Dakota (Mojica, *Princess* 53), and the taped portion of her song of "Transformation Twelve" is, in large part, a love song to her (then) husband Fernando Hernandez (Mojica, Personal Communication). This song recalls the first time she travelled to his home in Mexico. She remembers how he "tasted of salt and oranges"; she remembers how "the moon sang her happiest songs to [them]"; she remembers "the falling stars that took [their] breath away" (Mojica, *Princess* 55). But these moments of self-reflexivity serve to contextualize and deepen the bigger picture while tightly binding the descendant (Mojica) into relationship with those ancestral mothers of mixed-blood peoples who speak their stories through her.

Hence, when Borst-Tarrant set about developing *More Than Feathers and Beads*[15] several years later, she utilized her mother's process to document stories of contemporary women outside of herself and beyond the circle of her immediate family to interrogate the stereotypical categories of Indigeneity, which mainstream audiences expect to encounter within a performative event. Indigenous experience is often only recognized as such by these audiences if it is expressed through signifiers, which they have come to associate with "authentic" Indigeneity. But as Borst-Tarrant's characters reveal, contemporary Indigenous Peoples are exposed to and may allow ourselves to be influenced as much by pop culture and Western aesthetics as we are by the traditional praxis belonging to our communities of origin: There are as many budding Giselles among our children as there are Fancy Dancers. It is our choice. It should be our choice. At the same time, Borst-Tarrant was determined to "take no prisoners" ("Spiderwoman … Legacy" 79). As she interrogated the fabrications of the Western world, she turned her mirror towards Indigenous communities themselves to simultaneously interrogate the human brokenness, which has resulted from those misshapen containment units (physical, intellectual, and psycho-spiritual) into which the people have been forced. As Borst-Tarrant's Fancy Shawl Dancer explains after interrogating her father's admission of racial intolerance,

---

15 In 2000, *More Than Feathers and Beads* was the sole Indigenous production (from the United States) to be selected for inclusion in Australia's Global Indigenous Theater Festival (Mojica and Knowles, *Staging Vol. II* 113).

> I just couldn't figure out why he was so mean. Then I realize that it wasn't that my dad was afraid of Black people it was the change. When he said that to me, he was saying that change isn't good and it isn't good for us Indian people. My dad came from a different time of survival and that so much was taken away from us he had to hold on to something. He wanted me to know that this is his world and even though I am going to college, he wanted me to understand that his world he created for me to survive in is protected and change was no good. ("More Than Feathers" 123)

Still, as Borst-Tarrant reminded us, we have a choice. We can choose to shatter the lenses, which have distorted the Indigenous image, as we remember ourselves. We can confront and interrogate the root causes of our own dis-ease. We can choose not to be defined by the affliction. Indeed, we bear a responsibility to choose, and we are responsible for the choices we make. Borst-Tarrant answered (or, rather, allowed us to answer for ourselves) the core question around which *More Than Feathers and Beads* had been constructed: "Is survival enough?" (131). The answer I take is this: survival alone will not suffice. Survival is our inheritance. But if we are to honour those who came before and who sacrificed so much to ensure our coming, we must take up that inheritance and transform it into a life well lived.

In the final moments of her performance, Borst-Tarrant remembered and celebrated "the HIV infected men and women of our communities," "the men who survived," "the gay mothers [including her own], fathers, uncles and mentors [including her own uncle-in-law Louis Mofsie]," "our children," "the survivors of rape, incest and abuse," and finally Flying Eagle Woman ("Ingrid") who had given up her own chance to survive in the fight for cultural preservation and restoration ("More Than Feathers" 130). As she had done throughout the piece, Borst-Tarrant cheekily defied expectations by eschewing the use of "traditional" signifiers of Indigeneity in the dance she performed to honour these relations and the bundles they left for us. *Her* honour song is at once a sly comment on dominant notions of authenticity and a defiant exercise of her freedom to choose her own mode of expression.

Madonna's "Express Yourself" is the rebel yell of young women seeking to invent (or to re-invent) themselves in the late 1980s. It is still understood to assert the value of the individual and to celebrate the freedom to express our differences. Borst-Tarrant, a fiery young woman, quite naturally claimed Madonna's music for her own. Hits such as "Vogue" (used only seconds later in Borst-Tarrant's show) and "Express Yourself" belong to her generation just as "Let it Be" or "All Along the Watchtower" belong to the baby boomers who were just coming into their own when these songs first hit the airwaves. Borst-Tarrant's honour song weaves the living, dead, and yet unborn into this "brave new world" that has forever transformed the lifeways of Indigenous Peoples. But as Borst-Tarrant reminded us, even as we labour to preserve, recover, and transform what remains of our plundered cultures, we are engaged in a project of *remaking a world that has remade us*. Homophobia and HIV have transformed some communities, which once honoured their Two-Spirited members. Residential schools (Canada) and Indian boarding schools (USA) were designed to isolate and re-program generations of Indigenous children. Many who survived these murderous institutions to become parents themselves were forced to forget who they were and passed down to their children a legacy of silence, violence, and self-hatred. Still, there remain "Flying Eagle" women and men in every Indigenous community. And with each generation, their numbers grow. These young people are recovering those tools we thought lost – tools, which teach us to remember; which reconfigure themselves to repair broken bodies, hearts, and spirits; and which offer the possibility of affecting transformation upon the dominant culture surrounding us: it too is dis-eased; it too requires healing.

As Borst-Tarrant's honour song manifests itself within an unexpected (and unapologetically American) pop aesthetic, the aesthetic itself is transformed by the purpose for which it has been appropriated. An iconic anthem of individualism on Borst-Tarrant's stage has been transposed into a choral anthem that calls up a communal circle. It dissolves the comfortable boundaries that separate the *I* from the *we*, the living from the dead, the child from the Elder, the colonized from the colonizer, or the fancy shawl dancer from the ballerina. Even the product of Borst-Tarrant's autonomous act of creation does not stand alone. Her invocation of Ingrid Washinawatok El-Issa inextricably binds this world she has created and its inhabitants to the works and worlds created by Spiderwoman Theater and the ever-widening circle of its inheritors.

As we examine the artistic lives of Spiderwoman's genealogical issue, we begin to see not only the evolution of Spiderwoman's processual legacy (its movement beyond autobiography) but also the inter- and intra-dynamics which direct the transformative possibilities it holds for all the generations. The flow of legacy does not travel in one direction from one generation to the next; nor does it stay solely within the biological family. It follows an orbiculate trajectory – flowing in ever-widening circles … Within circles … Within circles …

Apart from her work as a performer, director, playwright, and instructor, Murielle Borst-Tarrant is also a writer of fantasy. In this, too, she has found an avenue through which to nurture and develop what she has inherited. As she was working on the first book in her *The Star Medicine* series, she enlisted her mother to help her edit it. Instead of listening as Borst-Tarrant read sections of her manuscript aloud, Muriel Miguel "read [*her*] book to [*her*]," so that she would hear her words carried on another's breath (Borst, "Spiderwoman ... Legacy" 76).

This editorial exercise, adapted by Miguel from a key processual stage in her Storyweaving Practice was in part inspired by the feminist Consciousness Raising (CR) Gatherings in which Miguel participated in the early 1970s. But where CR sessions opened space to allow women to tell their own stories, Miguel's process (detailed in chapter 4) requires the originator of a story to witness its retelling, as each member of her "audience" tells her story back to her in sound, movement, and / or both. This processual development privileges the idea that it is as important to witness one's own story (in multiple dimensions) as it is to voice that story. This is Enow'kin. This is "Native storytelling but taking it and putting it into a modern form" (Borst, "Spiderwoman ... Legacy" 76). Muriel Miguel and her sisters drew aesthetic understandings from their inheritance and developed these into a methodology that would serve their own project of resurgence and anti-colonial reworlding during the last gasp of the twentieth century; so, too, their daughters take up this processual legacy and tease out its elements to increase its breadth, reach, and potency as a model of anti-colonial poetics in the twenty-first century.

Just as we have seen Murielle Borst-Tarrant receiving her mother's bundle only to pass it back – reminding Muriel to remember her own teachings – and receiving it again, so we can see Borst-Tarrant passing the gift forward and outward, reminding others to remember themselves in the stories they have inherited. To illustrate, Borst-Tarrant has served as a creative consultant on several non-Indigenous productions in New York City and its environs. During one such association with a company, which was mounting Shakespeare's *The Tempest*, Borst-Tarrant was originally brought on to facilitate the integration of an American Indian aesthetic into this Euro-American production. But before layers, which were largely foreign to the cast and crew, could be woven into the story they were telling, the storytellers first had to become fluent in Shakespeare's language and to locate themselves within his text. Somehow, this was not happening. Precious rehearsal time was passing, and the company seemed to be getting nowhere. As Borst-Tarrant tells it, the director asked her to step in and try to "get [the actors] going" ("Spiderwoman ... Legacy" 76). To meet the challenge, Borst-Tarrant brought the troupe into "Spiderwoman's studio," as it were. She initiated a circle wherein the actors retold Shakespeare's story in their own words and in their own turn. And each actor *heard* the others' tellings. From there, they were able to isolate the core of the play and to connect that core to personal stories "about their individual ambitions." Then, Borst-Tarrant had the actors retell the stories kinetically. And finally, "the words started to come easier for the actors" (Borst, "Spiderwoman … Legacy" 76).

Shakespeare's *The Tempest* (1611) is eerily prophetic. In these early stages of imperial exploration and contact, it predicts and processually analyzes the stages through which colonization would unfold over three centuries in the Americas after its writing – predicting Indigenous enslavement, the reserve system, and the systems of Indigenous re-education through which the suppression of Indigenous language and culture was operationalized. This is a European story, and its lessons were intended for a British audience. Four hundred years later, from the perspective of one for whom this story was *not* intended, it is particularly exciting to consider the implications of and possibilities carried within such intercultural encounters of the processual kind. Murielle Borst-Tarrant's legacy has been built upon carefully preserved and recovered fragments of besieged ancestral lifeways. And she has utilized this legacy, in part, to link the descendants of those who struggled so mightily to annihilate Indigenous lifeways to *their own* ancestral stories, to languages and lifeways they have forgotten, to their abandoned inheritance. Moreover, Borst-Tarrant's use of Storyweaving in this context has served not only to foster memory but also to *implicate the storytellers in their own history* by linking the personal motivations of the descendants with the ancestral ambitions that drove the colonizing project. Again, it is only through full acceptance of and accountability to the bundles we have inherited that we can begin to move forward in a creative (as opposed to destructive) and healthy (as opposed to pathological) manner. Indeed, it is only through the manifestation of remembered connections, the acknowledgement of difficult truths, and a sustained and active programme of redress that conciliation between Indigenous and non-Indigenous Peoples on Turtle Island might be accomplished.

Weaving Relationship, Weaving Repair

Old stories will not be written over. We may cover them with our silence, refusing to lodge their actors in living memory or to breathe life into past misdeeds by speaking them out into the present world; still, they continue to plot a course through which new stories unfold and new ghosts are brought into being. For me, then, the potential to restore right relations or to engender conciliation is, perhaps, the most significant impact of Spiderwoman Theater's processual legacy.

In September 2019, Hart House Theatre (located on the St. George Campus of the University of Toronto) turned 100 years old. For over a century now, Hart House Theatre has contributed the development of the storytellers and to the dissemination of the stories that have sparked and upheld the Canadian imaginary. *It is Canadian theatre before Canadian theatre could be said to exist*, and it has played a significant role in shaping the identity of this nation: William Hutt, Don Harron, Kate Reid, Raymond Massey, Wayne and Schuster, Donald Sutherland, Norman Jewison, and Lorne Michaels honed their craft upon its boards. Toronto and regional theatres (i.e., Crest, Jupiter, The Shaw Festival, and the Stratford Festival) sprang into existence during the second and third generations of Hart House Theatre's life.

Two of Duncan Campbell Scott's[16] plays had graced its boards: *Pierre* in 1921 and *Joy, Joy, Joy,* in 1926. And Carroll Aikins's three-act play in "Redface" – *The God of Gods* was produced by Hart House Theatre in 1922. To mark this historical moment, while looking forward to a second century of seasons, Hart House Theatre solicited me (first, for suggestions, and later) for help in producing its first Indigenous show as an *intervention* through which to commit itself to the urgent project of re-*storying its role as a cultural cornerstone in the colonial* edifice that contains us all.

Entering this project, I was wrestling with a tangle of questions: What dramaturgical methods might I employ to safely navigate the frontier between witness and voyeur? How might I ensure that the Indigenous bodies on that stage were not performing simply as fodder for colonial consumption? How might I ensure that the burdensome work of relationship building was shared equitably between Indigenous and non-Indigenous company members and ultimately between storytellers and witnesses alike? To what extent would the specifically Indigenous methodologies and dramaturgical structures (with which I had chosen to work) serve the project of relationship building in this historical moment? The process of building this show (originally envisioned as a collaboratively devised address of the

16 Duncan Campbell Scott (Poet Laureate of Canada) served as both a treaty commissioner (i.e., Treaties 6 and 9) and as the Superintendent of Indian Affairs in the early twentieth Century. He viewed Indian policy in Canada as a mechanism by means of which to legislatively eradicate all Status Indians in Canada. In 1923, he amended the Indian Act to make it compulsory for all Status Indian children (7–15 years of age) to attend residential schools in Canada.

TRC's 45th Call to Action)[17] carried its participants into spaces in which they were compelled to see, to remember, and to respond to a tangled history of settlement, to long suppressed histories, buried waterways, silenced voices, and wounded Earth.

Spiderwoman's Storyweaving practice, I had decided, would constitute the processual base through which to carry the artists (settler, new Canadian, and Indigenous) through the stories that remember ancient treaty relationships, the violation of these relationships, the personal histories that had brought us together in this historical moment, and finally into a new space of contact where conciliation and re-treating might begin. I had envisioned us doing this work together. But as I prepared for rehearsals, I began to wonder if this were not a naïve impulse. I wanted the relationships that came out of this process to be underpinned by truth, transparency, and trust; I hoped that each individual in the company including myself would be in some way transformed by the experience. And for these goals to be achieved, absolute honesty was required. Indigenous participants and settlers alike needed to be able to speak hard truths, to engage in difficult conversations and to wrestle together with our fears, our hopes, and our most cherished biases and assumptions. Courage would be required if we were to break the dam together. But in forcing a premature togetherness, I could either be courting dysfunction and micro-aggression, or a politely false, distinctly Canadian encounter in which any possibility of authentic relations would be lost.

Storyweaving is a practice that is informed by immense bravery and utmost generosity, but could I expect the Indigenous storyteller to trust that the non-Indigenous listener would receive her story without inherited assumptions? Could she tolerate her story being retold by that witness? What ultimately emerged from these questions was a four-pronged process. Each prong of the process emerges from Indigenous intellectual traditions, adapted as theatrical pillars for contemporary public performance in this historical

17 Call 45 enjoins the Canadian government to collaborate with Indigenous leaders on the creation of a "Royal Proclamation of Reconciliation." This document would be supported by the pillars of the Royal Proclamation (1763) and the Treaty of Niagara (1764). However, it would repudiate the Doctrines of Discovery and *Terra Nullius* and would implement the procedural recommendations of the *United Nations Declaration on the Rights of Indigenous Peoples* (Truth and Reconciliation Commission of Canada, 94). *Encounters* asked its creators to consider their personal investment in and responsibility to Call 45 and the process of forging a new (and functional) relationship through which to move forward together.

moment. Resting on the pillars of land-based dramaturgical praxis and two traditions of Storyweaving, underpinned by Anishinaabe and Haudenosaunee protocols of consent, the emergent project *Encounters at the "Edge of the Woods"* signals the potential of this processual blend to evolve into an effective methodology that specifically addresses the project of relationship building with the context of "Truth and Reconciliation."[18]

I realized that it was imperative to curate spaces of retreat – spaces in which the Indigenous company members could identify and wrestle with the work we needed to accomplish and in which non-Indigenous company members could wrestle with their questions and do their own work. Before our fledgling project of re-worlding could begin, we would require a retreat from each other into what Métis Curator David Garneau has termed "irreconcilable spaces of Aboriginality" (see Garneau, "Imaginary"; Robinson, "Welcoming"). In these spaces we would begin the work of repairing the "split mind," and from these spaces, we could re-encounter each other and the biotas that sustain us with generative action powered by good intention. This is an incredibly complex task in this historical moment. Canadians do not stand, as if for the first time, at the "Edge of the Woods." Our peoples have stood there before: treaties were ratified then violated; promises, uttered then broken. Hence, trust in the retreating process cannot be assumed; it must be hard won.

Within (what I have come to term) "irreconcilable spaces of condolence," we began our work on the storied land atop which the St. George Campus of the University of Toronto has been built. Each group on its appointed evening followed the same route and listened to the same stories of the lands upon which we were working. We storied the manicured grounds of the house Sir John A. Macdonald occupied in the year he signed the Indian Act into legislation. We laid hands on the stones of the buildings in which so many teachers and administrators of Canadian residential schools had been trained. We considered our own training as artists, educators, and researchers as we encountered the imposing stone "wombs" in which theories of eugenics and nutritional experiments on residential school children were birthed:

---

18 The performance text of *Encounters at the "Edge of the Woods"* has been published with a series of essays about and reflections about the process of its creation and around the creators' experiences within the process (see The Collective Encounter with Jill Carter, *Retreating to Re-Treat*, Playwrights Canada, 2024)

KATIA: Witness of our sins
Piled together
A reminder
JENNIFER: … i swear i can hear the walls talk
And wonder what they need to say
What we need to hear
Maybe it's the voices of children who were exposed to nutritional experiments
Reminding us every time we feast to make them a spirit plate. (Collective Encounter)[19]

We recounted the treaties that govern Tkaron:to, the fraudulent "Toronto Purchase," the expropriated lands. And we listened for the whisper of befouled, then buried, waters that still rage beneath the campus grounds, remembering too that the year in which Taddle Creek was finally buried on this campus (1884) is the same year in which the Indian Act was amended to prohibit Indigenous ceremonial praxis. And, in moments, hope swelled, as we remembered how those irrepressible waters surge up even today to "unsettle" campus life and remembered that in our own resurgence, a re-creation story is beginning:

JENNIFER: Legends
Traditional ecological knowledges
Smudge whenever we need medicine
Celebrate with songs
And laughter
And feasts
It is truly a beautiful thing. (Collective Encounter)

Our earliest discussions and questions began in these irreconcilable spaces apart. And it was within these spaces that we began to work with yet another iteration of Storyweaving introduced to us by Stó:lō-Cree/

19 Katia Café-Febrissy is a racialized settler. She is an accomplished director, playwright, and performer. As a resident of Tkaron:to, Katia joined The Collective Encounter to learn more about the Indigenous history of these territories and to strengthen her own alliances with the original stewards of this land. Jennifer Alicia Murrin is a queer, mixed (Mi'kmaw/settler) storyteller and spoken word artist originally from Ktaqmkuk (Newfoundland). Jennifer currently resides in Tkaron:to and works in a University of Toronto building from which the infamous nutritional experiments (1940s–50s) in Canadian residential schools were, in part, funded.

Métis author, educator, and activist Lee Maracle with her daughter Columpa Bobb. Maracle began by telling us her iteration of a Stó:lō Origin Story, for which she has been granted permission to tell. The story chronicles an era of conflict. Assaulted on all sides by fatal visions and catastrophic memories, the human survivors of the Great Flood have no time to bury their dead, to mourn their beloved, or to properly care for the unfathomable numbers of carcasses of the non-human creatures who in life had sustained their lives. Driven by terror and unaddressed mourning, these survivors begin to turn on each other. A fearsome serpent is awakened by their violence. Bearing two heads, it is a creature of warring impulses with which it affects the human population and drives the behaviours of the people. One head "swallows human conscience," perpetuating escalating terror, mistrust, and violence within the human community, while the second head tries to "solve problems," perhaps, by swallowing the people's terror. After all, as Maracle observed, "terrified people cannot be trusted." Maracle enjoined us here not to concentrate on details but to let the story "wash over" us. What fear-fuelled assumptions did we nurture and what actions did we perpetrate that ran so horribly counter to our good intentions? Who were we and how were our stories woven into a centuries-old campaign of genocide on these shores?

Each of us told the story back to Maracle, as she instructed, "different but the same." Different, because each of us had found our unique place within this ancient story. And within the relative safety of irreconcilable space, we were able to articulate that place and to share our truths, in song, in verse, in fragmented memories. Next, under Maracle's guidance, each group engaged in writing exercises through which to interweave the stories of its members. And when the entire company met, finally, in a shared space of call and response, that space became a liminal zone of encounter. Here, we had at last retreated to the "edge of the woods," and from there, our investigations would be guided by the processual stages mapped out by Spiderwoman Theater, alternatively retreating from the edge of encounter to irreconcilable space and returning again with increasing frequency to call out and respond with devastating honesty and deepening trust.

Throughout the process, the cast members laboured to answer a key question: How might individuals, estranged by a history of relational violation "become friends" in this historical moment (Collective Encounter)? How can the beneficiaries of the colonial project eschew the impulse to deflect guilt and reject responsibility? How can a seed of trust between Indigenous and non-Indigenous Peoples begin to take root and flourish? In 2019, The Collective Encounter located, for themselves, a place from which to begin. In this space of meeting, Settler colleagues were enjoined to "listen." In this space of meeting, shared personal truths *offered without equivocation or obfuscation* – personal tragedies, violent encounters, confusion and ignorance, rage and pain, survivance, forgiveness, and joyous memory – became the "wafting threads" connecting erstwhile strangers into a bittersweet intimacy from which new-found understandings and good intentions might be manifested as affective actions of redress and repair.

PESCH: Once I sat on an edge like this before
MANNAN: At the edge of the woods
URI: At the water's edge
SARAH: This is not the first time this has happened ...
BRENDA: For 150 *years* ...
CAST: For 150 years.... *(whispered echoes)*
SARAH: Standing here at the edge of the edge of the woods
I tiptoe softly
Humbled by your power
Your compassion, your radical love rage
The beauty in the actions you have shown me
Born trespasser, and complicit in your pain
And I want to answer your beautiful call
And respond to your rightful demands for change
Because I pray your great great grandchildren into existence
And until everyone knows this is Indigenous land,
I want to be part of the resistance. (Collective Encounter)[20]

Perhaps we begin to see here a practical address of a crucial (and often unaddressed) step in the anti-colonial project of re-worlding. This processual stage has been identified by Spiderwoman Theater and briefly discussed in the previous chapter of this work – the possibility of forgiveness carried in the achievement of empathic connection. In each Spiderwoman project, as we have seen, this empathic connection realizes itself through the very act of working together within the process. But it is important to recognize that the facilitation of this connection has also been built into the Storyweaving practice, and it is predicated upon the unconditional acceptance of our inherited bundles in their entirety.

20 Pesch Nepoose identifies as a Cree playwright and performer. Brenda Wastasecoot is a Nêhiyaw storyteller and faculty member at the University of Toronto. (Abdul) Mannan Ahmad, Uri Livne-Bar, and Sarah Michaels are settler performers who have begun to learn, to embrace, and to activate their responsibilities as allies.

This process of unearthing the malignant spirits that haunt us to examine them in the light may be a crucial first step in the healing process, but it is only half of the equation. Condemnation and rejection, when they become part of a pattern that repeats itself, only weaken us and threaten to corrupt the legacies we are preparing for the next generation. It requires courage to peel back the layers, find the questions, and follow the pain. It requires the same type of courage exhibited by the little child Lee Maracle introduced to The Collective Encounter in her telling of the story of the double-headed serpent. It is a little child who takes it upon himself to find, face, and immobilize the monster and so restore peace in his community. His stated intention, when he sets out on the quest, is to kill the serpent. But when he has faced the serpent, certain of his power to do just this, he rejects the initial destructive impulse and negotiates a treaty with the serpent: the humans will honour and feast the serpent, and the serpent will protect them. Thus, balance will be preserved. Imbedded within the layers of this originary quest; within all the layers Spiderwoman has explored; and within the layers of the works that have taken up Spiderwoman's process gleams a shining moment of redemption and all its possibilities. Inarguably, this shining moment has yet to be fully realized, but it is possible that through the application of the Enow'kin Principle (the inclusion and full consideration of multiple, contradictory texts) and through the process of intra-generational (and perhaps, intra-cultural) self-examination and truth-telling, the establishment of right relations between our peoples is, perhaps, an achievable goal.

This potential for restoration and repair permeates the works of the Miguel sisters and of their genealogical inheritors. It reveals itself quite explicitly within an intra-generational partnership forged by their daughters. The little-known "A Valentine to my Grandmother," written and performed by Murielle Borst-Tarrant and Monique Mojica, is a contemporary honour song that documents the history of Creation (in the story of Sky Woman) and the history of their own maternal line. Armed with the stories passed down to them by the women who raised them, Borst-Tarrant and Mojica sing out the story of the barefoot women (the midwives) who ran to survive and who ran to ensure the survival of the daughters they would bear. In song, they herald the stores of hope that they, the issue of these women who ran on bare feet, have inherited. These stores they will increase and pass on to the generations to come.

> We are descendants from the river and the stars
> We are of the eternal Turtle Clan
> We are the next rememberers

> We carry the songs in our hearts
> We carry the stories in our blood,
> The hope in our souls
> We are the past, the present, the future
> Take this story and hear the hope
> Take this story and hear our voices of our nations.
> (Borst, "Spiderwoman … Legacy" 85)

The power of this intergenerational reconciliation lies not in some rigid adherence to a sugarcoated history in which unacknowledged human brokenness lies festering in the dark. This is not an act of forgetting or of denying portions of our legacy. Nor is it an act of capitulation, which traps coming generations in an unending cycle of brokenness. Instead, like running water, it carries the promise of new life, new beginnings. As Muriel Miguel has remarked of this song, "A new creation story is being made. It's going again, and it doesn't necessarily mean that it'll be in [Spiderwoman's] words or [Muriel Miguel's] words, but it goes on" (qtd. in Haugo, "Persistent" 66). The legacy that Spiderwoman Theater has prepared for its issue will shift and reconfigure, looking back to inform the present even as it moves forward articulating itself in new words carried on the breath of new human beings speaking out and back to new worlds.

Beginnings

In the summer of 2003 at a Conference of German and Canadian Universities in Berlin, Nêhiyaw playwright Tomson Highway told us a story. At a yearly dinner, during which Canadian artists and select corporate supporters meet to share ideas and network, a highly accomplished doctor was seated across the table from him. This doctor looked the playwright up and down and then observed laconically, "That's a very nice shirt, Tomson. Grants must have been good this year." Highway immediately grasped his inference and was so shocked by it that he could make no response. This doctor, Highway told us, was expressing his subtle distaste at the idea of a system wherein a nation's artists receive financial support from its citizens. And he was subtly accusing Highway of misusing that support (i.e., by wasting taxpayers' money on fine clothing). "What I should have said," Highway told us in Berlin, "is this: you are a good doctor, are you not? And you are paid well for this – by the taxpayers. You believe this is fair, because you are good at your job, and you fulfil a necessary function. I, too, am a healer. And through my work, I heal many people *before they ever have to come to you.*"

Highway's assessment of his personal and professional identity – of his role as artist within his community and the responsibility this entails – is one that is shared by Indigenous artists across Turtle Island: Art is medicine, and Indigenous artists are charged with the responsibility of healing.

Since 1976, Spiderwoman Theater has dedicated its labours to the fulfilment of this responsibility, and the legacy it has been preparing will enable others to continue and build upon their good work. Three little brown girls from "there" (Red Hook, Brooklyn) have spun a genealogical generation of Spider Women right "here" – an issue of artists who carry on, teach, and who are actively advancing and evolving the Spiderwoman practice of Storyweaving. And they have engendered countless aesthetic inheritors from all four directions in their work with communities around the world. Now, perhaps, it is time for those of us who stand upon Spiderwoman's shoulders to return the gift by supporting our Elders in accordance with their needs, not in accordance with what we have decided they need: chapan. It is in this spirit then that I wish to close this chapter.

I am still haunted by the idea that perhaps we – Indigenous artists, audiences, and communities – have not adequately expressed our awareness of the debt we owe to the Miguel sisters (although I want to believe that this project has begun to address and redress some of those areas in which we may have been remiss). And this haunts me, I think, because of doubts that Gloria Miguel has often expressed to me as she has reflected upon her life in art:

> You know the funny thing, Jill, when I talk about all of this experience, I think that I should be the healthiest, strongest woman in the world. And still, I find myself quite weak and stupid and dumb, because ... I don't know. It's good on stage, but it's so hard to do in real life. "You found all that power," you say. "You should be so strong and spiritual." And I'm not. You know, it's like we're left ...
>
> I don't know how my sister Elizabeth feels, and I don't know how Muriel feels. They have different stories with their power. But I feel now that people think ... There I go again with that clown character ... I'm spiritual, and I have strength, and I have all this. And I can't say, "Yeah, I'm ..."
>
> I'm strong, I realize, but I am not as strong as I want to be. And what did I learn from all that? I don't know.
>
> It's not always automatic and successful. It may come, because I feel that doing all that work should be useful in my life, and I find myself after a while without work, without money. Without. Without. Without. And I say,

> "What good is it to me? What did I get for it – *from* it? Is it here, and I don't see where I can use it? What good does it do?" (Interview 2007)

In the final analysis, we are fragile, finite flesh. However rich the legacy we have built, we are secretly tortured by fears that it is not enough – that regardless of all we may have accomplished, our best efforts count for naught. And so, I conclude here by offering a strong shoulder to the surviving Miguel sisters that they might, if they so desire, stand upon it. From this vantage point, I invite them to look upon all they have done and all that is being accomplished because of the good work they have begun. Indigenous sovereignty lives in our nations' stories. And the healthy, sovereign communities that we imagine for our children will ultimately emerge out of the stories "of our becoming, of our becoming whole" – stories told by artists who live the telling and "make creation story begin again in life as in art" (Mojica and Knowles, "Creation" 6). This is the "house" that Spiderwoman has built. This is the bundle the Miguel sisters have assembled for their heirs presumptive. Theirs is the blind leap that we must imitate – despite the doubts that may assail us – because without that leap, transformation cannot occur.

This is not a conclusion. Nor ought we try to write one. A "door has been left ajar" (G. Miguel, "Daughters"). And we stand on the threshold, ready to be transformed at the dawning of a new creation.

Appendix 1: *The Fittin' Room* (Spiderwoman Theater), "Pam's Ed. (March)"

From the Walter Havighurst Special Collections & University Archives (Miami University Libraries, Oxford, Ohio).

(Please note, I have attempted to transcribe a handwritten document, which is replete with crossed out phrases and some illegible sections, including marginalia.)

[PAGE ONE]

Cheer:	I said: straight, gay, young, fat, feminist, old It ain't fittin' – Shake that thing
"The Way We Were" (hum)	Eva – words
Class Photo Questions > beadwork > cancer/moon	 3 actress/fem.
Gloria's Testimony – I am a …	
Am I Paranoid	Lisa
It's hard being a woman [This is fem. Theatre	– Eva Lisa]
Spike & Sport	
Feelings	Pam/Eva
Questions	punk/pink/understand this
Psychotic Episode / Lesbian	Muriel
Lisa's Testimony	
Mood for Love / get real / I want I want	Muriel

Mood for Love (whistle) / 1st Encounter
I want [illegible] – Eliz. Gloria & Eva

Questions
[illegible]

Are you Punk – into S&M – Could tell by the way you turned around
whips & chains

Hey Butch Butchie
Fem. Could tell by the way you didn't turn around

Names
Do you like – – – – –
10 Little Indians
Grand Canyon – Hey Minnie ha ha / scalp
There goes the neighborhood
13 13 13

[PAGE TWO]

Straight
Gay
Short fat skinny
Blond & brown
Young & old
And
Wishy washy
That's the way we are
Throw Eva down
All look

[PAGE THREE]

Closet Radical (Eva & Gloria)
Spike & Sport
Blondes / Eva fem.
Esther Williams
Motherless Child
Opera
Dinner Party
But is she gay
(Lisa) 42nd St.
Spiderwoman mystique (1. Muriel 2. Eva 3. Gloria 4. Lisa)
I don't like you

Eat Momma
10 Little Indians
Indian Love Call
Ladies Room – Muriel: Excuse me! This is the ladies room / Pam: (scream) / Gloria: (looks and walks out)
Telephone never rings – G[loria]
Friendship
But is she sexy / Sexy on 7 > Gloria Questions
~~P Delilah~~
I used to have a lover
Now that I'm free, what do I do about being alone?
[illegible]
[illegible]
Eva's Chicken / Birth of a woman
Spike & Sport

[PAGE FOUR]

Eva: Am I not a woman – Has not a woman hands? Has not a woman eyes, organs, dimensions, senses, affectations [sic], feelings, passions
I'll buy my own (Puttin' on the Ritz)

Lisa & G[loria]	Can I buy you a drink? Eva – I'll have a glass of white wine
P[am]	Can I buy you a drink
M[uriel]	Hey, Can I buy you a drink (to Lisa)
E[va]	Hey Mama (to Lisa)
M[uriel]	Do you have a light (to Pam)
L[isa] & G[loria]	Are you lonely (reach [for each] other)
E[va]	Can I buy you a drink ([to] Muriel)
All	No thanks. I'll buy my own

After show comments
I just wanted to have a real conversation. Not Rhetoric.
March – Lisa begin march. Muriel last on – Eva begin Sat.

Appendix 2: From the Walter Havighurst Special Collections and University Archives (Miami University Libraries, Oxford, Ohio)

MARVEL COMICS ATTACKS SPIDERWOMAN
WILLIAM KUNSTLER DEFENDS THEATRE GROUP

To the NEWS MEDIA in New York City.

Ladies and Gentlemen:

We'd like to bring the following to your attention:

SPIDERWOMAN THEATRE is a woman's theatre group, founded in 1975 by director Muriel Miguel. SPIDERWOMAN THEATRE is named after Spiderwoman, the goddess of creation of ancient Hopi Indian legend, who taught her people the art of weaving. Three of the women in the group, including the director, are Native Americans.

On 10/01/80 we received a mailgram from Thea Kerman, assistant counsel of the Marvel Comics Group, informing us of Marvel's ownership of the copyrighted and trademarked character of Spiderwoman and stating that we have no right to any use of the name of this character. Our use of the name SPIDERWOMAN THEATRE is considered a "dilution of the distinctiveness of the Spiderwoman mark."

We question Marvel's or any company's right to appropriate and claim exclusive use of names from a people's cultural heritage: Spiderwoman, Winnebago, Thunderbird, Mohawk, etc.

At the present time we are preparing our defense against Marvel's demand that we "cease and desist from any further use of the name Spiderwoman." SPIDERWOMAN THEATRE's interests will be represented by William Kunstler.

We would greatly appreciate any coverage of this conflict by the news media. Please be so kind to relay this letter to whomever could make the right use of it.

Sincerely,

SPIDERWOMAN THEATRE
77 Seventh Ave.
New York, N.Y. 10011

Contact: Lisa Mayo
243–6209

Appendix 3: From the Walter Havighurst Special Collections and University Archives (Miami University Libraries, Oxford, Ohio)

Scene Analysis – *Women in Violence* – Spiderwoman Theater

Clown Song

Introduction of Clowns

GLORIA – The chameleon – doesn't know who she is and until she finds herself she wears a hardhat and cape for protection, a reflective skirt to reflect others' images of her, and carries a flashlight to look at herself.

MURIEL – The Trickster – Has a tail, which she uses to tickle and tease people with and which is responsible for all her actions and tricks.

LISA – The Perfect Woman – Has gorgeous looks, is loved by everyone, and always keeps everything perfectly smooth.

PAM [verge] – The Nun – Wears a habit, which she hopes to fly to heaven on and carries a scrub brush to clean the world and the other women.

LOIS [weaver] – The bag lady (rag woman) – wears layers and layers of clothes, lives on the streets, is tough and cynical and has a bad mouth.

NAJA [Beye] – The dejected one

The Violence in the Streets Story

Feeling guilty about the inability to act in a violent street situation – {Audrey}

The Rat Pack

Muggings, violence, killings

The Mass Murder of Women Dream

The Knife Story

Protecting a man who has just been a physical threat

***** Series of gross American, street, ethnic jokes *****

The Rope Story
Wanting to help another woman but not knowing how

The Suicide Stories
Physical and mental violence towards one's self [sic]

The Holtsville Story
Attempted rape by a man and betrayal by a woman

Jokes and Put-Downs (*humorous humiliation of another)

The Feminist Story
Violence between women

The Animal Story
Dehumanization by a man on a power trip (*flaunting of power)

The Princess and the Frog (A Fairy Tale)
Joke Vignettes

The Pill Story
How society controls women with drugs

The Caroline Story
Forced Institutionalization

SONG: "Santa Claus Is Comin' To Town"

The Shrimp Story
Violence between sisters

***** MORE JOKES*****

The Revolution Section
"IN A REVOLUTION A WOMAN IS EQUAL"

Wallace Black Elk's Plea for Peace and Unity
Battle of Wounded Knee, 1973

Romantic Songs

THE END

Works Cited

Page NA = Page not available. Citations bearing this notation belong to articles (generally theatre reviews from around the world), which I have been able to access in the Native American Women Playwrights Archive (NAWPA), which is part of the Walter Havighurst Special Collections and University Archives (Miami University Libraries, Oxford, Ohio). While the copies of such articles are quite legible, many are missing their page numbers.

Abbott, Larry. "Spiderwoman Theater and the Tapestry of Story." *The Canadian Journal of Native Studies*, vol. 16, 1996, pp. 165–80.

Allen, Paula Gunn. *Pocahontas: Medicine Woman, Spy, Entrepreneur, Diplomat*. HarperCollins, 2003.

– *The Sacred Hoop: Recovering the Feminine in American Indian Traditions*. 1986. Beacon, 1992.

"The American Indian Institute and the Traditional Circle of Indian Elders and Youth." *American Indian Institute*, Internet Archive, https://web.archive.org/web/20190412073627/https://twocircles.org/traditional-circle. Accessed 10 July 2021.

Archibald, Jo-ann. *Indigenous Storywork: Educating the Heart, Mind, Body, and Spirit*. Vancouver: UBC P, 2008, https://doi.org/10.59962/9780774855440.

Aristotle. *Poetics*. Translated by Malcolm Heath, Penguin, 1996.

Armstrong, Jeannette. "Excerpts." *Listening to the Land: Conversations about Nature, Culture and Eros*, Sierra Club Books, 1995, pp. 282–97.

Austen, Ian. "Report Denounces Canadian Police in Handling of Indigenous Man's Death." *The New York Times*, 22 Mar. 2021, https://www.nytimes.com/2021/03/22/world/canada/canada-police-discrimination-colten-boushie.html.

Baker, Rob, and Bonnie Davidson, editors. "Tonight: In Manhattan." *Daily News*, 6 Mar. 1981, Page NA.

Beaucage, Marjorie. "Strong and Soft. Excerpts from a Conversation with Muriel Miguel." *Canadian Theatre Review*, vol. 68, Fall 1991, pp. 5–8, https://doi.org/10.3138/ctr.68.001.

Beck, Julian. *The Life of the Theatre: The Relation of the Artist to the Struggle of the People*. City Lights, 1972.

Benedetti, Jean, editor. *The Moscow Art Theatre Letters*. Methuen, 1991.

Ben-Zvi, Linda. "Staging the Other Israel: The Documentary Theatre of Nola Chilton." *The Drama Review*, vol. 50, no. 3, Fall 2006, pp. 42–55, https://doi.org/10.1162/dram.2006.50.3.42.

Bhabha, Homi K. *The Location of Culture*. Routledge, 2005, https://doi.org/10.4324/9780203820551.

Billotte, Louise. "The Story of Muriel Miguel, a City Indian." *The Soho Weekly News*, 5 June 1975, Page NA.

Blaeser, Kimberly. *Gerald Vizenor: Writing in the Oral Tradition*. OU Press, 1996.

Blumenthal, Eileen. "Spinning Free." *The Village Voice*, vol. 25, no. 7, 18 Feb. 1990, Page NA.

Bonnell, Yolanda. *bug*. Scirocco Drama, 2021.

– "Why I'm Asking White Critics Not to Review My Show." *Vice Newsletter*, 14 Feb. 2020, https://www.vice.com/en_ca/article/dygxgw/why-im-asking-white-critics-not-to-review-my-show.

Borst, Murielle. "More Than Feathers and Beads." *Staging Coyote's Dream: An Anthology of First Nations Drama in English (Volume II)*. Edited by Monique Mojica and Ric Knowles, Playwrights Canada, 2008, pp. 111–32.

– "Spiderwoman Theater's Legacy." *Performing Worlds into Being: Native American Women's Theater*. Edited by Ann Elizabeth Armstrong, Kelli Lyon Johnson, and William A. Wortman, Miami UP, 2009, pp. 75–87.

Boyer, Yvonne, and Dr. Judith Bartlett. "External Review: Tubal Ligation in the Saskatoon Health Region: The Lived Experience of Aboriginal Women." 22 July 2017. https://www.saskatoonhealthregion.ca/DocumentsInternal/Tubal_Ligation_intheSaskatoonHealthRegion_the_Lived_Experience_of_Aboriginal_Women_BoyerandBartlett_July_22_2017.pdf.

Brunette, Candace. Personal Communication. 1 June 2008, Toronto, ON.

– Personal Communication. 24 June 2008, Toronto, ON.

– Personal Communication. 22 Aug. 2008, Toronto, ON.

Burns, Judy, and Jerri Hurlbutt. "Secrets: A Conversation with Lisa Mayo of Spiderwoman Theater." *Women and Performance: A Journal of Feminist Theory*, vol. 5, no. 2, 1992, pp. 166–83. https://doi.org/10.1080/07407709208571158.

Cajete, Gregory. *Igniting the Sparkle: An Indigenous Science Education Model*. Kivaki, 1999.

– *Look to the Mountain: An Ecology of Indigenous Education*. Kivaki, 1994.

Canning, Charlotte. *Feminist Theaters in the U.S.A.: Staging Women's Experience*. Routledge, 1996.

Carter, Jill. "Blind Faith Remembers … This Ain't No Love Story, This Ain't No Masque: *Princess Pocahontas and the Blue Spots* as Transformative Ritual for the Grandmothers, the Ones Who Remain, and for the Ones Who Are Yet to Come." *Performing Worlds into Being: Native American Women's Theater*, edited by Ann Elizabeth Armstrong, Kelli Lyon Johnson, and William A. Wortman, Miami UP, 2009, pp. 7–28.

– "*Chocolate Woman* Visions an Organic Dramaturgy: Blocking Notation for the Indigenous Soul." Macdonald Stewart Art Centre, Guelph U, Jan. 2008, pp. 1–15, https://artgalleryofguelph.ca/wp-content/uploads/2022/12/Chocolate-Woman-Dreams-the-Milky-Way-Jill-Carter.pdf.

– "Indigenous Rage Incarnate: Irreconcilable Spaces and Indigestible Bodies." *Women and Popular Culture in Canada*, edited by Laine Zisman Newman, Canadian Scholars' Press, 2020, pp. 224–38.

– "'My! What Big Teeth You Have!': On the Art of Being Seen and Not Eaten." *Canadian Theatre Review*, vol. 182, Spring 2020, pp. 16–21. https://doi.org/10.3138/ctr.182.003.

– "The Physics of the Mola: Writing Indigenous Resurgence on the Contemporary Stage." *Modern Drama*, vol. 59, no. 1, 2016, pp. 1–25. https://doi.org/10.3138/md.0739.

– "'Poisoned by the Same Dream': *Respect* for the *Challenge* that is Stanislavsky's Legacy." *Stanislavsky and Directing: Theory, Practice and Influence*, edited by Anna Migliarisi, Legas, 2008, pp. 299–340.

– "Processual Encounters of the Transformative Kind: Spiderwoman Theatre, Trickster, and the First Act of Survivance." *Troubling Tricksters: Revisioning Critical Conversations*, edited by Deanna Reder and Linda M. Morra, WLU Press, 2010, pp. 263–88, https://doi.org/10.51644/9781554582051-019.

– "Writing, Righting, 'Riting': *The Scrubbing Project* Re-members a New 'Nation' and Re-configures Ancient Ties." *Alt.Theatre: Cultural Diversity and the Stage*, vol. 4, no. 4, Summer 2006, pp. 13–17.

Cartwright, Diane. "Spiderwoman Theatre Workshop: Women in Violence." *Alternative Theater*, vol. 1, no. 3, Jan. 1976, p. 5.

Case, Sue-Ellen. Introduction. *Split Britches: Lesbian Practice/Feminist Performance*, edited by Sue-Ellen Case, Routledge, 1996, pp. 1–34.

Castellano, Marlene Brant. "Updating Traditions of Aboriginal Knowledge." *Indigenous Knowledges in Global Contexts: Multiple Readings of Our World*, edited by George J. Sefa Dei, Budd L. Hall, and Dorothy Goldin Rosenberg, U of Toronto P, 2000, pp. 21–36.

Chaikin, Joseph. *The Presence of the Actor*. Theatre Communications Group, 1972.

Chaillet, Ned. "Spiderwoman Theatre: Action Space." *The Times*, no. 60.352, 3 July 1978, p. 12.

Chamberlain, J. Edward. *If This is Your Land, Where are Your Stories: Finding Common Ground*. 4 Nov. 2003, Hart House Library, U of Toronto, Reading.

Chapin, Mac. "The World of Spirit, Disease, and Curing." Salvador, pp. 219–44.

Chekhov, Anton. "The Three Sisters." *Anton Chekhov: Plays*, translated by Michael Frayn, Methuen, 1988, pp. 187–280.

Cheng, Maria. "Indigenous Women in Canada Forcibly Sterilized Decades after Other Rich Countries Stopped." *AP News*, 12 July 2023, https://apnews.com/article/canada-indigenous-women-sterilization-apology-reparations-ebcacc0f27b8d4c12d8690718202531d.

Chocolate Woman Collective. *Izzie M: The Alchemy of Enfreakment*. Written by Monique Mojica and directed by Tara Beagan and Andy Moro, Wychwood Barns, Toronto, 13–22 July 2018.

Civilian Review and Complaints Commission for the RCMP. Chairperson-Initiated Complaint and Public Interest Investigation into the RCMP's Investigation of the Death of Colten Boushie and the Events that Followed. 7 Jan. 2021. Royal Canadian Mounted Police Act: Section 45.76(3). https://www.crcc-ccetp.gc.ca/en/commissions-final-report-cic-pii-ColtenBoushie-Events#toc2.

Collective Encounter with Jill Carter. *Encounters at the "Edge of the Woods."* Directed by Jill Carter, 6–7 Sept. 2019, Hart House Theatre, U of Toronto, Performance.

Commanda, Erica. "Spiderwoman Theatre's Muriel Miguel on Material Witness." *Muskrat Magazine*, 25 July 2017, http://muskratmagazine.com/spiderwoman-theatres-material-witness/.

Couchie, Penny. "Misdemeanor Dream in South Dakota." *Aanmitaagzi: He/She Speaks*, 23 Feb. 2024, https://www.aanmitaagzi.net/projects/misdemeanor-dream/.

Couchie, Penny, and Muriel Miguel. "Storyweaving, Indigenous Knowledge and Process in *Material Witness*." *Beyond Women's Words: Feminisms and the Practice of Oral History in the Twenty-First Century*, edited by Katrina Srigley et al., Routledge, 2018, pp. 223–35, https://doi.org/10.4324/9781351123822-21.

Crimmins, Sandy. "Spiderwoman Theatre; A Stage Manager's Notes." *American Writing: A Magazine*, vol. 13, 1996, pp. 43–50.

D'Aponte, Mimi Gisolfi. "Native Women Playwrights: Transmitters, Healers, Transformers." *Journal of Dramatic Theory and Criticism (Walter Havighurst Special Collections and University Archives, Miami University Libraries, Oxford, OH)*, supplement, vol. 14, no. 1, Fall 1999, pp. 99–108, https://journals.ku.edu/jdtc/article/view/3323/3252.

–, editor. *Seventh Generation: An Anthology of Native American Plays*. Theater Communications Group, 1999.

"The Dark Side of Discovery." *Communities Count: Equity Blogs*, 19 June 2019, https://www.communitiescount.org/blog/2019/6/19/the-dark-side-of-discovery.

Däwes, Birgit. *Native North American Theater in a Global Age: Sites of Identity Construction and Transdifference*. 2006. Universitätsverlag, published dissertation.

DeLeón Fernandez, Domitila, and Oswaldo DeLeón Kantule, "Mola Make – Making Molas," workshop, 16 June 2007, Textile Museum of Canada, Toronto.

Deloria, Philip J. *Playing Indian.* Yale UP, 1998.

Deloria, Vine, Jr. *God is Red.* New York: Dell, 1973.

Diamond, Beverley, M. Sam Cronk, and Franziska von Rosen. *Visions of Sound: Musical Instruments of First Nations Communities in Northeastern America.* Wilfrid Laurier UP, 1994.

Diner, Robyn. "Not-So-Exotic-Indians: Irony, Identity and Memory in *Spiderwoman's* Spectacles." *Thirdspace,* vol. 1, no. 2, Mar. 2002, https://bclabrowser.ca/index.php/thirdspace/article/view/diner.

Dolan, Jill. *The Feminist Spectator as Critic.* U of Michigan P, 1991. https://doi.org/10.3998/mpub.5169198.

– "Performance, Utopia, and the 'Utopian Performative.'" *TheatreJournal,* vol. 53, no. 3, Oct. 2001, pp. 455–80, https://doi.org/10.1353/tj.2001.0068.

– *Presence and Desire: Essays on Gender, Sexuality, Performance.* U of Michigan P, 1993. https://doi.org/10.3998/mpub.9850.

– *"Winnetou's Snake-Oil Show from Wigwam City." TheatreJournal,* vol. 42, no. 3, Oct. 1990, pp. 364–5, https://doi.org/10.2307/3208081.

Dunning, Jennifer. "Theater; Sisters in All Ways." *The New York Times,* 18 Oct. 1992, p. 6, https://www.nytimes.com/1992/10/18/theater/theater-sisters-in-all-ways.html.

Elm, Steve. "An Evening with Gloria Miguel." *AICH (American Indian Community House),* http://amerinda.org/newsletter/10-1/aneveningwithgloria.htm.

Faber, Roderick Mason. "Short Takes." *The Village Voice,* 11–17 Feb. 1981, p. 92

Favel, Floyd. "Poetry, Remnants and Ruins: Aboriginal Theatre in Canada." *Canadian Theatre Review,* vol. 139, Summer 2009, pp. 31–5, https://doi.org/10.3138/ctr.139.004.

– "Theatre: Younger Brother of Tradition." *Native Theatre Native Earth: Celebrating Twenty-Five Years of Native Earth Performing Arts Inc.,* Native Earth, 2007, pp. 30–4.

Favel Starr, Floyd. "The Artificial Tree: Native Performance Culture Research 1991–1996." *Critical Perspectives on Canadian Theatre in English (Volume One): Aboriginal Drama and Theatre,* edited by Rob Appleford, Playwrights Canada, 2005, pp. 69–73.

Ford, Clellan S. "Charlie Norwell Recalls the Winter Ceremonies." *Indians of the North Pacific Coast: Studies in Selected Topics,* edited by Tom McFeat, U of Washington P, 1967, pp. 198–208, https://doi.org/10.1515/9780773573482-022.

Forsythe, James. "Spirituality in Actor Training." *TheatreResearch in Canada,* vol. 17, no. 1, Spring 1996, pp. 67–82, https://doi.org/10.3138/tric.17.1.67.

France, Anna Kay, and P.J. Corso, editors. *International Women Playwrights: Voices of Identity and Transformation – Proceedings of the First International Women Playwrights Conference, October 18–23, 1988.* Scarecrow, 1993.

Frost, Robert. "The Road Not Taken." *Poetry Foundation*, https://www.poetryfoundation.org/poems/44272/the-road-not-taken.

Garneau, David. "Imaginary Spaces of Conciliation and Reconciliation: Art, Curation, and Healing." *Arts of Engagement: Taking Aesthetic Action in and beyond the Truth and Reconciliation Commission of Canada*, edited by Keavy Martin, et al., Wilfrid Laurier UP, 2016, pp. 21–41, https://doi.org/10.51644/9781771121705-003.

Gilbert, Helen. "Black and White and Re(a)d All over Again: Indigenous Minstrelsy in Contemporary Canadian and Australian Theatre." *Theatre Journal*, vol. 55, no. 4, Dec. 2003, pp. 679–98.

Giuliano, Mike. "Spiderwoman Theater Company Presents a 'Fittin' Cabaret Revue." *The News American*, 14 Nov. 1980, p. 9D.

Glancy, Diane. "Further (Farther): Creating Dialogue To Talk about Native American Plays." *Journal of Dramatic Theory and Criticism (Walter Havighurst Special Collections & University Archives, Miami University Libraries, Oxford, OH)*, vol. 14, no. 1, Fall 1999, pp. 127–30, https://journals.ku.edu/jdtc/article/view/3326/3255.

Global News. "Most Canadians Support Inquiry into Missing and Murdered Indigenous Women: Poll." *Global News*, 2 Mar. 2016, https://globalnews.ca/news/2552548/majority-of-canadians-support-mmiw-inquiry-poll/.

– "Trudeau Apologizes after Telling First Nations Mercury Poisoning Protester, 'Thank you for your Donation.'" *Global News*, posted 27 Mar. 2019, updated 28 Mar. 2019, https://globalnews.ca/news/5104937/justin-trudeau-protester-liberal-fundraiser/.

Global News with Amanda Connolly. "Trudeau Changes Course, Says 'Genocide' when Citing MMIWG Report's Findings." *Global News*, posted 3 June 2019, https://globalnews.ca/news/5349137/justin-trudeau-genocide-mmiwg-report/.

Goldstein, Richard. "Who Owns Spiderwoman?" *The Village Voice*, 18–24 Feb. 1981, p. 42.

Gómez-Peña, Guillermo. *Ethno-Techno: Writings on Performance, Activism, and Pedagogy*. New York: Routledge, 2005, https://doi.org/10.4324/9780203012765.

Grande, Sandy. *Red Pedagogy: Native American Social and Political Thought*. New York: Rowman & Littlefield, 2004.

– "Refusing the University." *Toward What Justice? :Describing Diverse Dreams of Justice in Education*, edited by Eve Tuck and K. Wayne Yang, Taylor & Francis, 2018, pp. 47–65, https://doi.org/10.4324/9781351240932-4.

Griffiths, Linda, and Maria Campbell. *The Book of Jessica: A Theatrical Transformation*. Playwrights Canada, 1997.

Gussow, Mel. "Theater: Spiderwoman Puts on 'Three Sisters.'" *The New York Times*, 11 Mar. 1982, posted 6 Jan. 2009, https://www.nytimes.com/1982/03/11/theater/theater-spiderwoman-puts-on-three-sisters.html.

Hagen, Uta, with Haskel Frankel. *Respect for Acting*. Macmillan, 1973.

Harjo, Joy, and Gloria Bird, editors. "Introduction." *Reinventing the Enemy's Language: Contemporary Native Women's Writings of North America*, W.W. Norton, 1997, pp. 19–32.

Harvey, Douglas S. *The Theatre of Empire*. Routledge, 2016.

Harvey, Kim Senklip. "To: Arts Leaders Re: Take Heed. This is a Reckoning." 8 June 2020, https://web.archive.org/web/20221001045024/https://www.kimsenklipharvey.com/post/to-arts-leaders-re-take-heed-this-is-a-reckoning. Accessed 22 June 2020.

–, writer and director. *Kamloopa: The Livestream*. Produced in partnership with the National Arts Centre, 27 Mar. 2020, Facebook Live.

Haugo, Ann. "'Circles Upon Circles Upon Circles': Native Women in Theater and Performance." *American Indian Theater in Performance: A Reader*, edited by Hanay Geiogamah and Jaye T. Darby, UCLA American Indian Studies Center, 2000, pp. 228–55.

– "Native Playwrights' Newsletter Interview: Lisa Mayo." *American Indian Theater in Performance: A Reader*, edited by Hanay Geiogamah and Jaye T. Darby, UCLA American Indian Studies Center, 2000, pp. 320–41.

– "Persistent Memories: An Interview with Spiderwoman Theater." *Performing Worlds into Being: Native American Women's Theater*, edited by Ann Elizabeth Armstrong, Kelli Lyon Johnson, and William A. Wortman, Miami UP, 2009, pp. 60–74.

– "Weaving a Legacy: An Interview with Muriel Miguel of the Spiderwoman Theater." *The Color of Theater: Race, Culture, and Contemporary Culture*, edited by Roberto Uno with Lucy Mae San Pablo Burns, Continuum, 2002, pp. 218–34.

– "Colonial Audiences and Native Women's Theatre: Viewing Spiderwoman Theatre's *Winnetou's Snake Oil Show from Wigwam City*." *Journal of Theory and Dramatic Criticism. (Walter Havighurst Special Collections & University Archives, Miami University Libraries, Oxford, OH)*, vol. 14, no. 1, Fall 1999, pp. 131–42, https://journals.ku.edu/jdtc/article/view/3327/3256.

Haye, Bethany. "Radical Spinsters." *The SoHo News*, 18 Feb. 1981, Page NA.[1]

Hogan, Linda. "A Different Yield." *Reclaiming Indigenous Voice and Vision*, edited by Marie Battiste, UBC P, 2000, pp. 115–23, https://doi.org/10.59962/9780774853170-012.

Holliday, Jon. "10 with an Acid View of Romance." *South Wales Echo*, 17 May 1979, Page NA.

1 I encountered this clipping in 2007 in the Native American Women Playwrights Archive in the Walter Havighurst Special Collections & University Archives, Miami University Libraries, Oxford, Ohio. When I later wrote to the archive to inquire about the page number, they informed me that this information had not been retained on the clipping provided to the archive by Spiderwoman Theater.

Holmes, Leilani. "Heart Knowledge, Blood Memory, and the Voice of the Land: Implications of Research among Hawaiian Elders." *Indigenous Knowledges in Global Contexts: Multiple Readings of Our World*, edited by George J. Sefa Dei, Budd L. Hall, and Dorothy Goldin Rosenberg, U Toronto P, 2000, pp. 37–53.

Howe, James. "The Kuna Portray Their Own Revolutionary History." Salvador, pp. 146–9.

Huntsman, Jeffrey F. "Native American Theatre." *American Indian Theatre in Performance: A Reader*, edited by Hanay Geiogamah and Jaye T. Darby, UCLA American Indian Studies Center, 2000, pp. 81–113.

Ikwe, Oogima. "This Way We Should Be Walking." *Algonquian Spirit: Contemporary Translations of the Algonquian Literatures of North America*, edited by Brian Swann, translated by Mary Magoulick, U of Nebraska P, 2005, pp. 188–200.

Isernhagen, Hartwig. *Momaday, Vizenor, Armstrong: Conversations on American Indian Writing*. U of Oklahoma P, 1999.

Jenkins, Linda Walsh. "Split Britches." *Women in American Theatre*, 3rd ed., edited by Helen Krich Chinoy and Linda Walsh Jenkins, Theatre Communications Group, 2006, pp. 298–302.

Joseph, Dione. "Cradling Space: Towards an Indigenous Dramaturgy on Turtle Island." *Performing Turtle Island: Indigenous Theatre on the World Stage*, edited by Jesse Rae Archibald-Barber, Kathleen Irwin, and Moira J. Day, U of Regina, 2019, pp. 169–83, https://doi.org/10.1515/9780889776579-009.

Jung, Cristina (Haw Song). "Crews Battle More than 170 Wildfires in B.C. as Drying Conditions Continue." *CBC News*, 3 July 2021, https://www.cbc.ca/news/canada/british-columbia/saturday-wildfire-evac-update-1.6089194.

Justice, Daniel Heath. "Renewing the Fire: Notes Toward the Liberation of English Studies." *English Studies in Canada (ESC)*, vol. 29, nos. 1–2, Mar./June 2003, pp. 45–54, https://doi.org/10.1353/esc.2003.0005.

– Personal Communication. 15 Jan. 2010, Toronto, ON.

Kafer, Kathy. "'Spiderwoman': Feminist Troupe Spins Web of Wacky Humor." *The News American*, 25 Nov. 1980, p. 2B.

Kantule, Oswaldo DeLeón. *Chocolate Woman Dreams the Milky Way*. First Developmental Workshop, U of Guelph, Macdonald Stewart Art Centre, 7–21 Nov. 2007.

– *Chocolate Woman Dreams the Milky Way*. U of Guelph, Macdonald Stewart Art Centre, 21 Nov. 2007, panel discussion.

Kaufmann, Donald L. "The Indian as Media Hand-Me-Down." *American Indian Theater in Performance: A Reader*, edited by Hanay Geiogamah and Jaye T. Darby, UCLA American Indian Studies Center, 2000.

Kershaw, Baz. *The Radical in Performance: Between Brecht and Baudrillard*. Routledge, 2013.

Kimmelman, Michael. "Karl May and the Origins of a German Obsession." *The New York Times*, 12 Sept. 2007, https://www.nytimes.com/2007/09/12/travel/12iht-12karl.7479952.html.

King, Thomas. *The Truth About Stories: A Native Narrative*. House of Anansi, 2003.

Koehler, Robert. "An Indian Message That Carries a Punch Line: Stage: Spiderwoman Theatre celebrates its Native American heritage with stories and comedy that counter stereotypes." *Los Angeles Times*, 12 Nov. 1990, https://www.latimes.com/archives/la-xpm-1990-11-12-ca-3380-story.html.

Laenui, Poka. "Processes of Decolonization." *Reclaiming Indigenous Voice and Vision*, edited by Marie Battiste, UBC P, 2000, pp. 150–60.

Little Bear, Leroy. "Jagged Worldviews Colliding." *Reclaiming Indigenous Voice and Vision*, edited by Marie Battiste, UBC P, 2000, pp. 77–85, https://doi.org/10.59962/9780774853170-009.

Lorde, Audre. "The Uses of Anger: Women Responding to Racism." *Sister Outsider*, The Crossing, 1984.

"The Magic of Working with Your Community: A Talk with Muriel Miguel and Henu Josephine Tarrant." *Facebook*, 15 Feb. 2020, https://www.facebook.com/watch/?v=131809138054262.

Manossa, Geraldine. "The Beginning of Cree Performance Culture." *Aboriginal Drama and Theatre: Critical Perspectives on Canadian Theatre in English (Volume One)*, edited by Rob Appleford, Playwrights Canada, 2005, pp. 124–33.

Maracle, Lee. *My Conversations with Canadians*. Book*hug, 2017.

Maurice Law. "Indigenous Women – Forced Sterilization Saskatchewan, Canada." 2018, https://ijrcenter.org/wp-content/uploads/2018/02/Fact-Sheet-Forced-Sterilization-in-Canada.

May, Karl. *Winnetou*. Translated by Michael Shaw, Seabury, 1977.

Mayo, Lisa. "Among the Living." *The Elders' Project*. Spiderwoman Theater and La MaMa ETC, New York City, NY, 2012.

– "Appropriation and the Plastic Shaman: Winnetou's Snake Oil Show from Wigwam City." *Canadian Theatre Review*, vol. 68, Fall 1991, pp. 54–5, https://doi.org/10.3138/ctr.68.017.

– Interview with Jill Carter. 28 Aug. 2007, New York City, unpublished.

Menakem, Resmaa. "Notice the Rage; Notice the Silence." *On Being with Krista Tippett*, 4 June 2020, https://onbeing.org/programs/resmaa-menakem-notice-the-rage-notice-the-silence/.

Mercredi, Morningstar, and Fire Keepers Collective. *Sacred Bundles Unborn*. Friesen P, 2021.

Miguel, Gloria. "Ibeler Uagan: Nietos del Sol/ Grandchildren of the Sun." *Canadian Theatre Review*, vol. 68, Fall 1991, pp. 30–2, https://doi.org/10.3138/ctr.68.010.

– Interview with Jill Carter. 26 Aug. 2007, Westbeth Artists' Housing, New York City, unpublished.

– *Something Old, Something New, Something Borrowed, Something Blue*. 10 Oct. 2008, Robert Gill Theatre, U of Toronto, Performance.

Miguel, Gloria, and Lisa Mayo. *Daughters from the Stars: Nis Bundor*. Directed by Renee Phillip, New York City: American Indian Community House, 1996, Hemispheric Institute, https://hemisphericinstitute.org/en/hidvl-collections/item/1702-daughters-from-the-stars-nis-bundor.html [permalink: https://hdl.handle.net/2333.1/1ns1rnh6].

Miguel, Muriel. Interview with Jill Carter. 17 June 2018, New York City, unpublished.

– Interview with Jill Carter. 27 Aug. 2007, New York City, unpublished.

– *Muriel Miguel: A Retrospective*. 24 Oct. 2019, Brown U, https://www.youtube.com/watch?v=TdPkpBXIIso.

– "Performance Lecture." *Aboriginal Studies Distinguished Lecture Series*, 13 Nov. 2006, U of Toronto, public lecture.

– Personal Communication. 16 Nov. 2006, Toronto, ON.

– Personal Communication. 7 July 2007, New York City, NY.

– Personal Communication. 15 July 2023, telephone.

– Personal Communication. 28 Aug. 2023, telephone.

– Personal Communication. 1 Sept. 2023, telephone.

– Personal Communication. 10 Sept. 2023, telephone.

– *RedTalk with Muriel Miguel: A Retrospective*. 10 Jan. 2020, Red Sky Performance, Artscape Sandbox, Toronto.

Miguel, Muriel, and Gloria Miguel. "Honouring Spiderwoman Theater Conference." 19–21 Feb. 2007. The Walter Havighurst Special Collections and University Archives, Miami University Libraries (Oxford, OH).

Mike, Chuck. Workshop. Centre for Indigenous Theatre. Oct. 2002, Toronto, ON.

Mojica, Monique. *Chocolate Woman Dreams the Milky Way*. Directed by Jose A. Colman, Helen Gardiner Phelan Playhouse, Toronto, 2–19 June 2011, performance.

– Developmental Rehearsals. *Chocolate Woman Dreams the Milky Way*. Nov. 2007, Macdonald Stewart Art Centre, U of Guelph.

– Developmental Rehearsals. *Chocolate Woman Dreams the Milky Way*. Oct. 2008, Toronto, ON.

– "Ethnostress: Women's Voices in Native American Theatre." *Footpaths & Bridges: Voices from the Native American Women Playwrights Archive*, edited by Shirley A. Huston-Findlay and Rebecca Howard, U of Michigan P, 2008, pp. 11–22.

– *Izzy M.: The Alchemy of Enfreakment*. Directed by Andy Moro Tara Beagan, b current Performing Arts Co., Wychwood Barns, Toronto, 13–22 July, performance.

– "In Plain Sight: Inscripted Earth and Invisible Realities." *New Canadian Realisms: New Essays on Canadian Theatre (Vol. Two)*, edited by Roberta Barker and Kim Solga, Toronto: Playwrights Canada, 2012, pp. 218–42.

– Personal Communication. 26 June 2008, London, ON.

Mojica, Monique. Personal Communication. 17 Jan. 2007, Toronto, ON.

– Personal Communication. 13 Mar. 2010, Toronto, ON.

– Personal Communication. 18 Feb. 2017, Toronto, ON.

– Personal Communication. 20 Aug. 2022, telephone.

– Personal Communication. 15 July 2023, Toronto, ON.

– *Princess Pocahontas and the Blue Spots: Two Plays by Monique Mojica*. Women's Press, 1991.

– "Stories from the Body: Blood Memory and Organic Texts." *Alt. Theatre: Cultural Diversity and the Stage*, vol. 4, nos. 2–3, May 2006, pp. 16–20.

Mojica, Monique, and Ric Knowles. "Creation Story Begins Again: Performing Transformation, Bridging Cosmologies." *Performing Worlds into Being: Native American Women's Theater*, edited by Ann Elizabeth Armstrong, Kelli Lyon Johnson, and William A. Wortman, Miami UP, 2009, pp. 2–6.

–, editors. Introduction to *Reverb-ber-ber-rations. Staging Coyote's Dream: An Anthology of First Nations Drama in English (Volume I)*. Playwrights Canada, 2003, pp. 99–101.

–, editors. *Staging Coyote's Dream: An Anthology of First Nations Drama in English (Volume II)*. Playwrights Canada, 2008.

Momaday, N. Scott. "The Man Made of Words." *Literature of the American Indians: Views and Interpretations*, edited by Abraham Chapman, New American Library, 1975, pp. 96–110.

Morrison, Toni. "A Humanist View." Portland State University's Oregon Public Speakers Collection (Part 2): Black Studies Center Public Dialogue, transcript by Keisha E. McKenzie, 30 May 1975, https://www.mackenzian.com/wp-content/uploads/2014/07/Transcript_PortlandState_TMorrison.pdf.

Naipaul, V.S. *The Mimic Men*. London: Penguin, 1969.

The Native American Women Playwrights Archive (NAWPA) in the Walter Havighurst Special Collections and University Archives, Miami University Libraries, Oxford, OH.

Needham, Fraser. "'The Bond is Broken': Data Shows Number of Indigenous Kids is Foster Care is Going Up." *APTN National News*, 21 Sept. 2023, https://www.aptnnews.ca/national-news/statistics-canada-indigenous-people-housing-issues-child-welfare/.

Nestruck, J. Kelly. "How Should Media Respond When an Artist Limits Reviews to Critics who are Indigenous, Black and People of Colour?" *The Globe and Mail*, posted 10 Feb. 2020, updated 18 Feb. 2020, https://www.theglobeandmail.com/arts/theatre-and-performance/article-how-should-media-respond-when-an-artist-limits-reviews-to-critics-who/.

Nolan, Yvette. *Medicine Shows: Indigenous Performance Culture*. Playwrights Canada, 2015.

– "Why It Matters Who Reviews Indigenous Theatre." *CBC Arts*, 19 Feb. 2020, https://www.cbc.ca/arts/why-it-matters-who-reviews-indigenous-theatre-1.5467785.

Ortiz, Simon J. "Land, Resistance, and Literature" Ontario Institute for Studies in Education, U of Toronto, 24 Jan. 2002, public talk.

– "That's the Place Indians Talk About." *Wicazo Sa Review*, vol. 1, no. 1, Spring 1985, pp. 45–9, https://doi.org/10.2307/1409426.

Ozawabineshi, Audrey Anne. "Debaj welcomes: Pulling Threads- A series of Fabric Workshops." *Facebook*, 28 Apr. 2017, https://www.facebook.com/events/debajehmujig-creation-centre/debaj-welcomes-pulling-threads-a-series-of-fabric-workshop/1287443484667321/.

Pasolli, Robert. *Book on the Open Theatre*. Bobbs-Merill, 1970.

Patraka, Vivian M. "*Split Britches* in Split Britches: Performing History, Vaudeville, and the Everyday." *Women & Performance: A Journal of Feminist Theory*, vol. 4, no. 2, 1989, pp. 58–67, https://doi.org/10.1080/07407708908571129.

Pearson, Tom. "Legacy and the Persistence of Memory: A Conversation with Muriel Miguel." *The Online Journal of the Public Theater's Native Theater Festival*, 26 Jan. 2009, pp. 1–16, http://thenativetheaterfestival.blogspot.com/2009/01/conversation-with-muriel-miguel.html.

Perkins, Kathy A. Interview with Lisa Mayo. 10 June 1992, Routledge Performance Archive, https://www.routledgeperformancearchive.com.

Perkins, Kathy A. and Roberta Uno, editors. *Contemporary Plays by Women of Color: An Anthology*. London: Routledge, 1996.

Phillips, Layli, editor. Introduction: "Womanism on its Own." *The Womanist Reader*, New York: Routledge, 2006, pp. xix–lv, https://doi.org/10.4324/9780203943670.

– Plato. "*Republic* (Book III)." *Dramatic Theory and Criticism: Greeks to Grotowski*, edited by Bernard F. Dukore, Boston: Thomson/Heinle, 1974, pp. 12–30.

Prince, Althea. "Stop Calling Us 'Slaves.'" *Access and Equity in the University*, edited by Keren S. Brathwaite, Toronto: Canadian Scholars' Press, 2003, pp. 259–68.

Puls, Herta. *Textiles of the Kuna Indians of Panama*. Buckinghamshire: Shire Publications, 1988.

Quan, Douglas. "Discovery of Children's Remains in Kamloops Stunned the Local Chiefs. Even the Radar Expert Wept." *Toronto Star*, 1 June 2021, updated 2 June 2021, https://www.thestar.com/news/canada/discovery-of-children-s-remains-in-kamloops-stunned-the-local-chiefs-even-the-radar-expert/article_748fb5f1-c5c2-5510-9704-53cccf85f5db.html.

Recollet, Karyn, and Jon Johnson. "'Why Do You Need to Know That?' Slipstream Movements and Mapping 'Otherwise' in Tkaronto." *Journal of*

Pedagogies: Walking Lab, vol. 4, 2019, pp. 177–90, https://doi.org/10.15209/jpp.1187.

Robinson, Dylan. "Welcoming Sovereignty." *Performing Indigeneity: New Essays on Canadian Theatre* (vol. 6), edited by Yvette Nolan and Ric Knowles, Playwrights Canada, 2016, pp. 5–32.

Romàn, David. *Acts of Intervention: Performance, Gay Culture, and AIDS*. Bloomington: Indiana UP, 1998.

Rosen, Bob, and Jane Zipp, directors. *Sun, Moon, and Feather: A Film by Bob Rosen and Jane Zipp. Perf. Lisa Mayo, Gloria Miguel and Muriel Miguel*. The Cinema Guild, 1989.

Russell, Andrew, Carolyn Jarvis, and Michael Wroebel. "'Throwaway Kids': Allegations of Trafficking, Mistreatment at Ont. Group Home Chain." *Global News*, 21 Nov. 2022, https://globalnews.ca/news/9283010/human-trafficking-mistreatment-ont-group-home-chain/.

Sainer, Arthur. "Arachne's Truths." *The Village Voice*, 17 Apr. 1978, p. 99.

Salvador, Mari Lyn, editor. *The Art of Being Kuna: Layers of Meaning among the Kuna of Panama*. UCLA Fowler Museum of Cultural History, 1997.

– "Looking Back: Contemporary Kuna Women's Arts." Salvador, pp. 151–211.

Schechner, Richard. *Between Theater & Anthropology*. U of Pennsylvania P, 1985, https://doi.org/10.9783/9780812200928.

– *Environmental Theater*. Applause, 1994.

– *Performance Theory (Revised Edition)*. Routledge, 1988.

Schneider, Rebecca. *The Explicit Body in Performance*. Routledge, 1997.

– *Segal Talks: Muriel Miguel and Gloria Miguel*. Martin E. Segal Theater Center, 22 June 2020,

Severi, Carlo. "Kuna Picture-Writing: A Study in Iconography and Memory." Salvador, pp. 245–70.

Shaw, Peggy, with Deborah Margolin, and Lois Weaver. "Split Britches: A True Story." *Women and Performance: A Journal of Feminist Theory*, vol. 4, no. 2, 1989, pp. 68–95, https://doi.org/10.1080/07407708908571130.

Sherzer, Joel. "Kuna Language and Literature." Salvador, pp. 103–36.

Shewey, Don. "Scathing Feminism." *The Boston Phoenix*, 10 Jan. 1978, Section Three, Page NA.

Silko, Leslie Marmon. *Yellow Woman and a Beauty of the Spirit: Essays on Native American Life Today*. Simon & Schuster, 1996.

Simpson, Audra. "Savage States: Settler Governance in an Age of Sorrow." 17 Jan. 2018, hosted by the Jackman Humanities Institute, U of Toronto.

Simpson, Leanne Betasamosake. *As We Have Always Done: Indigenous Freedom Through Radical Resistance*. U of Minnesota P, 2017, https://doi.org/10.5749/j.ctt1pwt77c.

Simpson, Leanne Betasamosake, and Edna Manitowabi. "Theorizing Resurgence from Within Nishnaabeg Thought." *Centering Anishinaabeg*

Studies: Understanding the World Through Stories, edited by Jill Doerfler, Heidi Kiiwetinepinesiik Stark, and Niigaanwewidam James Sinclair, Michigan State UP, 2013, pp. 279–93.

Sinclair, Raven. "Identity lost and found: Lessons from the sixties scoop." *First People's Child and Family Review*, vol. 3, no. 1, 2007, pp. 65–82, https://doi.org/10.7202/1069527ar.

Smith, Andrea. *Conquest: Sexual Violence and American Indian Genocide*. South End Press, 2005, https://doi.org/10.1515/9780822374817.

– "Men Only by Tradition: Women Can't Hit the Big Drum." *Windspeaker*, n.d., https://windspeaker.com/node/8873. Accessed 15 July 2023.

Smith, Annie. "Making Hope Actionable: The Cultural Work of *Weaving Reconciliation: Our Way*." *Canadian Theatre Review*, vol. 181, Winter 2020, pp. 81–5, https://doi.org/10.3138/ctr.181.015.

"Spiderwoman Papers." Walter Havighurst Special Collections and University Archives, Miami University Libraries (Oxford, OH).

Spiderwoman Theater. "About Muriel Miguel." https://www.spiderwomantheater.org/muriel-miguel. Accessed 18 June 2021.

– *MisdemeanorDream*. Third Developmental Workshop, Abrons Art Center (Henry Street Settlement), New York City, 4–6 Feb. 2020.

– "Persistence of Memory." *Performing Worlds into Being: Native American Women's Theater*, edited by Ann Elizabeth Armstrong, Kelli Lyon Johnson, and William A. Wortman, Miami UP, 2009, pp. 42–56.

– *Power Pipes* (1993 Performance). American Indian Community House, NYC Video Archives, Hemispheric Institute Digital Video Library (HIDVL), New York U, 2008, https://hemisphericinstitute.org/en/hidvl-collections/item/1703-power-pipes.html.

– "Power Pipes." *Seventh Generation: An Anthology of Native American Plays*, edited by Mimi Gisolfi D'Aponte, Theater Communications Group, 1999, pp. 149–200.

– "Re-verb-ber-ber-rations." *Staging Coyote's Dream: An Anthology of First Nations Drama in English*, edited by Monique Mojica and Ric Knowles, Playwrights Canada, 2003, pp. 103–32.

– *Reverb-ber-ber-rations* (1990 Performance). American Indian Community House, NYC Video Archives, Hemispheric Institute Digital Video Library (HIDVL), New York U, 2008, https://hemisphericinstitute.org/en/hidvl-collections/item/1704-reverb-ber-ber-rations.html.

Spiderwoman Theater. "Reverb-ber-ber-rations." Rehearsals, 1990. Tapes 6–9. Provided by Gloria Miguel. Quoted with Permission from Spiderwoman Theater.

– "Sun, Moon, and Feather." *Storiesof Our Way: An Anthology of American Indian Plays*, edited by Hanay Geiogamah and Jaye T. Darby, UCLA American Indian Studies Center, 1999, pp. 286–314.

– "Winnetou's Snake Oil Show from Wigwam City." *Keepers of the Morning Star: An Anthology of Native Women's Theater*, edited by Jaye T. Darby and Stephanie Fitzgerald, UCLA American Indian Studies Center, 2003, pp. 229–62.

Spiderwoman Theater and Aanmitaagzi. *Material Witness*. Producers: Spiderwoman Theater and Loose Change Productions, 12–29 May 2016, La MaMa Theatre (Safe Harbors Indigenous Arts Collective), New York City, performance.

Stanciu, Cristina. "'The Last Indian' Syndrome Revisited: Metamora, Take Two." *Intertexts*, vol. 10, no. 1, Spring 2006, 25–49. *Gale Literature Resource Center*, https://doi.org/10.1353/itx.2006.0012.

Standing Senate Committee on Human Rights. *The Scars that We Carry: Forced and Coerced Sterilizations of Persons in Canada – Part II*. July 2022, https://publications.gc.ca/collections/collection_2022/sen/yc32-0/YC32-0-441-4-eng.pdf.

Sur, Sanchari. "Decolonizing Theatre Practice as a Playwright and Performer: A Conversation with Yolanda Bonnell." *Intermission: Where All Great Theatre Discussions Happen*, 24 Feb. 2020, https://www.intermissionmagazine.ca/features/decolonizing-theatre-practice-as-a-playwright-and-performer-a-conversation-with-yolanda-bonnell/.

Tanner, Beccy. "29 Killed on Way to 1904 World's Fair." *The Wichita Eagle*, 11 Oct. 1904. http://www.eccchistory.com/TrainWreck1904.htm.

Thomson, Rosemarie Garland, editor. *Freakery: Cultural Spectacles of the Extraordinary Body*. New York UP, 1995.

Treuer, David. *Native American Fiction: A User's Manual*. Graywolf, 2006.

Truth & Reconciliation Commission of Canada (TRC). *Canada's Residential Schools: Reconciliation, The Final Report of the Truth and Reconciliation Commission of Canada*. McGill-Queen's UP, 2015.

– *Canada's Residential Schools: The Legacy: Final Report of the Truth and Reconciliation Commission of Canada*. McGill-Queen's UP, 2015.

– *94 Calls to Action*. McGill-Queen's UP, 2015.

Turner, Victor. *From Ritual to Theatre: The Seriousness of Human Play*. Performing Arts Journal Publications, 1982.

Turtle Gals Performance Ensemble. "The Scrubbing Project." *Staging Coyote's Dream: An Anthology of First Nations Drama in English (Vol. II)*, edited by Monique Mojica and Ric Knowles, Playwrights Canada, 2008, pp. 323–66.

Tyler, Mike. "What's in a Name? Marvel Comics Tells Spiderwoman Theater it Owns That One." *The Villager*, vol. 49, no. 9, 26 Feb. 1981, p. 5.

Vizenor, Gerald. *Manifest Manners: Narratives on Postindian Survivance*. U of Nebraska P, 1999.

Wane, Njoki Nathani. "Indigenous Knowledge: Lessons from the Elders – A Kenyan Case Study." *Indigenous Knowledges in Global Contexts: Multiple Readings of Our World*, edited by George J. Sefa Dei, Budd L. Hall, and Dorothy Goldin Rosenberg. U of Toronto P, 2000, pp. 54–69.

Weaver, Jace. *That the People Might Live: Native American Literatures and Native American Communities*. Oxford UP, 1997, https://doi.org/10.1093/oso/9780195118520.001.0001.

Wilmeth, Don B. "Noble or Ruthless Savage? The American Indian on Stage and in the Drama." *American Indian Theater in Performance: A Reader*, UCLA American Indian Studies Center, 2000, pp. 127–56.

Ya-Native: Preserving and Sharing our Cultures. 2018, https://www.ya-native.com/Culture_GreatPlains/firstpeople/1950-BlackElk.html.

Index

Note: Page numbers in *italics* indicate a figure.

Aanmitaagzi Big Medicine Studio, xivn10, 14–15n9, 15n10, 47, 60–3
activism. *See* communitism
Ahmad, Mannan (Abdul), 303n
Aikins, Carroll, 298
alcohol use, 76–7n
Alvis, Carmen (Cole), 59–60
American Indian, as term, 35n
American Indian AIDS Task Force, 3, 80, 94
American Indian Community House (AICH), xiii–xiv, 65–6, 80, 115, 180, 207, 254
Among the Living (Mayo), xiv, 4, 266
And My Sister Ate Dirt (Mayo), xiii, 137–9
Anishinaabeg: bear/mukwa as protector, 185–6; drum ceremony, 155–6; dualities, 10n6; Minobimaatisiiwin (living well), 37, 169n; Rappahannock relations, 152n; Seven Grandfather Teachings, 59; Sky Woman, 12–16, 57–8, 304; transformations, 27, 111–12
anti-colonization. *See* decolonization; healing of Indigenous dis-ease; resistance and refusals; re-worlding
Antonio. *See* Miguel, Antonio (father)
appropriation. *See* misappropriation and cultural theft
Aquash, Anna Mae, 291, 293
Aristophanes, *Lysistrata*, 135–7
Armstrong, Jeannette, 39, 192
"artificial tree" spirituality, 28–31, 66n2, 271
Ashkenazi, 16, 276n8
audiences: about, 134–5; complicity in racism and sexism, 50, 97n, 132–3; empowerment of, 134–5; incident in France (1977), 94–5, 114, 127–8, 134, 234; Indigenous community work, 55–6, 63; irreconcilable Indigenous spaces, 40, 45, 54, 58, 60–1, 300–2; male audiences, 115; pre-show on classism, 117–19; pre-show on intersectionality, 68–9; response to "show biz" Indians, 284
authenticity: identity, 106, 114–15; *More Than Feathers*, 293; "primitive authenticity," 187–8; *Reverb-ber-ber-rations*, 187–8; spirituality, 199–200, 234, 237–40; *Sun, Moon, and Feather*, 218; *Winnetou's Snake*

authenticity (*continued*)
Oil Show, 199–200, 234, 237–40. *See also* misappropriation and cultural theft

baluwala tree, 136n, 261n36
The Banana Bunch, xiii
beadwork, 24, 65–7, 169–70
Beaupré, Edouard, 284
Beck, Julian, 105, 125
Benton-Banai, Eddie, 155
Berghof, Herbert, 4, 4n2, 80, 89, 90, 93n
Beye, Naja, 113n1, 115n, 128, 137–8, 146, 282, 315
Bhabha, Homi, 31
Bilinsky, Barry, 284
biota: about, 179n; ecological disasters, 57, 184; forced removal from land, 228–30; as greater community, 198; harm from cult of individuality, 259; landscape as entire biota, 179n; liminal oneness with, 151–2, 157, 159n, 167, 178–9; non-Indigenous duty to heal, 257–8; story as belonging to, 175–6, 179, 186–8; struggle for harmony in, 153–4; waterway metaphor, 277–8. *See also* land; re-worlding
Bird, Gloria, 158–9
Black Elk, Wallace, 50–1, 165, 316
Black performers, 272–3n
Blau, Herbert, 99–100
Blood, Cherish Violet, 6, 48n10, 49, 62
Bobb, Columpa, 45n, 302, 304
Bobb, Sid, 11, 61
Bonnell, Yolanda, 59–60
Borst-Tarrant, Murielle (Muriel's daughter): about, 290, 295–7; dancer, 80, 263, 278; dramaturg and director, 290, 296–7; Guna name, 96n; marriage to Kevin, 80n; Miguel family, 80, 265, 278–9, 295–7; *More Than Feathers and Beads*, 267–8, 291, 293–5; non-Indigenous productions, 296–7; *Persistence of Memory*, 265, 278–9; *Power Pipes*, 200n, 253–4, 263; psychic gifts in family, 75, 211, 242; *Red Mother*, 290–1; Shakespeare's *The Tempest*, 296–7; *The Star Medicine* series, 295–6; Storyweaving, 291, 296–7; "A Valentine to my Grandmother", 304–5; writer, 295–6, 304–5
Bouman, Eva, 142–3, 145–7, 206, 309–11
Boushie, Colten, 22
Brecht, Bertolt, 81, 82–4n19, 92, 164, 290
Brougham, John, 272–3n
Brunette, Candace, 173–5, 287–90
bug (Bonnell), 59–60
burlesque, 4, 272–3n

Cabaret: An Evening of Disgusting Songs, xiii, 69, 139–41
Café-Febrissy, Katia, 301n
Cajete, Gregory, 26, 154–7, 163, 199
Campbell, Maria, 258
Canning, Charlotte, 106–7
Carter, Jill: about, 16–19, 37–40; Anishinaabe-Ashkenazi identity, 16, 20, 36, 38, 47, 195–6; collaborations, 39–40; communitism, 36–7, 40; dream experience, 193–6; Enow'kin principle, 39, 192, 296, 304; "Mean Men and Material Witnesses," 40–4; Miguel family as research partners, 16–17, 37, 38, 266; *Misdemeanor Dream* (2020), 6–16; misrepresentation challenges, 37–8; Muriel's workshops (2002, 2006), 176–9, 193–6; *Omushkego* workshop (2014), 288–90;

researcher as subject, 38, 47; respect for teachings, 19; response to *Red Mother*, 82–4n19, 84n; "restorative justice circle," 29–31; *Retreating to Re-Treat*, 300n18; simulation of survivance, 29–31; Spiderwoman Theater, 16, 36–7; workshop (2002–3), 181–6. See also *Encounters at the "Edge of the Woods"* (Collective Encounter)
Carter, Jill, views on: dualities vs. oppositional binaries, 10n6; genocide, 11–12, 23–5, 275–6n; Miguel sisters' life in art, 306–7; misappropriation harms, 165–7; story kernels and politics, 215–16n11; theatre's power to change violence, 51–2, 54–5
Cartwright, Diane, 131
Castellano, Marlene Brant, 37
ceremony: about, 26–7, 152, 234–5; "artificial tree" spirituality, 28–31, 66n2, 271; Cajete's pedagogical model, 155–6; Corn Dance, 130, 245–6; drums and pipes, 250–1, 259–60, 263; gender traditions, 250–1, 260–3; Guna culture, 123; for healing, 235, 261; liminality for transformation, 151–4, 157, 246; mechanics of illusion, 234–5; powwows, 79n14; *Reverb-ber-ber-rations*, 246–9; semblance vs. reality, 234–5; theatres as sites, 59–61; transformations, 26–7, 111, 246; *Winnetou's Snake Oil Show*, 233–5, 240; Yaqui deer dancers, 234–5. *See also* misappropriation and cultural theft; Sundance ceremony
Chaikin, Joseph: about, 80–9, 102–3; collaborative process, 125–6; dancers, 82–4n19; exercises, 81n16, 85–8, 177–8, 253n; Living Theater, 81, 88, 105, 125–6; Method acting, 81, 85, 111, 177–9; methodologies, 82–4n19, 125–6; Muriel's studies with, 81n16, 82–8, 100, 102–3; Open Theater, 81–2, 85–9, 102–4, 125–6, 177; political climate, 102–4; production credits, 103n33; Spiderwoman Theater processes, 16, 85–6, 125–6, 253n33; "Transformations," 85–6n, 87–8, 177–8, 190n
Chaillet, Ned, 97n, 114, 120, 123–4, 132
Chamberlain, J. Edward, 20
channeling, 185n. *See also* psychic gifts
chapan (wagon), 285, 306
Chapin, Mac, 241, 244n, 247n
Chekhov, Anton, 96–8, 204–7, 209, 225–6
children: Antonio as "scooped child," 73–4; Derrick's community model, 171–3, *172*; healing childhood pain, 113; sexual violence, 62. *See also* Borst-Tarrant, Murielle (Muriel's daughter); Mojica, Monique (Gloria's daughter); Tarrant, Henu Josephine (Murielle and Kevin's daughter)
Chilton, Nola, 81–2
Chocolate Woman Collective, 19, 283
Chocolate Woman Dreams the Milky Way (Mojica): about, 202, 264; development, 136n, 197n18, 241n23, 243, 264; Guna aesthetics, 264; Guna culture, 136n, 197n18, 241n23, 243n, 249, 261n36, 264; Mojica's visit to Gunayala (2008), 243n; nation-specific aesthetics, 202, 241–2, 243n, 245n, 264
Christians, 33n, 74, 75, 76
circular structures, 35, 133, 170–1, 173, 174–5, 264

class and classism: about, 103n32; Chaikin's theatre, 102–3; complicity in shameful jokes, 50, 97n, 132–3; financial precarity of artists, 103n32, 107; poverty in Miguel family, 34, 75, 76, 86–7, 101–2, 103n32, 208–9; poverty in *Split Britches*, 147; pre-show intervention, 117–19; Womanspace theatre, 107–8; *Women in Violence*, 117–19
clowns: *Material Witness*, 49, 51–2, 61–2; for teachings, 121, 123, 128–31; *Women in Violence*, 52, 86n, 118n, 119–21, 123, 128–31, 315
Coatlicue Theater, 200n
The Collective Encounter, 19, 300n, 301n, 302–4. See also *Encounters at the "Edge of the Woods"* (Collective Encounter)
colonization: assimilation as flawed mimesis, 31–2; assimilation in Gunayala, 123; essentialism, 238; genocide, 23–5, 186, 218, 229, 232, 274–5; *Indian Act*, 24, 298n, 300–1; knowledge systems, 17; overview of harms, 115; patriarchy, 36, 116, 119, 135–6, 237, 261; predictions in *The Tempest*, 297. *See also* Indigenous Peoples, misrepresentations; misappropriation and cultural theft; residential schools; shame; stereotypes
colonization, responses to. *See* decolonization; healing of Indigenous dis-ease; resistance and refusals; re-worlding; survivance
Colorado, Elvira, 200n, 206, 207n, 253, 282
Colorado, Hortencia, 200n, 233–4, 238, 253, 255, 261–2, 282
comedy. *See* humour
communitism: about, 34, 137, 160–1; activism for survivance, 34, 201; art for survivance, 92–4; Carter's projects, 36–7; culture workers, 55; kitchen table storytelling, 159–64; legacy of Spiderwoman Theater, 34, 92–5, 201; Miguel sisters, 80; quest for self in community, 137–9, 144–50; research partners, 37; re-worlding, 160, 163–4; talking circles, 94–5; womanist processes, 160–4. *See also* re-worlding; survivance
Corn Dance, Taos, 130, 245–6
cosmology, Guna. *See* Guna culture, cosmology
Couchie, Chris, 14–15n9
Couchie, Penny: *Material Witness*, 6, 47–9, 54, 61–2; *Misdemeanor Dream*, 6–9, 11; *Red Mother*, 82–4n19
Couchie-Waukey, Animikiikwe (Penny's daughter), 7, 9
Couteau, Donna, 6, *8*, 14, 48–9, 48n10, 282
COVID-19, 6, 15–16
creation stories. *See* stories, Indigenous
Crimmins, Sandy, 127, 282
critics, non-Caucasian theatre, 59
Cross, Joe (Caddo), 9–10n
cultural theft, 72, 227, 232, 235. *See also* misappropriation and cultural theft
Cycles (Womanspace), 105–8

dance and dancers: about, 79–80, 82–4; ceremony, 234–5, 246n29; Chaikin's influence, 82–4n19, 103n33; choreography, 82–4, 127; Little Eagles, 78; modern dance, 79, 82–4n19, 84; powwows, 79–80; Thunderbirds, 78, 80, 82–4n19. *See also* Miguel, Muriel, choreographer and dancer
D'Aponte, Mimi Gisolfi, 203n2, 256, 258, 261

Daughters from the Stars: Nis Bundor, xiv, 3, 6, 96n
Däwes, Birgit, 206, 213, 238
Debajehmujig Storytellers, 21
decolonization: art as medicine, 93, 95–6, 272, 304, 306; Cajete's pedagogical model, 26, 154–7, 163, 199; as creative project, 32; dualities vs. oppositional binaries, 10n6; Laenui's sociological model, 153–4, 156–7, 163, 199; liminality for transformation, 151–4, 157; Red Reading, 238, 292; respect and protection, 17, 95–6; TRC (Truth and Reconciliation Commission), 21, 24, 184, 299. *See also* healing of Indigenous dis-ease; resistance and refusals; re-worlding; survivance
Deloria, Vine, Jr., 91–2
Derrick, Jan, community model, 171–3, *172*
digital images: home movies, 157, 159, 209, 219, 224–5, 233, 238, 259, 284; *Rose-Marie* (film), 211–15, 217, 219–22
Diner, Robyn, 213
director, Spiderwoman Theater. *See* Miguel, Muriel, director
dis-ease. *See* healing of Indigenous dis-ease
Dolan, Jill, 162, 204, 207, 227–8n18
dramaturgy, Indigenous. *See* Mojica, Monique, dramaturgy; Spiderwoman Theater, dramaturgy
dualities vs. oppositional binaries, 10n6, 45n
Dunning, Jennifer, 260–1
Duran, Eduardo and Bonnie, 282
Durand, Yves Sioui, 21
Du Tu Kapsus (Flower of the Night), Gloria's Guna name, 49, 53, *53*, 54, 96n
Earth in Motion, 82–4n19
Eaton, Evelyn, 116
Eddy, Nelson, 212–13, 220–1
education, Cajete's model, 26, 154–7, 163, 199
education, theatre. *See* exercises, theatre; theatre training, Indigenous; theatre training, non-Indigenous
The Elders' Project: Among the Living, xiv, 4, 266
The Elders' Project: Something Old, Something New, Something Borrowed, Something Blue, xiv, 217–18
El-Issa, Ingrid Washinawatok (Flying Eagle Woman), 268–70, 275, 276, 294–5
Elm, Steve, xivn9
Encounters at the "Edge of the Woods" (Collective Encounter): about, 87n, 215–16n11, 298–305; Carter as director and dramaturg, 45n, 87n, 215–16n11, 298–9, 300n18; consent protocols, 300; development, 87n, 215–16n11, 299–303; forgiveness, 303; irreconcilable spaces, 45, 215–16n11, 300; kernels of stories, 215–16n11; key questions, 302; land-based praxis, 300; performers, 87n, 301, 303; productions (2019), 45n, 87n, 298; published text, 238, 300n; residential schools, 300–1; re-worlding, 215–16n11, 300, 303; "split mind" work, 45n, 87n, 300; Storyweaving, 87n, 299–302; University of Toronto history, 215–16n11, 298, 300–1
Enow'kin principle, 39, 192, 296, 304
Enriques, Virgilio, 156
Erdman, Jean, 82
Europe: genocide, 275–6n; incident in France (1977), 94–5, 114, 127–8, 134, 234; May's novel *Winnetou*, 230–3, 238–9; misappropriation,

Europe (*continued*)
230–3; tour of *Women in Violence*, 134n; *Winnetou's Snake Oil Show*, 227n16. *See also* colonization
exercises, theatre: about, 85–6n, 86n; body map and personal narratives, 14–15n9; Chaikin's exercises, 81n16, 85–8, 86n, 177–8, 253n; Chuck Mike's exercises, 126n; circles upon circles, 126n; "Clown in Us," 123; Derrick's community model, 171–3, *172*; drone or chord, 253n; Hagen's exercises, 16; "Improv Circle," 126n; Inside/Outside [Odets Kitchen] exercise, 85–6n, 86n; Laban exercises, 177; movement, 99–100, 126n; "object exercise," 178; Perfect People exercise, 85–6n, 86n; re-telling stories in own words, 296–7; scholarship on, 86n; sound, 177–8, 253n; Stanislavski movement, 99–100; "Transformations," 85–6n, 86n, 87–8, 177–8, 190n
extractivism, 18

fabric: finger weaving, 64, 109, 128; hand work, 63–4; Indigenous aesthetics, 124–5; *Material Witness*, 48, 49, 60–4; mola overview, 102n30, 121–3, *122*; mounds, 60–4; quilts, 102. *See also* mola; mola aesthetics
family, Miguel. *See* Miguel family
Farnell, Brenda, 289
Favel, Floyd: about, 170, 270–1; "artificial tree" appropriation, 28–31, 66n2, 271; on *chapan* (wagon), 285, 306; formulas for theatre, process, and tradition, 286–7; land's story, 170; nation-specific aesthetics, 271, 286; Native Performance Culture (NPC), 29, 270–2, 286–7; story as re-worlding work, 21
Fear into Sacred, xiv
Fear of Oatmeal (with Amerinda), 9–10n
feminism: complicity with Indigenous harms, 117; CR (Consciousness Raising), 85–6n, 104–5, 107, 108, 161, 296; feminist theatre, 104–9, 119; matriarchal power in *Lysistrata Numbah!*, 135–6; Miguel sisters as outsiders, 134; Muriel as feminist, 104–9; racism and classism, 134n; white middle-class feminists, 107, 146, 160; womanist processes, 160–4; Womanspace, 104–9. *See also* lesbian feminists; Split Britches Theater
First Daughter to Come from the Stars (Lisa's Guna name), 3n. *See also* Mayo, Lisa (Elizabeth Miguel)
First Peoples, terminology, 35n
Fishback, John Paul, 165
The Fittin' Room: about, 67–70, 309–11; performance (1980), xiii, 67–70, 309–11; performers' own identities, 67–70; pre-show on intersectionality, 68–9; publicity interview (Kafer), 142–6; script, 67n, 309–11
Flower of the Night (Du Tu Kapsus), Gloria's Guna name, 49, 53, *53*, 54, 96n
Flying Eagle Woman (Ingrid El-Issa). *See* El-Issa, Ingrid Washinawatok (Flying Eagle Woman)
Foner, Laura, 104–8
Fontaine, Tina, 22n2
Forsythe, James, 165, 167–8
1492: Blood Speaks (Coatlicue Theater), 200n
France, *Women in Violence* (1977), incident, 94–5, 114, 127–8, 134, 234
freaks, as term, 283n10
Friday Night, xiii, 137–9

Garneau, David, 45, 300
gender and sexual minorities (2SLGBTQQIA): honour

songs, 294–5; lesbian identity of Spiderwoman Theater, 72, 145n; Muriel's lesbian identity, 137, 139–47, 211; pre-show on intersectionality, 68–9; Two-Spirits in Derrick's model, 171–3, *172*. *See also* lesbian feminists
genocide, as term, 23–5, 275–6n
genocide, cultural, 186, 218, 229, 232, 274–5
Giroux, Tyree, 15
Glancy, Diane, 170, 203, 262
Gloria. *See* Miguel, Gloria
The God of Gods (Aikins), 298
Gómez-Peña, Guillermo, 110
Grande, Sandy, 107
Grandma. *See* Moore, Elizabeth Ashton (Elmira's mother, "Grandma")
Grosberg, Carol, 104–8
Guna connections with Miguels. *See* Miguel family, Gunayala, Panama
Guna culture: assimilation laws, 123; body adornments, 121–2; fetal caul, 247n; Gathering House, 123, 195–7, 210, 224, 248–9, 253n; gender traditions, 250–1, 260–3; hammock, 248–50, 252; kitchen table storytelling, 100, 159, 196–7, 210, 243n; male presence, 100, 159–60; medicine chants, 173, 197n18, 240–1; mola overview, 102n30, 121–3, *122*; nation-specific aesthetics, 162, 241–2, 243n, 245n; pictographs, 173, 197n18; psychic gifts, 247n; puberty ceremony, 261–2; sound in storytelling, 210; women, 102n30, 121–3, *122*, 260–2. *See also* mola; mola aesthetics
Guna culture, cosmology: about, 81n16, 196–7, 243–4; Baba Nana (deity), 9, 197n18; baluwala tree, 136n, 261n36; burba, 243, 249–50; chain of ancestors and descendants, 4–6; guardians, 249–50; healing, 81n16, 123, 197n18, 240–1, 243–4, 247n, 248–9; history as communal responsibility, 124–5; mola aesthetics, 102n30, 121–3, *122*, 196–7, 243n; sabbigarda tree, 243n; sabtur tree, 261–2; spiritual world, 81n16, 197n18
Gunayala, Panama. *See* Miguel family, Gunayala, Panama
Gunn Allen, Paula, 152n, 169–70
Guppy, Sherry, 14–15n9
Gussow, Mel, 207

Hagen, Uta: about, 88–98; on America's dis-ease, 93; art form as communal adventure, 94; Chaikin's studies with, 80, 89; Chekhov plays, 92, 96–8; exercise adaptations, 16, 178; HB Studio, 4, 88–9n23, 89–90; lack of safe spaces, 95–6; Lisa's studies with, 4n2, 84–5, 90, 96–7; method acting, 111; place and time in story, 91–3; quest for self in community, 91–3
The Halluci Nation, 283n
hand work, 24, 63–4, 65–7, 169–70
Harjo, Joy, 158–9
Harris, Frank, 278
Hart House Theatre, University of Toronto, 87n, 298
Harvey, Kim Senklip, 58–9
Haudenosaunee: Derrick's community model, 171–3, *172*; Sky Woman story, 12–16, 57–8, 304
Haugo, Ann, 88–9n23, 215n10, 228
healing of Indigenous dis-ease: art as medicine, 93, 95–6, 164, 272, 304, 306; ceremony of recovery, 233–5, 239–40; as choice, 294; Guna healing, 81n16, 123, 197n18, 240–1, 243–4, 247n, 248–9; healthy

healing of Indigenous dis-ease (*continued*)
balanced life, 37, 164–5, 169n; honour songs, 294–5, 304–5; inward vs. outward focus, 165, 175–6; medicine chants, 173, 197n18, 240–1; *More Than Feathers*, 293–5; Native Performance Culture, 272; *Persistence of Memory*, 279–81; "walking away," 57–8; *Winnetou's Snake Oil Show*, 233–5, 239–40; womanist processes, 160–4. *See also* ceremony; decolonization; resistance and refusals; re-worlding; Storyweaving

Henu. *See* Tarrant, Henu Josephine (Murielle and Kevin's daughter)

Hernandez, Fernando, 293

Hevey, David, 283n10

Highway, Tomson, 305–6

Hogan, Linda, 164

Holmes, Leilani, 38–9

home movies, 157, 159, 209, 219, 224–5, 233, 238, 259

homosexuality, 68–9, 72, 145n. *See also* gender and sexual minorities (2SLGBTQQIA); lesbian feminists

Honoring Spiderwoman Theatre Conference (2007), 88–9n23, 265

Hopi creatrix, Spiderwoman as, 71–2, 109

Hot Peaches, 139

Howe, LeAnne, 289

human beings, new, 82–4n19, 153–6, 163–4, 216n. *See also* biota; re-worlding

humour: Chekhov's plays, 96–8; Guna culture, 196; Lisa as comedienne, 4–5, 96–8, *98*, 131–2, 138–9; *Lysistrata Numbah!*, 134–7; *Material Witness*, 50; *Misdemeanor Dream*, 12–13; pedagogical function, 50, 129–30n, 132–3; shameful jokes, 50, 97n, 132–3; Trickster/Transformer figures, 129–30, 131–2; *Women in Violence*, 50, 97n, 132–3. *See also* clowns

Ibeler Uagan (Grandchildren of the Sun), 96n

identity: about, 133; authenticity, 106, 114–15; class and race in *Cycles*, 106–8; feminist, 134n; quest for self in community, 144–50

identity, Indigenous: about, 33–5, 110–12, 133; "becoming" processes, 111–12, 133; ceremony, 246–7; Derrick's community model, 171–3, *172*; history as communal responsibility, 124–5; mixed-blooded people, 110; Muriel's dissatisfaction with Womanspace, 106–9; quest for self in community, 144–50; stories for remaking, 26–7, 129–30; Storyweaving as quest, 33–5, 37, 86–7, 133, 144–50; survivance, 33–5, 37, 86–7; transformations by actions, 111–12

Ikwe, Oogima, 111–12

I'll Be Right Back, xiii, 2

Indian, as term, 35n

Indian Act, 24, 298n, 300–1

"Indian Love Call," 211–15, 217, 219–22. See also *Sun, Moon, and Feather*

Indigenous Peoples: art and activism, 35n; generational relations, 236; genocide, 23–5, 275–6n; invisibility, 25; non-heterosexual individuals, 145n; role models, 218; service organizations, 66n1; social harms, 23–5, 115, 275–6n; sovereignty, 269; terminology, 35n. *See also*

colonization; Indigenous women; residential schools
Indigenous Peoples, decolonization. *See* decolonization; healing of Indigenous dis-ease; resistance and refusals; re-worlding
Indigenous Peoples, knowledge. *See* biota; ceremony; knowledge, Indigenous; land; stories, Indigenous
Indigenous Peoples, misrepresentations: about, 37–8; enfreakment, as term, 283n10; *Izzie M*, 283–5, 289; literary representations, 28–31; Minstrelsy, 272–3; for nation building, 214; redface, 213–14, 272–3n, 273, 298; Red Reading, 238, 292; romantic nostalgia, 28–9; *Sideshow Freaks and Circus Injuns*, 283, 289; sideshows, 283–5, 289; simulation of survivance, 28–31. *See also* "show biz" Indians; stereotypes; *Winnetou's Snake Oil Show from Wigwam City*
Indigenous Peoples, theatre. *See* Spiderwoman Theater; Spiderwoman Theater, legacy; theatre, Indigenous; theatre training, Indigenous
Indigenous women: containment and pigeonholing, 62, 67–70; Derrick's community model, 171–3, *172*; at the drum, 250–1; fat-shaming, 62; matriarchies, 237; Missing and Murdered Indigenous Women and Girls (MMIWG), 21–3, 48–50, 54, 184; as transmitters, healers, and transformers, 256–8. *See also* Miguel family
intersectionality, 68–9, 117–19, 142
irreconcilable Indigenous spaces, 40, 45, 54, 58, 60–1, 215–16n11, 300–2
Irwin, Bill, 99–100
Iserhoff, Erika, 174–5, 287–9
Izzie M: The Alchemy of Enfreakment (Mojica), 283–5, 289

Jackson, Nadine, 82–4n19, 84n
Jamaica, Antonio's life in, 73–4
James Bay Cree, relocation, 287–8
Jamieson, Julia, 82–4n19
Jealousy, xiii, 137–9
Jews: anti-Semitic humour, 132–3; Ashkenazi, 16, 275–6n, 276n8; genocide, 275; Miguel marriages and descendants, 89, 100–1, 275–6n, 276n8
Johnson, Falen, 270n3
Johnson, Jon, 58
jokes. *See* humour
Joseph, Dione, 53
Josephine. *See* Mofsie-Tarrant, Josephine (Muriel's best friend, Kevin's mother)
Joy, Joy, Joy (Scott), 298
Justice, Daniel Heath, 228–9n

Kafer, Kathy, 142–6
Kamloopa (Harvey), 58–9
Kantule, Oswaldo DeLeón, 136n, 197n18, 241n23, 249, 264
kernels of the stories, 124, 190–3, 195, 215, 245, 264
Kevin. *See* Tarrant, Kevin (Josephine's son, Murielle's husband, Henu's father)
King, Thomas, 148n
kitchen table storytelling, 35, 100, 105, 158–64, 196–7, 210, 243n
knowledge, Indigenous: about, 26–7, 93, 153–4, 228–30; aesthetics, 124–5; art as medicine, 93, 95–6, 164, 272, 304, 306; "becoming" processes, 111–12; Cajete's pedagogical model, 26, 154–7, 163,

knowledge, Indigenous (*continued*) 199; communal vs. absolute truth, 124–6; context of relationships, 39; cosmologies, 10–11, 81n16, 111–12, 124–5; dualities, 10–11; history as communal responsibility, 124–5; Laenui's sociological model, 153–4, 156–7, 163, 199; land as source, 153–4, 168–9, 228–30; liminality for transformation, 151–4, 157; recovery of, 228–30; sacred geometry, 170–3, *172*; self-discovery processes, 96–7, 133; tribal specialists, 167; "validity test" for good life, 37; waterway metaphor, 277–8. *See also* biota; ceremony; land; oral tradition; stories, Indigenous; Storyweaving

knowledge, non-Indigenous: about, 27, 93; absolute truth, 124–5; dualities vs. oppositional binaries, 10n6; duty to heal biota, 257–8; essentialism in difference, 238; linear vs. circular structures, 173; mimesis, 27; misappropriation, 116; narratives, 148n; New Age movement, 28–9, 116, 227; self-discovery processes, 96–7; simulation of survivance, 28–31. *See also* colonization; Indigenous Peoples, misrepresentations; misappropriation and cultural theft; stories, non-Indigenous

Knowles, Ric, 202, 251, 254, 289

Kwakiutl ceremonies, 234n

Laenui, Poka, 153–4, 156–7, 163, 199

Lakota Sundance, 102n31, 245–6. *See also* Sundance ceremony

La MaMa Experimental Theatre Club, xiii, xiv, xvn10, 45–7

land: Derrick's community model, 171–3, *172*; kitchen table storytelling, 164; as knowledge source, 153–4, 168–9, 173–5; land acknowledgments, 11; land ethic, 168–9; mounds, 289; nation-specific aesthetics, 162, 241–2, 243n, 245n, 286, 289; Omushkego narratives, 174–5, 287–90; place as spiritual and physical, 153–4; place/land and time in story, 91–2; as primary text, 173–5; removals, 228–30; sense-memory exercises, 178; waterway metaphor, 277–8

Laronde, Sandra, 270

Lauzon, Jani, 21, 270, 276n8

learning. *See* exercises, theatre; theatre training, Indigenous; theatre training, non-Indigenous

legacy. *See* Spiderwoman Theater, legacy

lesbian feminists: about, 142–7; Hot Peaches troupe, 139; identity of Spiderwoman Theater, 141–7; mainstream feminists' lack of acceptance of, 134n; Marvel's conflicts with, 72; non-Indigenous communities, 145n; Weaver's direction of *Split Britches*, 147–9; white middle-class feminists, 107, 146, 160; womanism, as term, 160; Womanspace theatre, 104–5. *See also* feminism; gender and sexual minorities (2SLGBTQQIA)

Lesly, Jo, 165

liminality: about, 151–4; in ceremony, 246, 248–9; circular structures, 133, 170–1, 193; in daily life, 168–9; infinite meaning, 226; liminal events, 151–4, 157; *Persistence of Memory*, 268; *Power in Pipes*, 256; psychic visitations, 179–80, 185, 186–8, 236, 242; *Reverb-ber-ber-rations*, 248–9, 253; social necessity

for liminal, 151–4; Storyweaving, 193; transformative events, 82–4n19, 151–4, 157, 246; waterway metaphor, 277–8; Western impermanent liminoid events, 82–4n19, 151–2, 157, 159n, 167
Lisa. *See* Mayo, Lisa (Elizabeth Miguel)
Little Eagles Dance Co., 78
The Living Theater, 81, 88, 105, 125–6. *See also* Chaikin, Joseph
Livne-Bar, Uri, 303n
Loft, Angela, 6, 48n10, 49
Lois. *See* Weaver, Lois
Loose Change Productions, xivn10, 15n10
Lorde, Audre, 107, 187
Luna, James, 233n
Lynx Woman, 7–9
Lysistrata (Aristophanes), 135–7
Lysistrata Numbah!, xiii, 134–7, 261n36

MacDonald, Jeannette, 212–13, 220
Macdonald, John A., 300
males: audience members, 115; Derrick's community model, 171–3, *172*; Guna culture, 100, 159; kitchen table storytelling, 100, 159; male puppets in *Three Sisters*, 97–8, *98*; in *Misdemeanor Dream*, 9–10; patriarchal oppression, 36, 116, 119, 135–6, 141; reception of *Women in Violence*, 114–15; womanist inclusion, 9–10, 134n, 160
Malinche (Nahuatl), 291–2
manidoons collective, 59–60
Man is Man (Brecht), 81
Manitowabi, Edna, 57
Maracle, Cheri, 270n3
Maracle, Lee, 45, 87n, 159, 302, 304
marginalized artists. *See* racialized and marginalized people
Margolin, Deb, 115n, 149
Marvel lawsuit on "Spiderwoman," 70–2, 142, 313–14
Material Witness: about, 17–18, 44–54, *46*, 60–4; Aanmitaagzi partnership, xivn10, 14–15n9, 47, 60–3; ancestors and descendants, 4, 49; ceremonial space, 61; irreconcilable space, 61; Loose Change Productions, xivn10, 15n10; performances (2016, 2017), xivn10, 4, 4n3, *46*; power of theatre to change violence, 51–2, 54–5; refusals, 57–8; search for self, 49; survivance and healing, 6, 52–3, 57–8, 62–3; title, 61, 63; violence, 48–50, 62
Material Witness, development and performers: Carter's re-creation story, 40–4; Couchie, 47–9, 52, 54, 60–2; Gloria, 48n10, 49, 51–4, *53*, 57, 61, 64, 96n; Muriel as director and dramaturg, 4, 48n10; performers, 48n10; Pulling Threads workshops (2012–16), 47, 63; relation to *Women in Violence*, 48, 49, 51–2, 63; Sundance ceremony, 43–4
Material Witness, stage productions: backdrop, *46*, 47–8, 61, *122*; clowns, 49, 51–2, 61–2; dance, 62; Du Tu Kapsus, 49, 51–4, *53*, 57, 61, 64, 96n; fabric mounds, 48, 49, 60–4; Guna regalia (mola), 53, *53*; shameful jokes, 50, 97n
May, Karl, 230–3, 238
Mayer, Ginny, 282
Mayo, Lisa (Elizabeth Miguel): about, *2*, 2–5, 88–98; as an Elder, 266–7; birth (1924), 143–4; community work, 3–4, 80; death (2013), 40; education, 89; as eldest daughter, 3; glamour, 131, 139; Guna name, 3n, 5–6, 96n; humour, 96–8, *98*,

Mayo, Lisa (Elizabeth Miguel) (*continued*) 131–2, 138–9; illnesses, xivn8, 4, 84n, 265; Jewish family, 77, 89–90; Lisa Mayo as stage name, 73n6, 77, 132; marriage to Jules, 89–90, 134, 211; psychic gifts in family, 75, 179–80, 185, 186–7, 211, 236, 242; Rappahannock name (Feather), 149; shame, 282–3; singer, 3–4, 90, 220; visit to Gunayala (1994), 96n

Mayo, Lisa, identity: about, 77–9, 89–90, 133, 134n, 141, 264; ceremony, 246–7; as feminist, 134n, 138–9, 141, 143; as Guna woman, 96n, 136–7; as heterosexual, 134n, 142–3; as Indian, 79, 131, 138–9, 141, 143, 246–7; as mother, 139; quest for self in community, 144–50; Rappahannock woman, 149, 152n; religious beliefs, 77, 89; "show biz" Indians, *78*, 78–9, 219n, 282–5; as wife, 89, 144, 246

Mayo, Lisa, life in Brooklyn: about, 3–5; caregiving by aunt and grandmother, 73n7, 75, 210n7; caregiving for Muriel, 3, 211; feelings of abandonment, 75–6; home birth (1924), 73, 75, 143–4; "Mean Men and Material Witnesses," 40–4; Medicine Shows, *78*, 78–9, 282–3. *See also* Miguel family, life in Brooklyn

Mayo, Lisa, Spiderwoman Theater: acting as political resistance, 90–1; burlesque, 2, 4; clowns, 86n; co-founder, 3–4; as comedienne, 4, 96–8, 131–2, 135–6, 138–9; Inside/Outside [Odets Kitchen] exercise, 85–6n, 86n; intergenerational processes, 291; "make inside more like outside" motif, 4–5; with puppets, *98*; safe spaces for, 95–6; solo shows, 3; stereotype roles, 93; studies with Hagen, 84–5, 90, 96–7; as tragedienne, 4

Mayo, Lisa, Spiderwoman Theater productions: *Among the Living*, xiv, 4, 266; *Daughters from the Stars*, 6; *The Elders' Project*, 4, 266; *The Fittin' Room*, 67–70, 142, 309–11; *I'll Be Right Back*, 2; *Lysistrata Numbah!*, 135–6; *And My Sister Ate Dirt*, xiii, 137–9; *The Pause that Refreshes*, xiv; *Persistence of Memory*, 265–6, 278–80; *Power Pipes*, 259; *Reverb-ber-ber-rations*, 200n, 246–8; *Sun, Moon, and Feather*, 210–12, 220–2; *The Three Sisters from Here to There*, 98; *Voices from the Criss Cross Bridge*, xiv; *Winnetou's Snake Oil Show*, 233; *Women in Violence*, 4, 5, 85–6n, 86n, 119, 131, 315

Mayo, Lisa, views on: eternal chain of ancestors to descendants, 4–6; legacy, 6, 280; "make inside more like outside," 4–5; male puppets, 97–8; on self as mentor, 265

"Mean Men and Material Witnesses": (Carter), 40–4

Medicine Shows. *See* "show biz" Indians

Medicine Walk: Breath Track, 45n

Medicine Wheel, 164–5

Method acting, 81, 85, 111, 177, 178–9

Métis Nation, 291–2

metonyms, 69, 86, 110, 188, 214, 219. *See also* stereotypes

Michaels, Sarah, 303n

Midsummer Night's Dream (Shakespeare), 6–7

Miguel family: about, 18, 73–80, 143–4; cooperation, 222–6; identity as Indians, *78*, 78–80, 133; as partners in research on Spiderwoman Theater, 16–17, 37,

38; psychic gifts, 75, 179–80, 185, 186–7, 211, 236, 242. *See also* Mayo, Lisa (Elizabeth Miguel); Miguel, Antonio (father); Miguel, Elmira (mother); Miguel, Gloria; Miguel, Muriel; Moore, Elizabeth Ashton (Elmira's mother, "Grandma")

Miguel family, community members and relatives: aunt Lizzie, 209n4, 217–18, 219n; Jewish family members, 89, 100–1, 275–6n, 276n8; Joe, 101, 159, 209n4, 223, 233; "show biz" Indian visitors, 100. *See also* Borst-Tarrant, Murielle (Muriel's daughter); Mojica, Monique (Gloria's daughter); Tarrant, Henu Josephine (Murielle and Kevin's daughter)

Miguel family, Gunayala, Panama: Antonio's son, 74–5, 76, 101, 247–8; assimilation, 123; home movies, 209; Miguel family visits (1971, 1994), 96n, 101–2, *122*, 247–8, 262; Mojica's visit (2008), 243n; Nargana island, 197n19, 210; *Sun, Moon, and Feather* (film), 226n. *See also* Guna culture; Guna culture, cosmology; mola; mola aesthetics

Miguel family, life in Brooklyn: about, 40, 73–6, 143–4, 219n; Boat Story, 223–5; dreaming, 34, 224–5; drunkenness, 73, 74n, 76, 140; in *Fear of Oatmeal*, 9–10n; Gathering House Tradition, 195–7; home births, 73, 75, 143–4; home movies, 159, 209, 219, 224–5, 233, 238, 259; Indian stereotypes, 86–7; kitchen table storytelling, 100, 158–64, 196–7; "Mean Men and Material Witnesses," 40–4; mother's caul as artefact, 240, 242; poverty, 34, 75, 76, 86–7, 103n, 208–9; racism, 34, 75, 76, 86–7; "show biz" Indians, *78*, 78–9, 86–7, 99–100, 219n, 282–5; survivance, 220–6; violence, 34, 40–4, 222–3

Miguel, Antonio (father): about, 73–6, *78*; alcoholism, 73, 74n, 76, 113, 222–3; birth in Gunayala, 73n8, 197n19; death (1970), 226; marriage to Elmira, 3, 74–5; marriage to Guna woman, 74–5; personal qualities, 76, 225–6; as "scooped child," 73–4; seaman, 76; son in Gunayala, 74–5, 76, 101, 247. *See also* Miguel, Elmira (mother)

Miguel, Antonio (father), life in Brooklyn: about, 73–9, *78*; Boat Story, 159, 223–5; home movies, 159, 209, 219n, 224–5, 233, 238, 259; influence on theatre, 33n, 73–4, 76, 159, 243n; "Mean Men and Material Witnesses," 40–4; poverty, 73, 76, 103n; "show biz" Indians, *78*, 78–9, 86–7, 99–100, 219n, 282–5; in *Sun, Moon, and Feather* (film), 209n4, 219n; violence, 222–3. *See also* Miguel family, life in Brooklyn

Miguel, Elmira (mother): about, 73–7, *78*, 211; birth, 75; Christian, 33n, 74, 75, 76; daughters' forgiveness for, 251–2; death (1979), 139; emotional withdrawal, 33n, 73, 76, 77, 211, 224; honour song for, 304–5; personal qualities, 75; psychic gifts, 73, 75, 211, 236, 239–40, 242; Rappahannock, 3, 33n, 74, 210. *See also* Moore, Elizabeth Ashton (Elmira's mother, "Grandma")

Miguel, Elmira (mother), life in Brooklyn: Boat Story, 223–5; childbirth, 73, 143–4, 242; her caul as artefact, 240, 242; marriage

Miguel, Elmira (mother), life in Brooklyn (*continued*) to Antonio, 3, 74–5; Muriel as caregiver, 139–40; "show biz" Indians, *78*, 78–9, 86–7, 99–100, 219n, 282–5; in *Sun, Moon, and Feather* (film), 209n4; violence, 222–3. *See also* Miguel family, life in Brooklyn
Miguel, Gloria: about, 99–102, *222*; as an Elder, 266–7; birth (1937), 143–4; community work, 80; dis-ease, 280–1, 306–7; education, 99–100, 209n5; illnesses, 138n15; intergenerational processes, 291; life in Oberlin, 99, 100–1, 247; marriage and divorce (M. Szykowski), 52, 89, 100–1, 134; as middle sister, 144; mother, 99, 100; psychic gifts in family, 75, 179–80, 185, 186–7, 211, 236, 242; Rappahannock name (Moon), 54, 149; shame, 280–1, 282–5; singer, 99, 220; son, 278. *See also* Mojica, Monique (Gloria's daughter)
Miguel, Gloria, Guna culture: Guna name (Du Tu Kapsus), 49, 53, *53*, 54, 96n; identity as Guna woman, *53*, 53–4, 100–2, 123, 136–7, 151, 262; kitchen table storytelling, 100, 158; mola for Spiderwoman Theater, 102n30, 121–3, *122*; visits to Gunayala (1971, 1994), 96n, 101–2, *122*, 247–8, 262. *See also* Guna culture; Guna culture, cosmology; mola; mola aesthetics
Miguel, Gloria, identity: about, 77–9, 99, 133, 134n, 141, *222*, 264; ceremony, 246–7; as faculty wife, 99, 100–1, 247; as feminist, 134n, 141, 143; as heterosexual, 134n, 141, 143; as human being, 77, 100–1; as Indian, 79, 138, 141, 143–4, 246–7, 280–1; as mother, 144; quest for self in community, 144–50; as Rappahannock woman, 54, 149, 152n, 283–4; resistance to Indigeneity, 77; "show biz" Indians, *78*, 78–9, 99–100, 219n, 282–5; storytelling, 99
Miguel, Gloria, life in Brooklyn: caregiver for Muriel, 6, 211; childhood, 279–80; in *Fear of Oatmeal*, 9–10n; feelings of abandonment, 75–6; home birth (1937), 73, 75, 143–4; life with grandmother, 73n7; "Mean Men and Material Witnesses," 40–4; religious confusion, 77; "show biz" Indians, *78*, 78–9; violence, 54. *See also* Miguel family, life in Brooklyn
Miguel, Gloria, Spiderwoman Theater: *Daughters from the Stars*, 96n; *Fear of Oatmeal*, 9–10n; *The Fittin' Room*, 67–70, 142, 309–11; *Jealousy*, 137–9; *Material Witness*, 48n10, 49, 51–4, *53*, 57, 61, 64, 96n; *Persistence of Memory*, 265–6, 278–81; *Power Pipes*, 261–3; *Reverb-ber-ber-rations*, 200n, 246–8; *Sun, Moon, and Feather*, 210–12, 220–2, *222*; *Winnetou's Snake Oil Show*, 233; *Women in Violence*, 52
Miguel, Gloria, views on: aging, 49; life in Oberlin, 99–100; Miguel sisters' life in art, 306–7; writing, 290
Miguel, Muriel: about, 102–9; as an Elder, 266–7; birth (1937), 143–4; community work, 8, 80; forgiveness, 251–2; marriage, 89, 113, 134, 140; personal qualities, 40, 77, 84n, 101, 113, 280; psychic gifts in family, 75, 179–80, 185, 186–7, 211, 236, 242; Rappahannock name (Sun), 149; Sundance ceremony, 43–4, 102,

109, 245–6; as youngest sister, 144. *See also* Borst-Tarrant, Murielle (Muriel's daughter); Miguel family; Tarrant, Henu Josephine (Murielle and Kevin's daughter)

Miguel, Muriel, choreographer and dancer: about, 79–80, 82–4; Chaikin's influence, 82–4, 103n33; Little Eagles, 78; modern dance, 79, 82–4n19, 84; powwows, 79–80; Thunderbirds, 78, 80, 82–4n19; views on, 82–4n19. *See also* Chaikin, Joseph

Miguel, Muriel, director: about, 126, 137, 143; *Among the Living*, xiv, 4, 266; current director, 6; as "final eye," 137, 290; formulas for theatre, process, and tradition, 286–7; *Misdemeanor Dream*, 7–9; refusal of colonial control, 56; *The Scrubbing Project*, 276; Storyweaving, 5, 87–8, 126, 176–9, 193–6

Miguel, Muriel, identity: about, 77–9, 104, 112, 133, 134n, 139–47, 264; "becoming" processes, 111–12; ceremony, 246–7; clown persona, 130–1; as contemporary, urban artist, 82–4n19, 104; decision-making periods, 140–1; as director, 126, 137, 143; as feminist, 112, 134n, 140–1; as Guna woman, *122*, 136–7; as heterosexual, 134; as Indian, 77, 79, 82–4n19, 104, 140–1, 246–7; as lesbian, 137, 139–47, 211; as mother, 104, 140; quest for self in community, 137–9, 144–50; as Rappahannock woman, 149, 152n; as wife, 89, 113, 134, 140; as womanist, 112

Miguel, Muriel, life in Brooklyn: caregiving by Lisa and Gloria, 6, 211; caregiving for Elmira, 139–41; Elmira's emotional withdrawal, 73, 76, 211; home birth (1937), 73, 75–6, 143–4; Indian youth groups, 77; "Mean Men and Material Witnesses," 40–4; "show biz" Indians, *78*, 78–9, 86–7, 219n, 282–5. *See also* Miguel family, life in Brooklyn

Miguel, Muriel, Spiderwoman Theater: about, 85–7, 123–4; Chaikin's influence, 79–88, 81n16, 82–8, 100, 102–3, 253n; circular structures, 133, 170–1; as co-founder, 112; drone exercise, 253n; feminist influences (CR), 104–5, 296; Guna culture, 121–8, *122*, 176–9; kernels of stories, 245n; kitchen table storytelling, 105, 158–64; languages other than English, 89n; mola aesthetics, 121–8, *122*, 176–9; Open Theater productions, 103n33; organic continuity, 241n24; questions as focus, 35, 86, 148n, 163; resistance to stereotypes, 87; respect and protection, 95–6; safe spaces, 88–9n23; storytelling, 87; warm-up exercises, 177; Womanspace Theatre, 104–9, 112; workshops (2002, 2006), 176–9, 193–6. *See also* Chaikin, Joseph; Miguel, Muriel, director; Storyweaving

Miguel, Muriel, Spiderwoman Theater productions: *Fear of Oatmeal*, 9–10n; *The Fittin' Room*, 67–70, 142, 309–11; *Material Witness*, 4, 48n10; *Misdemeanor Dream*, 7–9, 12; *Persistence of Memory*, 265–6, 278–80; *Red Mother*, xiv, 82–4n19, 84n, 290–1; *Reverb-ber-ber-rations*, 200n, 245, 246–8; *Sun, Moon, and Feather*,

Miguel, Muriel, Spiderwoman Theater productions (*continued*) 211, 212n, 217; *Trilogy*, 137–9; *Winnetou's Snake Oil Show*, 233; *Women in Violence*, 122, 130–1

Miguel, Muriel, views on: beginning of Spiderwoman Theater, 44; classism, 119; origin stories, 57, 305; pedantry and pleasure, 113n2, 128; safe spaces, 88–9n23, 95; vision of Indigenous theatre space (NYC), 56–7

Mike, Chuck, 126

mimesis: "artificial tree" spirituality, 28–31, 66n2, 271; assimilation as flawed mimesis, 31–2; counter-mimicry, 213–15, 217; metaphysical vs. material, 29; simulation of survivance, 28–31; Western concept, 20, 27

Minstrelsy, 272–3

misappropriation and cultural theft: about, 71, 116–17, 164–7, 199, 227–30; "artificial tree" spirituality, 28–31, 66n2, 271; beadwork imitations (AICH), 65–7; complicity, 232–5; cultural theft, 72, 227, 232, 235; dis-ease from, 230, 239–40; Elders' call for action against, 199, 227; harms to health, 165–7, 235–6; Marvel's copyright lawsuit, 70–2, 142, 313–14; May's novel *Winnetou*, 229–32, 238–9; Medicine Wheel, 164–5; New Age charlatans, 227; pretenders, 232; re-appropriation of misappropriation, 29; *The Scrubbing Project*, 268, 270–6; shamanism, 75n, 116–17, 164, 199; spiritualists, 232; Storyweaving, 66n2; as violence, 116; *Winnetou's Snake Oil Show*, 75n, 116–17, 199, 227, 238–9. *See also* authenticity

Misdemeanor Dream: about, 6–16, *8*; Aanmitaagzi partnership, 14–15n9, 15n10; backdrop, 14–15n9, *122*; birth stories, 7–9; ceremony of recovery, 7–9; cosmology, 7–11; development, 7–15; humour, 12–13; male performers, 9–10; Muriel as director, 7–9, 12; origin stories, 7, 12–16; performance history (2017, 2021, 2024), xiv, 7, *8*, 15; performers, 7, 9, 11; pre-show address, 12; relation to Shakespeare's *Midsummer Night's Dream*, 6–7; re-worlding, 13–14; Sky Woman story, 12–16; title, 12–13; workshops (2020), 6–7, 11–12, 14–15n9

misrepresentations. *See* Indigenous Peoples, misrepresentations; stereotypes

Missing and Murdered Indigenous Women and Girls (MMIWG), 21–3, 48–50, 54, 184

Mofsie, Louis (Josephine's brother), 78, 80, 294

Mofsie-Tarrant, Josephine (Muriel's best friend, Kevin's mother): about, 71–2, 80, 108–9, 276–7; aesthetics and survivance, 72, 108–9, 128; co-founder of Spiderwoman Theater, 108–9; death (1975), 80n, 101, 109, 112; Miguel family, 80n, 101, 277, 280; namesake for Spiderwoman Theater, 11, 71–2, 80n, 108–9, 128; *Persistence of Memory* dedication, 276–7; Spiderwoman as creatrix, 109

MOHICANS spectacle, New York City, *78*, 78–9

Mojica, Monique (Gloria's daughter): Ashkenazi, 275–6n, 276n8; Guna name, 96n; Guna-Rappahannock, 276n8; Guna visits

(2008), 243n; intra-generational processes, 291; Native Performance Culture (NPC), 270–2; psychic gifts in family, 75, 179–80, 185, 186–7, 211, 236, 242; son, 278, 283; Sundance ceremony, 246n29; Turtle Gals Performance Ensemble, 268, 270, 274n6

Mojica, Monique, dramaturgy: about, 245n; digital images, 284; Favel's collaboration, 173; formulas for theatre, process, and tradition, 286–7; Guna structures, 173, 241n24, 243n; identity shaping, 110; "known sense," 241n24; land-based learning, 173; *More Than Feathers and Beads*, 291; nation-specific aesthetics, 162, 241–2, 241n24, 243n, 245n, 286, 288–9; "organic continuity," 241n24; performative mola, as term, 245n28; *Power Pipes*, 254; story as re-worlding work, 21; Storyweaving, 86, 292–3; "Transformations" exercise, 85–6n; workshops (2006, 2014), 190–3, 288–90

Mojica, Monique, views on: critical reception, 120n; euro-centric aesthetics, 120; invisibility of Indigenous harms, 25; kitchen table storytelling, 158, 162; Medicine Shows, 282–3; mola, 121

Mojica, Monique, works: *Izzie M: The Alchemy of Enfreakment*, 283–5, 289; *Princess Pocahontas and the Blue Spots*, xi, 267, 291–3; *The Scrubbing Project*, 270, 276; *Sideshow Freaks and Circus Injuns*, 283, 289; "A Valentine to my Grandmother," 304–5. See also *Chocolate Woman Dreams the Milky Way* (Mojica)

mola: about, 102n30, 121–3, *122*; assimilation laws, 123; asymmetry, 128–9; backdrop for Spiderwoman Theater, 121–3, *122*, 162, 252; fabric flaws, 128–9; Guna cosmology, 196–7, 243n; layers of fabric, 102n30, 122, 129; nation-specific aesthetics, 162, 241–2, 243n, 245n; women's dress, 53, *53*, 102n30, *122*

mola aesthetics: about, 121–3, *122*, 163–4, 196–7, 245n28; Chekhov's structures, 209n5; experience fragments, 124, 174–5; fours and eights, 197; history as communal responsibility, 124–5; humour, 196; kernel of the story, 124, 190–3, 215, 245, 264; kitchen table storytelling, 196–7; layering processes, 122–3, 196–7; linguistic patterns, 196; motifs, 197, 243n; multi-vocal perspective, 124; non-Indigenous reception, 162; performative mola, 124, 128, 163–4, 176–7, 201, 217, 245n28; race layer, 131; reception, 162; sharing moments, 235

Momaday, N. Scott, 26, 65, 91, 110, 164, 168–9, 198

Monique. *See* Mojica, Monique (Gloria's daughter)

Moore, Elizabeth Ashton (Elmira's mother, "Grandma"): about, 210–11, 217–18; ancestors, 210; caregiver for Lisa, 75, 210n7; as a grandmother, 217–18; medicinal knowledge, 75; midwife, 73, 210–11; opposition to Elmira's marriage, 74, 76; personal qualities, 217–18; psychic gifts, 211, 242; psychic visitation of Muriel, 179–80, 185, 186–7, 242; Rappahannock, 210

Moreno, Soni, 9–10n

More Than Feathers and Beads (Borst-Tarrant), 267–8, 291, 293–5

Morrison, Toni, 55

Mother Courage (Brecht), 82–4n19, 290
movement: exercises, 99–100, 126n; kitchen table storytelling, 158–9. *See also* dance and dancers
Murielle. *See* Borst-Tarrant, Murielle (Muriel's daughter)
Murrin, Jennifer Alicia, 301n
music and sound: drums and pipes, 250–1, 259–60, 263; exercises, 177–8, 253n; honour songs, 294–5, 304–5; "Indian Love Call," 211–15, 217, 219–22; mola aesthetics, 121–3; "Pale Moon," 233; *Persistence of Memory*, 278, 280; popular songs, 294–5; *Power Pipes*, 253, 253n; *Reverb-ber-ber-rations*, 188, 247–8, 250–2; sound in storytelling, 210; Storyweaving, 189–92; *Sun, Moon, and Feather*, 208–9; "Trail Song," 188; "Transformation Twelve," 293

Nana. *See* Moore, Elizabeth Ashton (Elmira's mother, "Grandma")
Native, as term, 35n
Native Performance Culture (NPC), 29, 270–2, 286–7. *See also* Favel, Floyd; Miguel, Muriel; Mojica, Monique (Gloria's daughter)
nature. *See* biota
Neihardt, John G., 145
Nepoose, Pesch, 303n
Neurotic Erotic Exotics (with AFOM), xiii
New Age movement, 28–9, 116, 227
new human beings, 82–4n19, 153–6, 163–4, 216n. *See also* re-worlding
noble savage, 230–2, 237–8, 272–3n. *See also* stereotypes
non-human beings. *See* biota
NPC. *See* Native Performance Culture (NPC)
Numbah!. See *Lysistrata Numbah!*

Off the Beaten Path Theater, 80
Oh, What a Life, xiii, 67
Ohoho, Shequish, 116
Olo Nadile-Naga Gilyai, 3n, 6. *See also* Mayo, Lisa (Elizabeth Miguel)
Omushkego Water Stories, 174–5, 287–90
The Only Good Indian (Turtle Gals), 270n3
The Open Theater, 81–2, 85–9, 102–4, 125–6, 177. *See also* Chaikin, Joseph
oral tradition: about, 27, 169–70, 176, 297; history as communal responsibility, 124–5; inclusive vision, 124; layers of knowledge, 124; multi-vocal perspective, 124; Spiderwoman tradition, 169–70, 175; story belongs to biota, 176; transformation of players, 27. *See also* stories, Indigenous
Ortiz, Simon, 26, 153n
O'Shinna "Fast Wolf," 116
other-than-human-beings. *See* biota

Palmater, Candy, 44
Panama. *See* Miguel family, Gunayala, Panama
pandemic, COVID-19, 6, 15–16
Parenteau, Tanis, 48n10
Pasolli, Robert, 86n
patriarchal oppression, 36, 116, 119, 135–6, 141
Paulin, Megan Lozicki, 14–15n9
The Pause that Refreshes (Mayo), xiv
Pearce, Stewart, 165
Peggy. *See* Shaw, Peggy
Penn, Brandy, 281
performative mola, 124, 128, 163–4, 176–7, 201, 217, 245n28. *See also* mola aesthetics
Perkins, Kathy, 3–4, 5
Persistence of Memory: about, 19, 267–9, 277–82, 285–6; ethics of

witnessing, 19; healing of dis-ease, 279–81; legacy as responsibility, 282, 285–6; liminal event, 268, 279; performances (2002, 2007), xiv, 141n, 263, 265, 290; published play (2009), 203, 238, 242n25; redemption, 19; re-worlding, 269, 282, 286; shame, 279–80, 282–3, 285; survivance, 19, 268–9, 278–81

Persistence of Memory, development: about, 267–9; Flying Eagle Woman (El-Issa) dedication, 268–70, 275, 276, 294–5; kernels of stories, 269; legacy, 279–80; Mofsie-Tarrant dedication, 276–7; nation-specific aesthetics, 267, 286, 289; waterway metaphor, 277–8

Persistence of Memory, performers: Borst-Tarrant, 265, 278; Gloria, 265–6, 278–81; Henu, 278–81; Lisa, 265–6, 278–80; Mojica, 265; Muriel, 265–6, 278–80

Persistence of Memory, stage production: music, 278, 280; opening declaration, 281–2

Persistence of Memory Conference (1998), 267

Phillips, Layli, 161

Pierre (Scott), 298

Plato, in inner/outer life, 110

Pocahontas (Powhatan), 74, 152n, 273, 274n5, 291–2

Powderface, Darylina, *8*

Power Pipes: about, 18, 201, 203, 253–63; ancestors and descendants, 203, 253, 259; female powers, 201, 254–5; harm from cult of individuality, 259; healing of dis-ease, 203, 256–60; performances (1992), xiv, 203n2; as published play, 201, 202–3, 238, 242n25, 254; relation to *Reverb-ber-ber-rations*, 254; stages (recovery, mourning, dreaming, commitment, action), 200–1

Power Pipes, development and performers: Borst-Tarrant, 200n, 253–4, 263; Colorado sisters, 200n, 253, 255, 261–2; Gloria, 261–3; Guna aesthetics, 197; Lisa, 259; Mojica, 200n, 254, 257n, 263n; shame, 255, 258–9; subway rape, 256–7, 261–2

Power Pipes, stage productions: backdrops, 254; ceremonial circle, 254; "Cuna Story," 261–2; drums and pipes, 250–1, 259–60, 263; "Gotcha," 254; light and darkness, 253, 254; Mesi Tuli Omai, 255–8; music and sound, 253, 253n; Owl Messenger, 259; painted bodies, 254–5; performative mola, 255, 258–9; "Shame Stories," 259; She Who Opens Hearts, 255–8; "Subway Rape," 256–7, 261–2; video archive (1993), 254

powwows, 79–80, 79n14, 183, 233

Prince, Althea, 32n

Princess Pocahontas and the Blue Spots (Mojica), xi, 267, 291–3

protection. *See* respect and protection

psychic gifts, 73, 75, 179–80, 185, 186–8, 211, 236–7, 239–40, 242

Pueblo stories, 124–5, 130

Puls, Herta, 243

puppets, 97–8, *98*, 206–7

Quechua women, 291

queer people. *See* gender and sexual minorities (2SLGBTQQIA)

quilts (mola). *See* mola

racialized and marginalized people: assimilation tactics, 56; audience complicity with racism, 50, 97n,

racialized and marginalized people (*continued*) 132–3; financial precarity, 107; languages other than English, 89n; refusals, 55–9; safe spaces for, 55, 58–9, 88–9n23, 95–6; white middle-class feminists and racism, 107, 146, 160; work within communities, 55–6, 63
Rappahannock: about, 74, 149–50, 152n, 210; Anishinaabe relations, 152n; Elmira's ancestors, 74, 210; Izzie M as Medicine Woman, 283–5; psychic gifts, 73, 75, 211, 242; sisters' names, 149. *See also* Moore, Elizabeth Ashton (Elmira's mother, "Grandma")
Ratelle, Deborah, 14n8
Raymore, Sheldon, 9–10n
Recollet, Karyn, 58
reconciliation. *See* decolonization; healing of Indigenous dis-ease; re-worlding
redface, 213–14, 272–3n, 273, 298
Red Mother (Muriel Miguel), xiv, 82–4n19, 84n, 290–1
Red Reading, 238, 292
Red Road, 169n
refusals. *See* resistance and refusals
Reilly, Charles Nelson, 90
religion. *See* Christians; Jews; spirituality, Indigenous
residential schools: about, 31–2, 298n; accountability, 12; assimilation as flawed mimesis, 31–2; genocide, as term, 23–5, 275–6n; Storyweaving, 186, 300–1; TRC report, 21, 24, 184, 299n; University of Toronto history, 300–1; unmarked graves, 11–12, 184; violence, 116
resistance and refusals: counter-mimicry, 213–15, 217; in Indigenous theatre, 215n10; irreconcilable Indigenous spaces, 40, 45, 54, 58, 60–1, 300–2; in *Lysistrata Numbah!*, 134–7; as "not done yet," 11; refusals, 55–9; re-integration of "split mind," 45n, 87n, 300. *See also* decolonization; re-worlding
respect and protection: about, 17, 95–6; Indigenous lifeways, 17, 59, 269; for Indigenous theatre workers, 17, 71, 95–6; Lisa's experiences, 88–9, 95; Miguel family as teacher/research partners, 16; safe spaces for performers, 55, 58–9, 88–9n23, 95–6; in womanist project, 260
Reverb-ber-ber-rations: about, 18, 179–80, 200–1, 239–52; ceremony of mourning, 200n, 237, 244–5, 248–9; liminal space, 248–9, 253; performances (1990), xiv; "primitive authenticity," 187–8; psychic visitations, 75n, 179–80, 185, 186–8, 236–7, 239–40, 242; as published play, 200–3, 238, 242n25; rehearsal tapes, 180n, 244–5, 249, 251–2; relation to *Power Pipes*, 254; shame, 236–7, 244–5; stages (recovery, mourning, dreaming, commitment, action), 200–1, 239, 252
Reverb-ber-ber-rations, development and performers: Corn Dance, 130, 245–6; forgiveness, 251–2; Gloria, 200n, 246–8; guardians (wooden figures), 249–50; Guna healing, 197, 240–1, 243–4, 247n, 248–51; kernels of the stories, 240, 245, 251; Lisa, 200n, 246–8; "Mama's Caul," 240, 242; Muriel, 200n, 245, 246–8; as own identity, 252; Rappahannock, 248; Sundance ceremony, 245–7
Reverb-ber-ber-rations, stage productions: backdrop, 252;

bullroar, 250; drum, 250–1, 252; "Grandma," 179–80; guardians (wooden figures), 249–50; hammock, 248–50, 252; light and darkness, 247–8, 252; "Mama's Caul," 240, 242; music, 247–8, 250; performative mola, 201, 245n28; sound, 247–8, 250–2; Sundance section, 246–7; "Trail Song," 188
re-worlding: about, 32, 58–9, 163–4, 282, 297; art as medicine, 32, 93, 95–6, 272, 304, 306; liminality for, 151–4, 157, 248–9; nation-specific aesthetics, 162, 241–2, 243n, 245n, 286, 289; "new human beings," 82–4n19, 153–6, 163–4, 215–16n11, 216n; storyweaver tradition, 176, 294–5
re-worlding processes: about, 32, 92–3, 163–4, 176; Cajete's pedagogical model, 26, 154–7, 163, 199; ceremony, 32, 59–60; communitism, 34, 92–4, 137, 157, 160–4; Derrick's community model, 171–3, *172*; forgiveness, 251–2, 303; history as communal responsibility, 124–5; honour songs, 294–5, 304–5; kitchen table storytelling, 158–64; Laenui's sociological model, 153–4, 156–7, 163, 199; land ethic and stories, 168–9, 173–5; mola aesthetics, 174–5; non-Indigenous influences, 92–3; recovery of knowledge, 32, 228–30; Sky Woman story, 12–16, 57–8; teachings in stories, 57, 148n; womanist processes, 160–4. *See also* ceremony; healing of Indigenous dis-ease; stories, Indigenous; Storyweaving; theatre, Indigenous
Richmond, Rosemary, 65–6
Robinson, Dylan, 45
Robyn, Jan, 282
Romàn, David, 38
Ronceria, Alejandro, 82–4n19
Rose-Marie (film, 1936), 211–15, 217, 219–22
Royal Proclamation of Reconciliation (TRC), 299n

Safe Harbors Indigenous Collective, 277
St. John, Michelle, 270, 275–6n, 276n8
Salvador, Mari Lyn, 196–7
Saraxin, Tasheena, 14–15n9
Schechner, Richard, 151–2, 176, 234–5
Schneider, Rebecca, 187–8, 213, 221, 227–8n18, 251
Scott, Duncan Campbell, 298
The Scrubbing Project (Turtle Gals), 268, 270–6
sexism, 50, 97n, 132–3
sexual orientation, 23, 68–9, 72, 145n. *See also* gender and sexual minorities (2SLGBTQQIA); lesbian feminists
Shakespeare, William, 6–7, 296–7
shame: about, 236–7; in bodies of descendants, 259; forgiveness, 251–2; internalized colonialism, 77, 195, 236–9, 252, 279–85; misappropriation's harms, 235–7; *Persistence of Memory*, 279–80, 285; *Power in Pipes*, 255–6, 258–9; redirection of shame, 273; *Reverb-ber-ber-rations*, 237; shameful jokes, 50, 97n, 132–3; spectacle as survivance, 282–5; for unconventional parents, 236–7, 240, 244–5, 279–80, 282–3
Shaw, Peggy: about, 142–3, 145–9; *Cabaret*, 69, 139; *The Fittin' Room*, 142; Hot Peaches troupe, 139; lesbian feminist, 139, 142–3, 145–7; *Split Britches* (with Weaver and Verge), xiiin2, 115n, 147–9; Split

Shaw, Peggy (*continued*)
Britches Theater, 139, 149; *Sun, Moon, and Feather*, xiii
Sherzer, Joel, 196
"show biz" Indians, *78*, 78–9, 86–7, 99–100, 219n, 282–5
Sideshow Freaks and Circus Injuns (Chocolate Woman Collective), 283, 289
sideshows, 283–4
Silko, Leslie Marmon, 124–5
SilverCloud Singers, 80
Simpson, Audra, 56
Simpson, Leanne Betasamosake, 10n6, 57
Sky Woman story, 12–16, 57–8, 304
Smith, Andrea, 116, 153, 228–9
Smukler, David, 165, 168
Snake Oil Show. See *Winnetou's Snake Oil Show from Wigwam City*
Soames, Danielle, xivn8
Solomon, Art, 37
Something Old, Something New, Something Borrowed, Something Blue, xiv, 217–18
sound. *See* music and sound
spectacles. *See* misappropriation and cultural theft; "show biz" Indians
spectators. *See* audiences
Spiderwoman Theater: about, 33–6, 80, 133, 306–7; archives, 71, 242n; authenticity, 114–15; communitism, 34, 92–4, 137, 157, 163–4; early history, 18, 141; exhibition (1997), 71; founding (1975), 3, 108–9; as intergenerational project, 9–10, 290–7; liminality for transformation, 151–4, 157; male presence, 9–10, 159–60; Marvel copyright lawsuit, 70–2, 142, 313–14; members, 137–8, 139, 142; performance history overview, xiii–xiv; published plays (1981–2002), 198–203, 238, 242n25, 263; reception, 120n; signature mola backdrop, 121–3, *122*, 162, 252; Spiderwoman as name, 71–2; split of troupe (1981), 141, 149–50, 204; stagecraft, 127, 282; as survivance, 33–4, 72, 80, 112, 206; waterway metaphor, 277–8; womanism, 10, 160–4. *See also* Mayo, Lisa (Elizabeth Miguel); Miguel, Gloria; Miguel, Muriel; Spiderwoman Theater, identity of company
Spiderwoman Theater, dramaturgy: about, 35, 50, 72, 87–8, 133, 163–4, 264; Chaikin's influence, 16, 85–8, 125–6, 253n33; circular structures, 35, 133, 170–1, 239; Guna culture, 33n, 121–3, 240–1, 243n; Guna structures, 264; Hagen's influence, 91–3; nation-specific aesthetics, 162, 241–2, 243n, 245n, 286, 289; performative metaphors, 121; published plays as documents of, 242n25; quest for identity, 33–5, 86–7, 133, 134n; questions as focus, 35, 86–7, 148n, 163; Spiderwoman metaphor, 72; stages (recovery, mourning, dreaming, commitment, action), 200–1, 239, 252; for survivance, 72, 80; waterway metaphor, 277–8. *See also* mola aesthetics; re-worlding; Storyweaving
Spiderwoman Theater, identity of company: about, 71–2, 133, 134n, 137–47, 264; as feminist, 115–16, 134n, 137, 141, 146; as heterosexual, 134n; as Indigenous, 18, 72, 143, 149–50; as lesbian, 72, 134n, 137, 141–7, 149–50; shifts in identity, 18, 149–50; whiteness, 146; womanist processes, 160–4

Spiderwoman Theater, legacy: about, 18–19, 80, 93–5, 285–6, 290–307; aesthetic heirs, 18–19, 80; Borst-Tarrant's *More Than Feathers*, 267–8, 291, 293–5; communitism, 34, 94–5, 137; freedom of choice, 294; genealogical heirs, 18–19; healing and survivance, 94–5; honour songs, 294–5, 304–5; inter- and intra-generational dynamics, 290–7, 305; Mojica's *Princess Pocahontas*, xi, 267, 291–3; re-worlding, 80, 163–4, 295–6; *The Scrubbing Project*, 268, 270–6; "Trail Song," 188. *See also* Borst-Tarrant, Murielle (Muriel's daughter); *Encounters at the "Edge of the Woods"* (Collective Encounter); Mojica, Monique (Gloria's daughter); Storyweaving

Spiderwoman Theater: The Real Marvel (exhibition, 1997), 71, 313–14

spirituality, Indigenous: alcohol use, 76–7n; "artificial tree," 28–31, 66n2, 271; Derrick's community model, 171–3, *172*; harms from misappropriation, 165–7; kernels of the stories, 124, 190–3, 215–16, 245, 264; knowledge specialists, 167; Medicine Wheel, 164–5; womanist processes, 160–4. *See also* ceremony; healing of Indigenous dis-ease

Split Britches (Weaver, Shaw, and Verge), xiiin2, 115n, 139, 147–9

Split Britches Theater, 115n, 128, 139, 148n, 149

"split mind," 45n, 87n, 300

Stanislavski, Konstantin, 80, 96, 99, 164

The Star Medicine series (Borst-Tarrant), 296

stereotypes: about, 86–7; countering of, 67, 135–6, 227, 293; *The Fittin' Room*, 67; *Lysistrata Numbah!*, 135–6; metonyms, 69, 110, 188, 214, 219; "Metonyndian," 69, 86–7; Minstrelsy, 272–3; *More Than Feathers and Beads*, 293; noble savage, 230–2, 237–8, 272–3n; redface, 213–14, 272–3n, 273, 298; roles for Indigenous actors, 87; *Sun, Moon, and Feather*, 212–14; Wild West shows, 233; *Winnetou's Snake Oil Show*, 227. *See also* Indigenous Peoples, misrepresentations; "show biz" Indians

Stó:lō, 11, 12, 45, 61, 301–2

Stone, John Augustus, 272–3n

stories, Indigenous: about, 20–1, 26–32, 133, 148n, 287–8, 296–7; art as medicine, 93, 95–6, 272, 304, 306; for becoming fully human, 26–8; and biota, 175–6; Cajete's pedagogical model, 26, 154–7, 163, 199; circular structures, 133, 170–1, 174–5; communal ownership, 126; Derrick's community model, 171–3, *172*; feminist influences (CR), 85n, 104–5, 107, 108, 161, 296; identity quest, 26–7, 121, 133; inward vs. outward focus, 175–6; kernels of the stories, 124, 190–3, 195, 215–16, 245, 264; kitchen table storytelling, 35, 100, 105, 158–64, 196–7, 210, 243n; knowledge transmission, 26–7; land-based structures, 173–5; mola aesthetics, 121–3; vs. non-Indigenous narratives, 148n; place/land and time, 91–2; possession of maker, 28–9, 177–8; re-worlding, 20–1, 28, 57–8, 154–6; right to control story, 26; shadow work, 287–8;

stories, Indigenous (*continued*) third person narrative, 27–9, 126n; waterway metaphor, 277–8. *See also* clowns; humour; oral tradition

stories, Indigenous, specific: baluwala tree, 136n, 261n36; creation/re-creation, 12–16, 57–8, 304; Doubled Headed Serpent, 45n; exile stories, 57–8; Lynx Woman, 7–9; Omushkego stories, 174–5, 287–90; origin stories, 7, 12–16, 45n, 57–8, 301–2; Sky Woman, 12–16, 57–8, 304; Spiderwoman creatrix, 109; Trickster/Transformer figures, 27, 85–6n, 119, 121, 129–30, 131–2

stories, non-Indigenous: Hagen's search for self, 91–3; vs. Indigenous narratives, 148n; individual ownership, 175–6, 178–9; inward vs. outward focus, 175–6; linear vs. circular structures, 173; mimesis as Western concept, 27; simulation of survivance, 28–31; Storyweaving, 66n2, 148n, 175–6

Storyweaving: about, 17, 18, 87–8, 108–9, 133, 176–93, 297, 306–7; biota connection to storyteller, 186–8; circular structures, 193; Enow'kin principle, 39, 192, 296, 304; feminist influences (CR), 85–6n, 104–5, 107, 108, 161, 296; formulas for theatre, process, and tradition, 286–7; Gathering House Tradition, 195–7, 253n; liminality, 193; mola aesthetics, 5, 121–3; Muriel's influence, 5, 87–8; non-Indigenous narratives, 66n2, 148n, 175–6; Spiderwoman tradition, 72, 169–70, 175, 176; terminology, as practice, 15n; unused stories, 126; waterway metaphor, 277–8. *See also* Spiderwoman Theater; Spiderwoman Theater, legacy

Storyweaving, practices: about, 181–93; ancestors, 186–8, 190–3; call and response, 302; Chaikin's influence, 79–88; consent protocols, 300; dreams, 193–6; empathic connections, 303; generous heart, 189; identity quest, 33–5, 37, 86–7, 133, 144–50; inhabitation of storyteller, 178–82, 185–8; Inside/Outside exercise, 85–6n; inward vs. outward focus, 175–6; "jam sessions," 191–3; kernels of stories, 124, 190–3, 195, 215–16, 245, 264; land-based praxis, 300; movement and sound, 189–92; multiple perspectives, 39, 192, 296; questions as focus, 148n, 163, 181–4, 193; remembered landscape, 181–6; retellings, 87n, 189–91, 302; self-reflection, 189–91; Transformations exercise, 85–6n, 190n; "Two Blonde Indian Sisters," 193–6; Weaver's adaptation, 147–8; wounded bear, 185–6; writing exercises, 302

Storyweaving, workshops: Carter's workshop (2002–3), 181–6; first workshop (1975), 108–9; Mojica's workshop (2006), 190–3; Muriel's workshops (2002, 2006), 176–9, 193–6

Strasberg, Lee, 16, 81–2n17, 176, 178

Sullivan, Chingwe Padraig, *8*

Sun, Moon, and Feather: about, 18, 149–50, 198–9, 208–26, *222*; authenticity, 218; counter-mimicry, 213–15, 217; dreaming, 34, 212, 217–19, 221–2, 225–6; identity quest, 149–50, 198–9, 209; Muriel's artistic statement on, 217; performance (1981), xiii, 206; as personal healing, 198–9, 203; poverty, 208–9, 212; as published play, 198–9, 202–3, 238, 242n25; reception, 213–16, 220–1; self in community, 149–50, 209; survivance, 150, 206, 208–9, 214–17, 220–6

Sun, Moon, and Feather, development and performers: family cooperation, 222–6; game of "Indian Love Call," 212, 220–2; Gloria, 210–12, 220–2, *222*; Guna culture, 159, 210; kernels in the stories, 208, 212, 215–16, 224; Lisa, 210–12, 220–2; Miguel family relationships, 149–50, 206, 209; Muriel, 211, 212n, 217; performative mola, 208–9, 214, 245n28; Rappahannock culture, 152n, 210; Rappahannock names, 98, 149, 198; relation to Chekhov's *Three Sisters*, 98, 204–7, 209, 225–6; relation to *Three Sisters from Here to There*, 204, 206–8

Sun, Moon, and Feather, stage productions: Boat Story, 223–5; English names of sisters, 206; home movies, 159, 209, 219, 224–5, 238, 259; "Indian Love Call," 211–15, 217, 219–22; music and sound, 208–9; Poverty Tape, 208–9, 209n4; *Rose-Marie* film images, 213, 220–1

Sun, Moon, and Feather (film, 1989), 209n4, 219n

Sundance ceremony: about, 102n, 183, 245–6; fabric and quilts, 102; Gloria's experiences, 246–7; misappropriation, 183; Mojica as dancer, 246n29; Muriel's experiences, 43–4, 102, 109, 245–6; *Reverb-ber-ber-rations*, 245–7; self-sacrifice, 102n31; at Wounded Knee (1973), 44

survivance: about, 28–31, 93, 214–17, 294; art as medicine, 93, 95–6, 272, 304, 306; communitism, 34, 92–4; counter-mimicry, 213–15, 217; dreaming, 217–19, 225–6; as identity quest, 33–5, 86, 133; mola as symbol, 123; as not enough, 294; pain as a gift, 211, 215; as pro-action, 214–17; role models, 218; "show biz" Indians, *78*, 78–9, 86–7, 219n, 282–5; simulation of survivance, 28–31; Spiderwoman Theater as, 33–4; stories for, 28; vs. survival, 225; threat to body, 214; waterway metaphor, 277–8; work within own communities, 55, 63

Szykowski, Mathis (Gloria's ex-husband), 100–1

Szykowski, Raphael (Gloria's son), 278

Tarrant, Henu Josephine (Murielle and Kevin's daughter), *8*, 14, 15, 80, 268, 277–82

Tarrant, Kevin (Josephine's son, Murielle's husband, Henu's father), 11, 15, 80, 268

The Tempest (Shakespeare), 296–7

theatre, Indigenous: about, 20–1, 29, 54–5; art as lifeway, 164; "artificial tree" spirituality, 28–31, 66n2, 271; authenticity, 114–15; as ceremonial sites, 59–60; history as communal responsibility, 124–5; irreconcilable Indigenous spaces, 40, 45, 54, 58, 60–1, 215–16n11, 300–2; languages other than English, 89n; as liminal, 151–2, 154, 157, 248–9; metaphysical mimesis, 29; Muriel's vision of space (NYC), 56–7;

theatre, Indigenous (*continued*) non-Caucasian reviewers, 59; respect for, 17, 71, 95–6; re-worlding, 21; safe spaces for performers, 55, 58–61, 88–9n23, 95–6; "traditional signifiers" of Indigeneity, 115; work within own communities, 55–6, 63. *See also* Chocolate Woman Collective; The Collective Encounter; Spiderwoman Theater; Storyweaving; theatre training, Indigenous; Turtle Gals Performance Ensemble

theatre, non-Indigenous: land acknowledgments, 11; as liminoid, 151–2, 157, 159n, 167; safe spaces for actors, 95–6; Womanspace, 104–9. *See also* Chaikin, Joseph; Hagen, Uta; Split Britches Theater

Theatre Passe Muraille, 59, 267

theatre training, Indigenous: about, 16–17, 164, 168–9; art as lifeway, 164; Carter's workshop (2002–3), 181–6; commonplace as sacred, 168; Derrick's community model, 171–3, *172*; Indigenous methodologies, 168; inward vs. outward focus, 175–6; land-based structures, 173–5; land's story, 168–70; limen (threshold), 168–9; Mojica's workshops (2006, 2014), 190–3, 288–90; mola-making, 174; Muriel's workshops (2002, 2006), 176–9, 193–6; *Omushkego* workshop (2014), 288–90. *See also* exercises, theatre; Storyweaving; theatre, Indigenous

theatre training, Indigenous and non-Indigenous. See *Encounters at the "Edge of the Woods"* (Collective Encounter)

theatre training, non-Indigenous: about, 16–17, 164–8, 175; accountability, 167–8; Carter's workshop (2002–3), 181–6; harms from misappropriation, 164–8; influence on Indigenous performers, 164; inward vs. outward focus, 175–6; land's story, 168. *See also* Chaikin, Joseph; exercises, theatre; Hagen, Uta; theatre, non-Indigenous

Thomas, Bear Witness (Mojica's son), 278, 283

3 Up, 3 Down, xiv

The Three Sisters (Chekhov), 97–8, 204–7, 209, 225–6

The Three Sisters from Here to There: about, 18–19, 97–8, 204–8; gender relationships, 207; history of co-creation, 204, 206–8; legacy of Storyweaving, 18–19; male puppets, 97–8, *98*, 206–7; performance (1982), xiii, 206; performers, 97–8, 206–7; philosophical and political questions, 207; reception, 207; relation to Chekhov's *Three Sisters*, 97–8, 204–7, 209; relation to *Sun, Moon, and Feather*, 204, 206–8

Thunderbird American Indian Dance Company, 78, 80, 82–4n19

Tobias, Lenore Keeshig, 218n

Toronto, University of. *See* University of Toronto

Traditional Circle of Indian Elders and Youth, 199, 227

Trail of the Otter, xiv

"Trail Song," 188

training. *See* theatre training, Indigenous; theatre training, non-Indigenous

trans people. *See* gender and sexual minorities (2SLGBTQQIA)

Treuer, David, 27
Trilogy: Friday Night, Jealousy, And My Sister Ate Dirt, xiii, 137–9
The Triple Truth (Turtle Gals), 270n3
Trudeau, Justin, 22–3, 25, 273n
truth, communal vs. absolute, 124–5
Truth and Reconciliation Commission (TRC), 21, 24, 184, 299
Turner, Victor, 151–2, 176
Turtle Gals Performance Ensemble, 18–19, 110, 268, 270–5
2SLGBTQQIA. *See* gender and sexual minorities (2SLGBTQQIA)
"Two Blonde Indian Sisters" (dream session), 193–6

University of Toronto: Graduate Centre for Study of Drama, 37, 181n, 233n; Hart House Theatre, 87n, 298; history in *Encounters*, 298–305. See also *Encounters at the "Edge of the Woods"* (Collective Encounter)

Valdez, Luis, 114n3
"A Valentine to my Grandmother" (Borst-Tarrant and Mojica), 304–5
Verge, Pam: about, 68, 142–3; *The Fittin' Room*, 67–70, 142, 309–11; *Friday Night*, 137–8; lesbian feminist, 142–3, 145n17; *The Persistence of Memory*, 282; Spiderwoman Theater, 68n, 115n, 137, 142–3, 149; *Split Britches*, xiiin2, 115n, 147, 149; Split Britches Theater, 115n, 149; *The Three Sisters from Here to There*, 206, 207n
violence: about, 112–13; child sexual abuse, 62; colonial harms overview, 115–16, 123; in Gunayala, 123; *Material Witness*, 48–50, 62; in Miguel family, 34, 40–4, 222–3; misappropriation as, 116; post-show on violence, 127–8; power of theatre to change violence, 51–2, 54–5; rape in *Power Pipes*, 256–7, 261–2; Sundance incident (1973), 43, 44; verbal and physical, 112–13; womanist approach, 115–16, 160. See also *Material Witness; Women in Violence*
visitations. *See* psychic gifts
Vizenor, Gerald, 28–9, 214
Voices from the Criss Cross Bridge (Mayo), xiv

Wastasecoot, Brenda, 303n
waterway metaphor, 277–8
Weaver, Jace, 33–4
Weaver, Lois: about, 108–9, 142–3, 145–9; as director, 126, 146–9; *The Fittin' Room*, 142; *Friday Night*, 137–8; lesbian feminist, 108, 109, 137, 142–3, 145–8; life in Blue Ridge Mountain, 109, 139, 145, 147; *The Persistence of Memory*, 282; Spiderwoman Theater co-founder, 33, 108–9, 137, 146–7; Spiderwoman Theater split, 142, 147–9; *Split Britches: A True Story*, xiiin2, 115n, 139, 147–9; Split Britches Theater, 115n5, 139, 147–9; *Women in Violence*, 118n, 315
Weston, Gayle, 14–15n9
Winnetou (May), 230–3, 238–9
Winnetou's Snake Oil Show from Wigwam City: about, 116–17, 199–200, 227–40; authentic spirituality, 199–200, 234, 237–40; ceremony, 233–5, 240; as communal recovery, 199–200, 203, 227–30, 239–40; controversy, 116–17; Elders call for (1988), 199, 227; Indigenous audiences, 228; misappropriation and cultural theft, 75n, 116–17,

Winnetou's Snake Oil Show from Wigwam City (*continued*) 199, 227, 238–9; performances (1988–2001), xiii, 116, 227n16; plastic shamanism, 75n, 116–17, 199, 227, 233, 292; psychic gifts, 75n, 237, 239–40; as published play, 199–200, 202–3, 238, 242n25; reception, 116–17, 162n, 227–8n18, 238
Winnetou's Snake Oil Show, development and performers: Elvira Colorado, 200n; Hortencia Colorado, 200n, 233–4, 238; Guna culture, 159; kernels of stories, 238; May's novel *Winnetou*, 230–3, 238–9; Miguel sisters, 233
Winnetou's Snake Oil Show, stage productions: Antonio's *MOHICANS* spectacle, *78*, 78–9; audience participation, 234–5; characters, 238; costumes, 237–8; home movies, 233, 238, 259; "Pale Moon" (song), 233; performative mola, 233, 235, 245n28; transformations, 235, 238
womanism: about, 10, 160, 163–4; approach to violence, 115–16, 160; communitism, 160–4; dualities vs. oppositional binaries, 10; kitchen table storytelling, 100, 159–64; respect and protection, 260; Spiderwoman Theater, 10, 160, 163–4; terminology, 160. *See also* feminism
Womanspace, 104–9, 112
women, Indigenous. *See* Indigenous women
Women in Violence: about, 17–18, 94, 112–33, 315–16; as autobiography, 94, 114, 120; communitism, 94–5; feminist identity, 114, 120, 133, 134n; Guna culture, 121; healing, 86n; humour, 50, 97n, 129–32; incident in France (1977), 94–5, 114, 127–8, 134, 234; Indigenous identity, 114, 120, 133; launch of Spiderwoman Theater, 4, 48; performances in Europe, 97n, 114n3; performance (1985) 10th Anniversary Celebration, xiii; performative mola, 5, 245n28; power of theatre to change violence, 51–2, 54–5, 94–5; reception, 114–17, 119–20, 131; relation to *Material Witness*, 48, 49, 51–2, 63; scene analysis, 113n1, 315–16; shameful jokes, 50, 97n, 132–3
Women in Violence, development and performers: about, 123–8, 133; Chaikin's exercises, 85–6n; circles upon circles, 133; clowns, 123, 130–1; consciousness raising (CR) sessions, 85–6n; Inside/Outside [Odets Kitchen] exercise, 85–6n, 86n; Lisa, 4, 5, 86n, 119, 131, 315; mola aesthetics, 128; Muriel, 130–1; new methodology, 50; Perfect People exercise, 85–6n, 86n
Women in Violence, stage production: backdrop, 102n30, 120–3, *122*; clowns, 52, 86n, 118n, 119–21, 123, 128–30, 315; costume, 131; Gloria, 52; lack of "traditional signifiers," 115; Perfect Woman, 4, 86n, 119, 131, 315; performances (1976–81), xiii, 4, 48, 54, 94, 117–18, 137; post-show on violence, 127–8; pre-show on classism, 117–19; scene analysis, 113n1, 315–16; self-revelations of performers, 120, 128–31; Trickster/Transformer figures, 85–6n, 119, 121, 129, 131–2
workshops, Storyweaving. *See* Storyweaving, workshops
world view. *See* knowledge, Indigenous
Wounded Knee, Battle of (1973), 44, 316

Yaqui deer dancers, 234–5